The Transformation of EU Competition Law

The Transformation of EU Competition Law

Next Generation Issues

Edited by

Adina Claici
Assimakis Komninos
Denis Waelbroeck

Wolters Kluwer

Published by:
Kluwer Law International B.V.
PO Box 316
2400 AH Alphen aan den Rijn
The Netherlands
E-mail: lrs-sales@wolterskluwer.com
Website: www.wolterskluwer.com/en/solutions/kluwerlawinternational

Sold and distributed by:
Wolters Kluwer Legal & Regulatory U.S.
920 Links Avenue
Landisville, PA 17538
United States of America
E-mail: customer.service@wolterskluwer.com

ISBN 978-94-035-0096-6

e-Book: ISBN 978-94-035-0116-1
web-PDF: ISBN 978-94-035-0126-0

Editors

Dr Adina Claici is a principal at the Brattle Group in Brussels, a Visiting Professor at the College of Europe and Barcelona School of Economics, and a member of the Executive Committee of the Global Competition Law Centre (GCLC) of the College of Europe.

Dr Assimakis Komninos is a Partner at White & Case LLP, a Visiting Professor at Université Panthéon Assas (Paris II) – LLM AWArDS, Visiting Research Fellow at University College London, and a member of the Executive Committee of the Global Competition Law Centre (GCLC) of the College of Europe.

Denis Waelbroeck is a partner at Ashurst LLP, a Professor at the Université libre de Bruxelles and a member of the Executive Committee of the Global Competition Law Centre (GCLC) of the College of Europe.

Contributors

Inge Bernaerts is Inge Bernaerts is Director for Strategy and Policy in the Competition Directorate General of the European Commission.

Fernando Castillo de la Torre is Director/Principal Legal Adviser in the Competition and Mergers team of the Legal Service of the European Commission.

Isabelle de Silva is President of the Sixth Chamber of the *Conseil d'Etat*, member of the *Tribunal des Conflits*, Associate Professor at Sciences Po, Scientific Adviser of the Publics Affairs School of SciencesPo, and Former President of the *Autorité de la Concurrence*.

Miguel Mota Delgado is a Doctoral Researcher at the Department of Law of the European University Institute.

Jacques Derenne is a member of the Brussels and Paris bars, a Partner at Sheppard Mullin, a Professor at the University of Liège and the Brussels School of Competition, and a member of the Executive Committee of the Global Competition Law Centre (GCLC) of the College of Europe.

Dr Krystyna Kowalik-Bańczyk is a Judge at the General Court of the EU and an Associate Professor at the Institute of Law Studies, Polish Academy of Sciences, Warsaw.

Alfonso Lamadrid de Pablo is a Partner at Garrigues (Brussels) and a Visiting Professor at the College of Europe.

Ina Lunneryd is a Managing Associate within the Antitrust & Foreign Investment Group at the Brussels office of Linklaters LLP.

Giorgio Monti is Professor of Competition Law at Tilburg Law and Economics Center and Research Fellow at the Centre on Regulation in Europe (CERRE).

Dr Jorge Padilla is a Senior Managing Director and Member of the Executive Committee at Compass Lexecon and a Visiting Professor at Toulouse School of Economics.

Luc Peeperkorn is a Professor at the Brussels School of Competition and previously a Principal Advisor on Antitrust Policy at DG COMP.

Nicolas Petit is Joint Chair in Competition Law at the European University Institute (EUI) and the Robert Schuman Centre for Advanced Studies (RSCAS) and invited Professor at the College of Europe in Bruges.

Marc van der Woude is a Judge at the General Court of the EU and a Professor at Erasmus University, Rotterdam.

Cani Fernández Vicién is the President of the Spanish National Markets and Competition Commission (CNMC) and has been a lawyer practising in EU and competition law for more than 30 years, a former *référendaire* at the Court of Justice of the European Union (1993-1997) and an associate professor at different academic institutions.

Adriana Meijide Vidal is a case handler at the Competition Directorate (Energy and Industry unit) of the Spanish National Markets and Competition Commission (CNMC).

Laurent Warlouzet is a Professor of History at Paris Sorbonne University and a Former Postdoctoral Fellow at the London School of Economics and the European University Institute.

Summary of Contents

Table of Contents

Introduction: Speech by Margrethe Vestager, Executive Vice-President of the European Commission

Good morning and thank you for the invitation to speak.

It is wonderful to be back in person in Bruges, with all of you. Because it is now more important than ever to come together. To unite forces.

Only a few weeks ago none of us could have imagined that by now we would be living in a different continent – one that again witnesses the tragedy of a large-scale war – and a different Europe altogether.

The decisions and actions that have been taken in the last few weeks and that will be taken in the days and weeks to come will shape the future of Europe for a long time. Whether they concern the imposition of sanctions in reaction to Russia's aggression against Ukraine, the provision of military support to Ukraine or the protection of refugees.

What is reassuring is to see that we are acting in unity and together with our democratic partners around the world. Because we have been reminded by the inspiring courage of the Ukrainian people that democracy and freedom have a price, and we must be willing to fight for it.

Also through our work, we try to do our part to preserve democracy and pluralism in our societies by protecting fair competition in the Single Market.

This is why I want to take the opportunity of being here today to share with you some thoughts on our ongoing work in each antitrust, mergers and State aid.

But before I do so, let me start with the most recent development on the Digital Markets Act (DMA). Last night, actually only a few hours ago, the Council and the European Parliament reached a political agreement on the Commission's proposal for a DMA. This is a historic moment for digital markets regulation in the European Union. For the first time, the Union will have in place a comprehensive set of rules regulating the conduct of gatekeeper platforms to keep markets open and contestable. And it all happened very fast, only 15 months after the Commission's proposal. I would like to thank the Council and the European Parliament for their commitment to achieve this shared goal, without which the DMA would not have seen the light of day so quickly. Of course, this is only the first step because one can only judge a law by the way it is enforced and its impact on the ground, but it is worth pausing for a second to appreciate all the work done to date.

1 ANTITRUST

The development of the DMA has not been happening in a vacuum. Our enforcement in digital markets and the in-depth market knowledge built through case practice enabled us to table the DMA. And our digital enforcement continues at a fast pace. Which is all the more remarkable, when you consider the challenges caused by the disruptions of the past two years.

It is precisely thanks to our digital enforcement that we continue to gain insights into these markets and the specific challenges they pose. For example in the *Facebook Marketplace* case opened last year, we raised concerns on how Facebook collects and uses certain types of data. You see similar issues addressed in certain provisions of the DMA itself.

In the *Google Adtech* case, we have concerns about Google's practices – including data-related practices – that may favour its own ad tech services. Again, we see parallels to what is being done through the DMA's ex ante approach – the provisions on transparency in the conditions for the supply of ad tech services in the DMA are aimed at promoting competition by other ad tech providers, and the requirements to obtain consent for data combination aims at reducing the data advantage enjoyed by gatekeepers.

The synergies between the DMA and the experience we gain from digital enforcement are working to our advantage, but that same experience shows that the two approaches are complementary – both will remain necessary. No one should expect the new regulatory instrument to replace Article 101 and 102 TFEU enforcement actions.

For example, we have recently opened an investigation into whether the so-called Jedi Blue agreement between Google and Meta restricted or distorted competition in markets for online display advertising. If so, it could hurt both publishers and consumers.

Nor has our work on digital markets come at the expense of antitrust work in other, more traditional sectors. On the contrary, the risks of harmful fragmentation are always there. Especially in times of disruption, some players may try to create unfair opportunities by fracturing the Single Market, for instance by restricting sales or hampering trade across the internal borders of the Union. Two of our recent investigations illustrate exactly this concern – one regarding Mondelez in the biscuit, chocolates and coffee markets; and one in the clothing market, regarding Pierre Cardin.

2 MERGERS

Moving now to mergers, an issue which is increasingly debated these days is the one of remedies. Which remedies, if any, a competition authority should accept as adequate and proportionate to address the competition concerns raised by a transaction? Our legal framework defines a clear preference for divestiture remedies, and if you look at our track record, you will see exactly this in the vast majority of cases.

Of course, the parties always have the initiative to propose solutions. The design of remedies is the outcome of cooperative negotiations.

In this, parties are well aware of our preference for 'clean slate' remedies, by which I mean stand-alone divestitures. Clean slate remedies address competition concerns, and there is no need for long-term monitoring, which is resource intensive and increases the risk of regulatory avoidance over time. This is why divestitures are the preferred remedy in the vast majority of cases, and the standard for our remedy policy. These have ensured in numerous cases over the past years that customers in Europe have as many choices after a merger as they had before, and that competitors in the market can continue to offer innovative products, at affordable prices.

But even when it comes to divestiture remedies, the reality is sometimes trickier, and we need guarantees the remedy will work in practice. So we need to mitigate the implementation risk. This is why we also rely on measures to make sure the divestitures are effective and safeguarded – that could be through provisions on suitable purchasers, upfront buyers and crown jewels.

A good example is the recent *Cargotec/Konecranes* case. In this case, we identified horizontal concerns in Europe for various types of port equipment. We cleared the merger with divestitures of viable stand-alone businesses from both parties, depending on the product. And we made sure these remedies fully removed our competition concerns. We ran two rounds of extensive market feedback with several competitors and customers to calibrate the remedy. Respondents were satisfied that, thanks to those remedies, there would be as many choices for European customers as before the merger. We also mitigated risks to the divestment process with an upfront buyer requirement, meaning that before the parties can consummate the merger that we need to approve suitable purchasers for each divestment business. The goal was to preserve competition in the market for port equipment, and together with the parties, we found a way to achieve this.

And we always need to make sure our assessment holds. We must issue a fully reasoned decision in every case we are called to review. And we do this on the basis of the evidence in our file, to which the parties have access once we formalise concerns in a Statement of Objections. That means we cannot ignore meaningful solutions that parties choose to offer. Our choice of remedy is not a matter of discretion. It is a question of assessing on a case-by-case basis the effectiveness of the parties' proposal, its ability to address the competition concerns in light of the market realities and the proportionality of the solution offered. And all this happens against the background of a strict judicial review of our decisions, both clearances and prohibitions.

That said, the remedy needs to fit the competition problem it is meant to address. It is clear that, in general, divestiture remedies are the most effective solution in horizontal cases, where a merger could eliminate a direct competitor. But in particular in some non-horizontal cases, we are open to considering other solutions.

In digital markets, for example, there might be concerns about interoperability or access to a service or product, but no overlap of activities. Structural remedies like a stand-alone divestiture might not be the most appropriate for solving that type of issue. In non-horizontal cases, outcomes quickly become rather binary if you exclude remedies implying access or interoperability. And neither a full clearance nor an outright prohibition is desirable when solutions can be found that preserve the opportunities for rivals to compete downstream or upstream.

For example, in the Meta/Facebook acquisition of Kustomer, our approach was to guarantee access to Meta's popular messaging channels - WhatsApp, Instagram and Messenger - for Kustomer's competitors offering consumer relationship management software, the so-called CRM software. This is because we found that Kustomer, although small, was an innovative and fast-growing player in the customer service and support customer relationship management - CRM - software market. These applications are used by businesses engaging with their customers to answer questions, solve problems and give advice. They rely significantly on Meta's popular messaging channels such as WhatsApp, Instagram and Messenger. We found that Meta would have the ability, as well as an economic incentive, to engage in foreclosure strategies vis-à-vis Kustomer's close rivals and new entrants.

To address these concerns, Meta offered comprehensive access commitments with a 10-year duration, ensuring that Kustomer's rivals will continue to have free and comparable access to Meta's important messaging channels. By keeping these channels open to all competitors, we preserved the possibility for more choice in the customer-relations software market. In this case, our intervention brought concrete safeguards for Kustomer's rivals in Europe, to make sure that they continue to compete on an equal footing, in the interest of consumers. Such safeguards are not available to Kustomer's rivals in other parts of the world.

Clearly, such measures are not possible in many cases. They are considered to the extent that they address targeted problems, and do not require excessive monitoring. But it is not in the interest of consumers to pretend that such issues of access or interoperability should not, in specific circumstances, be adequately remedied instead of either prohibiting the deal or not intervening at all.

Now to those who are concerned about the long list of acquisitions by large digital platforms and claim that there is limited oversight over such mergers, I would say that in this respect as well, our practice has moved on. A few years ago, many of these mergers were cleared, unconditionally after a Phase I investigation. Then, greater scrutiny led to some of these cases being subject to in-depth investigations, sometimes ending with unconditional clearances if no competition concerns were identified and sometimes ending with strings attached.

The DMA will give yet further means to complete our toolbox. First, by ensuring that both the Commission and national competition authorities are informed of transactions involving gatekeepers and core platform services in the digital sector, or transactions enabling the collection of digital data. Second, by enabling the Commission to impose a merger ban as a sanction for non-compliance, should the gatekeeper systematically be found non-compliant with its obligations under the DMA.

So both our practice and our rules are evolving with time, building on experience. And they will continue to do so, as we get to see and learn over time how our remedies have performed.

3 STATE AID

The need to use the in-built flexibility of our rules while continuing to preserve the level playing field in the Single Market have been central to our State aid work since the start of the pandemic. To say 'our State aid teams have been busy these past two years' is a huge understatement. As of February 2022, the Commission has taken more than 1,200 decisions and amendment decisions, approving around 900 national measures notified by 27 Member States under the COVID Temporary Framework.

The results of our latest survey show that this high workload really has paid off. Our goal was always to approve as much aid as was needed, as long as this did not create distortions in the Single Market. What we see from the survey results is that – yes – the aid disbursements remained proportionate to the impact of the pandemic crisis measures. No one Member State has completely outspent others. Thankfully the situation with COVID has improved to such a point, the question is not about whether to phase measures out, but rather 'how quickly'. This is what our dialogue with Member States is now focused on.

Our attention also turns towards using the flexibility in our State aid rules to help address the consequences of Russia's invasion of Ukraine. The Temporary Crisis Framework adopted on 23 March complements the existing State aid toolbox, which already includes many possibilities for Member States, including providing compensation to companies for damages directly suffered due to exceptional circumstances.

The new crisis framework enables Member States to grant limited amounts of aid to companies affected by the current crisis or by the related sanctions and counter-sanctions; ensure that sufficient liquidity remains available to businesses; and compensate companies for the additional costs incurred due to exceptionally high gas and electricity prices.

4 CONCLUSION

To conclude, I am convinced that, when the clouds of war finally lift, the work we put into preserving and strengthening our Single Market will equip us with the means to show the world that our path based on open trade and fair competition is truly better. After all, Bruges did not become great by conquest and ruthless occupation. It became great through commerce and industry.

CHAPTER 1

The Effects-Based Approach: Still Just as Necessary for an Effective and Coherent EU Competition Policy

Luc Peeperkorn[*]

1 INTRODUCTION

The history of European Union (EU) competition policy is the story of a gradual shift away from a focus on restrictions of the freedom of action of market participants, aimed at protecting the competitive process as such, and towards a focus on the effects of practices on the market, linked to a recognition that the goal should be the protection of consumer welfare. It was right and timely that the Global Competition Law Centre (GCLC) devoted its 2022 Annual Conference to looking back on this history and to questions about limitations in this shift in policy and challenges for the future.

For my presentation at the conference, the organisers, who are now the editors of this book, gave me a rather long title: *Twenty Years Later: Highlighting the Main Innovations of the Effects-Based Approach and Assessing Where We Stand – Does This Policy Still Offer the Right Responses to a Rapidly Changing World?*

As I had been involved in the introduction and development of the effects-based approach in EU competition policy, I guessed the organisers expected me to go into the main reasons invoked at the time to advocate the shift away from the more legalistic, form-based approach applied from the 1970s to the 1990s and towards the more economic, effects-based approach that was first introduced in the new area of merger control, before also being applied from the end of the 1990s to the assessment of supply

* The opinions expressed are strictly personal. While I previously worked for the European Commission, nothing in this chapter represents the views of the European Commission, DG COMP or any other institution, entity, person, etc. I would like to thank Paul Bridgeland and Magdalena Brenning Louko for their valuable comments. All errors and omissions are mine.

and distribution agreements and shortly afterwards for the other areas of application of Article 101 and finally also for Article 102.

Based on the question at the end of their long title, I gathered that the organisers also expected me to address whether the effects-based approach is still the right antitrust policy response in a world of concentrated digital markets and increasing demands for competition policy to address a range of societal concerns, including sustainability and the protection of privacy.

In summary, I concluded that the organisers wanted me to answer the following three questions about the evolution of EU antitrust policy towards an effects-based approach:

(1) Was this a necessary and desirable development?
(2) What are the main features of the effects-based approach?
(3) What are its proper boundaries and limits?

It is around these three questions that I organised my presentation, and which now provide the structure for this chapter.

2 WAS THE EFFECTS-BASED APPROACH A NECESSARY AND DESIRABLE DEVELOPMENT?

The short answer to this question is, yes it was! It was both necessary and desirable for a number of reasons.

First, the form-based approach casts the net of Article 101(1) too wide. Many agreements between firms go beyond simple one-off transactions and include clauses that limit the freedom of action of one or both the parties, for instance by stipulating a certain minimum volume or duration for their transactions, by requiring a degree of exclusivity, or by placing limits on how the parties may use the results of their cooperation. This meant that agreements were easily considered to be anti-competitive, no matter whether the parties were big or small, or whether they held any market power.

Combined with the notification system introduced by Council Regulation No 17 of 1962,[1] this led to a mass problem for the Commission. The Commission's competition report for 1971 (§48) mentioned a total of 30,000 notifications for exclusive dealing agreements alone. This meant that enforcers spent their time analysing and rubber-stamping harmless agreements, thereby undermining their capacity to focus on truly anti-competitive agreements and problematic markets.

The Commission's response was to adopt Block Exemption Regulations (BERs). However, the BERs of the 1970s, 1980s and early 1990s were also form-based: certain restrictions and combinations of restrictions were deemed to be legal regardless of the market position of the parties, while all other restrictions were excluded from the safe

1. Council Regulation No 17 of 6 February 1962, First Regulation implementing Articles 85 and 86 of the Treaty, OJ 13, 21.2.1962.

harbour (the so-called white-list approach). While these BERs did free up some enforcement resources, by reducing the need to assess large numbers of notifications of individual agreements, they also introduced a degree of under-enforcement, by creating safe harbours, at least for certain restrictions, up to 100 % market share.

Moreover, because these BERs only covered certain categories of agreements, many agreements were effectively excluded from the safe harbours. These other agreements were considered to be suspect, and were generally assumed to restrict competition, now not only because it was easy to show that they restricted the freedom of action ('Handlungsfreiheit') of one or the other party, but also because they fell outside the safe harbours provided by the BERs.

This context led to a high level of legal uncertainty, as well as high compliance costs for firms. Legal uncertainty in particular for agreements not covered by any of the BERs, because of the wide net cast by the form-based approach. And high compliance costs, because the form-based BERs created a straitjacket: firms wishing to avoid legal uncertainty by ensuring that their agreements fell within one of the BERs were unnecessarily hindered from adapting their agreements to economic reality and their business model, often to the detriment of both the firm and its customers.

Second, a point which is often overlooked, protecting the competitive process 'as such' provides no clear benchmark against which to decide cases. While a focus on consumer welfare gives direction and coherence to competition law enforcement, the same cannot be said of the goal of preserving a certain (not further defined) market structure, or of protecting the competitive process. The latter leads to a rudderless enforcement policy: for instance, it is not clear whether a merger that reduces the number of competing firms from five to four, but which also makes the remaining four firms more diverse in size, will result in an improvement or a deterioration of the market structure or the competitive process, unless we relate it to an outcome such as consumer welfare. Similarly, it is not clear how we should assess the effect on the competitive process of a manufacturer switching to a selective distribution system or of two firms creating a joint venture. The only way to conclude whether or not this harms the competitive process is by looking at the possible effects, i.e., at the outcome on the market.

The form-based approach, by creating a very wide net and an unclear benchmark, gave a lot of discretionary power to the Commission, which, because of its monopoly on the application of Article 101(3), was effectively the only enforcer of Article 101. Fortunately, the Commission's enforcement activity between the 1960s and 1990s was not as formalistic as this context might have led one to expect. But this was more due to the Commission exercising its discretion, rather than being a consequence of the rules that were in force at the time. In particular, the Commission did not apply the form-based approach systematically, by prohibiting thousands of agreements. Instead, it intervened selectively, and the case law of the form-based era was not devoid of effects analysis. Cases like *Liebig Spices* (Commission decision of 1977), *Fatty Acids* (decision of 1986) and *UK Tractors* (decision of 1992) all demonstrated a thorough understanding of the market context and applied a theory of harm that related to the (likely) effects.[2] The same can be said for judgments such as *Delimitis*.[3]

However, had the form-based approach been maintained, it would not have been possible to decentralise the application of Article 101 in an effective way. If multiple authorities had fished using a net with too fine a mesh, too many small fish would have been caught. And with many authorities, it would have been virtually impossible to ensure the discretionary restraint exercised by the Commission when it still held its enforcement monopoly. The shift to a systematic effects-based approach under Article 101 was not only part of but was a necessary precondition for the successful decentralisation of enforcement brought about by Regulation 1/2003. The effects-based approach, based on protecting competition for the benefit of consumers, provided both the appropriate limitation of the overall reach of EU competition policy and the benchmark to decide individual cases.

3 WHAT ARE THE MAIN FEATURES OF THE EFFECTS-BASED APPROACH?

Given the drawbacks of the form-based approach described above, it is no surprise that the call for reform came first from areas with a high number of agreements: mergers and vertical agreements.

Merger control by its nature requires an effects-based approach. Most mergers are beneficial or at least will not produce anti-competitive effects, and it is only in a limited number of cases that one would wish to intervene. The reasons for intervening will be linked to the market situation in which the merger takes place and the likely collusive or exclusionary effects that can be expected. This was recognised and put into practice by the Commission from the moment it obtained the power to vet mergers with an EU dimension in 1989 and was subsequently expressed in its horizontal and vertical merger guidelines of 2004 and 2008 respectively.[4]

In essence, the review carried out in the second half of the 1990s of the Article 101 enforcement policy towards vertical restraints was based on the same underlying idea. There are hundreds of thousands or even millions of supply and distribution agreements in the EU – as practically every firm needs to purchase inputs and/or find buyers and distributors for its output – and most of these agreements are beneficial or at least unobjectionable from a competition policy perspective. A policy that considered any restriction of the freedom of action of one of the parties as a potential restriction of competition was extending the reach of Article 101(1) far too wide, resulting in too many agreements being seen as potentially infringing Article 101.

2. *Liebig spices*, OJ 1978 L 53/20; *Fatty Acids*, OJ 1987 L3/17; *UK Tractors*, OJ 1992 L68/19.
3. Case C-234/89, *Stergios Delimitis v. Henninger Bräu AG*, judgment of the Court of 28 February 1991.
4. Guidelines on the assessment of horizontal mergers under the Council Regulation on the control of concentrations between undertakings, OJ C 31, 5.2.2004, pp. 5-18; Guidelines on the assessment of non-horizontal mergers under the Council Regulation on the control of concentrations between undertakings, OJ C 265, 18.10.2008, pp. 6-25; https://ec.europa.eu/competition-policy/mergers/legislation/notices-and-guidelines_en.

With the Vertical BER of 1999[5] and the Vertical Restraints Guidelines of 2000[6], the Commission for the first time adopted effects-based rules for the application of Article 101. And once this approach had been successfully introduced for supply and distribution agreements, it did not take long for the Commission to also apply it to the other areas of EU antitrust law, for horizontal agreements, for technology transfer agreements and finally for the assessment of abuses of dominance.

The main components of the effects-based approach can be grouped around three central features: (1) casting the net of EU competition law less wide, in particular for Article 101 and to a lesser extent for Article 102, by limiting their application to situations where anti-competitive effects can be expected, (2) providing guidance for a structured effects-based assessment in individual cases, and (3) bringing coherence to the assessment of different types of agreements and conduct, both within and between Articles 101 and 102.

As regards casting the net of Article 101 less wide, the main components are:

- A new *De Minimis* Notice, adopted in 2001 and revised in 2014, containing higher market share thresholds – 10% aggregate market share for agreements between competitors and 15% individual market share for agreements between non-competitors – below which it is assumed that agreements not containing by object restrictions will not have restrictive effects and will thus not infringe Article 101.[7]
- The introduction of wide umbrella BERs, each with its coverage capped by a market share threshold and a limited hardcore list, the so-called blacklist approach instead of the white-list approach of the form-based BERs.[8]
- The clear recognition in the various Article 101 Guidelines adopted by the Commission since 2000, accompanying the wide umbrella BERs, that there is no presumption of illegality for agreements that fall outside the safe harbour of a BER simply because the market share threshold is exceeded.[9]
- And last but not least, a narrower definition of by object restrictions, achieved by providing a clear list of hardcore restrictions in each BER.[10] The crux of these hardcore lists is that they only contain types of restrictions which either cannot be expected to create efficiencies or which are not indispensable to

5. Commission Regulation (EC) No 2790/1999 of 22 December 1999 on the application of Article 81(3) of the Treaty to categories of vertical agreements and concerted practices, OJ L 336, 29.12.1999, https://eur-lex.europa.eu/legal-content/EN/AUTO/?uri=OJ:L:1999:336:TOC.
6. Commission Notice – Guidelines on Vertical Restraints, OJ C 291, 13.10.2000, pp. 1, https://eur-lex.europa.eu/legal-content/EN/AUTO/?uri=OJ:C:2000:291:TOC.
7. Commission Notice on agreements of minor importance which do not appreciably restrict competition under Article 101(1) of the Treaty on the Functioning of the European Union (*De Minimis* Notice), OJ C 291, 30.8.2014, pp. 1-4, https://eur-lex.europa.eu/legal-content/EN/TXT/?uri=OJ:C:2014:291:TOC.
8. The BERs and accompanying Guidelines, which are regularly revised and updated, can be found at: https://competition-policy.ec.europa.eu/antitrust/legislation/block-exemption-regulations_en.
9. *See*, for instance, point 275 of Commission Notice – Guidelines on Vertical Restraints, OJ C 248, 30.6.2022, pp. 1-85.
10. The form-based approach is in essence the same as a very wide definition of by object restrictions: it leads to easy presumptions that restrictions fall within Article 101(1).

realise efficiencies. That is why the various Article 101 Guidelines not only indicate that these hardcore restrictions cannot benefit from the respective BER and are assumed to fall within Article 101(1), but also that they are generally unlikely to fulfil the conditions of the Article 101(3) exception.[11]

As regards the provision of guidance for structured effects-based assessments, the main components are:

- The Article 101 Guidelines adopted by the Commission since 2000 for the assessment of various types of agreement (vertical, horizontal, technology transfer, etc.), providing not only explanations for the application of the BERs but also a structured effects-based framework for assessing agreements in cases where the market share thresholds are exceeded or which are not covered by a specific BER.
- The Article 102 Guidance adopted by the Commission in 2008, in which it developed a full-blown effects-based approach for exclusionary conduct by dominant firms, including an efficiency defence in line with Article 101(3), and the extensive confirmation of this approach by the Court of Justice (CoJ) in its seminal *Post Danmark I* and *Intel* judgments.[12]
- The practice of formulating a theory of harm and collect the necessary evidence to test that theory in individual cases.

The detailed explanations of the – essentially identical – effects-based approach in the various Article 101 Guidelines and the Article 102 Guidance, together with the uniform safe harbours introduced by the various BERs, have been at least as important as the European Competition Network (ECN) for promoting coherent enforcement of Articles 101 and 102 throughout the EU. Without these policy instruments, which provide detailed explanations of the effects-based approach for different types of agreements and conduct, it would be much harder to coordinate the application of Articles 101 and 102 within the ECN.

The extension of the effects-based approach to Article 102 also restored coherence between the application of Articles 101 and 102.[13] This was not so self-evident in the late 1990s and early noughties, when the effects-based approach had been introduced for Article 101, whereas a form-based approach continued to be used for the application of Article 102.

There are several obvious reasons why coherence between the application of Articles 101 and 102 is important. First, this is necessary because in many instances the

11. For more background on the distinction between restrictions by object and by effect, *see* Luc Peeperkorn, *Defining 'By Object' Restrictions*, Concurrences No. 3-2015.
12. Guidance on the Commission's enforcement priorities in applying Article 82 of the EC Treaty to abusive exclusionary conduct by dominant undertakings, OJ C-45/7 of 24.2.2009; Case C-209/10 *Post Danmark A/S v. Konkurrencerådet*, judgment of the Court of Justice (Grand Chamber) of 27 March 2012, ECLI:EU:C:2012:172; Case C-413/14 P *Intel v. Commission*, judgment of the Court of Justice (Grand Chamber) of 6 September 2017, ECLI:EU:C:2017:632.
13. The following paragraphs until the end of this section are based on Luc Peeperkorn, *Coherence in the Application of Articles 101 and 102: A Realistic Prospect or an Elusive Goal?*, World Competition 39(3) (2016): 389-412.

same conduct can be, and sometimes is, assessed under both provisions of the Treaty. The Van den Bergh case is a good example, where – within the same case – the obligation on Irish retailers not to use freezers provided by Van den Bergh for the sale of competing ice cream brands was assessed under Article 101, while the inducement to use such freezers, by making them available for free/against a higher price for the ice cream, was assessed under Article 102.[14] While the existence of a dominant position and the related degree of market power must be taken into account under both articles, it would obviously not make sense if the outcome of the assessment depended on the choice of article being applied.[15]

This need for coherence in the application of Articles 101 and 102 holds not only for conduct such as tying and single branding/exclusive purchasing obligations, which are capable of infringing both articles, but also for other types of conduct, such as rebates, which, where they are not part of an agreement, can only be addressed under Article 102. The potential positive and negative effects of rebates, for instance, are very similar to the effects of single branding/exclusive purchasing obligations. Dealing with them using different approaches would therefore not only be unjustified from a policy perspective, it could also create an unwarranted bias in firms' conduct.

One could argue that when the effects-based approach was first introduced for Article 101, this did not necessarily lead to inconsistency with the application of Article 102. For a long time, the prevailing view was that the last condition of Article 101(3) – that of no elimination of competition – was in fact equivalent to an absence of dominance (i.e., a dominant position implied the elimination of competition). According to that view, a restrictive agreement could thus never be exempted where one of the parties held a dominant position.[16] It was therefore only logical to consider that the same applied to unilateral exclusionary conduct under Article 102. On that basis, a form-based approach to the application of Article 102 seemed perfectly consistent, as the same conduct in the form of an agreement was not capable of exemption under Article 101 either, as soon as one of the parties was dominant.

However, this view was not conducive to the development of a coherent policy.[17] While it is generally recognised that negative effects can only arise where one or more of the firms involved has a degree of market power, it is not coherent, for the reasons explained below, to create a category of restrictions or conduct which is considered

14. Case T-65/98, *Van den Bergh Foods v. Commission* [2003] ECR II-4653. In that case, the obligation to use freezers exclusively for the products of the dominant undertaking and the inducement to use such freezers were considered to lead to outlet exclusivity.
15. *See also* Ekaterina Rousseva, *Rethinking Exclusionary Abuses in EU Competition Law*, Hart Publishing, 445-455 (2010).
16. *See* for instance point 135 of the 2000 Guidelines on Vertical Restraints (OJ C 291, 13 October 2000, pp. 1-44): 'The last criterion of elimination of competition for a substantial part of the products in question is related to the question of dominance. Where an undertaking is dominant or becoming dominant as a consequence of the vertical agreement, a vertical restraint that has appreciable anti-competitive effects can in principle not be exempted.'
17. I make a distinction between a consistent policy and a coherent policy. A consistent policy ensures that similar cases receive the same or similar treatment. However, a consistent policy could still be wrong, in the sense that for some or all cases the treatment does not serve the goal of the policy. A coherent policy is a consistent policy where the consistency makes economic and legal sense, meaning that the actions undertaken systematically further the policy's stated goal.

using an effects-based approach/to be restrictive by effect below the level of dominance but is considered using a form-based approach/as having a restrictive object once one of the parties is dominant.

On the one hand, if a particular restriction or conduct truly has the object of restricting competition ('normally having a net negative effect on consumers'), treating it as by object only in cases of dominance will lead to under-enforcement and unnecessary complexity and enforcement costs. As explained before, if a particular type of agreement or conduct normally produces net negative effects, it is because it is unlikely to be used to create efficiencies. In that case, there is no reason to expect that the negative effects will only materialise where one of the parties is dominant. Having to prove that the threshold of dominance has been reached will thus lead to unnecessary enforcement costs and indeed under-enforcement.[18]

On the other hand, if a restriction or conduct is of the by effect type, i.e., a restriction or conduct that can be and regularly is used to create efficiencies, treating it as by object as soon as one of the parties is above the dominance threshold leads to over-enforcement and unnecessary legal uncertainty for firms. The main reasons are, first, that the likelihood of efficiencies is generally not negatively correlated with holding market power. In other words, generally restrictions which are treated as restrictions by effect below the dominance threshold do not suddenly change their character and start producing net negative effects above that threshold. Even though the firm in question is dominant, the restriction or conduct may very well still be used to create efficiencies. A second related point is that it is evidently wrong to consider that the effects will be very different depending on whether the firm is just above or below the dominance threshold. In other words, introducing a sharp break in the assessment ('by effect' below the threshold and 'by object' above the threshold) is not justified. Last, making the by object classification dependent on the existence of dominance will create significant legal uncertainty, as the threshold itself is not necessarily clear and predictable in all cases. Applying the classification in this way will thus also have an impact on the behaviour of non-dominant firms, whose incentives to grant rebates or enter into exclusive arrangements will be undermined, leading in many cases to a loss of competition and consumer welfare.[19]

However, the position that a restrictive agreement or exclusionary conduct could never be exempted where one of the parties held a dominant position started to shift,

18. As an example, classifying a naked price-fixing agreement as by object only in cases where more than 10% or 25% or 50% of the market is covered (on the grounds that negative effects are considered unlikely or even impossible below these levels) would simply lead to an increased risk of 'false positives' (unjust acquittals), due to the complexities and costs involved in defining the relevant market and assessing the exact coverage, while not reducing the risk of 'false negatives', due to the general absence of any efficiencies associated with this type of agreement.
19. That is why the use of a market power filter or a dominance filter, including the use of a market share threshold as a proxy, is not the appropriate tool to distinguish between by object and by effect restrictions. Using such a threshold to distinguish 'good' from 'bad' would place undue importance on defining and applying the parameters of the threshold. If a market share threshold were used, it would be likely to result in unhelpful disputes about the exact boundaries of the relevant market, about market share data, whether to use volume or turnover data, etc. As regards a dominance threshold, the focus would unfortunately shift to proving and prohibiting a dominant position, instead of assessing the allegedly abusive conduct and its effects.

slowly at first. The EU Courts ruled (e.g., in 2002 in *Atlantic Container Line* and in 2007 in *British Airways* and *Microsoft*) that the anti-competitive exclusionary effect arising from unilateral conduct or agreements of a dominant firm may have to be balanced with, or can be outweighed by, its pro-competitive effect in terms of efficiencies that benefit the consumer.[20]

In 2008 the Commission adopted its Article 102 Guidance, in which, as stated previously, it developed a full-blown effects-based approach for exclusionary conduct by dominant firms. This approach has by and large been confirmed by the CoJ in its *Post Danmark I* and *Intel* judgments. In the *Post Danmark I* judgment, the Court of Justice for the first time aligned the conditions for a successful efficiency defence under Article 102 with the conditions of Article 101(3), enumerating all the conditions for a successful efficiency defence in the same way as the Commission had already done in its Article 102 Guidance.[21] This implied the recognition of what is, in effect, a true 'Article 102(3)' defence. In the *Post Danmark I* and *Intel* judgments, the CoJ ruled that the conduct of dominant firms, and in particular pricing conduct, is generally only abusive if it can foreclose as-efficient competitors. This as-efficient-competitor principle needs to form a part of the assessment, together with other factors such as the extent of dominance, the market coverage of the conduct, the strategy and intent of the dominant firm, etc., in order to undertake a full effects analysis and conclude whether the dominant position has been abused.[22] Specifically on the application of the as-efficient-competitor test, the CoJ made clear in *Intel* that this test is deemed useful to assess pricing conduct, but it is not necessary.[23]

These developments, introducing the effects-based approach also for Article 102, were necessary to ensure coherence between the application of Articles 101 and 102 and reduce, if not eliminate, the risk of inconsistency that would result if and to the

20. Joined Cases T-191/98, T-212/98 and T-214/98 *Atlantic Container Line (TACA)* [2003] ECR II-3275, para. 939; Case T-395/94 *Atlantic Container Line* [2002] ECR II-875, para. 330; Case C-95/04 P *British Airways v. Commission* [2007] ECR I-2331, paras 69 and 86; Case T-201/04 *Microsoft v. Commission* [2007] ECR II-3601, paras 688-710 and 1144.
21. *See* paras 40-42 of the judgment and para. 30 of the Guidance, both referred to in footnote 12. In *Post Danmark I*, the Court of Justice followed the Article 102 Guidance almost word for word in its description of the efficiency defence. It also followed the Guidance when it distinguished this defence from the possibility for the dominant firm to show that its conduct is objectively necessary. These two defences together set out how firms can provide an objective justification for their conduct. Whereas the efficiency defence consists of a case-based balancing of effects, the objective necessity test is based on factors external to the parties themselves and unrelated to their position on the market, including for instance reasons of public health or safety protection. *See* point 29 of the Article 102 Guidance and point 18(2) of the Commission Guidelines on the application of Article 81(3) of the Treaty, OJ C 101, 27.4.2004, pp. 99.
22. In its *Google Android* judgment of 14 September 2022, Case T-604/18, ECLI:EU:T:2022:541, the General Court summarises in §§638-641 this 'Intel test' for pricing conduct, including application of the as-efficient-competitor principle ('an analysis of the intrinsic capacity of that practice to foreclose competitors which are at least as efficient as the dominant undertaking').
23. *See* §§142-144 of the CoJ *Intel* judgment, referred to in footnote 12. *See also* the General Court's *Google Android* judgment, §641, referred to in footnote 22, and §§538-539 of its *Google Shopping* judgment of 10 November 2021, Case T-612/17, ECLI:EU:T:2021:763. For more background on the Intel judgment and the distinction between the AEC principle and the AEC test and the usefulness of the latter for the assessment of conditional rebates: Luc Peeperkorn, *Conditional Pricing and the AEC Test: A Happy Marriage or an Awkward Couple?* – Concurrences No. 2-2019.

extent that an effects-based approach were applied under one article and a form-based approach under the other.

4 WHAT ARE THE LIMITS OF THE EFFECTS-BASED APPROACH?

This brings me to the third question posed by the organisers: to what extent is the effects-based approach still relevant and what are its boundaries and limits? I will first address some concerns regarding its application in general, then make some remarks about the challenges of applying competition law and the effects-based approach in the digital sector and I will finish by discussing the limits on how far other goals and in particular sustainability goals can be incorporated into EU competition policy.

4.1 Some Concerns about the Effectiveness of Effects-Based Enforcement

Let me start by addressing a false concern, namely that the effects-based approach, while in principle leading to correct outcomes, leads to slower decision making and more legal uncertainty, whereas form-based rules would be easier to apply and provide more certainty. Experience shows the opposite. The form-based approach of the 1970s to 1990s led to a high level of legal uncertainty and unjustified restrictions on commercial freedom. Moreover, the average time taken by the Commission to adopt Article 102 decisions in the five-year period before the adoption of the Article 102 Guidance was actually longer than the average time taken after the adoption of the effects-based approach. The average time taken to adopt Article 102 decisions is around four years and this is indeed too long, but the cause is not the effects-based approach, which helps to focus and structure the investigation, but the complex nature of these cases, the increasing number of procedural safeguards of the parties' rights of defence, the unwillingness of firms to cooperate and the decision-making process within the Commission, with different departments and checks and balances creating bottlenecks in the decision-making process.

A real concern for the proper functioning of the effects-based approach is the temptation of enforcement authorities to define the category of by object restrictions too widely. When a competition authority starts a case, it may be tempting to define the restriction(s) or conduct under investigation as restrictive by object, as that enables anti-competitive effects to be presumed, rather than having to prove them. If in a particular case, given the market situation, the market power of the parties and evidence of a clear intention to restrict competition, it seems unlikely that the agreement is driven by efficiencies, it may seem redundant to have to show likely or actual negative effects and may in that case seem efficient to categorise the restriction as by object. However, as rightly stated by the Commission in recital 15 of its recently adopted Vertical BER, 'The categorisation of a restriction as hardcore ... should not depend on market-specific circumstances or the individual characteristics of the parties.'[24] The same should obviously apply for the categorisation of a restriction as a by object restriction.

Not only the national competition authorities (NCAs) but also the Commission have at times been unable to resist the temptation to define the by object category too widely or loosely. In cases like Cartes Bancaires and International Skating Union (ISU), the Commission categorised certain restrictions as by object when they were an integral part of a true integration of assets and activities to jointly set up and operate a bank card system and to jointly set up and operate a skating organisation and race calendar.[25] These restrictions were not devoid of the potential to create efficiencies but were simply not proportionate in their particular market context. In all these cases, the balance of possible negative and positive effects depended very much on the exact content of the agreement and cooperation and the situation in the market. It was not the fact itself that a Multilateral Interchange Fee (MIF) was used or that exclusivity conditions were imposed for skaters to take part in the ISU calendar that was considered problematic. What was problematic was the level of the MIF and the unreasonable strictness of the exclusivity conditions.

In other words, these were not by object restrictions; they were restrictions that, as a category, could very well be efficiency-enhancing, possibly even necessary in order to operate a bankcard system/skating calendar, but which in their precise configuration and market situation were not acceptable. It is therefore no accident that in these cases, while describing the restrictions as by object, the Commission still conducted an extensive effects analysis before reaching its decision. If they had really been by object restrictions, the effects analysis would not have been necessary. A real by object restriction is not by object because the price is set too high or the conditions of participation are too onerous. Defining by object 'à la tête du client' sends the wrong signal and creates legal uncertainty for all those instances where the same type of restriction is used to create efficiencies. In the interest of a sound effects-based approach and a coherent enforcement policy, authorities would do well to resist that temptation.

Finally, there is a concern about the fragmentation of EU competition policy. This concern is not necessarily linked to the effects-based approach but derives from the decentralisation of enforcement which the effects-based approach enabled. While Articles 101 and 102 and the case law of the European Courts and the BERs adopted by the Commission bind not only the Commission but also the NCAs and national courts,

24. Commission Regulation (EU) 2022/720 of 10 May 2022 on the application of Article 101(3) of the Treaty on the Functioning of the European Union to categories of vertical agreements and concerted practices, OJ L 134/4 of 11.5.2022. What is rather strange in recital 15 is that this precautionary remark is made in relation to one particular hardcore restriction, while it obviously should apply to all hardcore restrictions.

25. Commission Decision COM(2007) 5060 final of 17 October 2007 relating to a proceeding pursuant to Article 81 EC Treaty in Case COMP/D1/38606 – Groupement des cartes bancaires 'CB', https://ec.europa.eu/competition/antitrust/cases/dec_docs/38606/38606_611_1.pdf; Commission Decision COM(2017) 8240 final of 8 December 2017 relating to proceedings under Article 101 of the Treaty on the Functioning of the European Union (the Treaty) and Article 53 of the EEA Agreement in Case AT. 40208 – International Skating Union's Eligibility rules, https://ec.europa.eu/competition/antitrust/cases/dec_docs/40208/40208_1579_5.pdf.

Commission Guidelines only bind the Commission itself. It is in these Guidelines that the effects-based approach is explained and structured for the various types of agreements and conduct. One solution to reduce the risk of fragmentation would be to turn the ECN into a club where, even more than today, the rules are designed and adopted by all and bind all. Thus there would be 'ECN BERs' and 'ECN Guidelines'. That would of course require some changes to the consultation and adoption procedures, in particular to ensure that the Commission and NCAs adopt identical Guidelines on the same day, but would in my view be worthy of consideration.

4.2 The Effects-Based Approach and Digital Markets

That brings me to the most topical and difficult issue: how well can the effects-based approach and competition policy in general ensure effective competition in digital sectors? I certainly do not claim to have all the answers but hope to be able to make a small contribution to this difficult and lively debate.

A first and fundamental question is to establish where ex-post competition policy enforcement is sufficient and where ex-ante regulation is required. I guess this is the distinction that drove the Commission to propose its Digital Markets Act (DMA), leaving aside whether it has succeeded in making the distinction correctly.[26]

In my view, ex-post competition policy enforcement cannot work where the most efficient outcome is to have only one firm, that is in the case of natural monopolies. A natural monopoly may result for a number of reasons. A natural monopoly may be the consequence of continuing economies of scale. This we already knew from old network industries such as rail transport. The question now is whether, in particular, the collection and ownership of data also creates continuing economies of scale, meaning that more data always leads to more and improved possibilities to operate on the market. If so, and in the absence of regulation that requires the data to be shared, the natural market outcome will be the existence of only one supplier, for instance only one search engine. A natural monopoly may also result from indirect network effects, if the participants on at least one side of a platform market are not able or willing to multi-home; i.e., they are not able or willing to use multiple platforms, either simultaneously or over time. In that case, the market could 'tip' and end up with only one platform. In such a situation, regulation may be necessary to take away possible barriers to multi-homing. Finally, a natural monopoly may result from direct network effects, if there are (currently) no efficient possibilities for interoperability. In such a case, the market may again tip, ending up with only one supplier, and it may be necessary to regulate to enforce interoperability in order to allow competition between different (network) suppliers.

A problem with the current debate, at least it seems to me, is that the above terms and distinctions are often used rather loosely and with insufficient empirical evidence, which is not helpful for the identification of markets in which the tendency towards

26. https://ec.europa.eu/info/strategy/priorities-2019-2024/europe-fit-digital-age/digital-markets-act-ensuring-fair-and-open-digital-markets_en.

natural monopolies requires regulation before competition policy enforcement can be effective.

Outside the area of natural monopolies, I see no particular reason why competition policy should not work. However, for a discussion on its effective application, it is useful to make a distinction between cases addressing indirect customer or input foreclosure and cases addressing direct input foreclosure.

In case of indirect customer or input foreclosure, the (dominant) firm prevents or limits access by competitors to third-party upstream suppliers or downstream customers. This concerns conduct and agreements involving tying, bundling, predatory pricing, rebates, exclusive purchasing and exclusive sourcing. I see no reason why the usual effects-based approach could not or should not be applied. The NCAs and the Commission regularly take action in such cases, applying in particular Article 102 to restore and protect competition. Commission cases in the high tech and digital sectors include Intel (2009 – indirect customer foreclosure), Qualcomm Exclusivity (2018 – indirect customer foreclosure), Google Android (2019 – indirect customer foreclosure), Qualcomm Predation (2019 – indirect customer foreclosure) and Google Adsense (2019 – indirect input foreclosure).[27] The annulment of the Commission's decisions in the Intel and Qualcomm Exclusivity cases and the annulment in part in the Google Android case should not lead to the conclusion that the effects-based approach does not work.[28] It merely shows that the Commission needs to apply more rigorously the approach that it set out in its Article 102 Guidance.

For situations of direct input foreclosure, it is more difficult to determine the correct balance between ex-ante regulation and ex-post competition policy enforcement. This concerns situations where the dominant firm refuses or obstructs (efficient) access by rivals to an input produced by the dominant firm or to an asset/facility owned by the dominant firm. In these situations, the dominant firm is active both at the input level and, as a (potential) competitor, at the downstream level where the input is used. Termination of supply, margin squeeze and de novo refusal to supply are all forms of what is labelled direct foreclosure of competitors.

27. Commission Decision COM(2009) 3726 final of 13 May 2009 relating to a proceeding under Article 82 [EC] and Article 54 of the EEA Agreement in Case COMP/C-3/37.990 — Intel; Commission Decision COM(2018) 240 final of 24.1.2018 relating to proceedings under Article 102 of the Treaty on the Functioning of the European Union and Article 54 of the Agreement on the European Economic Area in Case AT.40220 – Qualcomm (Exclusivity payments); Commission Decision COM(2018) 4761 final of 18.7.2018 relating to a proceeding under Article 102 of the Treaty on the Functioning of the European Union (the Treaty) and Article 54 of the EEA Agreement in Case AT.40099 – Google Android; Commission Decision COM(2019) 5361 final of 18.7.2019 relating to a proceeding under Article 102 of the Treaty on the Functioning of the European Union and Article 54 of the EEA Agreement in Case AT.39711 – Qualcomm (predation); Commission Decision COM(2019) 2173 final of 20.3.2019 relating to a proceeding under Article 102 of the Treaty on the Functioning of the European Union (the Treaty) and Article 54 of the EEA Agreement in Case AT. 40411 – Google Search (AdSense).

28. Case T-286/09 RENV *Intel v. Commission*, judgment of the General Court (Fourth Chamber, Extended Composition) of 26 January 2022; Case T-235/18 *Qualcomm v. Commission*, judgment of the General Court (Sixth Chamber, Extended Composition) of 15 June 2022; *Google Android* judgment referred to in footnote 22, which annulled the Commission decision in so far as it considered the portfolio-based Revenue Share Agreements to constitute an abuse.

In general, EU competition policy and the case law impose a more cautious approach for the finding of abuses consisting of direct foreclosure than for abuses consisting of indirect foreclosure. In particular, for cases involving a de novo refusal to supply, it is necessary to prove indispensability, that is, to establish that there are no actual or potential substitutes for the input/service/facility of the dominant undertaking (*see Oscar Bronner, Magill, IMS Health, Microsoft*).[29] However, whereas the Article 102 Guidance explicitly states that the stricter criteria for finding a direct foreclosure type abuse apply equally to cases of *de novo* refusal to supply, termination of supply, constructive refusal and margin squeeze, more recent case law, in particular *TeliaSonera*[30] and *Slovak Telekom*,[31] has made clear that the Union Courts distinguish between situations where a dominant firm refuses to start supplying a rival firm and situations where the two firms have an ongoing supply relationship, even though one of them may want to terminate the relationship, or the other may disagree with (some of) the conditions of supply (the latter type of situations are referred to in the rest of this chapter as 'termination of supply').

There are two main reasons to be more cautious when intervening against direct foreclosure than against indirect foreclosure. The first reason is linked to the potential negative effects of the intervention on the incentives to invest of the dominant firm and its competitors. The indispensability condition is intended to ensure that the dominant undertaking is not forced to share the benefits of its investments with its current or potential competitors, and that these competitors do not rely on the dominant undertaking's investments but rather invest and innovate themselves, provided duplication of the input is feasible. Where possible, it is preferable to incentivise market operators to compete independently of each other, instead of creating a situation where competitors depend on each other for an input.

If an input is indispensable and therefore competitors cannot duplicate it, obliging the dominant firm to share its input cannot undermine the incentives of the competitors to invest. Possible negative effects on the dominant firm's own investment incentives can then be assessed under the efficiency defence, i.e., where the burden is on the dominant firm to show that its incentives to invest are undermined.

The second reason to be more cautious when intervening against direct foreclosure than against indirect foreclosure is that in direct foreclosure cases the remedy will often be more intrusive and require monitoring and price setting by the authority. This means that the design of an effective remedy is generally more difficult, as it is not easy

29. Case 7/97 *Oscar Bronner v. Mediaprint Zeitungs- und Zeitschriftenverlag, Mediaprint Zeitungsvertriebsgesellschaft and Mediaprint Anzeigengesellschaft* [1998] ECR I-7791; Joined Cases C-241/91 P and C-242/91 *Radio Telefis Eireann (RTE) and Independent Television Publications (ITP) v. Commission (Magill)* [1995] ECR I-743; Case C-418/01 *IMS Health v. NDC Health* [2004] ECR I-5039; Case T-201/04 *Microsoft v. Commission* [2007] ECR II-3601.
30. Judgment of the CoJ of 17 February 2011 in Case C-52/09 *Konkurrensverket v. TeliaSonera Sverige AB*, ECR I-527. The Court held that indispensability is an important factor, but that even if indispensability cannot be established, an abuse can still be found if there is an anti-competitive effect by potentially excluding competitors who are at least as efficient as the dominant undertaking.
31. Judgment of the CoJ of 25 March 2021 in Case C-152/19 P *Deutsche Telekom AG v. European Commission*, ECLI:EU:C:2021:238, in particular paras 43-61.

to force a firm to effectively supply its competitors. If a dominant firm is forced to give access or not to limit access to its own input, this will often require the authority to determine the access conditions (price, quantity, etc.), and this often for prolonged periods and for various market scenarios. In general, it is considered that competition authorities are not well placed to assume such a (possibly long-term) regulatory role and should do so only in exceptional circumstances.[32]

For all termination of supply cases, the Commission and NCAs will have to decide how to use the 'enforcement freedom' created by *TeliaSonera* and *Slovak Telekom*. Whether to simply apply the general test used for indirect foreclosure conduct, i.e., to find the termination abusive if it leads to anti-competitive foreclosure (foreclosure that is likely to harm consumers), or to introduce another limiting principle, less stringent than the indispensability test. The Commission chose to use the general anti-competitive foreclosure test in its Google Shopping decision[33], while the General Court in its *Google Shopping* judgment seems on the one hand to apply a general non-discrimination principle and on the other hand alludes to a number of factors that might form the basis of a limiting principle, most notably super dominance, the product being intended to be open and neutral and the product having been made available at first and only denied later.[34]

While the choice of a limiting principle may have a limited practical impact for the assessment of traditional termination of supply cases in the telecoms sector, since in these cases a margin squeeze is generally applied by dominant firms that are already under a regulatory obligation to supply their (indispensable) input to competitors, this choice is important for the increasing number of complaints concerning termination of supply scenarios in digital markets.

It can be argued that the new termination of supply scenarios in (dynamic) digital markets differ on essential points from the more traditional essential facility cases, at least as regards the first reason for a higher intervention threshold.

In digital markets, market power is often based on (in)direct network effects. Firms generally start with an open access strategy, granting equal and possibly free access to all parties that want to use their platform or service. However, once the platform or service has become unavoidable for a large share of users, the firm may change its strategy. It may exploit its market power by starting to price the access, possibly applying different rates for different users. In addition, the dominant firm may wish to enter other markets, in particular markets on which some of its

32. Conversely, in indirect foreclosure cases, the parties want to deal with each other, but the competition authority may object to certain aspects of the dominant firm's conduct (such as an exclusive purchasing requirement, tying or a certain type of rebate) that forecloses third parties. As a remedy, in most cases it will be sufficient to adopt a cease and desist order, i.e., obliging the dominant firm not to impose a particular requirement on its customers or to stop applying a particular type of rebate. Once the remedy is in place, the dominant firm and its customers will continue to deal with each other, as that is what they wanted to do in the first place, and there will be no need for the authority to intervene in their future transactions.
33. Commission Decision COM(2017) 4444 final of 27.6.2017 relating to proceedings under Article 102 of the Treaty on the Functioning of the European Union and Article 54 of the Agreement on the European Economic Area in Case AT.39740 – Google Search (Shopping).
34. *See* in particular §§176-183 of the judgment referred to in footnote 23.

customers/users are active. To facilitate such entry, the dominant firm may reduce access to its own platform/service for these users while simultaneously entering the market(s) where these users are active.

It is obvious that in the above situation there is no reason to fear that intervention, or applying a lower intervention threshold, could create a bias for the dominant firm not to supply in the first place. As indicated, in digital markets an open access strategy is commercially necessary at the start, when the market is new and developing and market positions are still in a state of flux. This distinguishes these cases from the more traditional essential facility and intellectual property (IP) cases, where the firm in question often does not intend to grant access when it undertakes the (sometimes very significant) investments that create the (natural) monopoly situation.

More generally, it can be argued that if a dominant firm has found it to be in its interest to supply an input to one or more customers, this shows that it considered it efficient, at least at that point in time, to engage in such supply relationships. In other words, supplying had no negative effect on its incentives to invest.[35] This and the fact that customers are likely to have made investments connected to these supply relationships mean that in such a scenario it may be less appropriate to impose the higher threshold for intervention.

However, it seems that the new termination of supply scenarios in digital markets do not differ substantially from the more traditional essential facility cases as regards the second reason for exercising caution. This is because the nature of the intervention is and remains substantially different between indirect and direct foreclosure cases. It is no overstatement to say that also in termination of supply cases in digital markets there is a real risk that mandating competitive access is not easy to implement or to monitor.

This raises the question of whether it would be desirable to still have a limiting principle for termination of supply cases. If not, competition authorities may become the regulator that has to police the commercial relationships of many disgruntled competitors and their dominant supplier/buyer. Think of the dominant brewer which is also active on the pubs market. The Commission and the NCAs would be expected to deal with complaints by independent pubs about the pricing and delivery conditions of the dominant brewer's beer. Or the complaints of brand manufacturers that are not present or not satisfied with their position on the shelves relative to the position of the own brands of a dominant supermarket.

Vague terminology such as leveraging or new terminology such as self-preferencing will not help to define such a limiting principle. Leveraging, i.e., the use of market power in one market/part of the market to gain market power in another market/part of the market, is a generic term that can be applied to most exclusionary practices (refusal to supply, tying, bundling, exclusive purchasing, rebates). Self-preferencing seems to encompass any preference for a firm's own activity over the activities of its rivals in the same market, and raises the risk of imposing a general non-discrimination obligation.

---

35. The dominant firm may of course argue that extending its activities into neighbouring markets is necessary to fund its investments in the input.

There are also good reasons why the non-discrimination principle that the General Court seems to suggest in its *Google Shopping* judgment would not be a good choice. The discrimination concept should be reserved for discrimination between third parties; it should not include treating your own subsidiary company more favourably than third parties, if only because the dominant firm can make the discrimination disappear on paper by charging a higher price to the subsidiary and by other forms of transfer pricing. Attempting to apply such a principle would not limit the number of potential cases and would only add to the complexity of finding an effective remedy.

In view of the above-mentioned grounds for caution, I suggest that there is a need for a limiting principle. But of course such a limiting principle should be within the bounds of the case law, which means that indispensability of the input can no longer be a necessary condition in termination of supply cases. Finding a workable and coherent limiting principle seems to be the one-million-euro question. Although I do not have the answer, I would like to offer some tentative suggestions for defining a limiting principle:

- *By type of effect*: the conduct may only be found abusive if it eliminates effective competition for a substantial share of the market. This addresses situations where the dominant firm becomes the gatekeeper to a substantial share of customers, which is particularly likely in cases where the dominant position is based on indirect network effects in two- or multi-sided markets, and where one group of customers is single-homing.
- *By expected duration of the effects*: a finding of abuse should only be possible in cases where it cannot be expected that the market itself will rectify the anti-competitive outcome in the middle or long term.
- *By type of product*: the 'dominant' product is, in the eyes of consumers, intended to be 'universal, open and objective'. For instance, the pre-Internet telephone directory or yellow pages were expected to provide the address and phone number of all merchants and not a selection depending on the activities of the publisher on certain downstream markets.
- *By level of dominance*: the dominant firm should have a super-dominant position.
- *By availability of an administrable remedy*: a finding of abuse should only be possible in cases where an effective remedy would not impose a long-term regulatory burden on the competition authority or court.

A limiting principle could possibly be based on (a combination of) the first three suggestions. They seem best fitted to the new termination of supply scenarios in (dynamic) digital markets, without opening the floodgates for regulatory competition policy intervention. A requirement of super dominance has a number of drawbacks, in particular that it would add a concept that, although often used in the literature, is not patently clear and has no direct link with the effects on the market. Finally, the availability of an administrable remedy is likely to involve a sliding scale and therefore does not appear very suitable as a limiting principle while, at the same time, the availability of administrable remedies should always be a relevant criterium for intervention – not just for termination of supply cases.

4.3 The Effects-Based Approach and Incorporating Other EU Policy Goals

The Commission and NCAs are traditionally focused in their cases on specific markets, on protecting competition and preventing the negative effects of market power for the customers in those relevant market(s). However, there is an increasing demand, from various sides, to look beyond the effects in specific markets and to take into account wider societal interests.

Traditionally, this type of demand often becomes more vocal during merger investigations involving firms that are seen to be strategically important. For instance, when in 2019 the Commission prohibited the Siemens/Alstom merger, the French minister of Economics and his German counterpart argued for a change in EU competition policy, and in particular EU merger policy: they said that competition policy should form part of an EU industrial policy.[36] It should allow the creation of 'European champions', even if that meant creating or strengthening a dominant position in EU markets, with direct negative effects for EU consumers. In other merger cases, the preservation of jobs is raised as a goal that should be taken into account. Depending on the particular case, arguments are made for more or less competition policy intervention.

More recently a second type of demand, which generally comes more from the political left, argues that competition policy should pursue several different goals and should not prioritise any particular welfare standard. Thus competition policy should not only protect competition and consumer welfare; it should also, for instance, protect small firms and employment, and promote balanced regional development and conservation of the environment. According to this view, competition policy should actively balance these goals. This type of demand is often more interventionist, calling for action, for instance, to defend regional employment interests. However, in other contexts, it may also argue for less intervention, for example to allow anti-competitive private sustainability initiatives.

What both types of demand have in common is that, in order to take societal interests into account, they propose to replace the test that is currently applied by competition law, which focusses on the effects on consumers in the relevant market, with a broader test, which focusses on the effects for society at large. This broader test would apply either in general or at least for certain types of agreements/when certain societal interests are involved. In other words, instead of assessing whether consumers in the relevant market are harmed or benefit as the test for prohibiting or permitting an agreement between firms, it is proposed that the test should be whether the agreement harms or benefits the society at large. In the jargon of competition specialists, the

36. Federal Ministry of Economic Affairs and Energy (Germany) and Ministry of Economy and Finance (France), *A Franco-German Manifesto for a European industrial policy fit for the 21st Century*, available at: https://www.bmwi.de/Redaktion/DE/Downloads/F/franco-german-manifesto-for-a-european-industrial-policy.pdf?__blob=publicationFile&v=2.

assessment would not be limited to 'in-market' negative effects and efficiencies, but would also include 'out-of-market' effects. In other words, the effects-based approach would be applied to a (much) wider category of effects.

Both types of demand often refer to one or more of the EU's other policy goals to support their case for widening the goal of EU competition policy. It is of course true that the EU has always had a number of goals. Currently, around 20 goals are mentioned in the EU Treaties: peace, the well-being of citizens, the internal market, security, justice, sustainable development, social justice, a social market economy, economic and social cohesion, price stability, full employment, social and technical progress, gender equality, the protection of human rights and children's rights, combatting social exclusion and discrimination, animal welfare, free and fair trade, and the eradication of poverty.[37] While the wording of the Treaties has evolved, the Treaties have always required that the EU's various policies and decisions take a range of goals into account.[38]

The question is therefore what this means or should mean in practice for the implementation of each individual policy. In our case, how should EU competition policy take the various goals of the EU – of which sustainability is one – into account? Answering this question in fact means defining what is, or should be, the goal of EU competition law, both from a legal and a practical enforcement perspective.

For a legal answer to this question, it makes sense to start by looking at the text of Articles 101 and 102. In particular the text of Article 101 is instructive. Here we can apply what is called backward induction. This concept comes from game theory and is usually about reasoning backward in time, but is also useful in a sequence where one part (here Article 101(3)) only needs to be applied if another part (here Article 101(1)) applies.

The second and third condition of Article 101(3) make clear that as long as consumers benefit from the restrictions and the restrictions are indispensable for producing efficiencies, an agreement that restricts competition is allowed. It is allowed even though the process of competition may be harmed and, for that matter, also if other objectives, such as employment or economic and social cohesion or balanced regional development, may be harmed. The conditions of Article 101(3) are exhaustive: they do not provide or allow for other objectives to be taken into account. Or, more accurately, they do not allow other objectives to be weighed against the objective of consumer welfare.

This logically means that an agreement can only be prohibited under Article 101 in cases where the conditions of Article 101(3) are not fulfilled. As the conditions are cumulative, this means that a restrictive agreement that does not benefit consumers and/or is not indispensable to obtain the efficiencies, is not permitted. The condition that consumers should benefit indicates that the objective of Article 101 is indeed to protect competition as a means to promote consumer welfare. This is also expressed in

37. *See* in particular Article 3 of the Treaty on European Union.

38. *See* in particular Articles 7-13 of the Treaty on the Functioning of the European Union (TFEU).

various Commission Guidelines – *see* in particular the Article 101(3) Guidelines – and in the Commission's enforcement practice.[39]

That the four conditions of Article 101(3) are not only cumulative, but also exhaustive, i.e., when the conditions are met, the exception is applicable and cannot be made dependent on any other condition, is neatly summarised in paragraph 42 of the Article 101(3) Guidelines: 'Goals pursued by other Treaty provisions can be taken into account to the extent that they can be subsumed under the four conditions of Article 101(3).' In other words, positive effects that contribute to other goals, for instance positive environmental effects resulting from a potentially anti-competitive agreement between competitors, can only be taken into account under Article 101(3) to the extent that such positive effects benefit consumers.

It can thus be concluded that, as a matter of law, the Commission, the NCAs and national courts, when they apply EU competition law, are not free to replace the consumer welfare goal with a total welfare goal, or to balance the consumer welfare goal against other policy goals.[40]

In addition to this legal answer, there are also strong practical arguments against expanding the goal of EU competition policy and in particular against attempting, in individual competition cases, to balance the effects of firms' conduct and agreements on multiple EU goals.

The world has many problems, most prominently the climate crisis, but also, for instance, poverty, concerns about privacy in the digital world, the deplorable treatment of animals in factory farming and, at least in some parts of the world, increasing income inequality and social division. There is also widespread dissatisfaction with the speed at which governments and intergovernmental organisations adopt and implement regulation to address these problems.

It is therefore not surprising that there is a push for private firms to help solve these problems and for competition authorities and courts, when dealing with competition cases, to not only focus on 'in-market' negative and positive effects, but to also take into account 'out-of-market' effects.

If that choice is framed as a technical choice of how wide the cost-benefit analysis should be, the discussion will naturally focus on the possibilities and difficulties of assessing out-of-market effects. There will be those on one side who point to the advances made in cost-benefit analysis in general and environmental economic assessments in particular and those on the other side who point to the likely difficulties, lack of predictability, delays and costs for competition policy enforcement.

---

39. Guidelines on the application of Article 81(3) of the Treaty, OJ C 101/97, 27.4.2004, point 13. *See also* point 5 of the Guidelines on Vertical Restraints, OJ C 248, 30.6.2022, pp. 1-85 and point 5 of the Guidelines on the application of Article 101 of the Treaty on the Functioning of the European Union to technology transfer agreements, OJ C 89/3, 28.3.2014.
40. For a similar reasoning for the assessment of mergers, *see* Commission Decision in Case M.8084 – Bayer/Monsanto of 21.3.2018, paras 3010-3029, and Commissioner Vestager's response to petitions published in August 2017, https://ec.europa.eu/commission/presscorner/detail/en/IP_18_2282. Both texts make clear that non-competition concerns protected by other EU or national rules on human health, food safety, consumer protection and environmental and climate protection are of great importance but cannot form the basis of a merger assessment.

I have argued elsewhere that a requirement to take out-of-market effects into account would undermine the predictability, rigour and uniformity of EU competition policy, not just because it is very difficult to weigh different interests and goals in a particular case, but also in view of the large number of actors (Commission, NCAs, national courts, firms required to self-assess) and the very large number of agreements/mergers/conducts concerned. This loss of rigour and certainty might not be a problem for very big firms, with their armies of lawyers, economists and lobbyists, but it would harm the many smaller firms and, behind them, their customers and European consumers, all of whom depend on a rigorous competition policy for their protection. It would thus be a bad choice from an effective enforcement point of view.[41]

However, the choice between a test based only on in-market effects or also on out-of-market effects is not merely a technical choice between different cost-benefit analyses.[42]

The basic assumption underlying competition policy is that competition forces firms to listen to their customers and to make products that customers want at the best price and quality possible. Without competition, or where competition is restricted, firms will have a degree of market power, allowing them to increase their profits at the expense of their customers, by increasing the price and/or lowering the quality or innovativeness of their products. This means that, as a rule, competition produces good outcomes, and competition authorities only need to intervene where competition is distorted by certain conducts or agreements between firms. As a result, competition policy enforcement can be limited to intervening on an ad-hoc/case-by-case basis.

This does not mean that competition policy cannot function as a complement to and in support of (possibly insufficient) regulation. Where regulation aims to address situations of market power, in general or in particular sectors, case-by-case competition policy intervention can often help regulation to achieve its goal. Good examples from the past include the role played by competition policy enforcement in the liberalisation of telecoms and other regulated industries. The reason why that worked was that both the legislation in question and competition policy were (and still are) focused on addressing market power and improving the in-market effects. Finding the right balance between the enforcement of competition policy and regulation will also be one of the challenges for the DMA, if it is to achieve its goal of making digital markets more contestable and fair.

However, the situation is totally different where regulation is trying to address negative external effects, as in the case of environmental legislation. External effects are, as a rule, out-of-market effects. Suppliers and customers in the (relevant) market from which the external effects emanate may not take these external effects into account, or they may do so to an insufficient degree. As a result, too much of the polluting product is produced and consumed. This is not the result of market power or

41. Luc Peeperkorn, *Competition and Sustainability: What Can Competition Policy Do?*, Concurrences No. 4-2020, pp. 40-52, and a chapter about which test to apply in competition policy in the section *Agency Outlook – European Union* in S. Holmes, D. Middelschulte & M. Snoep (eds), *Competition Law, Climate Change & Environmental Sustainability*, Concurrences (2021).

42. The remainder of this section is taken directly from Luc Peeperkorn, *Competition Policy Is Not a Stopgap!*, Journal of European Competition Law & Practice 12(6) (June 2021), 415-418.

a distortion of competition. One could even argue the opposite: that competition, by lowering the price and increasing the quality and thereby the attractiveness of the product, leads to increases in output and demand and thereby aggravates the problem of the external effects.

One solution to this problem is of course to internalise the negative external effects, using regulation such as a CO_2 tax. Economists often favour such solutions because, by internalising the negative effects, all effects are again brought in-market and, subject only to the usual case-by-case competition policy interventions against competition-distorting agreements or conducts, competition can again ensure optimal outcomes, also from the perspective of sustainability.

However, this first best solution is not what the proponents of a society-wide balancing/total welfare test are proposing. Although they recognise the importance of adequate regulation, they argue that regulation is often 'too little and too late'. And it is where there is suboptimal regulation that they propose to take 'out-of-market' effects into account.

This raises two basic questions. First, whether it is appropriate to address one market failure by creating another one; whether the non-internalisation of external effects is best combatted by allowing the creation of market power. In other words, whether, if the first best solution of sufficient and timely regulation is not possible, allowing a restriction of competition is really a good second best. Second, whether taking out-of-market effects into account, with the aim of integrating external effects into competition policy assessments, is compatible with the nature of competition policy.

The practical enforcement problems related to taking out-of-market effects into account, referred to above, already point towards a negative answer to both questions. But there are also two more fundamental reasons why the answer to both questions is no.

As explained by Schinkel and Treuren, giving firms market power does not create incentives to produce more sustainably. Schinkel and Treuren see a danger in the growing enthusiasm to relax competition policy in order to enable out-of-market efficiencies. 'On the contrary: growing awareness of the vital importance of a sustainable planet, the rise of civil society, and an increasing willingness to buy from and invest in companies that take a more socially and environmentally responsible stance are ever stronger motivators for firms to offer more sustainably produced goods and services in competition. These hopeful gathering forces for green should be given free rein, rather than be allowed to be suppressed by collaborations that risk collusion.'[43] This is the reason why fighting one market failure with another market failure will generally make matters worse.

The equally fundamental reason for a negative answer to the second question is linked to the case-by-case nature of competition policy enforcement. Competition policy intervenes on a case-by-case basis as a means to address the negative effects of

43. Maarten Pieter Schinkel & Leonard Treuren, *Green Antitrust: Friendly Fire in the Fight Against Climate Change*, in S. Holmes, D. Middelschulte & M. Snoep (eds), *Competition Law, Climate Change & Environmental Sustainability*, Concurrences (2021).

market power. A case-by-case approach is not suited to a scenario in which it is necessary to (also) take out-of-market effects into account, because these effects have intrinsically no relation to the existence or use of market power. Negative external effects result from the legal production and consumption of certain products and they can arise in both competitive markets and less competitive ones.

For instance, if a manufacturer changes its distribution system, by terminating its distribution agreements with some independent distributors and entering into distribution agreements with others, this is likely to have an effect not only on the attractiveness and availability of the products in question, but also on the transport needs of the firms involved and of their customers, and thereby on the external effects created by those transport needs. For example, if the new distributors are located further outside city centres, this may make it less costly to supply the distributors, but it may require customers to travel further. It may also have other external effects, such as an effect on the liveability of city centres. While the in-market price effects may be absent or non-appreciable, under a broad societal welfare test the out-of-market effects may bring the agreements within Article 101(1) and onto the radar of a competition authority.

In order to address these external effects, whether negative or positive, a competition authority will no longer be able to rely on case-by-case interventions, assuming that competition will lead to satisfactory outcomes in most markets. Net negative external effects may arise also in situations where the firms in question have no market power. As the example in the previous paragraph shows, this may happen not only in cases involving agreements between competitors (horizontal agreements) but also in cases involving supply and distribution agreements between non-competitors (vertical agreements). The firms themselves, when they self-assess their agreements, and competition authorities or national courts, when they have to decide on the legality of such agreements, may often have to rule against the agreement in situations where the firms involved are incapable of harming their customers by increasing the price/reducing the quality of their product, i.e., where there are no negative in-market effects.

The proponents of taking external effects into account have so far conveniently ignored this, by concentrating on demands from industry to widen the test under Article 101(3) and by only discussing horizontal agreements, i.e., to allow negative in-market effects to be compensated by positive out-of-market effects in cases of cooperation between competitors.[44] However, it should be obvious that if the positive external effects of an agreement are to be taken into account, then also any negative external effects should be taken into account. Not only because the same agreement may create both positive and negative external effects, on the same or different aspects of sustainability for instance, but also because it would not make sense to ignore the negative external effects if the aim is to apply a societal balancing test. Firms should

44. Except for Simon Holmes: while mainly speaking about using Article 101(3) 'as a shield' for anti-competitive sustainability agreements, he also speaks of using Article 101(1) 'as a sword', *Climate Change, Sustainability, and Competition Law*, Journal of Antitrust Enforcement 8(2) (July 2020): 354-405.

therefore be careful what they wish for. Similarly, if the test is changed for horizontal agreements, there is no legal basis or obvious policy justification for not also changing it for vertical agreements, of which there are hundreds of thousands in the EU.

In other words, to take out-of-market effects into account would require competition policy to change fundamentally, from a policy that relies on consumer sovereignty and competition to prevent problems in most cases, and intervenes only on a case-by-case basis in situations where firms have market power and the negative effects of their agreement are not outweighed by the efficiencies that it creates, to a policy that polices agreements in all market situations, including competitive markets. In that scenario, the enforcing authority would, for example, no longer be able to apply safe harbours based on market share thresholds or other proxies for market power. Under the new test, competition policy would have to monitor agreements in competitive and less competitive markets and would become a bad substitute for the regulation that is lacking. That is the reason why an out-of-markets effects test is fundamentally at odds with the nature and purpose of competition policy.

5 CONCLUSION

To conclude, the effects-based approach will remain the central approach in competition policy, if only for lack of a better alternative, but it will only remain successful if it is applied with due regard for its limits and in a context of sufficient ex-ante regulation.

The effects-based approach was not only necessary to allow the enforcement of Article 101 to be decentralised, it also provides the necessary framework for a coherent application of EU competition policy that protects competition in the market in the interest of consumers. This framework, set out by the Commission in its various guidelines and guidance documents, will require continuous updating, to adapt the structured effects-based approach to new market developments. A particular pressing question, in view of developments in digital markets, is whether to develop a new limiting principle for termination of supply cases. As suggested, this could be based on a combination of the effect of the conduct/agreement being to foreclose a whole segment of the market, the length of the period before market forces themselves can be expected to rectify the anti-competitive outcome and the characteristics of the product indicating that it was intended to be 'universal, open and objective'.

A well-functioning and cost-effective effects-based approach will also require a continuous updating of the category of by object restrictions/conduct, i.e., those which justify the presumption of an infringement of the competition rules. This should be based on enforcement experience that certain restrictions and conduct generally have a net negative impact on market outcomes.

While efforts to integrate additional goals into EU competition policy and to incorporate a societal balancing exercise may be well-intentioned and may appear to offer a means to allow competition law to 'do more' and 'be part of the solution', in reality they are likely to throw the baby out with the bathwater. Attempting to assess agreements and conduct by reference to multiple goals, and to weigh up their effects across multiple groups and markets or for society at large would make the application of competition law not only more complex, more costly, slower and less certain, but it would also change the nature of competition policy and turn it into a defunct form of market monitoring and market regulation.

Contrary to what some of the proponents of a society-wide balancing test argue, focusing only on the in-market effects does not mean that EU competition policy is failing to comply with the requirement, set out in Articles 7-13 of the Treaty on the Functioning of the European Union, to take the goals mentioned in Article 3 of the Treaty on European Union, including sustainable development, into account. That requirement is respected by taking the negative and positive effects on other goals into account to the extent that they either harm or benefit consumers in the relevant market. Such in-market weighing of effects can and should be done by EU competition policy.[45]

Competition policy can play a useful role, also for sustainability, by keeping markets competitive. As sufficiently demonstrated elsewhere, competition spurs innovation, and it is widely recognised that innovation is key to addressing the climate crisis.[46] Competition also forces firms to use scarce resources efficiently and to listen to consumers when they demand more sustainable products. In other words, by protecting competition, competition policy will indirectly support climate policy (and other sustainability goals). However, it can only fulfil this role if it is applied coherently and is not used as a stopgap or an excuse when governments fail to regulate appropriately.

45. *See* paras 42-43 of the Commission Guidelines on the application of Article 81(3) of the Treaty [2004] OJ C101/97. For some suggestions on how EU competition policy could improve this in-market assessment where sustainability agreements are concerned, *see* sections VIII and IX of Luc Peeperkorn, *Competition and Sustainability: What Can Competition Policy Do?*, Concurrences No. 4-2020.

46. Higher product market competition not only causes the level of productivity to increase, but also reduces differences in the productivity levels of firms within a market, by eliminating less productive firms. Thus, competition not only increases productivity by providing more opportunities for entry and expansion for more innovative firms, at the expense of less productive firms (reallocation or selection effect), but it also incentivises incumbent firms to improve. *See* for instance C. Syverson, *What Determines Productivity?*, Journal of Economic Literature 49(2) (June 2011): 326-365; N. Bloom et al., *Management Practices Across Firms and Countries*, NBER Working Paper No. 17850, February 2012. *See also* research into the (inverted U) relationship between concentration and the ratio of industry R&D to industry sales: P. Aghion et al., *Competition and Innovation: An Inverted U Relationship*, The Institute for Fiscal Studies, WP02/04, February 2002; S. Martin, *Competition Policy for High Technology Industries*, Journal of Industry, Competition and Trade 1(4) (2001):441-465. More recent research on incentives to innovate in the hard disk drive industry indicates that in that sector the incentive to innovate increases with the number of competitors in the industry, but that this positive effect tapers off when more than four or five firms compete, without, however, the incentive to innovate declining again at higher numbers of competitors. In other words, instead of an inverted U, it is more like a plateau once the market becomes less concentrated, i.e., higher numbers of competitors in the market are associated with a stable high incentive to innovate. *See* M. Igami & K. Uetake, *Mergers, Innovation, and Entry-Exit Dynamics: Consolidation of the Hard Disk Drive Industry, 1996-2016*, The Review of Economic Studies 87(6) (November 2020): 2672-2702, https://doi.org/10.1093/restud/rdz044.

CHAPTER 2

Towards a Fourth Paradigm in European Competition Policy? A Historical Perspective (1957-2022)

Laurent Warlouzet[*]

1 INTRODUCTION

Since the Treaty of Rome of 1957, the articles defining European competition policy have remained unchanged, but their interpretations have evolved. This chapter argues that it is possible to identify four different paradigms, i.e., a broad set of beliefs about the right interpretation of the Treaty of Rome that is informed by the dominant intellectual, political and institutional context of the time. Economists, lawyers, civil servants and politicians are not computers implementing a coded-program, but rather fleshy human beings embedded into wider sets of ideological beliefs, values and scientific knowledge. The term 'paradigm shifts' designs in this article an overhaul of the main objectives and of the implementation tools of European competition policy. It does not refer to a complete revolution in this public policy, as European institutions are marked by continuity and a strong inertia: all new developments must incorporate past primary and secondary legislation. Within this institutional and legal framework, however, room for interpretation exists, and therefore 'paradigm shifts' may be observed. They depend on the intellectual evolution of legal and economic thinking, on

* Laurent Warlouzet most recent books in English include: *Reinventing Europe: The History of the European Union, 1945 to the Present* (Brigitte Leucht & Katja Seidel (eds), Bloomsbury, 2023); *Governing Europe in a Globalizing World: Neoliberalism and Its Alternatives* (Routledge, 2018). The author thanks David Gerber, Frédéric Marty, Heike Schweitzer and Anselm Küsters for constructive and sometimes conflicting comments on an earlier version of this chapter. All interpretations and errors are those of the author.

the economic and political context, and on the balance of power between decision-makers.

The continuity between the Treaty of Rome creating the European Economic Community (EEC) and the current Lisbon Treaty (Treaty on the Functioning of the European Union (TFEU)) provides the ground for the historical methodology that lies at the heart of this chapter. Indeed, Articles 85 and 86 of the Treaty of Rome, respectively on cartels and on abuse of dominant position, have found their way in the current Articles 101 and 102 TFEU. The debate on the interpretation of these articles was fought in the literature, during conferences - notably those similar to the one, where this volume stems from - but also within the closed premises of national and European institutions. Hence, this contribution will use archives of various governments (Britain, France, Germany) and of the European Commission to reconstruct the debates on the interpretation of Articles 85-86 EEC (Articles 101-102 TFEU).[1] It will also rely on the interviews of former commissioners, DG Competition officials and competition policy experts.[2] Thanks to these new primary sources, the article will underline the complex interplay of many Member States - West Germany and others - in this history, and the growing role of the European Commission.[3]

Four main paradigms have shaped the history of the European competition policy. The first - the public interest paradigm - was dominant in Western Europe up to the 1980s (section 2), but not within the EEC, where a more syncretic approach

1. This chapter was written without extensive references to archives in footnotes. For more details about the topics covered herein, *see*: Laurent Warlouzet, *Governing Europe in a Globalizing World: Neoliberalism and Its Alternatives Following the 1973 Oil Crisis* (Routledge, 2018), 156-179; Laurent Warlouzet, *Europe contre Europe. Entre liberté, solidarité et puissance depuis 1945* (Cnrs editions, 2022), 229-256 and 327-345; Laurent Warlouzet, *The Centralization of EU Competition Policy: Historical Institutionalist Dynamics from Cartel Monitoring to Merger Control (1956-91)*, Journal of Common Market Studies 54(3) (2016): 725-741; Laurent Warlouzet, *The EEC/EU as an Evolving Compromise Between French Dirigism and German Ordoliberalism (1957-1995)*, Journal of Common Market Studies, 57(1) (2019): 77-93. More generally on the history of competition policy, *see*: Hubert Buch-Hansen & Angela Wigger, *The Politics of European Competition Regulation: A Critical Political Economy Perspective* (Routledge, 2011); Michelle Cini & Lee Mc Gowan, *Competition Policy in the European Union* (Palgrave, 2019); Frédéric Marty, *Towards an Economics of Convention-Based Approach of the European Competition Policy*, Historical Social Research, 40, 1 (2015), 94-111; Kiran Klaus Patel & Heike Schweitzer (eds), *The Historical Foundations of EU Competition Law up to 1980* (Oxford University Press, 2013); Sigfrido Ramirez, Andy Smith & Matthieu Montalban, 'Competition Policy: Ever Present but Far from All Conquering', in Bernard Jullien & Andy Smith (eds), *The EU's Government of Industries: Markets, Institutions and Politics* (Routledge, 2014), 141-164; Wolf Sauter, *Coherence in EU Competition Law* (Oxford University Press, 2016); Xavier Vies (eds), *Competition Policy in the EU: Fifty Years on from the Treaty of Rome* (Oxford University Press, 2009).
2. The author interviewed former commissioners Frans Andriessen and Peter Sutherland, former DG Claus-Dieter Ehlermann, former DG Competition officials Jonathan Faull, Anne Houtman, Michel Petite, Armand Saclé, Helmut Schröeter, and John Temple-Lang, as well as competition expert Valentine Korah. He has also met Ernst-Joachim Mestmäcker. Bar the last two, all of those interviews are available on the website of the European Union Historical Archives: https://archives.eui.eu/en/oral_history.
3. For lack of space, this article disregards three major actors in this process: the national competition authorities, the European Court of Justice, and the US actors (both institutional and intellectual). *See, e.g.*: Julie Bailleux & Antoine Vauchez (eds), *Exploring the Transnational Circulation of Policy Paradigms: Law Firms, Legal Networks and the Production of Expertise in the Field of Competition Policies* (EUI Working Paper, 2014).

dominated in the Treaty of Rome (section 3), before the advent of a second paradigm - the ordoliberal paradigm - which prevailed from 1962 to 2002 (section 4), when it declined against the rise of the third paradigm - consumer welfare (section 5). The emergence of a fourth paradigm, tentatively called 'the excess of market power', since 2015, will then be assessed (section 6).

2 GENESIS: THE PUBLIC INTEREST PARADIGM (1890-1970s)

At the origin of competition policy was the public interest paradigm. It rests on two ideas: (1) competition concerns are only one element among many for state authorities willing to monitor the markets, alongside social, regional, industrial and strategic criteria; and (2) the state authorities are the best actors to balance those various criteria and decide accordingly.

The prevalence of the public interest paradigm during most of the twentieth century is logical, as it was a high point of state intervention in the economy, with two long world wars and the setting up of welfare states and of dirigiste industrial policies. A majority believed that, since the 1929 crisis had amply demonstrated the failure of laissez-faire, state or quasi-state authorities were the best placed to define the 'public interest', as a balance between different objectives, mostly high growth, low inflation, technical modernization, regional balance and social fairness.

Besides, competition policy - defined as an active monitoring of market by state authorities designed to promote their efficiency according to the neoclassical vision of the 'pure and perfect competition' - is a relatively recent phenomenon. Indeed, the sheer concept of 'pure and perfect competition' dates back to the late nineteenth century. Before that, state authorities promoted market competition mostly in exceptional circumstances, to avoid hoarding during food crisis for example - an intervention documented even under the Roman empire, when Emperors had to provide 'food and games' for the city of Rome's inhabitants including by tinkering with prices and business practices.[4] Later on, in 1791, a French law passed during the French Revolution banned corporations, and in the meantime forbade most forms of what we now call 'agreements' or 'cartels'. According to David Gerber, this statute was a watershed, as it 'embodied the idea that law could be used to protect economic freedom'.[5] A new law was then passed under Napoleon to ban concerted action to manipulate 'the price of foodstuffs or other commodities ... above or below that which natural and free competition would have set'. French jurisprudence developed along those lines in the nineteenth century, in particular around the notion of 'fair competition', but without a coherent policy.

4. Paul Veyne, *Bread and Circuses: The Historical Sociology of a Political Pluralism* (London, Penguin, 1990).
5. David Gerber, *Law and Competition in Twentieth Century Europe: Protecting Prometheus* (Oxford University Press, 1998), 183; *see also* for many examples of French case-law: Alessandro Stanziani, *Rules of Exchange: French Capitalism in Comparative Perspective, Eighteenth to Early Twentieth Centuries* (Cambridge University Press, 2012), 248-278.

The first modern competition law was the United States (US) Sherman Act, enacted in 1890.[6] It was called 'antitrust', as it aimed at combatting the excessive concentration of power of the most powerful businessmen sometimes stigmatized as 'robber barons', who were often organized in 'trusts' coordinating the collusion of companies. The primary example was oil, with the dominance of Standard Oil until its dismantling in 1911 after a lawsuit based on the Sherman Act.

In Europe, competition policy appeared in the aftermath of World War II under various influences: the European willingness to emulate the US model to increase productivity; the US active promotion of it; and the distrust of cartels, which were associated with totalitarian regimes.[7] In reaction to 1930s protectionism and cartelization, Western elites promoted 'embedded liberalism' - namely an association of free-market, free-trade, and strong state intervention in terms of industrial, monetary and welfare state policies.[8]

Within this framework, a few Western European states adopted provisions that are associated nowadays with competition policy, but which were referred to differently in those days: e.g., the fight against 'restrictive practices', price policy, the monitoring of 'monopolies'. Among the six founding members of the EEC, only three had some provisions in this regard when the Treaty of Rome was signed: the Netherlands, since 1956; France, since 1953; and Germany, with the allied decartelization laws. The United Kingdom (UK) passed a law on monopolies in 1948, and another one on 'restrictive trade practices' in 1956. With the exception of the new German law passed in 1957, the implementation was weak, since those provisions were embedded into wider economic policies following broader industrial, social, regional and strategic criteria.[9]

However, the promotion of competition did exist even within the public interest paradigm. France, for example, had suffered from food shortages in the 1940s, despite being one of the most important producers of agricultural goods in the world. In reaction, the state severely repressed all practices that could increase price, such as restrictive vertical distribution agreements. In the 1950s and 1960s, stringent legislation was enacted and implemented to force producers to sell their products to supermarkets. Edouard Leclerc, one of the pioneers of French supermarkets, actively lobbied the French government to pursue a stringent policy in this area. With regard to

6. On US competition policy, *see*: William E. Kovacic & Carl Shapiro, *Antitrust Policy: A Century of Economic and Legal Thinking*, Journal of Economic Perspectives, 14(1) (2000): 43-60; Stephen Martin, *The Goals of Antitrust and Competition Policy* (Purdue CIBER Working Papers, 2007-003).
7. A few provisions existed before 1945 in several European countries under different guise, *see*: Gerber, *Law and Competition, supra*, 115-165.
8. John Ruggie, *International Regimes, Transactions, and Change: Embedded Liberalism in the Postwar Economic Order*, International Organization, 36(2) (1982): 379-415; Marie-Laure Djelic, *Exporting the American Model: The Post-war Transformation of European Business* (Oxford University Press, 2001).
9. The Netherlands was described as a 'cartel paradise' for example: Wendy Asbeek Brusse & Richard Griffiths, 'Paradise Lost or Paradise Regained? Cartel Policy and Cartel Legislation in the Netherlands', in Stephen Martin (eds), *Competition Policies in Europe* (Elsevier, 1998), 15-40; in the UK, the Monopoly commission explicitly used a public interest test: Stephen Wilks, *In the Public Interest: Competition Policy and the Monopolies and Mergers Commission* (Manchester University Press, 1999).

industrial policy, the French state used the threat of what we would refer to today as 'competition policy provisions' to dismantle horizontal cartels among suppliers of the state-owned utility EDF.[10] Since EDF held a monopoly over electricity production in France, it was also a monopsony for the French suppliers, who tended to share the national markets alongside pre-war positions. Hence, in France, as in most European countries, competition provisions were embedded into price policy and industrial policy.

Only in West Germany was a genuine competition policy enacted, with the 1957 law, thanks to an ordoliberal impetus (*see* section 4). It was independent from other public policies and was self-referential, as it promoted free competition simply for its own sake, and not to attain another objective. However, even in West Germany, the influence of the public interest paradigm was clearly visible in the many exemptions to the 1957 law, not only in terms of sectors but also in terms of practices (export cartels during the first decades). Many scholars underlined the tolerance shown by Ludwig Erhard, the minister of economy who passed the 1957 law, for the concentration into large companies.[11] Some ordoliberals were also dissatisfied with a law they considered to be too soft. On a macro-level, public subsidies to companies were on a par in West Germany and France until 1981 if all types of subsidies (including regional ones) are taken into account.[12] Later on, a famous case of industrial policy trumping competition policy occurred in 1988, when the government overruled the decision made by competition authorities to ban the merger between Daimler-Benz and MBB in 1988.[13] In 1989, the minister of economy Helmut Haussmann and his deputy Otto Schlecht, both centre-right free-marketers, considered that the German competition authorities were sometimes too severe given that companies needed to grow. More generally, the West German welfare state was strengthened in the 1950s as well with co-determination laws and pension reform. To sum up, Western Germany was not a paradise of free market, but rather a 'coordinated economy' where competition policy rules were useful to avoid collusion and to maintain high competitiveness.[14]

Eventually, this public interest approach declined in the late 1970s and 1980s. State interventions to steer markets were now considered mostly inefficient: planning became impossible with the rise of international trade; price policies, which could be useful in times of shortages, seemed pointless in a world of mass consumption and diversified items; and industrial policies often ended up in regulatory capture (with

10. Claude Didry & Frédéric Marty, *La politique de concurrence comme levier de la politique industrielle dans la France de l'après-guerre*, Gouvernement et action publique, 5(4) (2016): 23-45.
11. Volker Berghahn, *The Americanisation of West German Industry, 1945-1963* (Berg, 1986), 157-181; Jan-Otmar Hesse & Eva-Maria Roelevink, 'Cartel Law and Cartel Register in German 20th Century History', in Susanna Fellmann & Martin Shanahan (eds), *Regulating Competition. Cartel Registers in the Twentieth Century World* (Routledge, 2016), pp. 191-207.
12. Warlouzet, *Governing Europe*, *supra*, 106.
13. Archiv des Liberalismus, Gummersbach, A 49-68, note on the FDP Bundestagfraktion meeting on 31 August 1989; A 49-272, note from 7 November 1989.
14. West Germany epitomized the 'coordinated market economy' for the 'Varieties of Capitalism' scholars. *See*: Peter Hall & David Soskice, *Varieties of Capitalism: The Institutional Foundations of Comparative Advantage* (Oxford University Press, 2001).

massive subsidies unloaded on companies close to the political leaders) and/or in excessive concentration leading to high consumer prices.[15] A market-based approach came to prevail.

3 SYNCRETISM: THE COMPROMISE OF THE ROME TREATY

The Treaty of Rome of 25 March 1957, which created the EEC that is still at the basis of the current European Union (EU), is a syncretic document in many ways, since it is simultaneously intergovernmental and supranational, market-oriented and regulatory. The same is true for the 'rules governing competition' of the Treaty of Rome, whose main aim was to ensure market integration: it was pointless to remove state barriers to trade if private barriers were erected through cartels and other market-sharing agreements. An additional motivation was the counter-model of the German cartelization under the Nazi regimes. These motivations explained why relatively stringent provisions regarding competition policy were enacted in the 1951 Treaty of Paris, which created the European Coal and Steel Community (ECSC), the direct ancestor of the EEC.

Strikingly, the provisions of the 1957 Treaty of Rome on competition policy have remained largely unchanged in the current TFEU, with the same three articles:

(i) Article 85 EEC (now Article 101 TFEU,) establishing a prohibition on certain agreements affecting intra-European trade (paragraphs 1-2), with exemptions (paragraph 3);
(ii) Articles 86 EEC (now Article 102 TFEU, ex article 82 TEC) prohibiting the abuse of dominant position;
(iii) Articles 90 EEC (now Article 106 TFEU, ex Article 86 TEC) stipulates that companies in charge of 'services of general economic interest' are both concerned by these rules, and at the same time partially exempted.

A historical enquiry into the origins of the Treaty of Rome's competition rules dismisses the simplistic interpretation that would ascribe the origins of European competition rules solely to German ordoliberal thinking, or to the US antitrust tradition. On the contrary, the cross-examination of European, French and German archives of the negotiations reveals that many actors played a part. The main negotiators of the provisions on competition were the French and Germans. US officials played a much less important role than during the ECSC negotiations: in 1956-1957, Stalin was dead, so the fear of Cold War turning hot was subsumed. Besides, since the Marshall Plan was over, Washington did not have any financial leeway over most of the original six EEC Member States.

In Bonn, German archives show that the main priority of the principal West German negotiator, Alfred Müller-Armack, who is usually associated with ordoliberalism, was not to promote an active European competition policy, but rather to avoid

15. Warlouzet, *Governing Europe, supra*, 164-166.

any European threat over the future German law.[16] German negotiators refused both European provisions too distant from the German model, and a powerful Commission.

In Paris, French negotiators wanted an effective competition policy, and they refused any strong centralization on the Commission.[17] The French had imagined a system based on a stringent harmonization of competition law by Member States themselves, but under close supervision from the Commission and the Council. If one Member State did not act, the Commission could inquire and propose a solution. If this solution was not implemented, then the Council could impose a compromise by qualified majority voting. It seems that the French feared a non-implementation of competition rules by their neighbours. During the 1950-1951 ECSC negotiations, Paris had always insisted on stringent rules against the biggest companies in order to avoid any reconcentration of West German industries.[18] During the period 1956-1957, the French remained wary of the larger West German companies, and thus insisted on the same treatments for restrictive practices and for dominant position (sometimes called 'concentration').

The final substantive compromise was based on the German distinction between cartels and abuse of dominant position, with French input in the detail of the wording and inspiration from the ECSC blueprint. Discriminatory practices particularly targeted by French price policy were included (*see* in particular those listed in Article 85 EEC, paragraph 1, a, d and e, and Article 86, a, c and d). The French also secured Article 90 EEC, which protected state-owned companies and most industrial policy provisions.

From an institutional point of view, since both the French and the German were relatively wary against the Commission, it fell to the Belgians (and to the three Benelux countries in general: Belgium, the Netherlands and Luxembourg) to insist on the need to empower the Commission.[19]

The syncretic nature of the Rome Treaty was recognized by different legal scholars having conducted historical research on the origins of Article 86 EEC.[20] The

16. German national archives, B 102/134647, note Deringer, 7 November 1958; note Albrecht, 13 November 1958; Reiner Schulze & Thomas Hoeren (eds), *Dokumente zum Europaïschen Recht, Band 3: Kartellrecht (bis 1957)* (Springer, 2000): notes of Meyer-Cording, 5 November 1956; Vermerk betreffend die Konferenz über den Gemeinsamen Markt vom 05.11-07.11.1956, 8 November 1956.
17. On the French influence and its limitations, *see*: Warlouzet, *Le choix de la CEE*, pp. 269-276; Historical Archives of the European Union, CM3, 236, document from the secretariat of 4 July 1956; Doc Mar. Com. 37, 4 September 1956.
18. Brigitte Leucht, 'Expertise and the Creation of a Constitutional Core Europe: Transatlantic Policy Networks in the Schuman Plan Negotiations', in Michael Gehler, Wolfram Kaiser & Brigitte Leucht (eds), *Transnational Networks in Regional Integration: Governing Europe, 1945-83* (Palgrave Macmillan, 2010), 18-37.
19. Historical Archives of the European Union, CM 236, doc. MAE 252/56, 3-5 September 1956; *see also* the account of von der Groeben, who chaired the negotiations as a representative of the German government: Hans von der Groeben, 'Europäische Integration aus historischer Erfahrung: Ein Zeit-zeugengespräch mit Michael Gehler', *Zentrum für europäische Integrationsforschung (ZEI) Discussion Paper* no. C108/2002, 2002, p. 17.
20. Pinar Akman recognizes: 'It is still puzzling to the author why Article 82 EC [former Article 86 EEC or 102 TFEU] was couched in such a vague term': Pinar Akman, *Searching for the Long-Lost Soul of Article 82 EC*, Oxford Journal of Legal Studies, 29(2) (2009): 297; Heike Schweitzer admits similar uncertainties: Heike Schweitzer, 'Parallels and Differences in the Attitudes

same is true for Article 85 EEC. Both articles are relatively clear in terms of targets, but not in terms of methodology (i.e., which legal and economist criteria are relevant) and of procedure (i.e., notification procedure or not, role of the various EEC institutions). Competition could be interpreted as a protection of private rights or as part of public law and of the regulatory role of the state. Similarly, its objective may be the promotion of economic efficiency, and/or of economic freedom. What we perceive today as vagueness was, however, logical in the context of 1956 Western Europe, where almost no competition policy in the contemporary sense of the word existed. Moreover, it mirrors the ambiguity of other chapters of the Treaty, for example those on agriculture, whose multiple objectives laid out in Article 39 EEC often contradicted themselves. This language translated the difficult political compromises that were reached to conclude the Treaty.

4 REVELATION: THE ADOPTION OF THE ORDOLIBERAL PARADIGM (1962-2002)

The ordoliberal paradigm revealed competition policy as a stand-alone policy. By contrast with the public interest approach, the ordoliberal paradigm curtailed the state's role as a guardian of a liberal political and economic order. It was developed by German-speaking scholars in reaction to the totalitarian experience of Nazi Germany, and even earlier, as a response to certain turbulent episodes of the Weimar Republic, such as hyperinflation.[21] In their understanding, political liberalism and economic liberalism are strongly intertwined: individual liberties had to be protected against any dominant power, be they state authorities or conglomerates. The state must not intervene in the economy in an attempt to steer it with discriminatory tools, but it has a key role to play by monitoring the markets in order to avoid any excessive concentration of power. Emphasis is laid on the defence of the small actors, such as small and medium companies. Despite the divisions among ordoliberals, it is possibly to sketch an ordoliberal-inspired competition policy through its focus on the preservation of the liberty of competitors, by establishing a level playing field (which does not

Towards Single-Firm Conduct: What Are the Reasons? The History, Interpretation and Underlying Principles of Sec. 2 Sherman Act and Art 82 EC', in Claus-Dieter Ehlermann & Mel Marquis (eds), *European Competition Law Annual: 2007 – A Reformed Approach to Article 82 EC* (Hart Publishing, 2008), 119-164.

21. A standard account on ordoliberalism and its influence in Europe is: Gerber, *Law and Competition*. More recently on ordoliberals and European integration, *see*: Quinn Slobodian, *Globalists* (Harvard University Press, 2018). A lively debate exists on David Gerber's book about the ordoliberal influence on the EEC/EU competition policy. Pinar Akman and Hussein Kassim tend to dismiss it as a myth: Pinar Akman & Hussein Kassim, *Myths and Myth-Making in the European Union: The Institutionalization and Interpretation of EU Competition Policy*, Journal of Common Market Studies, 48(1) (2010): 111-132. Conversely, Anselm Küsters's PhD seeks precisely to identify ordoliberal thinking and language within EEC/EU competition policy through a traditional and innovative (using data-mining) approach: Anselm Küsters, *The Making and Unmaking of Ordoliberal Language: A Digital Conceptual History of European Competition Law*, PhD, Univ. Frankfurt am Main, 2022 (forthcoming Klostermann, 2023), 452-453.

mean the shielding of sub-efficient competitors) and its emphasis on legal formalism rather than on a full effect-based economic analysis.

As alluded to before, the ordoliberal way of thinking did not translate fully in the 1957 German competition law, as indeed is always the case with all economic theories. Many exemptions remained, and senior ordoliberals were disappointed with the law. Besides, debates existed on how to define an ordoliberal competition policy from the technical point of view.[22] Suffice to say, however, that in a comparative perspective, the West German situation was quite unique in 1957, with a law explicitly promoting competition for its own sake, with stringent provisions against cartels and, more importantly, the setting up of an independent authority, the Bundeskartellamt, which quickly became a powerful institution.[23]

The translation of the ordoliberal model at the European level was not a preordained outcome. Most of the ordoliberals were opposed to, or at least wary of, the Rome Treaty.[24] Going further, the emergence of an ambitious European competition policy was not anticipated for three reasons: first, no strong competition policy existed in Western Europe; second, France and West Germany refused any major delegation of power to EEC institutions (even though German rhetoric often paid lip service to federalism); and third, the previous experience of the ECSC's competition policy was disappointing - despite ambitious provisions the 1951 Treaty of Paris, the High Authority imposed only a mild restrain on the reconcentration of German industry.[25]

Hence the real paradigm shift occurred in February 1962 with the adoption of Regulation 17/62, which interpreted Article 85 EEC on cartels and transformed the 'rules governing competition' of the Rome Treaty into a full-fledged supranational policy. It imposed two major shifts: (1) EEC competition policy was a stand-alone policy defined by the competition-only criterion, and not by the public interest assessment; and (2) the European Commission played a major role in its implementation, because the decision was made to impose a procedure of notification, whereby all agreements had to be notified to the Commission, which then decided alone on their compatibility with the Treaty of Rome.[26] Member States had only a minor consultative role, and the Court of Justice merely reviewed the Commission's decision (whereas it was up to the Court to settle a conflict in several schemes considered before that).

This system was presented as a logical consequence of the Treaty of Rome by its promoters. But, during the early years of the negotiation leading up to Regulation 17/62, a majority of Member States led by France defended a completely different system, based on the abuse principle (absence of notification) and a decision-making system associating the Member States and the Commission.[27] Only a change in

22. Schweitzer, *Parallels*, *supra*.
23. Gerber, *Law and Competition*, *supra*, pp. 280-294.
24. Slobobian, *Globalists*, *supra*.
25. Laurent Warlouzet& Tobias Witschke, *The Difficult Path to an Economic Rule of Law: European Competition Policy, 1950-91*. *Contemporary European History*, 21(3) (2012): 437-455.
26. Whereas 'TheTreaty of Rome did not dictate such centralization' according to Gerber, *Protecting*, *supra*, 349.
27. For a summary of the negotiation of Regulation 17/62: Warlouzet, *The Centralization*, *supra*; for a detailed account: Warlouzet, *Le choix de la CEE*, *supra*, 304-332; Sibylle Hambloch, *Europäische Integration und Wettbewerbspolitik* (Nomos, 2009), 79-125.

majority in Belgium in 1961 (the Belgians leaned on the French approach before that, and then shifted to the German one),[28] the lack of efficiency of French negotiators, and a trade-off with Germany over the common agricultural policy (decided in January 1962 as well) allowed Regulation 17/62 to be adopted. The role of the first commissioner for competition, Hans von der Groeben, who was a former top German negotiator of the Treaty of Rome, and who was surrounded in Brussels by a team mostly influenced by German ordoliberalism, was also instrumental.[29] Von der Groeben insisted on putting the Commission, and not the Council or the ECJ, at the centre of the system.[30] Hence, the shift to the ordoliberal paradigm with Regulation 17/62 was by no means a foregone conclusion: a cartel policy with a stronger involvement of the Council or of the Court and no notification procedure could have emerged. The final compromise on Regulation 17/62 was secured in December 1961 after Bonn accepted a French request for a tougher regime for distribution agreements, eventually embedded in Article 22 of the Regulation.[31] Initially, Regulation 17/62 was a Pyrrhic victory for the European Commission, as it was drowned under more than 36,000 notifications in a just few years. Ironically, this situation owes much to the French insistence on targeting vertical distribution, which made up the bulk of the agreement notified to the Commission. A US expert of comparative cartel law estimated in 1962 that the French law was stricter than the German one with regard to vertical restraints.[32]

The first cartel ban, the famous *Grunding-Consten* decision of 1964, was a vertical distribution agreement between a German producer and a French distributor. The West German government opposed the ban, but it was overruled by the Commission, a decision that shows how von der Groeben remained independent from its government.[33]

Eventually, the Commission progressively solved its backlog problem in the 1980s by multiplying the decisions and the block exemptions. The European Court of Justice usually supported this dynamic, as it contributed to the overarching goal of market integration, even if the Court was often critical of the soundness of certain economic judgments (starting with the first cartel ban, *Grunding-Consten*, in 1966)[34]

28. On this Belgian shift, *see* the Conseil national du Patronat Français (CNPF – the French Peak Business Organisation) archives (Roubaix), 72 AS 1504, note Lartisien for Villiers on the meeting of 21-22 November 1961.
29. On the Commission's: Katja Seidel, *The Process of Politics in Europe: The Rof European Elites and Supranational Institutions* (IB Tauris, 2010).
30. Hambloch, Europäische; Warluozet, The Centralization; and German national archives (Koblenz), B 102/259228, note BMWi, EA4, 13 November 1961.
31. German national archives (Koblenz), B 102/2592294, note BMWi, EA4, Epphardt, 16 décembre 1961.
32. Stefan A. Riesenfeld, *Antitrust Laws in the European Economic Community*, California Law Review, 50(3) (1962): 459, 473.
33. Warlouzet, *Governing Europe, supra*, 158.
34. EC Court of Justice: joined cases 56 and 58-64, judgment of the Court of 13 July 1966, *Établissements Consten S.A.R.L. and Grundig-Verkaufs-GmbH v Commission of the European Economic Community*; Gerber, *Protecting, supra*, 352-368; on the Court's critics and the role of lawyers: Lola Avril, 'How Lawyers Became Essential Intermediaries Between Firms and the European Commission: Procedural Reform in Competition Cases (1962-1983)', in Lennaert van Heumen & Mechthild Roos (eds), *The Informal Construction of Europe* (Routledge, 2019), 163-180.

and on the procedures. Besides, the Commission experienced many hurdles outside the cartel remit. In the 1960s, Hans von der Groeben and other German experts influenced by ordoliberalism considered extending competition policy to the control of mergers and state aids, but the dominance of national neomercantilist policies prevented the Commission to encroach on Member States in this area before the mid-1980s.[35]

5 REFORMATION: THE 'CONSUMER WELFARE' PARADIGM (SINCE 2003)

Major overhaul of competition policy occurred during 2003-2004 in what is generally described as a progressive transition from the ordoliberal approach to the consumer welfare paradigm, first from the procedural point of view, and then from the substantive point of view.[36] From the procedural point of view, the definition of common legal and economic criteria accepted across a vast community of competition policy experts, as well as the development of efficient national competition policies in all EU states since the 1990s, allowed the Commission to abandon the framework of Regulation 17/62. Regulation 1/2003, adopted by the Council in 2002, decentralized the implementation of some cartel rules to national authorities, while keeping a strong power of coordination. The notification procedure was shelved as companies were now obliged to assess the legality of their practices themselves. The main substantive characteristic was the adoption of a more economic approach, based on the recent development in industrial organization economics, whereas the previous approach was based more on legal formalism. The priority became the defence of 'consumer welfare', which could be calculated. In addition, cartel-busting was also fostered through the leniency procedure, which gave more initiative to private actors.[37] In merger control, Regulation 139/2004 kept a more centralized framework, while at the same time promoting the more economic approach. It was then proposed for block exemptions regulations and for the abuse of dominant position in a 2009 communication.[38] The EU Court of Justice adopted it rather belatedly.[39]

The roots of this evolution are located in the 1990s. First, from an administrative point of view, DG Comp felt the need to concentrate on the most salient cases – those that define the jurisprudence – and thus to be alleviated from the burden of the notification system. Archival document from 1995 shows that Claus-Dieter Ehlermann (who was then Director General for Competition) and Philip Lowe (Director of the

35. Warlouzet, *Europe contre Europe*, *supra*, 244.
36. For an overview: David J. Gerber, *Two Forms of Modernization in European Competition Law*, Fordham International Law Journal, 31(5) (2007): 1235-1265.
37. On the genuine efficiency of the leniency programme: José Manuel Ordóñez-De-Haro, Joan-Ramon Borrell & Juan Luis Jiménez, *The European Commission's Fight Against Cartels (1962-2014): A Retrospective and Forensic Analysis*, Journal of Common Market Studies, 56(5) (2018): 1087-1107.
38. Communication from the Commission, Guidance on the Commission's enforcement priorities in applying Article 82 of the EC Treaty to abusive exclusionary conduct by dominant undertakings, 2009/C 45/02.
39. Judgment of the General Court of 26 January 2022, *Intel Corporation Inc. v. European Commission*, Case T-286/09 RENV.

Merger Task Force) were still preoccupied by the problem of backlog, which could be further reinforced by the perspective of the Eastern Enlargement.[40] They actively sought solutions to enable DG Comp to concentrate only on the most serious case. Second, the legal formalism and paucity of economic judgment of several Commission bans was sternly criticized by the Tribunal of first Instance of the Court of Justice. It even reversed a merger ban for unsound economic judgment in 2002.[41] Third, the intellectual development of industrial organization economics provided a readily available toolkit shared on both sides of the Atlantic – sometimes called 'Post-Chicago Antitrust Economics'.[42] Fourth, this development was part of a wider 'Americanization' of Europe that had returned since the 1980s: whereas the US looked into Western Europe's exceptional high growth for inspiration in the 1960s, the reverse was true in the Reagan years, when the US enjoyed a higher growth rate than Germany and won the Cold War.

The intellectual debate between the ordoliberals and the Second Chicago School was indeed raging as of the 1980s. The first group was spearheaded by Ernst-Joachim Mestmäcker, a prominent second-generation ordoliberal who had been an advisor to von der Groeben in the 1960s.[43] The second group, the Second Chicago School scholars, insisted on the necessity to prioritize economic goals, mostly consumer welfare.[44] Legal scholars such as the British Valentine Korah and the Belgian René Joliet (who was judge at the ECJ between 1984 and 1995) criticized, beginning in the early 1980s, several decisions of the Commission that they considered as too legally formalistic and not grounded in economics. Korah stigmatized DG IV 'dogmatic' severity against vertical agreements, whereas, in her opinion, many of them were useful to avoid 'free-riders' (companies that benefit from a service without paying for it, such as after-sale services protected by exclusive distribution agreements). She criticized a policy that was meant to protect competitors (in particular small- and medium enterprises (SMEs)) at the expense of competition, and hence of consumers. At the same time, the US lawyer Barry Hawk levelled the same criticisms against the Commission and spread them through the Fordham conferences, a major transatlantic forum on competition policy. Those criticisms did not leave the Commission officials unscathed. Some of these officials envisaged a more economic approach as soon as the early 1980s – notably Claus-Dieter Ehlermann and John Temple-Lang, who were then members of the legal service – but the ordoliberal impetus was maintained.[45]

40. Laurent Warlouzet, 'The Internal Market and Competition', in *The European Commission, 1986-2000: Histories and Memories of an Institution* (EU Publications Office, 2018), 269-273.
41. EU Court of Justice, Order of the Court (Grand Chamber) of 9 June 2010, *European Commission v. Schneider Electric SA*, Case C-440/07P.
42. Steven Salop, Carl Shapiro & Jean Tirole's *Nobel Prize in Economics: the Rigorous Foundation of Post-Chicago Antitrust Economics*, Antitrust, 29(2) (Spring 2015): 78-81.
43. Mestmäcker was influenced both by ordoliberalism and by Hayek. He was adamantly hostile to the 'more economic approach'. *See*: Claire Mongouachon, 'Les difficultés d'une interprétation ordolibérale de la constitution micro-économique de l'Union européenne', in Guillaume Grégoire and Xavier Miny (eds), *The Idea of Economic Constitution in Europe* (Brill Nijhoff, 2022), 344-379.
44. Warlouzet, *Governing Europe*, *supra*, 162-163.
45. This debate occurred within the framework of the famous Philip Morris case (*British-American Tobacco Company Ltd and R. J. Reynolds Industries Inc. v. Commission of the European*

In the meantime, despite this administrative continuity, a major evolution occurred at the political level. Commissioners Peter Sutherland and Leon Brittan held the competition portfolio from 1985 to 1992. They used both the ordoliberal heritage of DG IV, and their Anglo-Saxon zeal (the Irishman Sutherland studied in the US; and Brittan, a British man, was a prominent Thatcherite), to expand the remit of European competition policy towards new areas: mergers, state aids, and the liberalization of telecommunication and or air transport.[46]

In the 1990s, Director General Claus-Dieter Ehlermann, a German man with a different vision than the ordoliberal one (originally, he came from a social-democrat background), agreed to consider a radical overhaul of EU competition policy.[47] Philip Lowe, the director of the Merger Task Force, responded enthusiastically and emphasized the need for a stronger economic approach. He later became Director General from 2002 to 2010, during the enforcement of Regulation 1/2003 and the adoption of Regulation 139/2004. Those two landmark texts were adopted under the stewardship of Commissioner Mario Monti (1999-2004), the first economist to hold this position. The creation of an independent cartel office was even envisaged to hermetically separate the instruction of competition case from political pressure, before being rejected by DG Comp, who wanted to keep undisputed leadership over the orientation of competition policy in all areas.

The new approach puts an emphasis on consumer welfare, but is not a strict copy of the Second Chicago School's prescriptions. EU competition policy has remained more interventionist than what neoliberal scholars such as Robert Bork or Richard Posner would have liked. A synthesis between the integrationist impetus (the necessity to unify the internal market), the ordoliberal heritage (which had remained prevalent notably in certain ECJ rulings), the Second Chicago school critique, and the industrial economics toolkit have emerged, known as the 'Brussels School'.[48]

6 COUNTER-REFORMATION: THE 'EXCESS OF MARKET POWER' PARADIGM? (SINCE 2014)

Since the advent of Margrethe Vestager, a Danish liberal, at the helm of the Commission's portfolio for competition in 2014, a new paradigm tentatively called the 'excess of market power' is slowly taking shape. It is a response to a phenomenon of reconcentration of companies, especially the so-called GAFAM, which usually enjoy a

Communities, 17 November 1987, cases 142 and 156/84, ECR 4487): Laurent Warlouzet, 'The Difficult Quest to Implement Cartel Control: Grundig-Consten (1966) and Philip Morris (1987)', in Bill Davies & Fernanda Nicola (eds), *EU Law Stories: Contextual and Critical Histories of European Jurisprudence* (Cambridge University Press, 2017), 261-277.

46. Warlouzet, *Governing Europe, supra*, 171-174; Warlouzet, *Europe contre Europe, supra*, 233-256; Michelle Cini & Lee Mc Gowan, *Competition Policy in the European Union* (Palgrave, 1998), 31-35.
47. Warlouzet, *The Internal Market, supra*, 279; *see also*: Stephen Wilks & Lee Mc Gowan, *Disarming the Commission: The Debate over a European Cartel Office*, Journal of Common Market Studies, 33(2) (1995): 259-273.
48. Catherine Prieto & David Bosco, *Droit européen de la concurrence. Ententes et abus de position dominante* (Bruylant, 2013).

dominant position in their respective sectors:[49] this position was fostered first by the rise of new network industries that enjoyed a winner-takes-all effect, and second by a lenient US antitrust enforcement. At some point, Facebook even projected to launch its own currency. In addition, the potential of control on private life that those IT giants wield is a worrying development, especially at a time of rising populism.

Both dynamics have been also criticized by US scholars, notably Luigi Zingales, who feared a new 'Medici Vicious Circle', when private companies took over the political structure, such as in late medieval Florence.[50] A new approach, sometimes called 'New Brandesian', in reference to US Supreme Court judge Louis Brandeis (1919-1939), underlines the inadequacy of standard antitrust and of the 'consumer welfare approach' to capture the breadth of the GAFAM's market power. It is embodied, among others, by the young law scholar Lina Kahn, who was hired as chairwoman of the Federal Trade Commission in 2021.[51]

The 'excess of market power' paradigm is defined here by three features: (1) a focus on the repression of new forms of market power in the digital economy, symbolized by high-visibility fines against Apple, Google and Amazon since 2016 (market power is targeted as a problem in its own right even if consumer welfare can be increased in the short term); (2) creativity in legal and economic reasoning, with, for example, a wide use of the notion of fiscal aid (against Apple, but also against actors in other sectors such as Fiat or Starbucks); and (3) attention to non-competition criteria such as the protection of privacy, media plurality, digital plurality, or the protection of the environment. Hence, although it targets mostly the GAFAM, it also concerns multinationals in more traditional business lines. Some elements hint at the more severe stance of commissioner Vestager compared to her predecessors Joaqim Almunia (who wanted to settle one of the Google cases that led to a fine under Vestager) and Neelie Kroes (who criticized the Apple ruling). In parallel, the previous approach against more traditional anticompetitive behaviours was still enforced, with record fines against cartels. However, some of the most prominent rulings, notably the 2016 Apple decision with a record EUR 13 billion reimbursement request, were overturned by the Tribunal of First Instance. These legal challenges in the courts, the lack of guidelines to regulate such a new sector, and the long delay of investigation (especially in the rapidly changing environment of digital technology) demonstrated the limitation of the legal framework in the eyes of the Commission.[52]

---

49. The widely used acronym GAFAM designates Google, Apple, Facebook, Amazon and Microsoft. Since Google's parent company is Alphabet, and Facebook's is Meta, the acronym has morphed but the original version still sticks. Those companies are also known as the 'Big Five'. Apple does not have a dominant position in the smartphone market but its brand is so powerful that it wields enormous market power.
50. Luigi Zingales, *Towards a Political Theory of the Firm*, Journal of Economic Perspective, 31(3) (2017): 113-130; *see also*: Thomas Philippon, *The Great Reversal: How America Gave up on Free Markets* (Harvard University Press, 2019).
51. Lina M. Khan, *Amazon's Antitrust Paradox*, The Yale Law Journal 126(3) (2017), available at SSRN. On Brandeis's doctrine: Patrice Bougette & Frédéric Marty, *Information Exchange among Firms: The Coherence of Justice Brandeis' Regulated Competition Approach*, Gredeg Working Paper No. 2020-56, available at SSRN.
52. On the process leading to the DMA: Michelle Cini & Patryck Czulno, 'Digital Single Market and the EU Competition Regime: An Explanation of Policy Change', *Journal of European Integration*,

Margrethe Vestager strove to reinforce her legal toolkit by obtaining two new pieces of legislations, the Digital Market Act (DMA) and the Digital Services Act (DSA), both adopted in 2022.[53] The DSA is less concerned with competition and more with regulating online content, both to avoid hate speech, misinformation, etc., and to promote transparency in transactions. The DMA marks a fundamental shift in EU competition policy, since (1) the Commission enacts specific sectoral rules, whereas its previous approach has often been sectoral-neutral (even if there are specific rules for telecommunications, energy and the banking sector, among others); (2) it aims at the largest companies in the digital sectors only (the so-called digital gatekeepers); (3) market power seems to be targeted per se through a list of ex-ante prohibition, and not only in case of blatant abuse observed ex-post through an economic analysis; and (4) many non-competition criteria are promoted, such as privacy and plurality.

The DMA led to diverging interpretations, all of them recognising it as a watershed. For Anselm Küsters, the DMA, as well as several landmark decisions taken under the leadership of Margarethe Vestager against the GAFAM, can be read in part as a return to an ordoliberal-inspired approach that protects competitors rather than consumer welfare.[54] Frédéric Marty estimated that this evolution echoes both ideas promoted in the US by Brandeis in the 1920s, and ordoliberal thinking (even though the DMA is not ordoliberal, since it follows a more regulatory approach).[55] Conversely, a fear to the return of the 'public interest' era, when many conflicting goals and systematic political interference paralyzed competition policy, had also been expressed.[56] So far, however, the examination of the case-law does not seem to vindicate the fear of 'greenwashing', namely the lenient exemption from competition rules of

44(1) (2022): 41-57. In particular: 'Perhaps because digital markets are relatively immature and the Commission has not yet had built up enough of a track record, online platforms have tended to resist Commission control. Indeed, one of the functions of the new draft legislation would be to help nudge gatekeepers into cooperating with the Commission' (p. 47). M. Vestager also benefited from an enlarged portfolio in the von der Leyen Commission (when she was vice-president in charge of competition and of the digital market), compared to the Juncker Commission (when she was merely a commissioner in charge of competition policy).

53. DMA: Regulation (EU) 2022/1925 of the European Parliament and of the Council of 14 September 2022 on contestable and fair markets in the digital sector; DSA: Regulation 2022/65 of the European Parliament and of the Council on a Single Market For Digital Services (Digital Services Act) of 19 October 2022.
54. Frédéric Marty, 'Évolution des politiques de concurrence en droit de l'UE: de la Wettbewerbsordnung ordolibérale à la More Economic Approach néolibérale?', in Guillaume Grégoire & Xavier Miny (eds), *The Idea of Economic Constitution in Europe: Genealogy and Overview* (Brill, 2022), 325-329; Küsters, *The Making and Unmaking, supra*, 452-453. Anselm Küsters also underlines the interlinkage between the debate on the 10th reform of the GWB and the DMA: Anselm Küsters, *Gestaltung des EU Wettbewerbsrechts im digitalen Zeitalter: Ein quantitativer und qualitativer Vergleich von Konsultationsverfahren, Expertenbericht und jüngsten Reformvorhaben* (Peter Lang, 2022).
55. Frédéric Marty & Thierry Warin, *Digital Platforms' Information Concentration: From Keystone Players to Gatekeepers* (22 December 2020). CIRANO Working Paper 2020S-70, available at SSRN.
56. This debate lies at the heart of the GCLC conference entitled 'The Transformation of EU Competition Law: Next Generation Issues' (25-26 March 2022), from which this collective volume originates. *See also*: Luc Peeperkorn, *Competition Policy Is Not a Stopgap!*, Journal of European Competition Law & Practice, 12(6) (2021): 415-418.

restrictive regulations for loose environmental justifications.[57] Another bone of contention would be the potential of conflicting implementation between the Commission (which is the sole enforcer of the DMA) and the 27 national authorities, as well as the parallel implementation of traditional competition rules and of the DMA (which is based on Article 114 TFEU on the approximation of laws rather than on Articles 101-102 TFEU).[58]

More generally, Vestager's move should be understood in the broader context of the global return of neomercantilism since 2014.[59] Neomercantilism means here the active promotion of national firms by open or disguised protectionism. It is akin to nationalism in the political sphere. EU trade partners have become more aggressive since the 2010s and especially since 2016, with the difficult negotiation on Brexit and the election of Donald Trump as US President. President Trump carried out an openly protectionist trade policy, with a massive increase of US custom duties. China has continued to wage an efficient neomercantilist trade policy, stoking growing fear in the EU – even in Germany, when Mittelstand firms were threatened by Chinese takeovers in 2016. As a result, more countries are calling for a more interventionist industrial policy, from France – where this rhetoric has never disappeared – to Poland – where the PiS government has pursued a policy of 're-Polonisation' of certain strategic companies. Even EU trade and industrial policies have been complemented with more proactive tools since the beginning of the Commission chaired by Jean-Claude Juncker in 2014, starting with the 'Juncker Plan' and the Important Projects of Common European Interest (IPCEI). Even the European central bank has appeared to move away from its cherished market neutrality, with its policy of actively promoting green bonds announced in July 2022.[60]

It is thus no surprise that EU competition policy is also reacting to this trend, particularly because the Digital challenge can also be read through a neomercantilist lens in two respects. From an economic point of view, a new strategic sector dominated by foreign firms is emerging. Even if those firms are mainly based in a staunch ally of the EU, the US, this situation could change in the future if digital giants based in authoritarian regimes rise, or if the US adopt a Trumpian orientation. From a political point of view, the digital challenge, while broadly positive in terms of lowering

57. This fear of greenwashing is expressed in: Maarten Pieter Schinkel, *Green Antitrust: (More) Friendly Fire in the Fight against Climate Change*, SSRN papers 3749147 (2021); For a more sobering assessment: Walid Chaiehloudj, *Le droit de la concurrence est-il un frein à la protection de l'environnement*, Contrats concurrence consummation, 4(4) (2022): 13-24; *see also* the convergence of competition and environmental policy in the condemnation of a German car cartel on 8 July 2021: 'The five car manufacturers Daimler, BMW, Volkswagen, Audi and Porsche possessed the technology to reduce harmful emissions beyond what was legally required under EU emission standards. But they avoided to compete on using this technology's full potential to clean better than what is required by law. … It is illegal under EU Antitrust rules. Competition and innovation on managing car pollution are essential for Europe to meet our ambitious Green Deal objectives.' (Commission press release, 8 July 2021).

58. On all those points, *see*: Assimakis Komninos, *The Digital Market Act: How Does It Compare with Competition Law*, SSRN papers 4136146, 20 July 2022.

59. On this neomercantilist shift: Warlouzet, *Europe contre Europe*, *supra*, 399-434.

60. 'Central Banks and Markets: The Visible Hand', *The Economist*, 16 July 2022.

consumer prices and disseminating knowledge, is also a problem: aggressive nationalism and parochial prejudices are fuelled by unregulated social media, which are sometimes hijacked by authoritarian regimes to subvert elections in Western liberal democracies.

However, Vestager's policy cannot be interpreted as protectionist, since (1) there is hardly any European competitors of the GAFAM to preserve;[61] (2) the fines levelled against the GAFAM remain minimalistic compared to their lavish profits; (3) the Commission did not depart from its non-neomercantilist stance, with a track record showing no evidence of particularly targeting US companies (rather the reverse);[62] and (4) the US administration under Joe Biden (2021-present) has also embraced a more regulatory discourse against the GAFAM. The ban of the Alstom-Siemens merger in 2019 illustrates this point: Vestager took the rare decision of prohibition despite intense pressure from the French and the German governments to accept it.

Arguably, Vestager's policy fits more into the social-liberal vision of European integration that was promoted since the Marshall Plan, rather than in any kind of neomercantilist reflex.[63] According to this vision, which associates the notions of 'liberty' and 'solidarity', European integration rests on the creation of a unified internal market open to its neighbours, as well as on a set of rules protecting the weakest against the detrimental effect of trade liberalization. This is consistent with the fact that, at the national level, competition policy has also been defended by some centre-left leaders keen on curbing big business.[64] In 1961, for example, it was the arrival of centre-left parties in the Belgian government that prompted its shift to the German position, which was seen as more severe against cartels.

On the whole, the recent turn against market power could be interpreted as a reaction towards a new context, marked both by the emergence of new monopolies in the digital sector and by a global return of neomercantilism, rather than as a sheer return to the public interest principle. The situation is not the same as in 1962: policies based on the competition-only criterion have now been in force for decades in all EU countries; the jurisprudence still exists; and even if the Rome Treaty articles have remained the same, other treaties put a stronger emphasis on competition than before. In particular, the objectives of the Lisbon Treaty include the development of 'a highly competitive social market economy' (Article 3 Treaty on European Union (TEU)), and its Protocol 27 defines the internal market as 'a system ensuring that competition is not distorted' (Article 3 TEU).

61. However, the DMA could concern a couple of European companies, such as SAP.
62. Sebastian Billows, Sebastian Kohl & Fabien Tarissan, *Bureaucrats or Ideologues? EU Merger Control as Market-Centred Integration*, Journal of Common Market Studies, 59(4) (2021): 762-781; Anu Bradford, Robert J. Jackson Jr. & Jonathan Zytnick, *Is EU Merger Control Used for Protectionism?: An Empirical Analysis*, Journal of Empirical Legal Studies, 15(1) (2018): 165-191.
63. On the opposition between market-oriented, social and neomercantilist Europe: Warlouzet, *Europe contre Europe, supra*; and on the years spanning 1973-1986: Warlouzet, *Governing Europe, supra*.
64. David Spector, *La gauche, la droite et le marché* (Odile Jacob, 2017). In Germany, *see, e.g.*, the book authored by the far-left politician Sarah Wagenknecht, *Freiheit statt Kapitalismus: über vergessene Ideale, die Eurokrise und unsere Zukunft* (Campus Verlag, 2012).

7 CONCLUSION

Even if incongruous in publications dealing with competition policy, the religious vocabulary is a useful reminder that all public policies are based on a set of beliefs. In this religious war, the Treaty of Rome was a syncretic document, open to multiple interpretations, and written at a time when competition policies were feeble. This relative flexibility explains the four paradigm shifts, each of them dependent on a particular intellectual and political context: (1) The public interest approach, which was dominant before the EEC competition policy took off, was a 'Genesis', since it laid the ground for a state intervention to monitor the markets. (2) The ordoliberal impetus was a 'Revelation', since it invented the self-referential European competition policy. It left a deep mark on the EEC/EU since 1962, notably by inventing a system hugely centralized on the Commission, which was not imposed by the Treaty of Rome. (3) Then came the 'Reformation', a radical overhaul meant to rationalize, albeit within the same framework (self-referential competition policy). And finally, (4) the 'excess of market power' paradigm is a sort of 'Counter-Reformation', since it is not a simple return to ordoliberalism, but rather an adaptation to a more neomercantilist world. Those paradigm shifts are not surprising, especially in light of the history of US antitrust, where constant reinterpretation of ancient texts and doctrines are carried out, as witnessed by the very name of the current 'Neo-Brandesian' approach, which refers to an interwar judge.

Those changes were not brutal and clear-cut. Overlaps between the approaches have persisted. Obviously, those paradigms are ideal-type: they never materialize as such in reality, as they are mainly categories of thoughts. The flexibility of the Treaty is not absolute, as its wording, the secondary legislation and the case-law must be taken into account; but a certain room of manoeuvre exist to adapt to the evolution of the intellectual, institutional and economic framework. The solution of relying more on a coordination of national competition policies, which was promoted by the French in 1956, was discarded in 1962, only to be revamped in 2003 once the Commission had established a firm doctrine and could depend on efficient national authorities.

Compared to a traditional account of EU competition policy history, this article has confirmed the US antitrust and the German ordoliberal influences, while at the same time emphasizing four neglected factors. First, the Treaty of Rome still remains in place today, as it was both relatively flexible and bold, delivering a genuinely European competition policy at a time when hardly any policy of this kind existed in Western Europe. Second, this flexibility was used by many actors to shape the EEC/EU competition policy, and not only by the Germans. The French were insistent on getting an effective competition regime, and they imprinted their mark with a focus on restrictive vertical agreements. Belgian actors were also important during critical junctures. Third, the 'modernization' of the 2000s started with controversies between ordoliberal and promoters of the Second Chicago School as of the early 1980s. Fourth, in this field marked by a firm centralization of the European Commission, several European commissioners played an instrumental role in promoting paradigm changes, notably von der Groeben, Sutherland, Brittan, Monti and Vestager.

Nowadays, the urge is to go beyond religious war by defining more clearly what the new paradigm means. Gauging the economic effects in terms of consumer and global welfare of environmental, social, societal (privacy, plurality) and strategic criteria is almost impossible, especially because the timespan to judge the impact of an agreement can be very long; but certain guidelines and principles can be laid out. After all, the *Altmark* ruling was instrumental in defining a set of principles that were helpful in establishing which state aids were acceptable, despite the large number of conflicting logics at stake.[65] This debate on the measurability of non-economic criteria is all the more important as it overtakes competition policy, and concerns all EU policies more broadly.[66]

65. EU Court of Justice, Judgment of the Court of 24 July 2003, *Altmark Trans GmbH and Regierungspräsidium Magdeburg v. Nahverkehrsgesellschaft Altmark GmbH, and Oberbundesanwalt beim Bundesverwaltungsgericht*, case C-280/00.
66. *See* more generally on the relationship between law, economics and politics: Jedediah Britton-Purdy et al., *Building a Law-and-Political-Economy Framework: Beyond the Twentieth-Century Synthesis*, Yale Law Journal, 129(6) (2019): 1784-1835.

CHAPTER 3

The Genesis and Main Features of the Digital Markets Act*

*Inge Bernaerts***

1 THE ANTECEDENTS: REGULATION WAITING TO HAPPEN

By 2020, the emergence of a handful of digital conglomerates, their sheer size, economic power and societal influence, had given rise to a global debate on whether and how to rein in big tech. The debate was multifaceted, ranging from questions around fair taxation, working conditions of platform workers, social media's responsibility for illegal or harmful content and their role in democracy. In the antitrust community, however, the debate concentrated on whether existing antitrust rules were sufficient to keep the economic power of large digital platforms in check.

In the European Union (EU), the European Commission had since the early 2000s pursued a vigorous antitrust enforcement policy in the digital sector, relying in particular on Article 102 of the Treaty on the Functioning of the European Union (TFEU), which prohibits abuses of dominance. Hefty fines had been imposed and, overall, antitrust interventions undeniably resorted effect. For example, the competitive dynamics in the browser market increased substantially after the Commission intervened against Microsoft for tying its web browser, Internet Explorer, to its client PC operating system, Windows.[1] National competition authorities (NCAs) across the EU followed suit.[2]

* Regulation (EU) 2022/1925 of the European Parliament and of the Council of 14 September 2022 on contestable and fair markets in the digital sector and amending Directives (EU) 2019/1937 and (EU) 2020/1828 (Digital Markets Act), OJ L 265 of 12 October 2022, pp. 1 et seq.

** All views expressed in this chapter are strictly personal to the author and do not represent the views of the European Commission. The author wishes to thank Gunnar Wolf for his valuable comments.

1. Case AT. 39530 Microsoft (Tying), Commission Decision of 16 December 2009.
2. For an overview of national enforcement decisions in the digital sector, *see* Joint Paper of the heads of the national competition authorities of the European Union, How national competition

Nevertheless, concerns remained that antitrust enforcement alone was insufficient to keep digital markets open and contestable, and to deliver fair outcomes for business customers and consumers.

First, enforcement agencies were confronted with a harsh reality that their actions often had insufficient deterrent effect. Problematic behaviour kept popping up, in slightly different forms and shapes, by different undertakings or for different services, but in essence representing broadly similar patterns of behaviour, by which providers of key platform services entrenched their positions and leveraged market power into neighbouring areas.

Second, antitrust intervention proved to be slow and sometimes unable to prevent irreparable harm to the market structure. Such criticism was aired for example when the Commission in 2017 intervened against Google and imposed a EUR 2.42 billion fine for giving preferential treatment to its own online price comparison services when displaying results in Google search.[3] The General Court fully upheld the Commission's enforcement action,[4] but consumer organisations and competing price comparison providers complained that the intervention came too late as the market had moved on.

Third, abuse of dominance cases in the EU require a lot of resources. The case-by-case approach that characterises antitrust enforcement requires the enforcer in every case afresh to define the relevant market(s), to establish dominance, to demonstrate that the contested conduct is capable or likely to restrict competition, and to assess potential efficiency arguments brought forward by the defendant. The Commission's digital enforcement practice had shown that case files tended to become enormous[5] and procedures lengthy, with tech companies challenging substantive and procedural aspects almost systematically in both the administrative procedure before the Commission and in court. Whilst it is obviously legitimate for any company to make the fullest possible use of its rights of defence, from a public interest perspective the question arose whether the status quo was satisfactory. Experts had rung the alarm bell on the substantial risk of under-enforcement and the damage it could do to innovation, quality and choice for consumers.[6] Public consultations confirmed those concerns[7]

agencies can strengthen the DMA, endorsed by national competition authorities at the ECN Directors General's meeting of 22 June 2021, Microsoft Word – DMA – Joint EU NCAs paper – 21.06.2021_Final.docx (europa.eu).

3. Case AT.39740 *Google Search (Shopping)*, Commission Decision of 27 June 2017.
4. Case T-612/17 *Google and Alphabet v. Commission*, judgment of the General Court of 10 November 2021.
5. European Court of Auditors, Special Report 24/2020: EU audit report: merger control and antitrust proceedings, 19 November 2020, EU audit report: European Commission's merger control and antitrust proceedings: a need to scale up market oversight (europa.eu).
6. European Commission, Directorate-General for Competition, Y. Montjoye, H. Schweitzer & J. Crémer, Competition Policy for the Digital Era, Publications Office, 2019, https://data.europa.eu/doi/10.2763/407537.
7. Impact Assessment Report, Accompanying the document proposal for a Regulation of the European Parliament and of the Council on contestable and fair markets in the digital sector (Digital Markets Act), Commission staff working document (2020) 363 of 15 December 2020, Annex 2: Stakeholder consultation.

and the European Parliament had called upon the Commission to assess the possibility of imposing ex ante regulatory obligations to address the enforcement gap.[8]

Fourth, the global debate and economic literature converged that digital markets displayed a number of distinctive economic features, which make them prone to tipping and winner-takes-all outcomes. These include the presence of strong economies of scale, extreme network effects, the role of data as critical input and a data-driven feedback loop that further strengthen the network effects, conglomerate effects, customer lock-in and behavioural biases.[9] These systemic market features, if unaddressed, would always provide digital incumbents with very strong incentives to behave in an anticompetitive manner. In other words, the only root-cause solutions would be to lower barriers to entry in a structural manner, to facilitate customer switching and multi-homing to overcome network effects, and to break the data feedback loop.

In short, the antitrust instrument had proven to be a useful and sophisticated instrument to examine afresh potentially anticompetitive conduct, but going forward it was simply too heavy and too slow to tackle effectively the most egregious conduct by large digital platforms. The time had come for a new instrument.

2 COMMISSION PROPOSAL: BALANCING SPEED AND FLEXIBILITY

On 15 December 2020, the Commission adopted a proposal for a Digital Markets Act (DMA), a proposal for ex ante regulation, covering the largest platforms holding an entrenched gatekeeper position with respect to a limited number of core platforms services, and centrally enforced by the European Commission with far-reaching investigative and sanctioning powers.

2.1 Regulation

The fact that the Commission opted for regulation, a different type of instrument compared to the new antitrust tools developed in other jurisdictions such as the United Kingdom (UK) and Germany, is no doubt influenced by two factors: the EU's institutional set-up and its positive experience with the regulation of other sectors.

Institutionally, the Commission has a very particular position in the governance of the EU, as it does not only enforce EU law, including competition law, but also has the monopoly right to initiate new legislation in areas of EU competence. For example, the Commission is the sole authority that can initiate EU legislation to foster the internal market. That double - executive and legislative - hat, which spans all matters of EU competence, implies that the Commission had a broader spectrum of potential solutions at its disposal, beyond competition law. Moreover, it is well established in EU

8. European Parliament resolution on competition policy - Annual Report 2019 (2019/2131(INI), 18 June 2020.
9. OECD, Ex ante regulation in digital markets - Background Note, DAF/COMP(2021)15, 19 November 2021, section 2.1.; J. Crémer, Y.-A. de Montjoye & H. Schweitzer, Digital Policy for the Digital Era (2019).

case law[10] that competition law and sectoral regulation can coexist and be applied in parallel, which generates a natural vision of complementarity of both instruments, including in different departments of the European Commission.[11]

Historically, the Commission had good experiences with sectoral regulation, for example in the electronic communications sector, the energy sector and the financial services sector. Regulation, often inspired by competition law and co-developed by the Commission's competition department, had been successful in bringing down market entry barriers, in overcoming network effects and in facilitating consumer switching. Concepts such as access regulation, interoperability, unbundling or portability were tried and tested. Although not perfect and certainly unfinished, EU internal market legislation had been effective in removing regulatory barriers between Member States and creating a (more) harmonised framework for the EU internal market in those sectors.

The speed of technological and market developments in the digital sector, however, was new. It emphasised, on the one hand, the need for regulation to resort effect quickly and, on the other hand, the need for sufficient flexibility in order not to become outdated very soon. The search for a balance between speed and flexibility transpires in the basic design features of the DMA.

2.2 Asymmetric Regulation

The DMA targets only the largest platforms, with a presence in at least three Member States and very high customer numbers on both sides of the platform. Furthermore, it zooms in on a limited number of exhaustively defined core platform services, namely those where gatekeeper issues were considered most likely to emerge. The rules and obligations laid down in the DMA bind only those platforms that are designated as gatekeeper for one or more of the listed core platform services. In that sense, the DMA is asymmetric regulation.

The mechanism for designating platforms as gatekeepers contains a light, fast process whenever its provider exceeds a limited number of *quantitative* thresholds. That quantitative designation mechanism reflects the will to have the rules and obligations contained in the DMA kick in rapidly, following a straightforward procedure, for the most obvious candidate gatekeepers. According to the Impact Assessment Report accompanying the Commission proposal, a limited number of companies are expected to exceed the quantitative thresholds.[12]

10. For example, Case C-280/08 P *Deutsche Telekom AG v. European Commission*, judgment of the Court of 14 October 2010, paras 80 et seq.
11. DG Competition and DG Connect could build on their positive joint experience in shaping and enforcing the regulatory framework for electronic communications (the so-called Article 7 framework, referring to Article 7 of Directive 2002/21/EC of the European Parliament and the Council of 7 March 2002 on a common regulatory framework for electronic communications networks and services) and it is noteworthy that several of the senior officials involved in the development of the Digital Markets Act at some point had been involved in the Article 7 framework.
12. Impact Assessment Report, Rn. 180.

There is, at least on paper, a possibility for a company that fulfils the quantitative criteria to rebut the presumption that it is a gatekeeper, creating a limited degree of flexibility with a view to avoid 'false positives'.

In addition, the Commission has the possibility to designate companies as gatekeepers based on a set of *qualitative* criteria, after a market investigation. Although it can reasonably be expected that the Commission will designate first those gatekeepers that meet the quantitative thresholds, the DMA hence provides it the flexibility to designate also other companies, or the same companies for other core platforms services, should gatekeeper situations emerge, raising contestability and fairness issues, despite the quantitative thresholds not being met. The Commission can also designate 'emerging gatekeepers', reflecting once more the will to be able to intervene quickly and have a limited set of the rules and obligations kick in before a market tips and a gatekeeper position becomes entrenched.

Finally, the Commission can open market investigations to inquire whether services other than the core platform services listed exhaustively in the DMA should be added to the DMA. If it concludes positively, it can table a legislative proposal with a view to amend the DMA.

Whilst the DMA hence contains some flexibility to designate additional gatekeepers or, exceptionally, to rebut the gatekeeper presumption, the process for the Commission to designate gatekeepers on the basis of a limited number of quantitative thresholds foreseen in the DMA is straightforward and fast.

2.3 Ex Ante Regulation

A second important element of speed lies in the fact that the rules and obligations set out in the DMA kick in automatically, as a direct consequence of the gatekeeper designation decision, six months from designation. The DMA hence has impact (much) faster than an antitrust-based system under which remedies are imposed after a case-by-case assessment and the choice of remedies needs to be calibrated and motivated by the enforcer. It has been argued that the DMA is therefore a blunt instrument, which imposes one-size-fits all obligations ignoring the differences between core platform services. The benefits in terms of speed, administrative efficiency and predictability are, however, substantial. Furthermore, it should be underlined that several rules and obligations are explicitly limited to one or some core platform services only.

Also, for the majority of rules and obligations it is possible for a gatekeeper to request, or for the Commission to open ex officio, a dialogue process at the end of which the Commission may specify how exactly the gatekeeper shall ensure compliance. That specification process provides the necessary flexibility to go beyond the relatively general formulation of some obligations and clarify them in further detail. The process, however, does not suspend the obligation, or absolve the gatekeeper from compliance pending the process.

2.4 Enforcement Centralised with the European Commission

When the electronic communications and energy sectors were opened up for competition in the 1990s and early 2000s, a central role was granted to newly created, independent national regulatory authorities (NRAs) in the Member States. They acted under the oversight of the European Commission, who reviewed, and on some key points had the power to veto, draft decisions of NRAs. Similarly, the modernisation of competition law in 2003 introduced a system of parallel competences, whereby the Commission and NCAs share the public enforcement task of EU antitrust rules, with the Commission playing an oversight role to ensure consistency.

So why did the Commission propose to centralise the DMA enforcement at EU level?

Partly, it can be explained by the fact that the DMA targets a limited number of platforms, which mostly are global companies providing the relevant core platform services across the EU or at least in three Member States. It was considered most effective and most efficient to designate gatekeepers centrally, to specify compliance modalities centrally in order to avoid a fragmentation of the internal market through potentially differing modalities across Member States, and to take (public) enforcement action centrally. The Commission was of the view that centralised enforcement would best serve the internal market objective of the DMA, as it would guarantee the same level of protection to consumers and business users, no matter where they were established.

The Commission proposal foresaw investigative and sanctioning powers that were broadly similar to those in EU competition law. However, the DMA proposal also contained a few noteworthy add-ons. In case of systematic non-compliance, where fines proved not to be a sufficient deterrent, the Commission was empowered to impose behavioural or structural remedies. On the procedural front, the DMA proposal included novelties such as mandatory confidentiality rings and retention orders.

3 OUTCOME OF THE LEGISLATIVE PROCESS: BROADER, FASTER, SHARPER AND STRONGER

From the outset the DMA proposal was positively received in both the European Parliament and the Council of the European Union and the co-legislators committed to deal with the dossier as a matter of priority. The common will to act decisively and fast, and the intense rhythm of discussions and negotiations within and between the institutions, allowed for a political agreement to be reached on 24 March 2022, less than 16 months from the date of the proposal.[13] The DMA was formally adopted on 14 September 2022.

13. Digital Markets Act (DMA): agreement between the Council and the European Parliament – Consilium (europa.eu).

Whilst all provisions of the proposal were discussed and negotiated in detail, the debate concentrated on the DMA's scope, obligations and prohibitions, governance framework and enforcement mechanism.

3.1 Broader Scope and More Far-Reaching Obligations

Regarding the DMA's scope, co-legislators agreed to set the quantitative criteria for qualifying as a gatekeeper at a high level, confirming the asymmetric approach of the DMA.[14] They also agreed with the possibility for the Commission to designate additional gatekeepers on the basis of qualitative criteria and fine-tuned those criteria.

At the same time, they added web browsers and virtual assistants, to the list of core platform services, thus expanding the DMA's scope.[15] During the legislative process on the DMA, the Commission had published the results of its sector inquiry into the 'Internet of Things',[16] which concluded, inter alia, that virtual assistants might give rise to similar concerns as the ones the DMA was seeking to address for other platform services. Furthermore, indications had emerged from antitrust proceedings in several jurisdictions that platforms could shift gatekeeper behaviour, notably around the collection and cross-use of data, from search engines to web browsers, if web browsers were not also included as a core platform service within the scope of the DMA.

More substantially, the co-legislators furthermore widened the rules and obligations applicable to gatekeepers. An entirely new provision obliging gatekeepers to ensure interoperability of so-called number-independent interpersonal communications services (essentially messaging services) was added.[17] The scope of the FRAND obligation for access to app-stores was expanded to cover also search engines and online social networking services.[18] To facilitate consumer switching, the final text obliges gatekeepers to not only allow and technically enable the uninstallation of software applications, but also to allow and enable changes to default settings and to foresee choice screens in certain circumstances.[19] And beyond wide parity clauses,

14. Article 3(2) DMA sets the quantitative thresholds as follows: annual union turnover equal to or above EUR 7.5 billion in each of the last three financial years, or average market capitalisation or equivalent fair market value of at least EUR 75 billion in the last financial year, and providing the same core platform service in at least three Member States; at least 45 million monthly active users and at least 10,000 yearly active business users in the EU, in each of the last three financial years.
15. Article 2(2) DMA: 'A core platform service means any of the following: (a) online intermediation services; (b) online search engines; (c) online social networking services; (d) video-sharing platform services; (e) number-independent interpersonal communications services; (f) operating systems; (g) web browsers; (h) virtual assistants; (i) cloud computing services; (j) online advertising services, including any advertising networks, advertising exchanges and any other advertising intermediation services, provided by an undertaking that provides any of the core platform services listed in points (a) to (j).'
16. Final report – sector inquiry into consumer Internet of Things, Brussels, 20 January 2022, COM(2022) 19, internet-of-things_final_report_2022_en.pdf (europa.eu).
17. Article 7 DMA.
18. Article 6(12) DMA.
19. Article 6(3) DMA.

co-legislators decided to also ban narrow parity clauses.[20] These are only some examples of the rather significant way in which co-legislators expanded the set of regulatory rules and obligations applicable to gatekeepers.

3.2 Faster Procedures

To counter one of the main downsides of competition law enforcement, which the European Parliament had said was too slow to keep fast moving digital markets contestable and fair, both Parliament and Council sought to speed up processes and to close loopholes which potential gatekeepers could use to delay the impact of the DMA.

Importantly, the co-legislators narrowed down the possibility for platforms to rebut the gatekeeper presumption when it meets the quantitative designation criteria. The final text stresses that a rebuttal would be exceptional and that the Commission should only take into account those elements which directly relate to the quantitative criteria. To avoid unnecessary delays in the designation procedure, the Commission is empowered to reject a rebuttal without further market investigation if the arguments do not manifestly put into question the presumption.[21] Co-legislators also shortened the deadline for undertakings meeting the quantitative thresholds to notify the Commission thereof, and for the Commission to adopt a decision. They introduced hard deadlines in case the Commission intends to adopt a decision specifying compliance measures, and soft deadlines in case the Commission intends to adopt a non-compliance decision.

The co-legislators furthermore adopted unaltered elements of the Commission proposal intended to prevent or overcome potential procedural bottlenecks, such as the possibility for the Commission to impose mandatory confidentiality rings.

3.3 Sharper Sanctions

The 10% of worldwide turnover fines cap for first time violations of the DMA was preserved. However, co-legislators empowered the Commission to impose fines up to 20% in case a gatekeeper commits the same or a similar infringement a second time within a period of eight years.

Furthermore, the sanction arsenal in case of systematic non-compliance was extended to include the possibility for the Commission to impose on a gatekeeper a temporary acquisition ban, where this is 'proportionate and necessary in order to maintain or restore fairness and contestability as affected by the systematic non-compliance'. Systematic non-compliance requires that the Commission has found the gatekeeper to have infringed the DMA at least three times in eight years.[22]

20. Article 5(3) DMA.
21. Article 3(5) DMA and recital (23) DMA.
22. Article 16 DMA.

3.4 A Stronger Governance Framework

One of the elements most extensively discussed, not only between co-legislators, but also in the media, academia and stakeholder fora was the governance framework for the DMA. The Commission had made clear that it wanted to cooperate closely with NCAs, and other authorities, for monitoring the digital sector and for ensuring consistency in the enforcement of the DMA and other sets of legislation. It recognised the expertise held by those bodies and the limits of its own resources, but had proposed to leave the details of cooperation to be spelled out in subsequent implementing acts.

The co-legislators wanted to embed more details on such cooperation and coordination in the DMA itself. Without altering the Commission's role as sole enforcer of the DMA, the final text hence puts more flesh on the bone as regards concrete forms and fora of cooperation. It sets out that the Commission and NCAs shall cooperate and exchange information through the existing European Competition Network (ECN).[23] Where they are enabled to do so by national law NCAs can conduct investigations into possible cases of non-compliance with the DMA, but they cannot themselves adopt non-compliance decisions. They can, however, report their findings to the Commission supporting a possible non-compliance decision adopted by the Commission. First indications are that many NCAs will be empowered with such investigative competences by their Member State, and some have indicated a willingness to play an active role, including through joint investigation teams.[24] The DMA also provides for a mechanism whereby NCAs must inform the Commission of investigative steps and draft decisions concerning gatekeepers, complementing the mechanism of cooperation foreseen in Regulation 1/2003.[25]

As regards other national authorities, the DMA provides in more general terms that the Commission and Member States shall work in close cooperation and coordinate their enforcement actions to ensure 'coherent, effective and complementary' enforcement of various legal instruments applied to gatekeepers.

Interestingly, it furthermore establishes a 'high-level group for the DMA', composed of representatives of five European bodies and networks competent in related regulatory disciplines.[26] The high-level group has as mandate to provide the Commission with advice and expertise, including with a view to promote a consistent regulatory approach across different regulatory instruments. It shall meet at least once per year, upon the request of the Commission or of the majority of its members.

23. Article 38 DMA.
24. Tech giant 'gatekeepers' should face enforcers drawn from EU and national authorities, Snoep says, Natalie McNelis and Nicholas Hirst, 9.9.2022, MLex.
25. Article 11 of Council Regulation (EC) No. 1/2003 of 16 December 2002 on the implementation of the rules on competition laid down in Articles 81 and 82 of the Treaty.
26. The Body of the European Regulators for Electronic Communications, the European Data Protection Supervisor and European Data Protection Board, the ECN, the Consumer Protection Cooperation Network and the European Regulatory Group of Audiovisual Media Regulators, Article 40 DMA.

4 FROM ENACTMENT TO ENFORCEMENT

The publication of the DMA in the Official Journal of 12 October 2022 has fixed the time frame in which the DMA will become applicable. Undertakings fulfilling the quantitative criteria must file their notifications by 3 July 2023 at the latest. The Commission will then have 45 working days from notification to adopt a decision and the obligations will become applicable 6 months after designation, i.e., around March 2024.

It remains to be seen what the compliance strategy of different candidate gatekeepers will be. Will they seek to engage with the Commission – and with their customers on both sides of the platform – in a genuine spirit of compliance, or will the rather litigious relationship between the Commission as antitrust enforcer and tech firms continue? The future will tell and the truth may lay somewhere in the middle.

What is clear, however, is that, like with other sets of sectoral regulation, the implementation of the DMA will be an iterative process. There will be pressure from the public and the European Parliament for the DMA to show quick results for some of the most egregious problems. Therefore, it can be expected that, when needed, the Commission will not hesitate to adopt non-compliance decisions relatively soon. But the DMA also leaves ample room for regulatory dialogue and it entrusts the Commission with a longer term task of monitoring and regulating the digital sector. Enforcing the 'hard core' provisions of the DMA in its current form, will only be the starting point in that regard. Longer term, the Commission will be conducting market investigations under the DMA and may be tabling proposals for adjusting the scope of the DMA. It will be in a position to provide, based inter alia on its enforcement experience, more horizontal guidance and regulatory details on how some of the provisions are to be implemented.

The adoption of the DMA is in that sense only a first step, albeit it a major one.

CHAPTER 4

The New Drive Towards 'Economic Sovereignty' in Europe: What Changes for Competition Policy?

Isabelle de Silva

Now is a special time for Europe. The pandemic of COVID-19 has led European Member States and institutions to engage, since 2020, in unprecedented levels of European cooperation in order to fight the sanitary crisis and provide the necessary vaccines. The crisis also revealed some of the challenges created by the globalization of the economy, such as supply chain issues in basic goods or medicines.[1] When one considers the way Europe adapted to the COVID-19 crisis, maintaining its unity in the face of very daunting challenges, there are reasons to rejoice. But since then, the war in Ukraine has created the most serious threat to European stability since World War II. In that context, the issue of European sovereignty takes on yet another meaning.

Over the past few years, the notion of 'economic sovereignty' has made a striking comeback in the European political debate, and has remained central in the discussions around competition policy. What are the reasons for this renewed interest, and should we expect a major shift in competition policy? Or are we likely to witness a new 'policy mix', where traditional competition law tools will be used in conjunction with new legal instruments? Will the sovereignty debate leave its mark in competition enforcement? These are the questions we will try to answer.

1. This led the European Medicines Agency (EMA) to put in place special measures to help prevent and mitigate possible disruptions to the supply of medicines in the EU, with the EMA acting as 'central coordinator' in supporting Member States activities in this area during the pandemic.

1 THE 'ETERNAL RETURN' OF THE SOVEREIGNTY DISCOURSE

1.1 The Sovereignty Theme Has Come Back in Full Force over the Past Few Years, and Encompasses Several Subthemes

As we approach the twentieth anniversary of Regulation 1/2003,[2] the economic landscape has changed: the acceleration of the digitization of the economy and the emergence of major digital platforms raise new challenges for competition enforcers. We also witness a form of 'disenchantment' over globalization, and the fear that de-industrialization has gone too far. In a context where industrial policy appears as a key priority in Europe, sovereignty has become, once again, a 'must' of the political discourse, taking sometimes precedence over the notions of European integration or competition. It has certainly been the case, over the past few years, in France, but also in other Member States such as Germany.

1.1.1 During the French Presidency of the Council of the European Union (First Semester of 2021) Sovereignty Was Presented as the Foremost Priority

The French presidency of the Council of the European Union (EU) in 2021 chose as overarching motto the 'sovereignty agenda'. Sovereignty was thus the key word for the different areas of European policies, including the economy: 'The majority of European citizens no longer complain that Europe does too much, but rather that it does too little … . In 2017, with the Sorbonne speech, the President of the French Republic put forward the notion of a "sovereignty agenda" to our European partners, meaning Europe's ability to exist in the world to defend our values and interests.' This presentation of the priorities of the French presidency illustrated, as examples of this agenda for a 'sovereign Europe', some measures related to the ecological transition, social issues or defence, and underlined the following topics related to digital and economic issues: 'With regard to digital issues, copyright reform and the removal of terrorist content online have been passed, and platform regulation and accountability will soon be a reality;/With regard to economic issues, a historic recovery plan funded by joint European borrowing has helped Europe overcome the crisis. And Europe is progressively acquiring commercial protection instruments to no longer be naive when it comes to globalization.'[3]

Several initiatives pushed forward through this European presidency were presented as a means of promoting European sovereignty, notably the twin acts establishing a new regulation of digital platforms, the Digital Services Act (DSA) and the Digital Markets Act (DMA).

The theme of economic sovereignty has remained an important component of French policy since. The presence of the term 'sovereignty' in the official titles of two

2. Council Regulation (EC) No. 1:2003 of 16 December 2002 on the implementation of the rules on competition laid down in Articles 81 and 82 of the Treaty.
3. https://presidence-francaise.consilium.europa.eu/en/programme/priorities/.

ministers of the current French government[4] (economy and agriculture) is a testimony of the lasting importance of this notion, across different sectors of public policy.

1.1.2 Even Before the French Presidency of 2021, Europe Had Seen the Return in Full Force of the 'National' or 'European Champions' Discourse, Which Crystallized over the Controversial Proposed Merger Between the 'German' Siemens and the 'French' Alstom

The management of both companies advocated for the merger, touted as creating a 'global giant' in the rail market. Siemens and Alstom being Europe's largest suppliers in the rail markets, it was argued that a merger between them would allow the creation of a single 'European champion' that would be a major force in the industry. The merger also received very strong support from the governments of France and Germany. The the merger faced an in-depth scrutiny by the European Commission. This 'phase 2 investigation', was, in its turn, criticized in governmental and political spheres in both France and Germany.

The merger, beyond its intrinsic complexities – it involved a number of different markets and raised difficult questions about the size of the markets and the intensity of competition from Chinese companies, *inter alia* – was marked by an unusual level of intervention from national governments.

The European Commission finally prohibited,[5] in February 2019, the Siemens-Alstom merger under the EU Merger Regulation of 2004.[6] The Commission found that this merger would have harmed competition in markets for railway signalling systems and very high-speed trains, and noted that merging parties had not offered remedies sufficient to address these concerns.

Commissioner[7] Margrethe Vestager, presented the decision in the following terms: 'Millions of passengers across Europe rely every day on modern and safe trains. Siemens and Alstom are both champions in the rail industry. Without sufficient remedies, this merger would have resulted in higher prices for the signalling systems that keep passengers safe and for the next generations of very high-speed trains. The Commission prohibited the merger because the companies were not willing to address our serious competition concerns.'

4. When he was reappointed under the current government, the Minister Bruno le Maire received the title of 'minister of economy, finance and industrial and digital sovereignty'. And the current minister for the agriculture, M. Marc Fesneau is 'minister for agriculture and Food sovereignty'.
5. Decision M.8677, 6 February 2019, https://ec.europa.eu/commission/presscorner/detail/en/IP_19_881.
6. Council Regulation (EC) No. 139/2004 of 20 January 2004 on the control of concentrations between undertakings.
7. As she was then, before her nomination as executive Vice-President of the European Commission under Ursula von der Leyen presidency.

1.1.3 *The Debate about European Competition Policy: Too Demanding for European Firms or Necessary to Protect the European Consumer?*

The Siemens–Alstom case,[8] throughout the examination, and in the aftermath of the prohibition, led, in some political circles, to severe criticism of merger enforcement by the European Commission. Some stakeholders expressed the view that such 'strict' merger control risked to weaken the European economy and industry, was ' 'naïve', and put European companies at a disadvantage, in comparison to companies operating outside of Europe (in the United States (US) and China), which were deemed to 'benefit' from a less taxing scrutiny of mergers and state subsidies.

This led to a call for a 'reboot' of European competition policy, some players advocating a renewed focus on industrial policy and the creation of European champions, others being in favour of a 'modernization' of European competition policy, so as to better take into account the specificities of the digital economy.

In the days that followed the Siemens-Alstom merger prohibition, France and Germany published, on 19 February 2019, a 'Joint Franco-German manifesto on Industrial Policy' calling for EU merger rules to be changed. French Minister Bruno Le Maire, and German Economy Minister Peter Altmaier both regretted what they considered to be a 'massive disadvantage' of European companies in comparison to their Chinese and American counterparts.

'In order to be able to create a new European champion, it is necessary to change the European regulatory framework', Minister Bruno Le Maire declared, while underlining that countries such as China were able to subsidize heavily their own companies without being subject to state subsidies control. The Franco-German plan expressly aimed at fostering the creation of 'European champions'.

This Industrial Manifesto was followed, the 4 July 2019, by a Common Proposal from France, Germany and Poland for a 'Modernized Competition Policy', which was prepared by a report from the French Inspection générale des Finances and the Conseil Général de l'Economie on the EU competition policy and industrial strategy.[9] The Common Proposal issued a vast range of proposals, such as 'taking into account third countries state interventions in merger control', 'tackling excessive market power of big tech firms', modernizing merger control, or encouraging behavioural remedies.

The French Senate also decided to take part in the debate, and published, after a vast consultation, an information report on the 'Modernization of European competition policy'[10] in July 2020, which underlined the benefits of sound competition enforcement and proposed targeted changes.

---

8. The decision was commented in several articles. *See* 'Beyond Alstom-Siemens: Is There a Need to Revise Competition Law Goals? EU Policy after Siemens/Alstom: A Look into the Right Tools to Preserve the EU Industry's Competitiveness at Global Level', B. Amory, C. de Navacelle & H. de la Barre, Concurrences No. 4-2019, p. 3; 'European Champions: What Now for EU Merger Control after Siemens / Alstom?', Alex Nourry Dani Rabinowitz (2020) 41 European competition Law Review, Issue 3, p. 116.
9. The report was published on 2 June 2019 and has been translated in English.
10. Information report No. 603, by Senators Alain Chatillon and Olivier Henno for the Commission of European Affairs and the Commission of economic affairs of the French Senate, 8 July 2020, http://www.senat.fr/rap/r19-603/r19-603.html.

Some participants in the debate wanted a major shift in competition policy. They felt that economic sovereignty and industrial policy should become the new overarching objectives of competition law, and of its enforcement by competition agencies. At the same time, voices were heard, in Europe and in the US, to adapt competition policy, to adjust the consumer welfare standard, and to better take into account other considerations, such as labour markets or sustainability.[11]

If European competition policy was 'under fire' for being too strict, it received in the meantime very strong support in other spheres. For instance Patrick Rey and Jean Tirole, the 2014 Nobel Laureate in economics, took up their pens to defend 'keeping politics out of Europe's competition decision'.[12] The European Commission and several national competition agencies (NCAs) supplied evidence that when they acted to maintain a sufficient level of competition in European markets, treating all companies equally irrespective of their 'nationality'. they were not only protecting the European consumers, many companies large and small being included in that category, but also allowed all European players to become more competitive, in Europe and abroad. The case was also made that the 'politicization' of competition policy in Europe would make enforcement unpredictable for companies and expose European companies to retaliation in other regions of the world, if it was perceived that Europe was 'protecting its own' by applying more lenient merger control. In this advocacy effort, it was recalled that the number of blocked mergers over the years is extremely small, and that European merger control has not prevented the development of powerful international companies in European soil. As Commissioner Vestager expressed in a speech in 2019[13] 'we can't build those champions by undermining competition. We can't build them with mergers that harm competition, or by looking the other way when Europe's businesses break our rules ... . Our competition rules are in place to ensure that European companies can compete on their merits ... businesses do best when they can compete on a level playing field.'

1.2. Sovereignty and Industrial Policy: A New Priority or a Constant in the European Debate?

1.2.1. Before European Champions There Were 'National Champions': From Seventeenth Century Lace to Twenty-First Century Batteries

The idea that 'European champions' should be created or encouraged by a public policy – and not left to the competitive process in the market – is, in many ways, the

11. *See* for instance the discussion of this issue of 'sustainability and competition' by the OECD. In 2020 and 2021, and the OECD paper on 'Environmental considerations in competition enforcement' DAF/COMP(2021)4.
12. Published in Le Monde, on 20 March 2019, the authors wrote 'Upset by the decision, France and Germany now want to rewrite EU merger rules and give member states more say over proposed tie-ups. But although such an approach may seem tempting, Europe would be wise not to leave competition policy enforcement in the hands of its politicians.'
13. 'The champions Europe needs', Margrethe Vestager, WELT Economic Summit, Berlin, 9 January 2019.

direct heir of a very common theme in economic policy history: the creation of 'national champions'. The idea that 'having' national champions is a desirable policy objective for a government is not new. And neither is the view that competition law or enforcement may run counter to that objective.

Encouraging the development of national champions has long been a constant feature of the national discourse in many countries. France and Germany jump to mind, but it is safe to say that other EU countries share the pride to have a 'national champion' (Fiat or Ferrari have been national passions in Italy as Saab or Ikea in Sweden). Many governments have felt, over past centuries, that fostering the national prominence of 'their' national companies was a desirable goal and an integral part of their political power of sovereignty. This school of thought has very ancient roots, particularly in countries with a tradition of intervention by the State in the economy, under the guise of dirigiste economy.

In France, few figures exemplify this school of thought as well as Jean-Baptiste Colbert. In his time, the great trade battle was not waged about semiconductors or high-speed train, but about Lace. The statesman endeavoured to shape what was at the time a very 'strategic' industry. Colbert remains, to this day, a national figure in France, as First minister of State of Louis the XIV, because he had a lasting impact on the organization of the country's politics and economy. What would later be called the 'Colbertisme' doctrine is firmly rooted in the belief that state intervention is needed to secure the largest part of limited resources. Colbert tried to reorganize industry and commerce in order to increase French influence among nations. One of his goals was to grow France's share of international trade and reduce the commercial hegemony of the Dutch. This led to the establishment of monopoly privileges for lace manufacturers, of protective tariffs on imported lace and, finally, to the prohibition of all foreign lace. At the same time, Colbert enforced quality standards on production and trade. These measures were later viewed as having had a freezing effect on the French economy and having prevented it from benefiting from innovation in technologies and production from other regions of the world.

Colbert remains an iconic figure due to the perception that intervention by the French State led to a form of 'grandeur' of the economy.

Since Colbert time, the treaty of Rom introduced a systemic change: the construction of a single market and European integration.

As a consequence of the withdrawal of internal trade barriers and other restrictions to the unified market in Europe, the discourse about the protection of National champions had to be toned down somewhat. But as Europe was becoming a global economic power, the creation of 'European champions' became a new legitimate objective of the European leaders, the more so if it allowed to further European leadership in strategic industries.

In that respect, the best 'success story' remains the creation of Airbus,[14] a major European player that could compete with giants such as the American Boeing, and

14. The Airbus programme began in 1965, based on a Franco-German initiative to form a consortium to build a European high capacity, short-haul jet transport.

would rely on the assets of several European companies. Airbus, now EADS[15], has become a motive of national pride in the participating countries, and often serves as benchmark for other European projects in the field of technology and industry. A project launched by the European Commission in October 2017 to boost the European capacity in efficient batteries – crucial to answer the growing demand for electric cars –, the 'European Battery Alliance', has been touted as the 'Airbus of batteries'.

The Airbus precedent was also used as a parallel to justify the Siemens-Alstom merger, the proponents presenting it as an 'Airbus of trains'.

1.2.2 What Are the Reasons for the Current Return of the Theme of European Champions and of Economic Sovereignty?

First, the Siemens-Alstom merger had an unusual echo because of several elements. Notwithstanding the obvious difficulties this merger presented – given the market shares of both parties – the parties seemed unwilling to consider any major remedies. They approached the merger as a 'question of principle', with the expectation that strong support from both governments would pave the way for an unconditional approval.

Second, the case raised important issues related to the development of powerful Chinese companies in the railway industry, benefiting from strong State support or subsidies, and not subject to the same kind of competition scrutiny as practised under EU law. It came after other delicate merger cases, in the steel industry for instance, where the geographic market definition and the actual competitive pressure exercised by Chinese companies had already been much debated.

Third, these technical debates within the competition sphere resonated with a more global issue, mixing economic and political considerations: the perception that the extreme globalization of the economy has come at a cost. Many European countries are now facing the long-term consequences of deindustrialization and loss of industrial capacities, in basic industries, but also in sophisticated technologies, such as the car industry, electronics or trains. Globalization, which led many European industries to outsource part of their manufacturing process in lower wages regions, had already started to be challenged in recent years. Some governments, parliaments and elected officials feel that the process has gone too far, given its impact on regions affected by de-industrialization and the difficulty to find alternate employment sources after plant closures.

The COVID-19 pandemic recently gave a powerful new boost to the industrial policy discourse. It revealed the risk of shortages that affect Europe when global trade stops or is severely impacted, as was the case in 2020 and 2021. Europe was faced with serious difficulties to secure face masks, medicines or vaccines, and various categories of goods (including, for limited periods, basic food items during lockdown such as flour in France). This led European governments to encourage industries to reshore their

15. EADS stands for European Aeronautic Defence and Space company.

manufacturing in Europe, and to have a more cautious approach in terms of supply chain and minimum inventory.

As it regained ground, the notion of economic sovereignty and independence acquired a new facet, with the emergence of 'digital sovereignty'. Europe, in many ways, has fully embraced the digitization of the economy and the systemic changes it entails, from online shopping to social media or the 'platform economy'. But it seems to lag behind the US or China, because it has not created on its soil giant platforms such as Google, Facebook, Alibaba or TikTok. The European electronics industry – phone, computers, and microprocessors – has been almost completely wiped out by its American and east Asian competitors., Europe has not yet managed to jump aboard new strategic sectors emerged, such as cloud computing and to create players comparable to Amazon Web Services (AWS), Microsoft or Google. The COVID-19 pandemic also revealed that European companies and consumers had to depend, for their crucial digital activities, be it videoconferencing or online shopping, on companies raised and directed outside of Europe.

2 HOW HAS THE NEW PRIORITY GIVEN TO ECONOMIC SOVEREIGNTY AFFECTED EUROPEAN COMPETITION POLICY?

The 'European champions debate' has led to a limited but focused adjustment – rather an *aggiornamento* – of competition policy, but the basic principles of merger control in Europe have remained untouched. The main outcome has been the adoption of new, additional regulatory instruments intended to answer the ills identified in the sovereignty debate.

2.1 The Siemens-Alstom Debate Led to Several Proposals to Adjust European Competition Policy and to Create Additional Tools

As mentioned previously, a number of proposals were put on the table, through the Franco-German manifesto of 2019, the Franco-German-Polish proposal to adapt competition policy, and several other parliamentary, expert reports or scientific literature.

The Franco-German manifesto laid down several ideas in order to strengthen the European industry, an objective voiced with urgency: 'The choice is simple when it comes to industrial policy: unite our forces or allow our industrial base and capacity to gradually disappear.' In addition to proposals related to 'massive investing in innovation' (artificial intelligence, microelectronics, batteries) and to an effective 'protection' in trade policy, adapting the regulatory framework was the 'third pillar' of this manifesto.

The following options were considered:

- Taking into greater consideration the state-control of and subsidies for undertakings within the framework of merger control.
- Updating current merger guidelines to take greater account of competition at the global level, potential future competition and the time frame when it comes to

looking ahead to the development of competition to give the European Commission more flexibility when assessing relevant markets. This would enable a more dynamic and long-term approach to competition, at the global scale. This could entail adapting regulation no 139/2004 and current merger guidelines.
- Considering whether a right of appeal of the Council which could ultimately override Commission decisions could be appropriate in well-defined cases, subject to strict conditions.
- Adapting further European State-aid rules to enable Member States to finance major research and innovation projects including the first industrial deployment (IPCEI) in Europe. 'The IPCEI is a useful tool for financing large scale innovative projects, but it is very complex to implement. It may be appropriate to revise the implementing conditions to ensure that the IPCEI is easier and more effective to implement. More generally, state-aid guidelines must provide a clear framework, taking into account the aim to develop innovative industrial capacity in Europe.'

Intending to pursue these proposals with a more in-depth study, the French government commissioned a report by the Inspection générale des finances and the Conseil général de l'Economie[16] (under the supervision of Anne Perrot) on 'European competition policy and EU's strategic interests'.

This document summarized the 'industrial policy and economic sovereignty' doctrine, and considered various avenues to solve what it perceived are ills.

Interestingly, the report gives a positive account of European competition policy, stating it 'seems to have been generally effective in fulfilling its role without hindering the rollout of European industrial projects in terms of numbers. Merger control has led to the rejection of a small number of transactions: since 2000, only sixteen refusals have been issued from over 6000 reported transactions'. However, the report lamented the fact that merger enforcement relies heavily on structural remedies, and found it would often lead to the sale of strategic assets to competitors outside Europe.

The report recognized that the relevant criteria used by the European Commission, based on Regulation 2004, to determine if a merger 'significantly impairs competition in a market' were in line with what most Organisation for Economic Co-operation and Development (OECD) countries apply, and acknowledged the efficiency of the fight against abuses and cartels, and the modernization of the State-aid control system.

Overall, the report considered that European competition law was 'more strictly enforced' in the EU than elsewhere (the US and where the level of concentration has increased, and China), and advocated an update of the legal EU framework based on the concept of 'strategic interests of the EU'. It issues a number of proposals, some - the so-called disruptive options - requiring to revise the Treaties: for example (1) examining the merger taking into account all criteria, competition-related or not, such as employment, environment, health, industrial development, technological sovereignty; (2) granting a special right of evocation to the president of the Commission for competition matters; (3) giving the Council of the EU a right of evocation concerning concentration cases based on the French and German institutional model; (4) setting

16. Inspection générale des finances et Conseil général de l'économie, Rapport sur la politique de la concurrence et les intérêts stratégiques de l'UE, publié le 3 juin 2019.

up an independent authority (mirroring the French competition authority) in place of DG COMP, with a 'right of evocation' given to the Commission.

The favoured scenario consists in improving existing instrument and their implementation, to make them 'more agile and effective in the face of digital challenges': one of the ideas is to establish a European level digital systemic stakeholder supervisory body. Another is to address the issue of below the notification threshold mergers when they involve innovative startups.

Finally, the report recommended a targeted approach to modernize competition enforcement by the Commission, such as updating the notice on relevant markets, and focusing on alternative policy tools, outside of the realm of competition law: trade instruments, public bidding, reciprocity, etc.

2.2 The Outcome of the Debate: New Priorities for the European Commission, New Regulatory Tools, and Some Adjustments to Competition Policy

2.2.1 The Mandate of the New von der Leyen Commission for 2019-2024 Was Influenced by the Sovereignty Debate

The new European Commission presided by Ursula von der Leyen defined a political mandate[17] that clearly placed sovereignty among its priorities.

President von de Leyen defined six priorities for the Commission for 2019-2024, one of which was to prepare a 'Europe fit for the digital age', with the idea that 'Europe must now strengthen its digital sovereignty and set standards, rather than following those of others – with a clear focus on data, technology, and infrastructure.' The new Commission also put a clear focus on revitalizing European industry, with Executive Vice-President Margrethe Vestager and Commissioner Thierry Breton in charge of this digital agenda.[18]

DG Competition adopted a communication, on 18 November 2021, on a 'competition policy fit for new challenges', which detailed the initiatives planned. One was to review the criteria used by the EC to analyse the internal market compatibility of State aid, so as to promote the execution of important projects of common European interest (IPCEIs): the criteria had to align with the new priorities, such as the digital decade and supporting Small and medium enterprises (SME).

Several initiatives were taken to fostering the development of European industry, especially in the digital field (artificial intelligence, cloud computing) and in 'strategic' sectors such as batteries.

17. *See* 'A Union That Strives for More, My Agenda for Europe' by candidate Ursula von der Leyen, Political guidelines for the next European Commission 2019-2024.
18. As President von der Leyen told the European Parliament in her speech of November 2019 as President-elect: 'Our industry is world class in high value sectors, for instance making a third of the world's space satellites. And our companies are at the cutting edge, holding 40% of the world's renewable technology patents. We should harness this transformative power of the twin digital and climate transition to strengthen our own industrial base and innovation potential.'

2.2.2 *A New Tool to Achieve a Level Playing Field for All Undertakings Operating in the EU: The 'Regulation on Foreign Subsidies Distorting the Internal Market'*

The adoption of a new regulatory tool to take into account foreign subsidies granted to companies outside of Europe can be described as one of the direct consequences of the sovereignty debate following Siemens-Alstom.

This legal initiative is quite innovative and was adopted in record time. A white paper was published in June 2020,[19] followed by a formal proposal by the European Commission of a Regulation on foreign subsidies distorting the internal market on 5 May 2021,[20] and a provisional political agreement reached between the Council and the European Parliament on 30 June 2022. French Minister Bruno le Maire presented the agreement in the following terms: 'The French Presidency of the Council of the European Union was built on the principle of economic sovereignty. Economic sovereignty depends on two key principles: investment and protection. The agreement reached on this new instrument will make it possible to combat unfair competition from countries that grant massive subsidies to their industry. This is a major step towards protecting our economic interests.'

Under the Regulation, the Commission will have the power to investigate financial contributions granted by non-EU governments to companies active in the EU. If the Commission finds that such financial contributions constitute distortive subsidies, it can impose measures to redress their distortive effects. The Regulation introduces three new legal tools:

(i) a notification-based tool to investigate concentrations involving a financial contribution by a non-EU government, where the EU turnover of the company to be acquired (or of at least one of the merging parties) is equal or higher than EUR 500 million and the foreign financial contribution is at least EUR 50 million;
(ii) a notification-based tool to investigate bids in public procurements involving a financial contribution by a non-EU government, where the estimated value of the procurement is equal or higher than EUR 250 million; and
(iii) a general market investigation tool to investigate all other market situations, and smaller concentrations and public procurement procedures, which the Commission can start on its own initiative (ex-officio) and may request ad-hoc notifications.

This new legal tool will allow the European Commission to use investigative tools that are quite similar to those it currently uses for merger control and antitrust investigations. It illustrates the development of new additional procedures in merger control, such as the creation or expansion of national foreign direct investment controls.

19. COM(2020) 253 final.
20. COM(2021) 223 final 2021/0114 (COD).

2.3 The New Competition Policy Landscape: An *Aggiornamento* and a New Combined Application with a Specialized Tool, the DMA

2.3.1 A Swifter, Broader and Updated Competition Enforcement

Under both mandates of Margrethe Vestager (as commissioner for competition, then as executive Vice-President in charge of the political priority 'Europe fit for the Digital Age'), many changes have been introduced in order to achieve a swifter, more effective competition enforcement. Competition enforcement has undergone various important changes in recent years. The 'sovereignty debate' undoubtedly spurred and accelerated these evolutions.

A major shift has been the return of the interim measures tool, a power laid down by Regulation 1/2003,[21] but which had been shelved for many years.[22] The fact that the Commission was not using the tool, deeming the legal test too challenging, had been lamented by many stakeholders, including the French government and the Parliament. When the European Commission imposed interim measures on Broadcom,[23] the world's leading supplier of chipsets used for TV boxes, it signalled its clear intention to use the instrument in the future. The 'success' of this new approach was sealed by a swift conclusion of the case, through a commitments decision.[24]

Another cornerstone in the updating of the competition toolkit was the new approach to 'Article 22 referrals' under the 2004 Merger Regulation. The announcement that the Commission would now be open to examine referrals by Member States national competition authorities, even when the merger was not subject to notification under national rules, was a momentous change.[25] The Illumina Grail case, where the French competition authority (Autorité de la concurrence) referred the merger to the European Commission, thus starting an enforcement and judiciary saga[26] that ended, after gun jumping[27] and interim measures proceedings,[28] with a prohibition of the acquisition,[29] was the first illustration of this new approach.

---

21. *See* Article 8 of Council Regulation (EC) No. 1/2003 of 16 December 2002. Before that, the European Court of Justice had ruled that the Commission had the implied power to adopt interim measures, *see* 'Interim measures in EU competition cases: origins, evolution and implications for Digital markets', Despoina Mantzari, 23 February 2020.
22. Or had faded 'into oblivion', to quote Mel Marquis in his definition of 'Interim measures', Global Dictionary of Competition Law, Concurrences, Article No. 12304.
23. AT.40608 Broadcom, interim measures decision 16 October 2019.
24. AT.40608 Broadcom commitments decision 7 October 2020, less than a year after the interim measure decision.
25. *See* Margrethe Vestager speech 'The future of EU merger control', the International Bar Association Annual Conference, 11 September 2020, and the Commission Guidance on the application of the referral mechanism set out in Article 22 of the Merger Regulation to certain categories of cases.
26. *See* the decision of the Commission on 19 April 2021 to accept a request from France, joined by Belgium, Greece, Iceland, the Netherlands and Norway, to assess the proposed acquisition of Grail by Illumina, and the judgment of the General Court in Case T-227/21, *Illumina v. Commission*, 13 July 2022.
27. M. 10483, statement of objections issued 19 July 2022.
28. M. 10493, statement of objections 20 September 2021, and decision to adopt interim measures to prevent harm to competition 29 October 2021.
29. 6 September 2022, M. 10188.

Finally, an important step in the updating of competition policy tools is the review of the 'Market definition notice' of 1997.[30] Although this document is not often well known by the general public, its importance for practitioners and competition enforcers is crucial: it sets the general principles which allow to apply market definitions, the stepping stone in EU competition law to identify the boundaries of competition between firms.[31]

The European Commission launched an evaluation process of the market definition notice, which led on 12 July 2021 to a staff working document summarizing its findings.

The final notice will likely incorporate the existing 'jurisprudence', but will also give answers to many questions that had been raised during the Siemens-Alstom debate. The new revised notice will take into account the questions related to market power in digital market, the way in which foreign subsidies benefitting companies outside of the European market can have an impact on the competition analysis, or the definition of the relevant time frame when identifying a possible competitor.

The revised market definition notice should also introduce more flexibility in the use of market definition per se in the context of merger control, and allow for a broader perspective on the competition analysis.

2.3.2 The DMA, A New Regulatory Tool Complementary to Competition Law Enforcement

The DMA, like the Regulation on foreign subsidies, was adopted in an exceptionally short period, given the complexities of the subject and the hurdles it faced.

The DMA has taken up some of the issues raised on the debate on 'digital sovereignty' or 'economic sovereignty', such as a possible 'under enforcement' of competition law vis-à-vis digital platforms, and an insufficient protection of smaller European companies against certain practices.

If the DMA has not been defined, from the point of view of its legal basis, as a competition instrument, but as a single market instrument, it is very much a competition tool, inasmuch as its objective is to make sure that digital Europe remains a fair and competitive market for all players.

3 CONCLUSION

The Siemens-Alstom case will certainly remain one of the most debated mergers of recent years. After the cancellation of the wedding, Alstom found a new 'bride' in

30. OJ C 372, 9.12.1997, pp. 5-13, 'The Notice'. About the review, *see* 'Market Definition Notice under Review', 20 July 2021, Latham &Watkins Carles Esteva Mosso, Adrien Giraud and France-Helene Boret, Concurrences award 2022 for Antitrust client briefing.
31. Market definitions encompass defining relevant products but also setting geographic market boundaries. It is according to a given market definition that market shares will be calculated, that dominant firms will be revealed. This analytical exercise governs both antitrust and mergers.

Bombardier, a merger that went altogether more 'smoothly'.[32] The Siemens-Alstom parties did not challenge the prohibition decision in the General Court, thus not allowing jurisprudence to examine some of the questions that had been raised, on market definitions for instance.

Beyond the fact that it was a 'difficult case', the Siemens-Alstom case allowed for a very in-depth debate about competition policy, its goals, its tools, its legitimacy and a number of other important issues, from the absence of a scrutiny of foreign subsidies comparable to State-aid control in other parts of the world. This debate was not limited to competition specialists (practitioners, lawyers, economists). Political stakeholders (governments, parliaments, think tanks or professional bodies) were at the forefront of the discussion, which stimulated innovative proposals, including by the European Commission.

By exploring the ways in which European companies felt they were subject to more intense competition scrutiny than their American or Chinese counterparts, novel approaches were devised. Trade policy was identified as a way to achieve fair competition across the globe, and a new, groundbreaking legal tool was adopted to tackle foreign subsidies, if and when they have an impact on the competition dynamics in Europe. The need to adapt to the digital economy led to the adoption of the DMA, introducing a very different approach to ensuring fair competition, through ex ante obligations or prohibitions. Rather than leading to a destruction of competition policy as we know it, one could say that the sovereignty debate has, in the end led to its reinforcement and rejuvenation.

32. M. 9779, Alstom Bombardier transportation, 31 July 2020, the Commission cleared the acquisition of Bombardier by Alstom, with remedies including divestitures.

CHAPTER 5

Neoclassical Competition Policy Without Apology

Jorge Padilla

1 NEOCLASSICAL COMPETITION POLICY: A PRIMER

By neoclassical competition policy, I understand a policy seeking to protect and promote competition according with the principles of neoclassical economics, which specify that the production, consumption and pricing of goods and services are driven by the interaction of supply and demand, which in turn reflect the utility maximization of rational consumers and the profit maximization of firms.[1]

A neoclassical economist considers that free markets typically yield the best allocation of scarce resources (i.e., goods and services end up in the hands of those that value them most so that all gains from trade are exhausted), ensure that production is efficient (i.e., output is produced with fewer and less costly inputs), and provide the right incentives in terms of process and product innovation.[2]

Neoclassical economists recognize that in some circumstances the market may fail to deliver such efficiency. Such *market failures* may be caused by departures from rationality, imperfect and/or asymmetric information, externalities, etc.[3] Most importantly, the existence of market power may cause the market to deliver inefficient outcomes.[4]

1. *See* E. Roy Weintraub, Neoclassical Economics, *The Concise Encyclopedia of Economics* (2007). Available from http://www.econlib.org/library/Enc1/NeoclassicalEconomics.html.
2. *See* Gerard Debreu, *Theory of Value*, Yale University Press (1959). Available from http://efaidnbmnnnibpcajpcglclefindmkaj/https://cowles.yale.edu/sites/default/files/files/pub/mon/m17-all.pdf.
3. *See* Diane Coyle, *Market, State and People*, Princeton University Press (2020).
4. *See* Jean Tirole, *The Theory of Industrial Organization*, MIT Press (1988).

A market where a firms holds monopoly power, for example, will be characterized by prices well above the incremental or marginal costs of production. As a result, some consumers with willingness to pay in excess of those costs may not be able to afford to acquire the monopolized goods and services. Not all gains from trade will be materialized and thus the monopoly would generate a *deadweight loss*.[5] Markets where one or more firms have the ability to charge supra-competitive prices may also be characterized by inefficient production and too little innovation.[6] Quality may also be lower than optimal when market power exists.[7]

However, market power is not a problem per se; as it most often reflects efficiency, superior business skill and entrepreneurial ingenuity.[8] Not all entrepreneurs are born equal and not all firms are equally efficient. Thus, the dynamics of competition in a free market may well give rise to positions of market power, which may or may not be temporary, depending on whether the competitive advantages of the firms with pricing power are replicable or not.

Neoclassical economists are not against market power as such, since they understand that the prospect of *supra* competitive profits drives entrepreneurs to work hard, rewards investment and innovation, creativity and originality, and are convinced that the pursuit of profit is what benefits consumers and society the most in the long run.[9] Of course, they understand that in the short run firms with market power extract rents from consumers and may even set prices at a level that excludes some consumers and leaves their demands unsatisfied. Yet, they believe that those are social costs worth incurring because of the long-term benefits of the positive incentive effects of market power.

It follows that the goal of neoclassical competition policy, and more generally regulation, is not to eliminate market power but to control it, so that it is not misused to distort the competitive process and harm consumers and society. When there are reasons to believe that existing market power is temporary, then the focus of neoclassical competition policy is to ensure that the integrity of the competitive process is preserved so that the most efficient firms, whether actual competitors or new entrants, can effectively exert a competitive constraint on the actions and policies of the incumbent(s) with market power. When the competitive process is unlikely to produce the waves of creative destruction that could check market power in the long run, neoclassical regulators intervene to influence or, if needed, control the pricing and non-pricing decisions of those with market power, but always in order to increase welfare and, in particular, consumer welfare.[10]

Neoclassical economists are fully aware that regulating markets is no easy task. Addressing market failures may be too costly or may even be impossible. Regulatory

5. *See* Oliver Williamson, Economies as an Antitrust Defense: The Welfare Tradeoffs, *American Economic Review*, 58.1 (1968), pp. 18-36.
6. *See* Tirole (1988) *supra* n. 4.
7. *Ibid*.
8. *See* Harold Demsetz, Information and Efficiency: Another Viewpoint, *Journal of Law & Economics*, 12.1 (1969), pp. 1-22.
9. *See* Milton Friedman, *Capitalism and Freedom*, University of Chicago Press (1992).
10. *See* Coyle (2020), *supra* n. 3.

intervention entails all sort of direct and indirect costs: setting up a regulatory apparatus is costly; regulators may be captured and then do more wrong than good; and, most importantly, regulatory interventions may have unintended consequences that end up causing more harm than the market failure that motivated them in the first place. The possibility and the social costs of *regulatory failure* cannot be ignored.[11]

This is especially true because regulators, including those working at the most reputed competition agencies, are human and therefore prone to error. They may overestimate the benefits of intervention and/or underestimate the costs of intervention, or vice versa.[12] The job of a regulator is to decide whether to intervene or not in response to a market failure in light of the available evidence. Importantly, because of human fallibility, the regulator can make two types of error: it may conclude that the right decision is to intervene when it is not (a Type I error or a false positive), or that the right decision is not to intervene when intervention is indeed needed (a Type II error or a false negative). Each of these errors involves a cost—i.e., a loss of competition to the detriment of consumers. If the regulator chooses its decision to minimize the expected cost of error, that decision will likely be the one that maximizes welfare and, if market power is the source of the market failure, protects the competitive process.[13]

From the above, it follows that a competition policy can be considered compatible with neoclassical economics if it respects the following principles:

(1) It sets as the ultimate goal of its interventions the maximization of consumer welfare or, more broadly perhaps, economic efficiency.
(2) It limits interventions to situations when there is a clear market failure—e.g., when a company with market power is acting to erect barriers to entry to protect its dominance.
(3) It does not treat market power or dominance as a problem per se and understands the motivating role of the pursuit of economic rents.
(4) It is cognizant of the limitations imposed by human fallibility and, therefore, it adopts the so-called error cost framework, which states that intervention should be limited only to situations where the expected cost of no intervention (the expected cost of Type II errors) is greater than the expected cost of intervention (the expected cost of Type I errors).

11. *Ibid.*
12. *See* Frank H. Easterbrook The Limits of Antitrust, *Texas Law Review*, 63 (1984), pp. 1-40. This error cost approach has been applied to legal rules generally as well as antitrust in particular. *See, e.g.*, Richard A. Posner, An Economic Approach to Legal Procedure and Judicial Administration, *Journal of Legal Studies*, 2 (1973), pp. 399, 400. For more recent applications *see* C. Frederick Beckner III and Steven C. Salop, Decision Theory and Antitrust Rules, *Antitrust Law Journal*, 67 (1999), pp. 41-76; Keith N. Hylton and Michael Salinger, Tying Law and Policy: A Decision-Theoretic Approach, *Antitrust Law Journal*, 69 (2001), p. 469; David S. Evans and Jorge Padilla, Designing Antitrust Rules for Assessing Unilateral Practices: A Neo-Chicago Approach, *University of Chicago Law Review*, 72 (2005), pp. 73-98.
13. Easterbrook (1984), *supra* n. 12.

2 NEOCLASSICAL COMPETITION POLICY UNDER ATTACK: THE NEO BRANDESIANS

Each of these four principles is now being seriously questioned by policymakers, practitioners, academics and pundits.[14] The ultimate rationale for this attack lies in certain adverse macroeconomic developments on both sides of the Atlantic that are blamed on the ineffectiveness and extreme forbearance of neoclassical competition and regulatory policies. The alleged consequences of the lack of appropriate intervention are said to be the increase in concentration and the increase in mark ups in most industries, especially in the high-tech ones, the decline in the labor share, the reduction of investment and the fall in productivity, and the increase in inequality in the West.[15]

Not everybody agrees with the alleged increase in concentration and profitability. Some argue that the increase in concentration is negligible in most industries,[16] the result of incorrect statistical methods, or irrelevant because it is calculated at a level of aggregation that is meaningless.[17] Others dispute the claimed increase in markups,[18] or argue that it merely reflects a redistribution of rents between leaders and laggards within industries.[19]

Many others disagree that competition policy and regulation are the causes of such changes. Rather they consider that, e.g., the decline in the labor share is the result of globalization (in particular the impact of the imports from China and other low-wage economies),[20] technological change (which has displaced labor with capital),[21] and the decline in union power.[22] Likewise, the increase in concentration and markups would not be due to unchecked market power but rather to fundamental developments, like the emergence of the digital giants and, more generally, the reduced rate at which technological innovation diffuses within and across industries.[23]

---

14. *See* Lina Khan, Amazon's Antitrust Paradox, *Yale Law Journal*, 126 (2017), pp. 710-805.
15. *See, e.g.*, Branco Milanovic, *Global Inequality*, Harvard University Press (2018); Thomas Philippon, *The Great Reversal*, The Belknap Press (2019); and Jan Eeckhout, *Profit Paradox*, Princeton University Press (2021).
16. *See* Gregory J. Werden, Concentration and Rising Market Power: Fears and Facts in *Research Handbook on Abuse of Dominance and Monopolization*, Pinar Akman, Or Brook, and Konstantinos Stylianou (eds.), Edward Elgar (2021). Available at SSRN: https://ssrn.com/abstract=39 09838.
17. *See ibid.*
18. *See* Jordi Jaumandreu, The Remarkable Stability of the US Manufacturing Markups (2022). Available from http://www-2.rotman.utoronto.ca/userfiles/brownbags/businesseconomy/fil es/markup_stability_09102022.pdf.
19. *See* John C. Haltiwanger, Henry R. Hyatt and James R. Spletzer, Industries, Mega Firms, and Increasing Inequality. IZA DP No. 15197 (2022).
20. *See* David H. Autor, David Dorn and Gordon H. Hanson, The China Syndrome: Local Labor Market Effects of Import Competition in the United States, *American Economic Review*, 103 (2013), pp. 2121-2168.
21. *See* David H. Autor et al., The Fall of the Labor Share and the Rise of Superstar Firms, *Quarterly Journal of Economics*, 135.2 (2020), pp. 645-709.
22. *See* Henry S. Farber et al., Unions and Inequality over the Twentieth Century: New Evidence from Survey Data. NBER working paper 24587 (2021).
23. *See* Diego Anzoategui et al., Endogenous Technology Adoption and R&D as Sources of Business Cycle Persistence. *American Economic Journal: Macroeconomics*, 11(3) (2019), pp. 67-110.

While in my opinion the jury is still out as regards the causes, consequences and relevance of these macroeconomic developments, it seems clear that the prevailing view among regulators and politicians is that competition policy, merger control and economic regulation, need to be reinvigorated for both macroeconomic and, also, for political reasons.[24]

For the so-called Neo Brandesians, as some of the most outspoken critics of neoclassical competition policy call themselves,[25] market power is bad per se. Like the U.S. Supreme Court Justice Louis Brandeis,[26] they believe that "We may have democracy, or we may have wealth concentrated in the hands of a few, but we cannot have both."[27] That is, they are not only concerned with the potential distortions of the competitive process caused by the abusive unilateral conduct of firms with market power, or the potential anticompetitive effects of mergers and other agreements. They are worried that unchecked economic power may translate into unfettered political power and distort the very foundations of our liberal democracies.[28] For them this is the hour of fate when twenty-first century capitalism, especially in its surveillance form, needs to be reformed.[29]

Neo Brandesians also criticize the consumer welfare goal of neoclassical competition policy. They regard it as inherently subjective and consider it invites tolerance of anticompetitive practices. In their view, the consumer welfare standard places undue emphasis on prices (and output) and fails to weigh appropriately the importance of preserving rivalry in the long run even when that implies tolerating higher prices in the short run.[30]

According to Federal Trade Commission (FTC) Chair Lina Kahn, current chairperson of the FTC:[31]

> [T]he undue focus on consumer welfare is misguided. It betrays legislative history, which reveals that Congress passed antitrust laws to promote a host of political economic ends—including our interests as workers, producers, entrepreneurs, and citizens. ... Antitrust law and competition policy should promote not welfare but competitive markets. By refocusing attention back on process and structure, this approach would be faithful to the legislative history of major antitrust laws. It would also promote actual competition—unlike the present framework, which is overseeing concentrations of power that risk precluding real competition.

24. *See* Carl Shapiro, Protecting Competition in the American Economy: Merger Control, Tech Titans, Labor Markets, *Journal of Economic Perspectives*, 33.3 (2019), pp. 69-93.
25. Not all critics of the neoclassical consensus are Neo Brandesians. *See, e.g.*, Jonathan B. Baker, Finding Common Ground among Antitrust Reformers. *Antitrust Law Journal*, 84(3)(2022), pp. 705-752. *See also* Nicolas Petit and Thibault Schrepel. (2022). Complexity-Minded Antitrust. Available from https://papers.ssrn.com/sol3/papers.cfm?abstract_id=4050536.
26. *See* Melvin I. Urofsky, *Louis D. Brandeis: A Life*, Pantheon Books (2009).
27. As quoted in Raymond Lonergan, *Mr. Justice Brandeis, Great American*, The Modern View Press (1941), p. 42.
28. *See* Jamie Susskind, *The Digital Republic*, Pegasus Books (2022).
29. *See* Shoshana Zuboff, *The Age of Surveillance Capitalism*, Profile Books (2019).
30. *See* Maurice E. Stucke, Reconsidering Antitrust's Goals, *Boston College Law Review*, 53 (2012), p. 551.
31. *See* Khan (2017), *supra* n. 14.

They are also critical of the market failure principle—which requires investigating the existence of a market failure and assessing its likely effects prior to intervention. In their opinion the effects-based approach, according to which intervention is only justified when there is evidence that market outcomes are undesirable and that there is a causal link between the alleged market failure and those undesirable outcomes, has turned competition law into an ineffective policy tool: lengthening investigations, making them highly complex endeavors, and exposing them to challenge in court.

Lina Khan states:[32]

> In today's formulation, the rule of reason serves as a supposed balancing test of harms and benefits. In practice, gauging the effects of particular conduct ends up turning on the "conflicting testimony of the parties" retained expert economists. Indeed, ..., the evolution and increasing centrality of the rule of reason approach has meant a "delegation of authority from judges and juries to economists," who now determine "the application, and sometimes even content, of antitrust rules."

Instead, they favor the adoption of a more formalistic approach which would prescribe intervention when certain formal conditions (such as the market share of the company under scrutiny or the form of the conduct at issue) are met.[33] For example, they advocate the reinvigoration of the so-called structural presumption (which posits that mergers should be blocked if they increase concentration in the relevant market without further enquiry into their likely price effects) in horizontal merger control.[34]

Finally, they are against the error cost framework, regard any reference to unintended consequences as a fairy tale and any discussion of Type I errors as a "do-nothing charter," constantly used and abused by the incumbents' lobbyists.[35] They believe Type II errors have been systematically underestimated under the false pretense that markets self-correct,[36] which of course is unlikely to be the case when market power is entrenched by the existence of insurmountable barriers to entry.

In short, Neo Brandesians sustain the following beliefs:

(1) The ultimate goal of antitrust intervention is not the maximization of consumer welfare or economic efficiency, but rather the protection of rivalry.
(2) Antitrust intervention should not be limited to situations when there is evidence that certain conduct may prove inefficient, but rather should be based on a series of per se rules that condemn certain forms of conduct without the need for investigating their efficiency.

32. *See* Lina M. Khan, The Ideological Roots of America's Market Power Problem. *The Yale Law Journal Forum* (2018). Available from https://www.yalelawjournal.org/forum/the-ideological-roots-of-americas-market-power-problem.
33. *See* Tim Wu, *The Bigness Curse*, Columbia Global Reports (2018).
34. *See* John Kwoka, The Structural Presumption and the Safe Harbor in Merger Review: False Positives or Unwarranted Concerns?, *Antitrust Law Journal*, 81.3 (2017), pp. 837-872.
35. Visit, e.g., the pages of well-known and much liked economists Tommaso Valletti and Cristina Caffarra on Twitter.
36. *See* Ariel Ezrachi and David Gilo, Are Excessive Prices Really Self-Correcting?, *Journal of Competition Law & Economics*, 5.2 (2009), pp. 249-268.

(3) Market power or dominance is as a problem per se. Rivalry and innovation go hand in hand.
(4) The so-called error cost framework is merely a reactionary rhetorical tool.

3 A NEOCLASSICAL SYNTHESIS

The competition policy debate has become extremely polarized, especially as regards the optimal approach to adopt in respect of the so-called Big Tech companies: Alphabet, Amazon, Apple, Meta and Microsoft. Neo Brandesians believe that these corporate giants abuse their proprietary information technologies to distort competition and that this has increased economic inequality and social division and slowed down innovation. These companies are said to act as big robber barons, smashing innovation and exploiting consumers.[37] Some call for the breakup of the largest Big Tech companies, others demand to surpass the competition policy straitjacket to compel them to share technology, data, and knowledge through the use of ex ante regulation.[38]

At the other end of the spectrum, some consider the Neo Brandesian proposals as a form of "hipster" antitrust, and the Neo Brandesians as "caviar socialists" or "bourgeois bohèmes," who oppose and misunderstand the close relationship between antitrust and economics.

According with Elyse Dorsey, Jan M. Rybnicek and Joshua D. Wright:[39]

> Hipster Antitrust, or the "New Brandeis Movement," ... proposes to divorce antitrust law from economic analysis, to abandon the well-established consumer welfare framework that introduced the rule of law to antitrust, and to replace that standard with a vague and pliable socio-political approach. Hipster Antitrust claims the consumer welfare standard invites excessive corporate control over antitrust agencies and outcomes. Hipster Antitrust claims it would reduce corporate control over antitrust institutions and their decision-making by relaxing the constraints imposed upon them by the consumer welfare standard and simultaneously granting them greater discretion under a broader, multi-factored public interest test.

Neo Brandesians are said to cherry pick from Justice Brandeis' views, ignoring his hate for big government.[40] More importantly, they are accused of fostering

37. *See* Ariel Ezrachi and Maurice E. Stucke, *How Big-Tech Barons Smash Innovation—And How to Strike Back*, Harper Business (2022).
38. *See* James Bessen *New Goliaths: How Corporations Use Software to Dominate Industries, Kill Innovation, and Undermine Regulation*. Yale University Press (2022).
39. *See* Elyse Dorsey, Jan M. Rybnicek and Joshua D. Wright, Hipster Antitrust Meets Public Choice Economics: The Consumer Welfare Standard, Rule of Law, and Rent Seeking. *Competition Policy International* (2022). Available at https://www.competitionpolicyinternational.com/wp-content/uploads/2018/04/CPI-Dorsey-Rybnicek-Wright.pdf.
40. "Louis Brandeis, who was confirmed to the Supreme Court exactly 100 years ago, was America's greatest critic of bigness since Thomas Jefferson. Denouncing big banks as well as big government as symptoms of what he called a 'curse of bigness', Brandeis was determined to diminish concentrated financial and federal power, which he viewed as a menace to liberty and

confusion and maximizing discretion; of trashing the consumer welfare standard,[41] because it is administrable, predictable, and credible; and, most ominously, of abandoning the rule of law and its limiting principles, so that agencies can challenge any conduct that they find ideologically objectionable.[42]

3.1 The Consumer Welfare Standard

Abandoning the consumer welfare standard would be a serious mistake. I concur with Daniel Sokol when he states:[43]

> Antitrust works well because it is technocratic in that a singular (but flexible within its economics) goal is administrable institutionally. To introduce the world of political imperfections into a technical process that examines markets would create further distortions affecting consumers. Antitrust does well dealing with antitrust problems. To the extent that there are other related problems, the right answer is not to create an antitrust that lacks democratic accountability (because antitrust becomes regulation via the backdoor) and exceeds its mandate of the past forty years. Rather, the better solution is to identify the underlying problem and solve it with more effective tools.

I also agree with Commissioner Christine Wilson that:

> Injecting additional goals will undermine credibility and predictability while leading to subjectivity and politicization.[44]

And I also agree with Carl Shapiro that for the last 40 years or more:

> there has been a broad consensus among antitrust scholars and practitioners in favor of the "consumer welfare" standard. No evidence whatsoever has been put forward calling this consensus into question. Indeed, I know of no serious antitrust experts who favor abandoning the "consumer welfare" standard, and no workable alternative has been propose.[45]

democracy." *See* Jeffrey Rosen, The Curse of Bigness, *The Atlantic* (2016). Available from https://www.theatlantic.com/politics/archive/2016/06/the-forgotten-wisdom-of-louis-d-brandeis/485477/.

41. "This analysis reveals that the current framework in antitrust—specifically its equating competition with 'consumer welfare', typically measured through short-term effects on price and output—fails to capture the architecture of market power in the twenty-first century marketplace." Khan (2017), *supra* n. 14, p. 716.
42. *See* Christine S. Wilson, The Neo-Brandeisian Revolution: Unforced Errors and the Diminution of the FTC, U.S. Federal Trade Commission (2021). Available at https://www.ftc.gov/system/files/documents/public_statements/1598399/ftc_2021_fall_forum_wilson_final_the_neo_brandeisian_revolution_unforced_errors_and_the_diminution.pdf.
43. *See* D. Daniel Sokol Antitrust's "Curse of Bigness" Problem, *Michigan Law Review*, 118 (2020), pp. 1259.
44. *See* Wilson (2021), *supra* n. 42.
45. *See* Hearing Before the S. Comm. on Antitrust of the S. Comm. on the Judiciary, 115th Cong. at 3-4, (2017) (statement of Carl Shapiro, Transamerica Professor of Business Strategy, Walter A. Haas School of Business, University of California at Berkeley). Available at: https://www.judiciary.senate.gov/download/12-13-17-shapiro-testimony.

As noted by Leah Samuel and Fiona Scott-Morton:[46]

> The problem with the debate on these issues is that parties on both sides are talking past each other, each side using a different definition of the term "consumer welfare." Academic economists—unless they are already deep in the weeds of this debate—don't understand the confusion because the concept of "consumer welfare" appears in every introductory microeconomics textbook. But policymakers and judges today do not use the textbook definition, nor does the media.

When Neo Brandesians criticize the consumer welfare standard, what they criticize is a policy of minimal intervention whereby only actions that are likely to lead to higher prices and lower output are prosecuted. For Neo Brandesians, the consumer welfare standard:

> now often means a defendant-friendly antitrust standard that dismisses the benefit of quality and innovation, rounds uncertain harms down to zero, ignores input suppliers, and is unduly deferential to claims of efficiencies. Modern textbook economics rejects this weakened standard, and in this way is aligned with the Neo-Brandesians.[47]

Yet, for most economists, that is not the correct interpretation of the consumer welfare standard. The right interpretation is that competition policy interventions must be directed at protecting the welfare of consumers by preserving the integrity of the competitive process, noting that anything that influences demand creates consumer welfare. Higher prices reduce consumer welfare, as lower quality does. Consumer welfare increases when firms innovate introducing new and/or better product and services. Consumer welfare may fall when consumer privacy is violated and/or as a result of the consumption and production decisions of other individuals and firms.

In my opinion, therefore, abandoning the consumer welfare principle that guides neoclassical competition policy would be a serious mistake and it would also be wrong to dilute this standard by incorporating new and ill-defined goals. What we need to do is clarify the notion of consumer welfare so that agencies and courts understand that it is an encompassing concept, which can and should accommodate all price and non-price factors that provide utility and, hence, affect consumer choice and market demand.

Following Kaplow and Shavell (2002), I believe that:

> legal rules should be selected entirely with respect to their effects on the well-being of individuals in society and that notions of fairness ... should receive no independent weight in the assessment of legal rules.[48]

The relevant question is not whether consumer welfare ought to be the main the main (or sole) goal of competition policy in our time. Rather the focus should be placed on the appropriate time dimension for consumer welfare. Given the paramount

46. *See* Leah Samuel and Fiona Scott Morton, What Economists Mean When They Say "Consumer Welfare Standard." Promarket (2022). Available at https://www.promarket.org/2022/02/16/consumer-welfare-standard-antitrust-economists/.
47. *Ibid.*
48. *See* Louis Kaplow and Steven Shavell, *Fairness Versus Welfare*, Harvard University Press (2002).

importance of innovation as a driver of consumer satisfaction, competition assessments should focus less on the short-term price effects of certain actions and strategies and instead consider their long-term implications on innovation and welfare.

3.2 Market Failure Versus Government Failure

Neo Brandesians also err when they dismiss the relevance of the effects-based approach to antitrust intervention. I believe their position in this respect is fundamentally ideological.

First, Neo Brandesians consider that market power is bad per se, and that hence intervention is warranted unless the firm with market power behaves "as if" it were a price taker (i.e., in a perfectly competitive manner).

In this respect, the Neo Brandesians are close to the ordoliberal economists and philosophers that inspired European competition law.[49] For ordoliberals, firms with market power—dominant firms—have "a special responsibility not to allow its conduct to impair undistorted competition on the common market."[50]

As explained by Ahlborn and Padilla (2007):

> the origin of the "special responsibility" doctrine can be traced back to the ordoliberal "as if" principle, according to which firms which are not price takers, i.e., which possess (significant) market power have not only have a negative obligation (i.e., not to commit certain harmful acts) but also a positive obligation (i.e., to behave as if they do not have any market power).

However, as a matter of economics, a firm with market power may compete on the merits, and hence benefit consumers, even when it does not act as a price taker. This is why per se illegality rules are rarely justified in antitrust, other than in price-fixing cases, and why it is therefore important to assess the likely effects of a given action, balancing its likely pro- and anticompetitive effects before any intervention takes place. Distinguishing between exclusionary acts, which reduce social welfare, and competitive acts, which increase it, is typically very difficult. Courts and competition regulators using a simplistic form-based approach are bound to make gross mistakes: some practices will be found legal when they are welfare-reducing and vice versa. As it is often said, *if it ain't broke, don't fix it*.

Second, Neo Brandesians tend to underestimate the cost of intervention because they are overoptimistic about the ability of the state to effectively address market failures. In his well-known paper "Competition and Democracy," Nobel Prize Laureate Gary Becker famously noted:[51]

---

49. *See* Christian Ahlborn and Jorge Padilla, From Fairness to Welfare: Implications for the Assessment of Unilateral Conduct under EC Competition Law. In Claus-Dieter Ehlermann and Mel Marquis (eds.), *European Competition Law Annual 2007: A Reformed Approach to Article 82 EC*. Hart Publishing (2007).
50. *See* Case 322/81, *Michelin v. Commission* [1983] ECR 3461, para. 57.
51. *See* Gary Becker, Competition and Democracy. *Journal of Law & Economics*, 1 (1958), pp. 105-109.

> Economists have often argued that if an industry acts as a monopolist it would be desirable government policy either to break up the monopoly or, if this is undesirable because of increasing returns, to regulate and perhaps even nationalize it. This proposition, although extremely well known and often accepted as obvious, turns out upon close examination to be far from obvious, and to involve several assumptions of doubtful validity. The argument supporting this proposition goes something as follows: Monopolies cause a maldistribution of resources, since the price charged by a monopolist exceeds marginal costs and an optimal distribution requires price equal to marginal cost. An optimal allocation would occur if the industry were made competitive, since price equals marginal costs in competitive industries. If the industry were a "natural" monopoly, price could be made equal to marginal cost either indirectly by government regulation or directly by government administration. Therefore, the recommendation is an antitrust law to prevent or break up contrived monopolies and government regulation or government administration of natural monopolies.
>
> The non-sequitur in this argument is the sentence beginning with "therefore"; the recommendation of government intervention does not follow from the demonstration that government intervention could improve matters. Demonstrating that a set of government decisions would improve matters is not the same as demonstrating that actual government decisions would do so. This kind of inference is logically equivalent to identifying the actual workings of the market sector with its ideal workings.

Government failure is common. Regulatory intervention may have unintended consequences. Regulators may fail to deliver optimal outcomes because they have insufficient information or because they are ideologically captured. So, *even if it is broke, don't try to fix it if you are not sure about the end result.*

3.3 Market Power Is Not Necessarily Bad

Economic theory shows that, under fairly general conditions, increased rivalry tends to improve the allocation of resources. Industry fragmentation brings prices closer to (incremental) costs and enhances short-term consumer welfare. However, in the long term, consumer welfare is not only influenced by the relative efficiency with which the scarce resources of an economy are allocated; it is also positively affected by the emergence of new products, technologies and services.

In industries where firms compete by launching new products and developing new technologies, having numerous firms with no market power, and hence low prices, is not necessarily ideal. In fact, the opposite may well be true: the prospect of lower prices may reduce the incentives to invest and innovate. There is no support in economic theory or evidence for the oft-stated proposition that product market fragmentation necessarily promotes innovation. In other words, while on many occasions rivalry and innovation go hand in hand, that is not always the case.

As recently stated by Katz and Shelanski (2007):[52]

> enforcement authorities cannot confidently presume as a matter of economic theory or experience that more competitors are beneficial or that market power is detrimental for R&D, except in the limited case of merger to monopoly where the evidence supports a moderate presumption of harm.

3.4 In Defence of the Error Cost Framework

The job of a competition agency is to produce a decision by assessing the Plaintiff's narrative or "theory of harm," S_p, and the Defendant's efficiency defence, S_D, considering the available evidence, E (factual evidence, documentary evidence and economic evidence).

3.4.1 *The Error Minimization Principle*

In reaching a decision, the agency can make two types of error: it may conclude that the Plaintiff is right when it is not (a Type I error) or that the Defendant is right when it is not (a Type II error). Each of these errors involves a cost—i.e., a loss of competition to the detriment of consumers. Let c_1 denote the cost of a Type I error and c_2 the cost of a Type II error.

To achieve its ultimate goal, a competition agency should choose the decision that minimises the expected cost of error. Let us denote as $P_r\ (S_D \mid\mid E)$ the probability that the Defendant is right given the available evidence and, likewise, as $P_r\ (S_p \mid\mid E)$ the probability that the Plaintiff is right given the available evidence. Then, the expected cost of a Type I error equals $P_r\ (S_D \mid\mid E) \times c_1$ (where $\times$ is the multiplication operator) and expected cost of a Type II error equal $P_r\ (S_p \mid\mid E) \times c_2$. Thus, according to the *Error Cost Minimization Principle*, the agency should find that the Defendant infringed the competition laws when

$$R = \frac{Pr(S_P \parallel E) \times c_2}{\Pr(S_D \parallel E) \times c_1} > 1, (1)$$

i.e., when the likelihood ratio R is greater than 1, because it is then that error costs are minimized when the agency finds that the Plaintiff is right given the available evidence.

3.4.2 *Relative Plausibility and the Threshold of Persuasion*

Let π_p be the prior that infringement decision is correct and π_D be the corresponding prior that the decision is flawed. Let $P_r\ (E \mid\mid S_p)$ measure the fit (or consistency) of the Plaintiff's theory of harm S_p with the evidence E, and likewise $P_r\ (E \mid\mid S_D)$ measure the

52. *See* Michael Katz and Howard Shelanski, Mergers and Innovation. *Antitrust Law Journal*, 74.1 (2007), pp. 1-85.

fit (or consistency) of the Defendant's pro-competitive narrative S_D with the evidence E. Then, using Bayes's formula, we have that:

$$\frac{Pr(S_P \parallel E)}{Pr(S_D \parallel E)} = \frac{Pr(E \parallel S_P) \times \pi_P}{\Pr(E \parallel S_D) \times \pi_D}, (2)$$

And, therefore, we can re-write equation (1), as:

$$\frac{Pr(E \parallel S_P)}{Pr(E \parallel S_D)} > \frac{c_1}{c_2} \times \frac{\pi_D}{\pi_P}. (3)$$

The test in equation (3) is known in the legal literature as the *Relative Plausibility Test*,[53] which is no other than Easterbrook's error cost minimization principle (*see* equation (1) above). In plain English, the agency should minimize the expected cost of error by finding that the defendant infringed the competition laws when, other things equal, the Plaintiff's narrative is relatively more plausible given the facts.

But how much more plausible? The *Threshold of Persuasion* equals the ratio on the right hand side of equation (3). It is greater when (a) the cost of the Type II error is low relative to the cost of a Type I error, and (b) the theory of harm is a priori less plausible than the alternative pro-competitive motivation.

3.4.3 Reinvigorating Neoclassical Competition Policy

There is nothing objectionable about the error cost minimization principle and the equivalent relative plausibility test. Agencies, whatever their ideology, should only entertain intervention in response to a fully specified and cogent theory of harm, S_p. They should also consider the efficiency defence provided by the Defendant, S_D, and should balance the relative plausibility of the two narratives by confronting them to all available evidence, E.

This balancing exercise is inherently complex and, therefore, it would be incorrect to intervene, or not, by reference only to the plausibility of the anticompetitive narratives. Because agencies are fallible, they must factor in their assessment (i) the cost of the Type I and Type errors, c_1 and c_2, respectively; and (ii) the priors, π_p and π_D, by considering the legal and economic context, the prior case law and the lessons of extant economic theory and evidence.

The error cost framework may therefore result in more or less interventionist policies depending on the relative weight given to the costs of Type I and Type II errors, as well as on the credibility attributed to certain theories of harm and to the efficiency claims made by defendants—i.e., the agency's priors.

U.S. competition agencies and courts, though not their European counterparts, have typically regarded the cost of the Type I errors as greater than the costs of the Type

53. Ronald J. Allen and Michael S. Pardo, Relative Plausibility and Its Critics, *International Journal of Evidence & Proof*, 23 (2019), pp. 5-59.

II errors. They have acted under the presumption that the cost of prohibiting efficient practices always outweighs the costs of perpetuating monopolies, because, as Judge Easterbrook stated:

> There is no automatic way to expunge mistaken decisions of the Supreme Court. A practice once condemned is likely to stay condemned, no matter its benefits. A monopolistic practice wrongly excused will eventually yield to competition, though, as the monopolist's higher prices attract rivalry.[54]

It is true that if an anticompetitive business practice is mistakenly permitted, the resulting monopoly profits may attract competition and new entrants at least in the long run, whereas market forces play little corrective role for pro-competitive business practices deemed anticompetitive. It is also true that, by restraining legitimate acts, antitrust intervention may reduce the value of being a legitimate market leader—the goal that drives innovation. Yet, monopolies can slow their eventual destruction sometimes through anticompetitive methods and sometimes through the political process. As a result, the forces of competition, and creative destruction, may not provide sufficient limitation on the magnitude and duration of monopoly profits. Moreover, bad decisions can and do get expunged or worked around.

The differences between the U.S. and Europe in terms of their willingness to intervene are not limited to their different assessment of the relative costs of Type I and Type II errors. They also relate to their views on the credibility of certain theories of harm and the relative weight given to efficiency justifications.

Their disparate priors seem to reflect a different understanding of the relevant economic theory as well as the different economic realities on both sides of the Atlantic. Until recently, U.S. agencies, and especially U.S. courts, endorsed the so-called Chicago school of antitrust.[55] The Chicago school revolutionized antitrust by using price theory to develop a series of "impossibility theorems," which showed that, under some circumstances, it was not possible for firms to have the incentive to engage in certain anticompetitive practices even if they had the ability to do so. The most famous is the "single monopoly profit theorem,"[56] which was considered fatal (or so it appeared) to the leverage doctrine. Variants of the single-monopoly profit theorem have been applied to tying, essential facilities, and, more broadly, to the analysis of vertical integration. The implication of these theorems was that the true motivation for certain practices was efficiency: *if it cannot be anticompetitive, then it must be efficient.* More formally, the Chicago School sustains that many unilateral practices should be per se legal because these practices usually create efficiencies and firms with monopoly power typically lack incentives to engage in unilateral practices that reduce welfare.

54. Easterbrook (1984), *supra* n. 12.
55. *See* Robert H. Bork, *The Antitrust Paradox: A Policy at War with Itself*, Free Press (1993). *See also* Edmund W. Kitch, The Fire of Truth: Remembrance of Law and Economics at Chicago, 1932-1970. *Journal of Law & Economics*, 26 (1983), pp. 163-175.
56. Under some assumptions, in a vertical chain of production, there is fixed potential for monopoly profit. A firm with a monopoly at one level of the chain gets all of the monopoly profit if it charges a monopoly price and everyone else in the chain charges a competitive price. Indeed, it serves the monopolist to encourage competition at every other level because any monopoly profit earned by others will reduce its own.

In the 1980s, economists found that it was possible to develop models in which a firm could use a monopoly in one market to affect adjacent markets in ways that reduced social welfare.[57] Other economists subsequently identified other situations in which a monopoly could generate more profits or protect existing profits by foreclosing competition in a second market.[58] A further strand of modern economics undercuts the proposition that firms had no incentive or ability to engage in predatory pricing.[59] This so-called post-Chicago literature[60] provides a collection of "possibility theorems," showing that certain practices reduce social welfare if specific parameters (e.g., elasticity of demand, the magnitude of fixed costs, etc.) fall within a particular range of values.[61]

While the post-Chicago approach had an impact on both U.S. and European antitrust law, thus far the impact on the U.S., especially on its courts, has been more limited. This explains in part why European competition agencies have been relatively more open to certain theories of harm and more willing to intervene.[62] But it may not explain it all. Differences in priors across the Atlantic may also reflect differences in their economies. The U.S. economy is much more flexible and dynamic, and therefore much more likely to self-correct, than the economies of most European countries.

As stated by Jonathan Baker:[63]

> In applying decision theory, a *neutral economic tool*, to the analysis of antitrust rules, contemporary conservatives have made a series of erroneous assumptions, which collectively impart a non-interventionist bias to their conclusions. These assumptions systematically overstate the incidence and significance of false positives, understate the incidence and significance of false negatives, and understate the net benefits of various rules by overstating their costs. (Emphasis added.)

4 MORE ECONOMICS NOT LESS

The neoclassical approach to antitrust can accommodate the legitimate criticisms of the Neo Brandesians in a more effective way than the ill-defined policy changes they propose would be able to deliver. Current calls for disruption are dangerous despite the benevolent intentions of their proponents. As Justice Brandeis said:

57. *See* Michael D. Whinston, Tying, Foreclosure, and Exclusion, *American Economic Review*, 80(4) (1990), pp. 837-859.
58. *See* Dennis W. Carlton and Michael Waldman, The Strategic Use of Tying to Preserve and Create Market Power in Evolving Industries, *Rand Journal of Economics*, 33 (2002), pp. 194-220.
59. *See*, Patrick Bolton, Joseph F. Brodley and Michael H. Riordan, Predatory Pricing: Strategic Theory and Legal Policy, *Georgetown Law Journal*, 88 (2000), pp. 13-89.
60. *See* Antonio Cucinotta, Roberto Pardolesi and Roger Van den Bergh (eds.), *Post Chicago Developments in Antitrust Law*, Edward Elgar (2002).
61. *See*, Patrick Bolton, Joseph F. Brodley and Michael H. Riordan, Predatory Pricing: Strategic Theory and Legal Policy, *Georgetown Law Journal*, 88 (2000), pp. 13-89.
62. *See* Ken Heyer, A World of Uncertainty: Economics and the Globalization of Antitrust. *Antitrust Law Journal*, 72 (2005), pp. 375-422.
63. *See* Jonathan Baker, Taking the Error out of "Error Cost" Analysis: What's Wrong with Antitrust's Right, *Antitrust Law Journal*, 80 (2015), pp. 1-38.

> Experience should teach us to be most on our guard to protect liberty when the government's purposes are beneficent. Men born to freedom are naturally alert to repel invasion of their liberty by evil-minded rulers. The greatest dangers to liberty lurk in insidious encroachment by men of zeal, well-meaning but without understanding.[64]

In my opinion, the opposite of revolution is not stagnation but reform. The macroeconomic developments discussed in Section II above, and in particular the (more or less significant) increase in concentration and markups and the increase in the economic and political power of a number of large corporations, most prominently high-tech companies, should lead competition agencies and courts to reconsider the threshold of intervention (i.e., the threshold of persuasion).

They should first reconsider their priors, being more receptive to leveraging theories of harm and more skeptical about efficiency justifications. They should also revise their estimations of the relative costs of Type I and Type II errors, likely giving extra weight to the latter. What they should not do is to throw the baby out with the bathwater, giving up the discipline imposed by the error cost minimization principle and the associated relative plausibility test.

More concretely, the response to the challenges posed by the Big Tech platforms should not be the adoption of per se prohibition rules without justification in economics, because it is simply not true that Type I errors are no longer possible. The response of those that (overly) rely on creative destruction arguments to advocate for no, or limited, intervention in platform markets is also incorrect. The evidence of the last twenty years demonstrates that disruptive innovation cannot be taken for granted and that market power in platform markets is often not transient. In short, Type II errors are also likely and costly.

Presumptions of legality and illegality should be grounded on solid economic theory and evidence. They should not be driven by ideology. Identifying the circumstances under which such presumptions fail to hold and thus should be rebutted is also an exercise for economists and management scientists. The right response to the current disappointment with competition policy is more economics not less. This was indeed the conclusion of Kovacic and Shapiro in their survey of the first century of antitrust, who noted:

> The availability of new data sources like electronic point-of-purchase data, the refinement of flexible game theoretic models, and the new emphasis on innovation assures that robust arguments over the proper content of competition policy will flourish in the 21st century.[65]

64. *Invasions of Privacy: Government Agencies*. Hearings, Eighty-ninth Congress, First Session, Pursuant to S. Res. 39, Vol. 10, 1-3. United States Congress-Senate Committee on the Judiciary. Subcommittee on Administrative Practice and Procedure. U.S. Government Printing Office, 1965.
65. William E. Kovacic and Carl Shapiro, Antitrust Policy: A Century of Economic and Legal Thinking, *Journal Economic Perspectives*, 14 (2000), pp. 43-55.

The good news is that over the last few years the economics and management literature has improved our understanding of how platform markets work.[66] The not so good news is that hitherto such literature has mainly produced "possibility" theorems and thus has failed to develop in ways that could help antitrust agencies to assess the cost and likelihood of Type I and Type II errors. It is this vacuum that may explain why the neoclassical consensus is under siege by the Neo Brandesians but also the libertarians. This is the void that we need to fill, and I am confident that we (academic economists, economic consultants and agency economists) can and we will (working together).

66. *See, e.g.*, Paul Belleflamme and Martin Peitz, *The Economics of Platforms*, Cambridge University Press (2022) and references therein.

Chapter 6

Challenges of Decentralisation of Competition Law Enforcement: A Retrospective Overview in Case Law

*Krystyna Kowalik-Bańczyk**

The decentralisation of the enforcement of EU competition law was a novelty when ten new Member States joined the European Union on 1 May 2004, the date upon which Regulation No. 1/2003[1] entered into force. Therefore, for at least some countries in the EU, the decentralised implementation of EU competition law is the only enforcement model they have known. Since May 2004, decentralisation has been a common feature of competition law enforcement, so common and accepted that there is no significant debate around its effectiveness.

The process of decentralisation consisted in conferring various EU-level tasks upon the national competition authorities (NCAs) in the EU and formed part of a process of reform of the EU governance.[2] The decentralisation of EU competition law enforcement has meant that the European Commission and NCAs[3] have parallel competences to enforce Articles 101 and 102 TFEU, and together they form the so-called European Competition Network (ECN). Within ECN, the attribution of cases

* All opinions expressed in this chapter are those of the author alone, the usual disclaimer applies.

1. Council Regulation (EC) No. 1/2003 of 16 December 2002 on the implementation of the rules on competition laid down in Articles 81 and 82 of the Treaty, OJ L 1, 4.1.2003.
2. Paul Craig, *EU Administrative Law* 29 (Oxford University Press 2006). The concept of 'decentralisation' is used, for example, by Laura Parret, *Side Effects of the Modernisation of EU Competition Law: Modernisation as a Challenge to the Enforcement System of EU Competition Law and EU Law in General* 159 (Wolf Legal Publishers 2011).
3. Commission Notice on cooperation within the Network of Competition Authorities (Text with EEA relevance), OJ C 101, 27.4.2004.

and exchange of information are regulated by Regulation 1/2003[4] and a certain level of procedural harmonisation has occurred since the entry into force of this regulation.

The years of decentralisation has had two main practical consequences for EU competition law enforcement. First, it has obliged NCAs and national judges to be on the frontline of EU competition law enforcement, what EU Court of Justice President Koen Lenaerts has called 'throwing into arena of EC competition law enforcement'.[5] Indeed, the decentralisation of EU competition law enforcement has led NCAs to implement Articles 101 and 102 TFEU on a very frequent basis. Second, even if the decentralisation started in 2004 in itself covered only public enforcement, it was designed to increase the private antitrust enforcement and has had precisely that effect, by further enabling the enforcement of EU competition law by national courts.[6] The multi-level system of competition law enforcement, founded upon Articles 3, 11, 12 and 13 of Regulation 1/2003 has resulted, therefore, in most EU competition law cases in the EU being enforced at national level.

Decentralisation of the application of the EU competition law has not only led the national competition authorities to frequently apply Articles 101 and 102 TFEU. In addition, decentralisation has also brought about a much higher level of harmonisation and coherence in both substantive and procedural competition rules across EU Member States.

The case law of the EU Court of Justice and EU General Court on the issues related to decentralisation covers different aspects and can be analysed from different angles. As Advocate General Mazák stated in one of the first cases on decentralisation:

> The decentralisation of the enforcement of EU competition law goes further than simply requiring NCAs and national courts to apply Articles 101 and 102 TFEU. To enable the decentralisation to be properly implemented, Regulation No 1/2003 provides for at least three distinct mechanisms: (i) the conferral of power on NCAs and the national courts, with a resultant decrease in the Commission's direct enforcement activity; (ii) the requirement for the NCAs and the national courts to apply Articles 101 and 102 TFEU within a system regulating the relationship between national and EU law; and, last but not least, (iii) arrangements to facilitate cooperation and control of the work of the NCAs and the national courts in order to safeguard a uniform and coherent application of the EU competition rules. As we will see below, a consequence of the important role which NCAs (and the

4. Alison Jones & Brenda Sufrin, *EU Competition LawL Text, Cases and Materials* 884 (6th ed. Oxford University Press 2016); Damien M.B. Gerard, *Regulation 1/2003 (and Beyond): Balancing Effective Enforcement and Due Process in Cross-Border Antitrust Investigations*, in: *International Antitrust Litigation: Conflict of Laws and Coordination* 365-392 (Jürgen Basedow, Stéphanie Francq & Laurence Idot eds, Bloomsbury Publishing Plc 2012); Barry J. Rodger, *The ECN and Coordination of Public Enforcement of EU Law: Can Lessons Be Learned from International Private Law Jurisdiction Rules and Vice Versa?*, in: *International Antitrust Litigation: Conflict of Laws and Coordination* 345-364 (Jürgen Basedow, Stéphanie Francq & Laurence Idot eds, Bloomsbury Publishing Plc 2012).
5. Koen Lenaerts & Damien Gerard, *Decentralisation of EC Competition Law Enforcement: Judges in the Frontline*, World Competition, Vol. 27, No. 3 (2004), 9.
6. Assimakis Komninos, *EC Private Antitrust Enforcement: Decentralised Application of EC Competition Law by National Courts* (1st ed. Hart Publishing 2008); Karoline Hjelmtvedt, *The Decentralization of Enforcement of EU/EEA Competition Law*, 38(2) European Competition Law Review 60-71 (2017).

> national courts) play in the functioning of the new system is that, under Regulation No 1/2003, they are subject to strict rules as regards both the powers conferred on them and the exercise of those powers.[7]

The question of whether or not the rules to which NCAs are subject are very strict and whether their supervision is equally strict will be further analysed. What is clear is that the very framework of decentralisation has never been contested. It can be summarised in most cases as being a discussion centred on 'who does what, how and in what circumstances'.

In this paper, the objective is to look back on and assess the input of decentralisation for the effective implementation of EU competition law. That assessment will be conducted mainly through the lens of the case law of the Court of Justice and General Court, as it provides the topics of real discussion on the functioning of the decentralised system. In order to do this, the following questions will be examined. First, what is the role of NCAs and that left for the European Commission as a result of decentralisation. Second, what happens if there are too many volunteers to handle a case. Third, what happens in an opposite scenario, when there are no volunteers to undertake an antitrust investigation. Case law on these questions remains relatively sparse, which might hint, already at this stage, to the conclusion that judicial reaction to doubts has been a sufficient way for improvement or clarification of decentralisation as it stands. Before looking at these questions, it is useful to look at procedural harmonisation within the EU.

1 HARMONISATION OF ANTITRUST PROCEDURE

Part of the discussion on decentralisation was long centred on procedural solutions in areas that had not been harmonised in the first place at the national level. Regulation 1/2003 as such concerns, first and foremost, the procedure before the European Commission. The procedural rules to be applied by NCAs are, in principle, less affected by this regulation and remain within the realm of national procedural autonomy. Indeed, when an NCA applies Article 101 or Article 102 TFEU, Regulation 1/2003 does not lay down the procedural rules to be followed. Irrespective of whether an NCA applies national law or Article 101 or 102 TFEU, procedural questions are governed by national law, unless a different solution stems from Regulation No. 1/2003, however.[8] First, Article 5 of Regulation 1/2003 contains an exhaustive list of the types of decisions which NCAs are required to take when they implement EU law,[9] which Judge von

7. Opinion of AG J. Mazák in Case C-375/09, *Prezes Urzędu Ochrony Konkurencji i Konsumentów v. Tele2 Polska sp. z o.o. (now Netia SA)*, ECLI:EU:C:2010:743, 7.12.2010, point 14.
8. Ute Zinsmeister, *Sanctions in View of the Reform of European Competition Law of a Practitioner's Experience*, in: *Competition Law Sanding in the European Union. The EU-Law Influence on the National Law System of Sanctions in the European Area* 188 (Gerhard Dannecker & Oswald Jansen eds, Kluwer Law International 2004).
9. Alison Jones & Brenda Sufrin, *EU Competition Law* ... 1153; Silke Hossenfelder, *Reform of European Competition Law: Exchange in the Cooperation Between Competition Authorities and the Effects on the Sanctioning System*, in: *Competition Law Sanding in the European Union: The*

Danwitz viewed in an article as implying 'procedural decentralisation' of EU competition law.[10] Second, Articles 11 and 13 of Regulation 1/2003 define the arrangements for cooperation between the Commission and the national competition authorities, as well as the question of concurring powers. Third, Article 12 of Regulation 1/2003 specifies the manner in which the exchange of information between those authorities is to take place (developing what has been described by a commentator as a free market of evidence[11]). Fourth, Article 35 of Regulation 1/2003 requires Member States to set up a competition authority responsible for the enforcement of Articles 101 and 102 TFEU, in accordance with the detailed rules laid down in that provision. Although it mentions only the fact that the Member States designate a competent competition authority, that obligation was interpreted by the Court of Justice in 2010 as necessarily interfering with the procedural framework of Member States.[12]

In Case C-375/09 *Tele 2,*[13] the Court of Justice expressly stated that the procedural autonomy of Member States cannot be upheld where it 'risks jeopardising the attainment of the objective, set out in the first recital in the preamble to the Regulation, of ensuring the uniform application of Articles 101 TFEU and 102 TFEU'.[14] In Case C-360/09 *Pfleiderer v. Bundeskartellamt*, the Court of Justice interpreted Regulation 1/2003 in the context of a national procedure for access to the case file by a third party seeking to bring an action for damages. The Court of Justice held that such access could be granted 'to the victim of an infringement of EU competition law seeking damages' on the basis of national law, but after 'developing the interests protected by EU law'.[15]

EU-Law Influence on the National Law System of Sanctions in the European Area 167 (Gerhard Dannecker & Oswald Jansen, Kluwer Law International 2004). That is confirmed by AG J. Mazák opinion in Case C-375/09 *Prezes Urzędu Ochrony Konkurencji i Konsumentów p. Tele2 Polska sp. z o.o., currently: Netia SA*, ECLI:EU:C:2010:743, 7.12.2010.

10. Thomas van Danwitz, *La protection des droits fondamentaux lors de la mise en oeuvre décentralisée du droit communautaire de la concurrence*, Concurrences 4 (2008), 31. Similarly, by emphasising principally that Regulation No. 1/2003 lays down the detailed rules for the decentralised application of EU competition law in the Member States, Konrad Ost, *Die VO 1/2003 – Grundlage des Netzwerks und grundrechtskonformes Modell eines Kartellverfahrensrecht*, in: *Rechtsschutz und Wettbewerb in der neuen europäischen Rechtsentwicklung* 33 (Jürgen Schwarze ed., Nomos 2010).
11. Andriani Kalintiri, *Evidence Standards in EU Competition Enforcement: The EU Approach* (Hart Publishing 2019).
12. Judgment of the Court of Justice in Case C-439/08 Vlaamse federatie van verenigingen van Brood- en Banketbakkers, Ijsbereiders en Chocoladebewerkers (VEBIC) VZW, ECLI:EU:C:2010:739, 7.12.2010, cf.: Joana Goyder, *'VEBIC': The Role of National Authorities in Appeals Against Their Own Decisions*, Journal of European Competition Law & Practice Vol. 2, No. 3 (2011), 238.
13. Judgment of the Court of Justice in Case C-375/09 *Prezes Urzędu Ochrony Konkurencji i Konsumentów p. Tele2 Polska sp. z o.o. (now Netia SA)*, ECLI:EU:C:2011:270, 3.5.2011. Cf: Bernard Van de Walle de Ghelcke, *Limits to the Power of National Authorities in the Application of European Competition Law*, Journal of European Competition Law & Practice Vol. 2 No. 5 (2011), 477 to 489; Marco Amorese, *Case C-375/09, President of the Office of Competition and Consumer Protection v. Tele 2, Now Netia: The First Part of the Commission in the European Competition Network as a Safeguard Against National Competition Policies and the Revision of 'primus inter pares' Doctrine*, Columbia Journal of European Law Vol. 18 (2011), 177.
14. Judgment of the Court of Justice in Case C-375/09 *Prezes Urzędu Ochrony Konkurencji i Konsumentów v. Tele2 Polska sp. z o.o. (now Netia SA)*, ECLI:EU:C:2011:270, 3.5.2011, para. 28.
15. Judgment of the Court of Justice in Case C-360/09 *Pfleiderer v. Bundeskartellamt*, ECLI:EU:C:2011:389, 14.6.2011, para. 32.

That case law clearly indicated that until implementation of Directive 2019/1[16] ('ECN + directive'), Member States were free to apply their own procedural rules when implementing Regulation No. 1/2003, even if that entailed a different level of protection for the undertakings concerned as compared to, for example, in other Member States or the procedure before the Commission.[17] The only exception was Article 12(1) of Regulation 1/2003, which precludes the possibility that information communicated in the context of a competition law investigation be used against a natural person, if that was to give rise to criminal liability.[18] Regulation1/2003 does not provide for any guarantee of direct protection, however, for the parties or participants in the decentralised EU competition procedures; a lacuna filled by the ECN + Directive.[19]

The works on the ECN + Directive brought about a more structural, broader discussion on the functioning of decentralisation. The directive was designed to complement Regulation 1/2003, strengthening both institutional and procedural powers and providing for further procedural harmonisation. Under the ECN + Directive, NCAs have been granted the same guarantees of independence, resources, and enforcement and fining powers necessary to ensure that convergent outcomes are reached (recital 3 of the directive). Indeed, the modernisation introduced by ECN + Directive had three objectives: first, to increase effectiveness in enforcement by enhancing the autonomy and independence of NCAs;[20] second, to introduce better cooperation between NCAs; and, third, to harmonise national procedural standards[21] also in purely national enforcement proceedings (Article 3 of the directive). Because of

16. Directive 2019/1 of the European Parliament and of the Council of 11 December 2018 to empower the competition authorities of the Member States to be more effective enforcers and to ensure the proper functioning of the internal market, OJ 2019, L 11, 14.1.2019.
17. For example, in Poland, information obtained in the context of *regularisation* requests was not disclosed to other parties to the proceeding or to third parties, whereas such a practice existed on the part of the European Commission. Maciej Bernatt, *Sprawiedliwość proceduralna w postępowaniu przed organem ochrony konkurencji* 170 (Wydawnictwo Naukowe Wydziału Zarządzania Uniwersytetu Warszawskiego 2011); Katarzyna Róziewicz-Ładoń, *Postępowanie przed Prezesem Urzędu Ochrony Konkurencji i Konsumentów w zakresie przeciwdziałania praktykom ograniczającym* konkurencję 206 (Wolters Kluwer 2011).
18. Peter Oliver, *Le règlement 1/2003 et les principes d'efficacité et d'équivalence*, 3-4 CDE 370 (2005).
19. Directive 2019/1 of the European Parliament and of the Council of 11 December 2018 to empower the competition authorities of the Member States to be more effective enforcers and to ensure the proper functioning of the internal market, OJ L 11, 14.1.2019.
20. But point 22 of the preamble clearly underlines that '(22) The operational independence of national administrative competition authorities should not preclude either judicial review or parliamentary supervision in accordance with national law ... National administrative competition authorities might also be subject to control or monitoring of their financial expenditure, provided this does not affect their independence.'
21. Preamble to the Directive lists: right to good administration, rights of defence, right to be heard, Article 8 – right not to self-incriminate. For instance, recital 14 of the Preamble: 'The exercise of the powers, conferred by this Directive on NCAs, including the investigative powers, should be subject to appropriate safeguards which at least comply with the general principles of Union law and the Charter of Fundamental Rights of the European Union, in accordance with the case law of the Court of Justice of the European Union, in particular in the context of proceedings which could give rise to the imposition of penalties ... Parties to whom preliminary objections about an alleged infringement of Article 101 or Article 102 TFEU have been notified should have the right to access the relevant case file of NCAs, to be able to exercise their rights of defence effectively.'

this, NCAs have been provided with inspection powers covering both the enforcement of Articles 101 and 102 TFEU on a stand-alone basis and the parallel application of national competition law to the same case. The ECN+ directive has provided NCAs with the power to obtain all information related to the undertaking subject to the investigation, including in digital form, irrespective of the medium on which it is stored. As regards the protection of leniency statements and settlement submissions, the directive also covers the enforcement of national competition law on a stand-alone basis. Previously, the marked differences between the leniency programmes in the Member States lead to legal uncertainty for potential leniency applicants. This weakened their incentives to apply for leniency. Member States are now able to implement clearer and harmonised rules for leniency in the area covered by the directive, which guarantees a level playing field for undertakings operating in the internal market. The ECN+ Directive does not apply to national laws insofar as they provide for the imposition of criminal sanctions on natural persons, with the exception of the rules governing the interplay of leniency programmes with the imposition of sanctions on natural persons. It also should not apply to national laws that provide for the imposition of administrative sanctions on natural persons that do not operate as an independent economic actor on a market.

2 RENATIONALISATION OF EU ANTITRUST ENFORCEMENT?

Following the entry into force of Regulation 1/2003, many commentators viewed the legislative development as having the effect of 're-nationalising' EU competition law. This was also followed by the presumption that undertakings might attempt to opt for the national system of competition law enforcement which was the most favourable to them.[22] Those concerns proved to be unfounded since, as Giorgio Monti rightly observed, most systems for protecting competition law in the EU Member States were akin to the EU-level framework.[23] Regulation 1/2003 itself also constituted a certain procedural model before the competition authority, *de jure* or *de facto* reproduced in

22. The arguments put forward, although it seems unfollowed later by actual practice, by: Ivo Van Bael & Jean-François Bellis, *Competition Law of the European Community* 1025 (Wolters Kluwer 2005); Marek Kolasiński, *Decyzje Prezesa Urzędu Ochrony Konkurencji i Konsumentów w sprawach dotyczących naruszenia wspólnotowego prawa konkurencji*, 4 PPH 4 (2009), states that that would be likely to undermine the effectiveness of EU law and undermine the protection of the rights of economic operators.
23. Giorgio Monti, *EC Competition Law* 394 (Cambridge University Press 2007); John Temple Lang, *Decentralized Application of Community Competition Law*, World Competition Vol. 22 No. 3 (1999); Joana Goyder & Albertina Albors-Llorens, *Goyder's EC Competition Law*, 519 (5th ed., Oxford University Press 2009). More broadly, the tendency to harmonise solutions in the various countries of the European Union and in the world: Jürgen Basedow & Stefan L. Pankoke, *General Report*, in: *Limits and Control of Competition with a View to International Harmonisation*, 1-62 (Jürgen Basedow ed., Hart Publishing 2002). However, it should be noted that those prohibitions are similar to Articles 101 and 102 TFEU. On the historical development of the cartel law harmonisation process, *see*: Hanns Ullrich, *Harmonisation within the European Union*, European Comparative Law Review Vol. 3 (1996), 178.

most EU Member States[24] and which has been further aligned by ECN + Directive. The possibility of *forum shopping* was not specifically high, as in most cases it is the competition authority which decides whether or not to initiate a procedure. While it is true that it is possible to speculate on the possibility of initiating proceedings against a particular undertaking under a national (for example, highly restrictive) system for the implementation of competition law following a complaint by a competitor, the threat to the undertaking concerned appears no more significant than when the procedure is initiated on the authority's own initiative and certainly does not correspond to the classic sense *of forum shopping*.

The essential criterion for distinguishing between the question of whether a procedure must be conducted on the basis of EU legislation or national law on cartels is the condition of an effect on trade between Member States,[25] expressly laid in Articles 101 and 102 TFEU which has remained unchanged since the first formulation of the equivalent provisions in the EEC Treaty. That condition establishes a boundary between separate, albeit interconnected, legal orders. Under Article 3 of Reg. 1/2003, NCAs and national courts are required to apply Articles 101 and 102 TFEU where they apply national competition law to agreements and practices which may affect trade between Member States.[26]

The question whether a practice affects trade between Member States has two effects.

First, it has certain consequences for competence. Where a practice affects trade between Member States, the NCA is competent to pursue a decentralised EU competition law procedure. It is a subsidiary competence, where the European Commission is not involved. If the Commission commits or declares its intention to investigate, the

24. Konrad Ost, *Die VO 1/2003 – Grundlage des Netzwerks und grundrechtskonformes Modell eines Kartellverfahrensrecht* in: *Rechtsschutz und Wettbewerb in der neuen europäischen Rechtsentwicklung* 37 (Jürgen Schwarze ed., Nomos 2010).
25. Kris Dekeyser & Maria Jaspers, *A New Era of ECN Cooperation. Achievements and Challenges with Special Focus on Work in the Leniency Field*, World Competition Vol. 30, No. 1 (2007), 8. David Bosco et al., *Effect on Trade Between Member States and Anti-competitive Practices: A Topical Question*, Concurrences No. 2 (2011), 17-32, in that text, mention the similarity between that clause and the *American interpretation clause* contained in the Sherman Act at 30.
26. There is no doubt that this is an obligation and not an option, Ivo Van Bael & Jean-François Bellis, *Competition Law of the European*. The very condition of an effect on trade will not be more detailed here, it is the subject of the Commission's analysis in the 2004 Communication, the guidelines on the effect on trade concept contained in Articles 81 and 82 of the Treaty, OJ 175, 27.4.2004. Cf.: David Bosco et al., *Effect on Trade Between Member States and Anti-competitive Practices: A Topical Question*, Concurrences No. 2 (2011), 21; Ivo Van Bael, *Due Process in EU Competition Proceedings*, 32-35 (Wolters Kluwer 2011); Laura Hiljemark, *Enforcement of EC Competition Law in National Courts: The Perspectives of Judicial Protection*, in: *The Internationalisation of Antitrust Policy* 86 (Maher Dabbah ed., Cambridge University Press 2003). In the case law of CJEU, *see, e.g.*, the judgment of the Court of Justice in Case C-309/99, *Wouters v. Algemene Raad van de Nederlandse Ordre van Advocaten*, ECLI:EU:C:2002:98, 19.2.2002, para. 95; judgment of the Court of Justice in Case C-475/99, *Ambulanz Glöckner v. Landkreis Südwestpfalz*, ECLI:EU:C:2001:577, 25.10.2001, para. 49; judgment of in Case C-215/96, *Bagnasco v. Banca Popolare de Novara*, ECLI:EU:C:1999:12, 21.1.1999, para. 51; judgment of the Court of Justice in Case C-111/94, *Job Centre Coop*, ECLI:EU:C:1995:340, 19.10.1995, para. 37; judgment of the Court of Justice in Case C-41/90, *Höfner and Elser v. Macroton GmbH*, ECLI:EU:C:1991:161, 23.4.1991, para. 33; judgment of the Court of Justice in Case T-199/08, *Ziegler v. Commission*, ECLI:EU:T:2011:285, 16.6.2011, para. 73.

NCA automatically loses its competence to investigate a matter in which the Commission has initiated its own procedure. The NCA is then required to close the procedure in so far as it related to Article 101 or 102 TFEU (Article 11(6) of Regulation 1/2003).[27] That solution ensures that the rules on competition are enforced uniformly within the EU.[28]

Second, the finding that the practice in question has an effect on trade between Member States has consequences for the choice of the applicable law. The determination of an 'effect on trade' means that not only national provisions are applicable to the practice or conduct but also Articles 101 and 102 TFEU.[29] An antitrust case is thus a 'Union' case[30] as well as a national law case. Indeed, it is not a choice between the various applicable provisions (the choice 'either ... or ...'), but the addition of another legal framework for assessing the practice or conduct (in general 'in accordance with' the application of the relevant provisions of national law).[31] Alternately, Member States may adopt national competition rules (as regards the 'characterisation') which prohibit or penalise specific unilateral practices of undertakings not expressly foreseen by Article 102 TFEU.[32] The Member States are also free to adopt and apply within their

27. The interpretation of that provision became clearer after CJEU replied to the question referred for a preliminary ruling by the Czech court in *Toshiba Corp. and Others* in Case C-17/10, *the Úřad pro ochranu hospodářské soutěže*, by which that court endeavoured to clarify whether, from the date of accession (1 May 2004), the Czech competition authority had lost its jurisdiction to deal with the case against Toshiba, since the proceedings had been brought by the European Commission only in relation to the application of the case against Toshiba — judgment of the Court of Justice in Case C-17/10 Toshiba *Corporation and Others, p. Úřad pro ochranu hospodářské soutěžei*, ECLI:EU:C:2012:72, 14.2.2012.
28. Van Bael & Bellis, *Competition Law of the European...* 1027; Luis Ortiz Blanco & Konstantin Jörgens, *National Authorities for Upholding Competition* in: *EC Competition Procedure*, points 1.54, 1.55 (Luis Ortiz Blanco ed., Oxford University Press 2013).
29. The initial proposal for Regulation No. 1/2003 provided that only Community law (now the European Union) and not national law would be applicable in the event of an effect on trade. However, the final version of the regulation provides for the parallel application of the national and EU provisions, por. Jean-François Bellis, *La decentralization* in : *La modernisation dans l'application du droit de la concurrence* 62 (Paul Nihoul Brussels 2004); Van Bael & Bellis, *Competition Law of the European...*, p. 1032; Giorgi Monti, *Modernisation: From Policy to Practice*, 28 European Law Review 463 (2003); Silke Hossenfelder, *Reform of European Competition Law: Changes in the Cooperation Between Competition Authorities and the Effects on the Sanctioning System*, in: *Competition Law Sanctioning in the European Union: The EU-Law Influence on the National Law System of Sanctions in the European Area* 166 (Gerhard Dannecker & Oswald Jansen, Kluwer Law International 2004).
30. Dawid Mąsik, *Sprawa wspólnotowa przed sądem krajowym*, Europejski Przegląd Sądowy Vol. 9 (2008), 16-22.
31. There is nothing to suggest that the national legislature 'waives', in such circumstances, the application of the provisions of national law, so that both EU and national law would be applied, where appropriate, cf. the approach taken by the Italian legislation described by Giorgio Monti, *EC Competition ...* 403. It may also be noted that, in the United Kingdom, the national competition authorities did not have the power to apply EU competition law prior to the reform. Gian Luigi Tosato & Leonardo Bellodi (eds), *EU Competition Law: Volume I – Procedures*, 32 (Claels and Casteels 2006); Opinion of AG J. Mazák, *Prezes Urzędu Ochrony Konkurencji i Konsumentów v Tele2 Polska sp. z o.o. (now Netia SA)*, C-375/09, 7.12.2010, para. 19.
32. Ivo Van Bael, *Due Process ...* p. 90 states that those solutions are to be found in law: France, Greece, Germany, Portugal, Lithuania, Hungary and Ireland. These may be rules relating to abuse of economic dependence, the prohibition of selling at a loss, etc. Giorgio Monti, *EC Competition ...* pp. 406 to 407 states that the French legislation justified that solution, first, that

territory legislation protecting interests other than the protection of competition on the market as enshrined in Articles 101 and 102 TFEU.[33] Thus, in principle, in assessing a practice affecting trade between Member States, NCAs apply both the provisions of EU substantive law (Article 101 or 102 TFEU) and national substantive law.

There is no doubt that, in conjunction with Article 3 of Regulation 1/2003, the national courts and NCAs must examine of their own motion whether a practice is liable to affect trade. In that sense, it is a 'binding' requirement.[34] The non-application of provisions of the TFEU, even where the condition of an effect on trade is met, would result in potential infringement proceedings under the TFEU and Regulation No. 1/2003 against a Member State under Article 258 TFEU. However, as yet, there has not been the initiation of proceedings on that ground. Any other type of consequences of such a non-application of EU law remains fully speculative, as to our knowledge, it has not brought about the consequences at the national level. One probably would need to deal with the possible differing national practice by applying the usual doctrine of *Simmenthal* and dis-apply the solutions of national law (or rather the national decision?), without however formally invalidating them, once identified that they hinder the effectiveness of EU competition law. It is easier said than done in such circumstances, because it seems that the non-application of EU rules with respect to an undertaking can foremost have the consequence that this undertaking cannot benefit from the *ne bis in idem* principle and avoid any prosecution for the same infringement penalised under national law, providing that the criteria of *idem* is identified.[35] This also undermines the general effectiveness of the application of EU competition law.

The paradox and 'inconclusive' example of possible diversity in approach to the same practice, depending on the court deciding upon a case, when no effect on trade is invoked, might be due to the interpretation of Article 7 of Regulation No.

---

it was a question of continuing, by the French competition authority, an infringement of French competition law consisting of an abuse of economic dependence. Second, it had to ensure that it was possible to apply the prohibition on selling at a loss, a prohibition which in 1990s. was subject to an analysis of CJEU in the judgment of the Court of Justice in Joined Cases C-267/91 and C-268/91 P. *Keck and Mithouard* ECLI:EU:C:1993:905, 24.11.1993, cf. Laurence Idot, *France*, in: *The Modernisation of EU Competition Law Enforcement in the EU* 151 (Dermot Cahill ed., Cambridge University Press 2004).

33. Giorgio Monti, *EC Competition …*, on the contrary, notes that it is the solution adopted in the judgment of the Court of Justice in Case C-41/96 *VAG-Händlerbeirat eV v. Colrad-Consult*, ECLI:EU:C:1997:283, 4.6.1997, paras 12 to 14, in which the German court applied the German rules on unfair competition (and not antitrust legislation) in order to cancel the contract. Hanns Ullrich maintains that that provision is such as to 'reverse' the scope of the national provisions relating to unfair competition – Hanns Ullrich, *Anti-unfair Competition Law and antitrust Law: A Continental Conundrum?*, 1 EUI Working Paper in Law 45 (2005); Similarly, Monti, *EC Competition …* 422.
34. Judgment of the Court of Justice in Case C-151/20 *Bundeswettbewersbehörde v. Nordzucker AG, Südzucker AG, Agrana Zucker GmbH*, ECLI:EU:C:2022:203, 22.3.2022, para. 53: 'Where the national competition authority applies provisions of national law prohibiting cartels to an agreement of undertakings which may affect trade between Member States within the meaning of Article 101 TFEU, the first sentence of Article 3(1) requires Article 101 TFEU also to be applied to it in parallel.'
35. Judgment of the Court of Justice in Case C-151/20, *Bundeswettbewersbehörde v. Nordzucker AG, Südzucker AG, Agrana Zucker GmbH*, ECLI:EU:C:2022:203, 22.3.2022, paras 42, 58.

1215/2012.[36] In this regard, the case before the Court of Justice, C-59/19 *Wikingerhof GmbH & Co. KG v. Booking.com BV*[37] is illustrating. It concerned a reference for preliminary ruling from a German Bundesgerichtshof in proceedings between a hotel in Schleswig-Holstein, and Booking.com BV, the accommodation booking platform established in the Netherlands, relating to certain booking practices which Wikingerhof claimed constituted an abuse of dominance. The Bundesgerichtshof had been asked to assess an appeal based on the contention that the appeal court in question had erred in finding that the action before it did not come within its jurisdiction in matters relating to tort, delict or quasi-delict within the meaning of Article 7(2) of Regulation 1215/2012.[38] In its answer to the Bundesgerichtshof, the Court of Justice stated that the action brought by the hotel, based on the legal obligation to refrain from any abuse of dominant position, is a matter relating to tort, delict or quasi-delict within the meaning of Article 7(2) of Regulation No. 1215/2012. There was however no follow up on the issues of effect on trade and the lack of taking it into account.

3 CHOICE OF THE BEST PLACED AUTHORITY

As already mentioned above, according to Article 11(6) of Regulation 1/2003, the initiation by the Commission of proceedings for the adoption of a decision under Chapter III of that regulation relieves the NCA of their competence to apply Articles 101 and 102 TFEU. If the NCA is already acting on a case, the Commission initiates proceedings after consulting that NCA. In case C-17/10 *Toshiba*,[39] Advocate General Kokott took the view, that despite the fact that Article 11(6) contains a procedural rule which provides that the initiation of proceedings by the Commission would relieve the national competition authorities of their competence to apply Article 101 or 102 TFEU,[40] this does not preclude proceedings based on national competition law from continuing unless the application of national law is excluded for the reasons referred to in Article 3 of Regulation 1/2003.[41] It was in that sense that Court of Justice,[42] in paragraph 91 that:

36. Regulation (EU) No. 1215/2012 of the European Parliament and of the Council of 12 December 2012 on jurisdiction and the recognition and enforcement of judgments in civil and commercial matters (recast), OJ 2012, L 351.
37. Judgment of the Court of Justice in Case C-59/19, *Wikingerhof GmbH & Co. KG v. Booking.com BV*, ECLI:EU:C:2020:950, 24.11.2020.
38. The referring court invoked judgment of the Court of Justice in Case C-27/17, *flyLAL-Lithuanian Airlines*, EU:C:2018:533, 5.7.2018, where it was stated that an action concerns matters relating to tort, delict or quasi-delict within the meaning of point 2 of Article 7 of Regulation No. 1215/2012 where it relates to claims for civil liability or an injunction that are based on the fact that the conduct complained of amounts to an abuse of a dominant position. Such an abuse of a dominant position could result from making the conclusion of a contract subject to the acceptance of unfair trading terms.
39. Critically on this case: Marco Botta, *Testing the Decentralization of Competition Law Enforcement: Comment on Toshiba*, European Law Review Vol. 38, No. 1 (2013), 107-117.
40. Opinion of AG Kokott in Case C-17/10, *Toshiba and Others*, ECLI:EU:C:2011:552, 8.9.2011, para. 74.
41. *Ibid.*, para. 79.
42. Judgment of the Court of Justice in Case C-17/10 *Toshiba Corporation and Others v. Úřad pro ochranu hospodářské soutěže*, ECLI:EU:C:2012:72, 14.2.2012, para. 91.

> a national competition authority does not, pursuant to Article 11(6) of Regulation No 1/2003, read in combination with Article 3(1) of the same regulation, permanently and definitively lose its power to apply national competition law where the Commission opens a proceeding for the adoption of a decision under Chapter III of Regulation No 1/2003. A fortiori, in a situation such as that at issue in the main proceedings, in which the competition authority of a Member State penalises, by the application of national competition law, the anti-competitive effects produced by a cartel in the territory of the said Member State during periods prior to the accession of the latter to the Union, the combined provisions of Articles 11(6) and 3(1) of Regulation No 1/2003 cannot, in respect of those periods, prevent the application of national provisions of competition law.

The manner in which cases are divided between the national authorities and the Commission has been declared not amenable to direct judicial review.[43] Appeals may be brought only against acts (decisions) adopted after a decision on competence has been made. In *France Télécom*[44] the General Court expressly stated that:

> although Regulation No 1/2003 establishes cooperation between the Commission and the national competition authorities, it retains the predominant role of the Commission in investigating infringements. In particular, Article 11(6) Regulation [1/2003] provides that, subject to consultation with the competent national authority, the Commission is entitled to initiate a procedure for the adoption of a decision, even if a competition authority of a Member State is already dealing with a case. Moreover, there is no such prohibition either in the Commission Notice on Cooperation within the Network of Competition Authorities, which, moreover, does not confer on the undertakings concerned an individual right to require that their case be assisted by a specific authority, or from a joint declaration of the Council and the Commission on the functioning of the network of competition authorities, which is political and does not create rights, legal obligations or the principle of subsidiarity, that principle not calling into question the powers conferred on the Commission by the Treaty.[45]

Certain Commission decisions relating to its functioning within the ECN are subject to judicial review, however. Under Regulation No. 1/2003, the Commission adopts decisions on cooperation within the network of competition bodies, which are subject to normal judicial review under Article 263 TFEU. These include decisions to transmit documents (under Article 11(2) of Regulation 1/2003), decisions requesting disclosure of documents collected by an NCA in a case examined by that authority (Article 11(2)); decisions to refer the case back to an NCA (Article 11(6)), decisions to exchange information (Article 12), decisions to suspend proceedings on the ground that the case is dealt with at a different level (Article 13(1)) and the decision rejecting the complaint on the ground that an NCA is dealing with the case (Article 13[46]).

---

43. Konrad Ost, *Die VO 1/2003: Grundlage des Netzwerks* ... 34.
44. Judgment of the Court of First Instance in Joined Cases T-339/04 and T-340/04 *France Télécom SA v. Commission of the European Communities*, ECLI:EU:T:2007:80, 8.3.2007.
45. Judgment in joined Cases T-339/04 and T-340/04 *France Télécom v. Commission* ECLI:EU:T:2007:80, 8.3.2007, paras 79 to 83, 85, 88 and 89.
46. Judgment of the General Court in Case T-201/11, *Si.mobil telekomunikacijske storitve d.d. v. European Commission*, ECLI:EU:T:2014:1096, 17.12.2014; judgment of the General Court in Case T-355/13, *easyJet Airline v. Commission*, EU:T:2015:36, 21.1.2015.

As regards the latter type of decision, Article 13 effectively prevents dual proceedings occurring. According to Article 13(1), when NCAs of two or more Member States have received a complaint or are acting on their own initiative under Article 101 or Article 102 TFEU against the same agreement, decision of an association or practice, the fact that one authority is dealing with the case shall be sufficient grounds for the others to suspend the proceedings before them or to reject the complaint. The Commission may likewise reject a complaint on the ground that an NCA is dealing with the case. Similarly, if the case has already been dealt with by a different authority, the Commission or a different NCA can reject the complaint.

There are not many cases that explain the notion of 'dealt with'. In its judgment in LL-Carpenter/Commission,[47] the General Court stated that the words 'deal with' does not simply mean that another authority has received a complaint or that it has before it a case of its own motion. A referral by a complainant or a referral by a competition authority of a Member State on its own initiative is an act which, considered in itself, does not attest either to the use of its powers by the competition authority of a Member State or, a fortiori, to an examination of the matters of fact and of law relating to the case in question. Thus, the Commission would not fulfil its general supervisory role under Article 105(1) TFEU if it were authorised to reject a complaint solely on the ground that an NCA had received a complaint or that it had lodged a complaint with it without those acts giving rise to any dealing with the case at issue within the meaning of Article 13(2) of Regulation No. 1/2003. Still, according to settled case law, the Commission is required to define and implement the orientation of EU competition policy. In order to perform that task effectively, it is entitled to give differing degrees of priority to the complaints brought before it[48] and even the fact that the national authority has not dealt with the case on the merits cannot oblige it to proceed with the full examination of the case at hand. The Commission can also reject the complaint if the applicant's rights are satisfactorily protected.[49] However, particular circumstances may oblige the Commission to investigate the case that normally could be dealt with at the national level. In this regard, in its judgment of 9 February 2022 *Sped-Pro*,[50] the General Court relied on the right to effective judicial protection (Article 2 TEU, Article 19 paragraph 1 TEU, Article 47 of the Charter) to state that an NCA has to be absolutely independent in order to assure effectiveness of EU competition law[51] and if there are serious reasons to presume that there is a risk of violation of fundamental rights of the undertaking concerned if the case is handled at the national level.[52]

47. Judgment of the General Court in Case T-531/18, *LL-Carpenter s. r. o. v. European Commission*, ECLI:EU:T:2020:91, 12.3.2020.
48. Judgment of the General Court in Case T-480/15, *Agria Polska sp. z o.o. and Others v. European Commission*, ECLI:EU:T:2017:339, 16.5.2017; judgment of the General Court in Case T-531/18, *LL-Carpenter s. r. o. v. European Commission*, ECLI:EU:T:2020:91, 12.5.2020, para. 64.
49. Judgment of the Court of First Instance in Case T-458/04, *Au Lys de France SA v. Commission*, ECLI:EU:T:2007:195, 3.7.2007.
50. Judgment of the General Court in Case T-791/19, *Sped-Pro S.A. v. European Commission*, ECLI:EU:T:2022:67, 9.2.2022.
51. *Ibid.*, para. 86.
52. *Ibid.*, para. 98.

4 THE ROLE OF (OR THE ROLE LEFT TO) THE EUROPEAN COMMISSION

When one looks at the scope and functioning of decentralisation of competition law enforcement, unavoidably there is a question of what is left at the centralised EU-level? The role of the European Commission can be described as three-fold. First, the Commission deals a lot with the negotiated proceedings,[53] in particular based on Article 9 of Regulation 1/2003 for non-cartel cases and the settlement procedure introduced for cartels since 2008.[54] Second, the Commission still handles the biggest, pan-European infringements – in particular abuse of dominance cases under Article 102 TFEU. Third, the Commission can intervene as a unifying actor, in cases where it is 'particularly well placed' to investigate. The result of the change in the Commission's involvement in competition law enforcement is that there have been less decisions in recent years that have been contested before the EU General than was previously the case. The Commission's decisions are also often followed by private enforcement actions before national courts.[55] Thus, at least partly, the decentralisation has caused that the control of competition rules to take place ex post (also for Article 101(3) TFEU) and before national courts. There is a relatively low level of preliminary references relating to the interpretation of Articles 101 and 102;[56] the *ne bis in idem* principle,[57] the parallel application of EU and national rules[58] and private enforcement.[59] As one of the

53. The hybrid version of those proceedings has been an object of series of judgments since 2016: first on the question if such hybrid procedure is legitimate – judgment of the General Court in Case T-95/15, *Printeos, SA and Others v. European Commission*, ECLI:EU:T:2016:722, 13.12.2016; second on the question if it was not discriminatory to use it, judgment of the Court of Justice in Case C-411/15 P, *Timab Industries and Cie financière et de participations Roullier (CFPR) v. European Commission*, ECLI:EU:C:2017:11, 12.1.2017; third on the question of drafting of decisions referring to a parallel different proceedings – content of the decision should not mention those who did not take part in settlement proceedings – judgment of the Court of Justice in Case C-440/19 P, *Pometon v. Commission*, ECLI:EU:C:2021:214, 18.3.2021; fourth on the methods of setting fines for different situations – judgment in Case C-39/18 P, *Commission v. Icap Management Services and Icap New Zealand*, ECLI:EU:C:2019:584, 10.7.2019.
54. Commission Notice on the conduct of settlement procedures in view of the adoption of Decisions pursuant to Article 7 and Article 23 of Council Regulation (EC) No. 1/2003 in cartel cases, OJ C 167, 2.7.2008.
55. Cf. the consequences of truck cartel – judgment of the Court of Justice in Case C-882/19, *Sumal, S.L. v. Mercedes Benz Trucks España, S.L.*, ECLI:EU:C:2021:800, 6.10.2021; judgment of the Court of Justice in Case C-30/20, *RH v. AB Volvo and Others*, ECLI:EU:C:2021:604, 15.7.2021; judgment of the Court of Justice in Case C-724/17, *Vantaan- -kaupunki- v. -przeciwko- -Skanska-Industrial Solutions Oy i in.*, ECLI:EU:C:2019:204, 14.3.2019; judgment of the Court of Justice in Case C-267/20, *Volvo and DAF trucks*, ECLI:EU:C:2022:494, 22.6.2022.
56. Judgment of the Court of Justice in Case C-307/18, *Generics (UK) Ltd and Others v. Competition and Markets Authority*, ECLI:EU:C:2020:52, 30.1.2020, judgment of Court of Justice in Case C-228/18, *Gazdasági Versenyhivatal v. Budapest Bank Nyrt. and Others*, ECLI:EU:C:2020:265, 2.4.2020.
57. Judgment of the Court of Justice in Case C-857/19, *Slovak Telekom v. Protimonopolný úrad Slovenskej republiky*, ECLI:EU:C:2021:139, 25.2.2021; judgment of the Court of Justice in Case C-617/17, *Powszechny Zakład Ubezpieczeń na Zycie S.A. v. Prezes Urzędu Ochrony Konkurencji i Konsumentów*, ECLI:EU:C:2019:283, 3.4.2019.
58. Judgment of the Court of Justice in Case C-308/19, *Whiteland Import Export*, ECLI:EU:C:2021:47, 21.1.2021.
59. Judgment of the Court of Justice in Case C-882/19, *Sumal, S.L. v. Mercedes Benz Trucks España, S.L.*, ECLI:EU:C:2021:800, 6.10.2021; judgment of the Court of Justice in Case C-30/20, *RH v. AB*

recent cases, *Whiteland Import Export*[60] indicated, the Court of Justice is of the opinion that if national courts should choose the legal basis that guarantees the full efficiency of EU competition law, stating for instance that: 'national courts are not required to apply Article 25(3) Regulation 1/2003 to the time-barring of a national competition authority's powers to impose penalties for infringements of EU competition law'.[61] It places great responsibility on the national courts, as expressly stated by the Court of Justice at paragraph 58 of the judgment: 'it would in principle be for the referring court, without waiting until the national legislation at issue is amended by legislation or by any other constitutional procedure, to give full effect to the obligations ... by interpreting that legislation so far as at all possible in the light of EU law, and particularly the rules of EU competition law, ..., or, as necessary, by disapplying that legislation'. This is done in order to fully implement the principle of effectiveness because according to the Court of Justice at paragraph 65: 'Article 4(3) TEU and Article 101 TFEU, read in the light of the principle of effectiveness, must be interpreted as precluding national legislation, ... where it becomes apparent, having regard to all elements of the limitation rules at issue, that such an exclusion presents a systemic risk that acts constituting such infringements may go unpunished, which it is for the referring court to verify.'

5 *NE BIS IN IDEM* IN VARIOUS CONTEXTS

There is interesting case law relating to the *ne bis in idem* principe in competition law proceedings. In his Opinion of 2 September 2021, *bpost v. Autorité belge de concurrence*[62] C-117/20, Advocate General Bobek explains very clearly complications linked with the application of this principle in a competition law context. He states that the implementation of the idea of *ne bis in idem* within EU law has been difficult for a number of reasons (paragraph 2). First, in a composite legal space such as the EU, be it horizontally (Member States – Member States) or vertically (Member States – European Union), the practical implementation of that idea results in an enhanced level of complexity. There are simply too many variables. Second, new segments, layers, and sub-fields of regulation are being introduced, including the creation of new bodies or authorities responsible for regulatory supervision. This sometimes leads to an overlap in mandates and confusion as to where the competence to investigate and sanction lies. Third, according to AG Bobek, there is the 'Engel-multiplication'. The rather expansionist criteria, originally coined by the European Court of Human Rights

Volvo and Others, ECLI:EU:C:2021:604, 15.7.2021; judgment of the Court of Justice in Case C-724/17, *Vantaan- -kaupunki- v. -Skanska- Industrial Solutions Oy i in.*, ECLI:EU:C:2019:204, 14.3.2019; judgment of the Court of Justice in Case C-267/20 Volvo and DAF trucks, ECLI:EU:C:2022:494, 22.6.2022.

60. Judgment of the Court of Justice in Case C-308/19, *Whiteland Import Export*, ECLI:EU:C:2021:47, 21.1.2021.
61. *Ibid.*, para. 41.
62. Opinion of AG Bobek in Case C-117/20 *bpost v. Autorité belge de concurrence*, ECLI:EU:C:2021:680.

to broaden its jurisdiction under Article 6(1) of the European Convention of Human Rights, are now also being used in other contexts. That includes the assessment of what constitutes a 'criminal offence'[63] for the purposes of Article 50 of the EU Charter of Fundamental Rights. As a result, many rules and procedures that were in the past perceived on a conceptual level as being administrative, are now considered to be criminal.

In PZU Życie/UOKIK, C-617/17, the Court of Justice stated that the principle of *ne bis in idem* enshrined in Article 50 of the Charter must be interpreted as not precluding an NCA from fining an undertaking in a single decision for an infringement of national competition law and for an infringement of Article 102 TFEU. In such a situation, the NCA must nevertheless ensure that the fines are proportionate to the nature of the infringement. Thus, Article 50 of the Charter in a competition law context means that both EU and national law applied by the same authority and the principle of *ne bis in idem* does not preclude the use of national rules in parallel to EU rules.

In case C-857/19 Slovak Telekom, both the EU authority and national authority reacted to the same or similar behaviour. The Court of Justice interpreted, as in Toshiba case, the first sentence of Article 11(6) Regulation 1/2003, saying that NCAs are relieved of their competence to apply Articles 101 and 102 TFEU where the European Commission initiates proceedings for the purposes of adopting a decision finding an infringement of those provisions as meaning that the Commission's intended formal act relates to the same alleged infringements of Articles 101 and 102 TFEU committed by the same undertaking or undertakings on the same product market or markets and the same geographical market or markets during the same period or periods as those concerned by the proceeding or proceedings previously brought by those authorities. The principle *ne bis in idem* does not apply, therefore, where proceedings are brought against or sanctions imposed on an undertaking separately and independently by an NCA and the European Commission for infringements of Article 102 TFEU relating to separate product markets or separate geographical markets.

In the case C-151/20 *Nordzucker et al.*[64] the Austrian Court initially dismissed the action brought by the Austrian authority on the ground that the agreement at issue had already been subject to a penalty imposed by German competition authority, stating that it would be contrary to the *non bis in idem principle*. Following the appeal from the Austrian competition authority, the Supreme Court of Austria signalled doubts as to the definition of *idem* in such circumstances. The Court of Justice confirmed that the doubts were legitimate and that the *idem*, even if its identification remains the competence of national court,[65] might possibly not be fully there. The criterion of

63. Very clearly stating that proceeding for the imposition of fines under competition law should considered as criminal proceedings: judgment of the Court of Justice in Case C-17/10 *Toshiba Corporation and Others*, EU:C:2012:72, 14.12.2012, para. 94, judgment of the Court of Justice in Case C-617/17, *-Powszechny- Zakład Ubezpieczeń na Zycie*, EU:C:2019:283, 3.4.2019, para. 28; judgment of the Court of Justice in Case C-151/20, *-Bundeswettbewersbehörde v. Nordzucker AG, Südzucker AG, Agrana Zucker GmbH*, ECLI:EU:C:2022:203, 22.03.2022, para. 32.
64. Judgment of the Court of Justice in Case C-151/20, *Bundeswettbewersbehörde v. Nordzucker AG, Südzucker AG, Agrana Zucker GmbH*, ECLI:EU:C:2022:203, 22.3.2022.
65. *Ibid.*, para. 42: 'It is for the referring court, which alone has jurisdiction to rule on the facts, to determine whether the dispute before it relates to the same facts as those which led to the

assessing the existence of the same offence is 'identity of the material facts, understood as the existence of a set of concrete circumstances which are inextricably linked together and which have resulted in the final acquittal or conviction of the person concerned'.[66] In the case at hand, two parallel proceedings based on both national law and EU law remained possible, provided that the second (time-wise) national decision was not based on a finding of an anti-competitive object or effect in the territory of the first Member State.[67] The possibility of having two national proceedings for infringing Article 101 TFEU was thus confirmed, as long as the national authorities base themselves on findings limited to their respective territories.

At the same recent date, in the case C-117/20 bpost,[68] in the context of the parallel application of regulation and competition law, the Court of Justice interpreted Article 50 of the Charter of Fundamental Rights of the European Union, read in conjunction with Article 52(1) thereof, as not precluding a legal person from being fined for an infringement of EU competition law where, on the basis of the same facts, that person had already been the subject of a final decision in proceedings relating to an infringement of sectoral rules on the liberalisation of the relevant market. This is permitted so long as: first, there are clear and precise rules making it possible to predict which acts or omissions are liable to be subject to a duplication of proceedings and penalties and also that there will be coordination between the two competent authorities; second, that the two sets of proceedings have been conducted in a sufficiently coordinated manner within a close timeframe; and, third, that the overall penalties imposed correspond to the seriousness of the offences committed.

The existing case law seems to confirm that the principle of *ne bis in idem* is applicable to competition law proceedings in different configurations, but the Court of Justice has, up until now, never identified the violation of this principle in the context of decentralisation.

6 FINAL REMARKS

Since the adoption of ECN+ Directive, no broader reflection on decentralisation has taken place. The directive brought about harmonisation of procedural standards and higher guarantees and requirements as to the independence of NCAs. Some issues pending before its adoption, mainly as regards coherence and convergence, have been finally resolved. First, as to the coherence in what is done at national and EU levels, NCAs have at present identical powers to the Commission and they can cooperate fully

adoption of the German authority's final decision, having regard to the territory, product market and period covered by that decision.'

66. Judgment of the Court of Justice in Case C-151/20, *Bundeswettbewersbehörde v. Nordzucker AG, Südzucker AG, Agrana Zucker GmbH*, ECLI:EU:C:2022:203, 22.3.2022, para. 38; judgments of the Court of Justice in Case C-524/15, *Menci*, EU:C:2018:197, 20.3.2018, para. 35, and in Case C-537/16, *Garlsson Real Estate and Others*, EU:C:2018:193, 20.3.2018, para. 37.
67. Judgment of the Court of Justice in Case C-151/20 *Bundeswettbewersbehörde v. Nordzucker AG, Südzucker AG, Agrana Zucker GmbH*, ECLI:EU:C:2022:203, 22.3.2022, para. 58.
68. Judgment of the Court of Justice in Case C-117/20, *bpost SA v. Autorité belge de la concurrence*, ECLI:EU:C:2022:202, 22.3.2022.

with each other. They are also, at least nominally, to be more independent and self-sufficient. As to convergence, in particular of procedural standards, national procedures became more and more aligned to the model represented by the European Commission in an organic rather than being forced to do so. That convergence was deemed not sufficient, however, and so the directive has sought to require further harmonisation.

The result of the decentralisation of competition law enforcement is the existence of a composite legal space – there might be a drive to an enhanced level of complexity and risk of overlaps. But no real return to centralisation has been witnessed; the Commission remains active in only a few fields, whereas NCAs and national courts are still at the frontline of competition law enforcement in the EU and the Commission intervenes in their activity only in exceptional cases (like to risk for fundamental rights). The big unanswered question remains on the concrete consequences of possible inaction of national authorities if the practice in question affects trade between Member States. Despite almost twenty years of decentralisation this issue is still waiting for a clarification.

CHAPTER 7

Article 3 of Regulation 1/2003 and the Doctrine of Pre-emption

Miguel Mota Delgado & Nicolas Petit

1 INTRODUCTION

Which rule takes precedence in a case of parallel application of European Union (EU) and national competition law?[1] The Rome Treaty had not foreseen the question,[2] leading early commentators to propose to resolve conflicts in favour of the strictest rule and others to support the prevalence of EU law, whether or not it was stricter.[3]

In *Walt Wilhelm*, the European Court of Justice (ECJ) held that the application of national law should 'not prejudice the uniform application throughout the [EU] of the [EU] rules on cartels and of the full effect of the measures adopted in implementation of those rules'.[4] Consequently, 'conflicts between the rules of the [EU] and national rules in the matter of the law on cartels [should] be resolved by applying the principle that [EU] law takes precedence'.[5] *Walt Wilhelm* passed to posterity as one of the earliest applications of the principle of primacy of EU law by the ECJ.

The *Walt Wilhelm* Court, however, made clear that such judicial regulation of the parallel application of EU and national competition rules was not necessarily the end of

1. This chapter's references to the 'European Union' and to 'Articles 101 and 102 TFEU' shall include all previous designations, such as 'European Economic Community' and 'Articles 85 and 86 ECC'.
2. The first regulation implementing Articles 101 and 102 TFEU did not address the issue either. *See* Regulation No. 17: First Regulation implementing Articles 85 and 86 of the Treaty, OJ 13, 21.2.1962, pp. 204-211.
3. For a review of the doctrinal discussion about the parallel application of EU and national competition rules until 1969, *see* Lúcio Tomé Feiteira, *The Interplay Between European and National Competition Law after Regulation 1/2003: 'United (Should) We Stand?'* (2016), pp. 29-37.
4. *See* Case 14-68 *Walt Wilhelm and others v. Bundeskartellamt*, 13.7.1969, ECLI:EU:C:1969:4 (1969), para. 9.
5. *See ibid.*, para. 6.

the discussion. In fact, the Court's judgment opened the door to the possibility of a different arrangement under a regulation adopted pursuant to the relevant treaty basis.[6]

The Commission came back to the question in the early 2000s. In a policy reform known as the 'modernisation' of EU competition law, the Commission proposed to explicitly introduce a principle of exclusion of national competition law:[7]

> *Article 3*
>
> *Relationship between Articles 81 and 82 and national competition laws*
>
> Where an agreement, a decision by an association of undertakings or a concerted practice within the meaning of Article 81 of the Treaty or the abuse of a dominant position within the meaning of Article 82 may affect trade between Member States, Community competition law shall apply to the exclusion of national competition laws.

The legislative compromise ultimately reached in the Council led to the promulgation of a different and more complicated arrangement. The Commission's principle of exclusion was abandoned in favour of a complex model that safeguards the application of specific types or provisions of national law. Article 3 of Regulation 1/2003 reads as follows:[8]

> *Article 3*
>
> *Relationship between Articles 81 and 82 of the Treaty and national competition laws*
>
> 1. Where the competition authorities of the Member States or national courts apply national competition law to agreements, decisions by associations of undertakings or concerted practices within the meaning of Article 81(1) of the Treaty which may affect trade between Member States within the meaning of that provision, they shall also apply Article 81 of the Treaty to such agreements, decisions or concerted practices. Where the competition authorities of the Member States or national courts apply national competition law to any abuse prohibited by Article 82 of the Treaty, they shall also apply Article 82 of the Treaty.
> 2. The application of national competition law may not lead to the prohibition of agreements, decisions by associations of undertakings or concerted practices which may affect trade between Member States but which do not restrict

6. In the ECJ's words, '[c]onsequently, *and so long as a regulation adopted pursuant to Article 87(2)(e) of the Treaty has not provided otherwise*, national authorities may take action against an agreement in accordance with their national law, even when an examination of the agreement from the point of view of its compatibility with Community law is pending before the Commission, subject however to the condition that the application of national law may not prejudice the full and uniform application of Community law or the effects of measures taken or to be taken to implement it.', *see ibid.*, para. 9, emphasis added.
7. *See* Proposal for a Council Regulation on the implementation of the rules on competition laid down in Articles 81 and 82 of the Treaty and amending Regulations (EEC) No. 1017/68, (EEC) No 2988/74, (EEC) No. 4056/86 and (EEC) No. 3975/87 ('Regulation implementing Articles 81 and 82 of the Treaty'), OJ C 365E, 19.12.2000, pp. 284-296.
8. *See* Council Regulation (EC) No. 1/2003 of 16 December 2002 on the implementation of the rules on competition laid down in Articles 81 and 82 of the Treaty, OJ L 1, 4.1.2003, pp. 1-25.

competition within the meaning of Article 81(1) of the Treaty, or which fulfil the conditions of Article 81(3) of the Treaty or which are covered by a Regulation for the application of Article 81(3) of the Treaty. Member States shall not under this Regulation be precluded from adopting and applying on their territory stricter national laws which prohibit or sanction unilateral conduct engaged in by undertakings.

3. Without prejudice to general principles and other provisions of Community law, paragraphs 1 and 2 do not apply when the competition authorities and the courts of the Member States apply national merger control laws, nor do they preclude the application of provisions of national law that predominantly pursue an objective different from that pursued by Articles 81 and 82 of the Treaty.

Article 3 is not an easy read. On the one hand, Article 3(1) and the first sentence of Article 3(2) work towards convergence. Article 3(1) requires that national competition authorities and national courts apply national competition law in parallel with EU competition law if the agreement or abuse affects trade between Member States. And the first sentence of Article 3(2) embodies a hard rule that prevents national competition law from prohibiting agreements that do not infringe Article 101(1) of the Treaty on the Functioning of the European Union (TFEU).

On the other hand, the second sentence of Article 3(2) and (3) work towards divergence. Both sentences embody exceptions.[9] Article 3(2) says that Member States can apply stricter national laws in relation to unilateral conduct by undertakings. Article 3(3) permits the application of national laws that predominantly pursues an objective different from that pursued by Articles 101 and 102 TFEU.

Different interpretations have been submitted in regard to the meaning of both exceptions. One thesis is that these legislative exceptions allow for more internal market fragmentation than the judicial arrangement in place since *Walt Wilhelm*, which did not provide any exception regarding the adoption or application of stricter national rules on unilateral conduct.

That reading, however, rests on a strong legal assumption. The assumption is that Article 3 insulates specific national rules from the displacing effects of the principle of primacy of EU law. The problem with the assumption lies in the fact that it is far from unanimous that Article 3 – more generally a provision of secondary law – can modulate the *primacy* of Articles 101 and 102 TFEU – more generally of provisions of primary law.

Still debated to this day, the issue of the appropriate reading of Article 3 of Regulation 1/2003 requires a reexamination. The text of Article 3 is so convoluted that it may be one of the most cryptic provisions of the EU competition law system. This paper seeks help in the explanatory power of the constitutional law doctrine of pre-emption to shed light on the legal significance of Article 3.[10]

9. We refer to these rules as 'exceptions' because they are drafted as such. As we will see, the precise content of these exceptions is the subject of much debate.
10. On the doctrine of pre-emption and EU law, *see generally* Robert Schütze, *Supremacy Without Pre-emption? The Very Slowly Emergent Doctrine of Community Pre-emption*, 43 Common Market Law Review 1023 (2006) and Amedeo Arena, *The Twin Doctrines of Primacy and Pre-Emption*,

The chapter starts by considering the scope of Article 3, determining which national rules are regulated by Article 3(2) and (3) (section 2). The paper then construes Article 3 through the lenses of the doctrine of pre-emption (section 3). As will be seen, reading Article 3 through a pre-emption lens not only clarifies the situations covered in the provision but also yields interesting practical consequences.

2 THE SCOPE OF ARTICLE 3 OF REGULATION 1/2003

Article 3 is a difficult provision. The text uses vague, abstract and imprecise words. What is meant, for instance, by 'stricter' and 'national laws' or by national law that 'predominantly pursue an objective different from that pursued by Articles [101 and 102 TFEU]'? In addition, the text of Article 3(2) and (3) employs disconcertingly varying language. For example, Article 3(2) talks about 'adoption' and 'application' of national laws, when Article 3(3) only mentions 'application'. What legal significance should be attached to small variations between the two clauses?[11] Conventional methods of interpretation allow us to derive some general points concerning the proper interpretation of the situations covered by Article 3(2) and (3).

2.1 Which National Rules Are Covered by Article 3(2) and (3)?

The Article 3 exceptions allow for the application of certain national rules. The exception of Article 3(2) benefits to 'stricter national laws which prohibit or sanction unilateral conduct engaged in by undertakings'. And the exception of Article 3(3) safeguards 'national merger control laws' and 'provisions of national law that predominantly pursue an objective different from that pursued by Articles [101 and 102 TFEU]'.

Every lawyer confronted with the text of Article 3 will come away with questions. Is it for the Member States to decide which national rules are 'stricter' or pursue an objective 'predominantly different' from that pursued by Articles 101 and 102 TFEU? Is the concept of 'national laws' in Article 3(2) restricted to national *competition* laws? And how to say if national law pursues an objective 'predominantly different' from the one pursued by Articles 101 and 102 TFEU? We deal with all three questions in turn.

2.1.1 EU or Member State Power over the Article 3 Exceptions?

The question of who has the authority to decide whether a national law is stricter or pursues predominantly different objectives is critical. In a case against Facebook, the

---

in Oxford Principles of European Union Law: The European Union Legal Order: Volume I (Robert Schütze & Takis Tridimas eds, 2018).

11. Judicial guidance is, in this regard, scarce. *See*, for instance, Opinion of AG Trstenjak in Case C-484/08 *Caja de Ahorros y Monte de Piedad de Madrid*, 29.10.2009, ECLI:EU:C:2009:682; Opinion of AG Kokott in Case C-681/11 *Schenker & Co and Others*, 28.7.2013, ECLI:EU:C: 2013:126; Case T-466/17 *Printeos, SA and Others v. European Commission*, 24.9.2019, ECLI: EU:T:2019:671; and at the national level *Expedia Inc/Autorité de la concurrence e.a*, Cour de Cassation 10-14.881, 82011FR0510(01) (2011).

German Competition Authority (GCA) seized the authority to declare its national competition law 'stricter' than Article 102 TFEU, allowing itself to intervene below the threshold of unlawful abuse of dominance.[12]

A well-established interpretative principle of EU law states that 'the terms of a provision of [EU] law which makes no express reference to the law of the Member States *for the purpose of determining its meaning and scope* must normally be given an autonomous and uniform interpretation throughout the [EU]'.[13] The language chosen by the ECJ in this case law matters. Article 3 expressly mentions Member States' law. But there is no reference (or renvoi) to the legal order of the Member States to define the meaning and scope of 'stricter national laws' or 'provisions of national law that predominantly pursue an objective different from Articles [101 and 102 TFEU]'.[14]

In view of this interpretative principle, Article 3 regulates the application of the law of the Member States without '[deferring] to national authorities the task of classifying internal provisions in accordance to their primary goal [...]'.[15] Indeed, and contrary to what some authors appear to suggest,[16] the words 'stricter' or 'predominantly different' in Article 3 embody *autonomous concepts of EU law*.[17] Thus, classificatory authority over Article 3 is vested with the EU, not the Member States.[18] This means that any classification of national competition law as 'stricter' than Article 102 TFEU may be overruled by the ECJ.[19]

2.1.2 National (Competition) Laws

The next question is whether the Article 3(2) exception covers national laws stricter than EU competition law or only national *competition* laws. In concrete terms, the issue

12. *See* Decision of the German Competition Authority in Case B6-22/16 *Facebook*, para. 914. An English translation of this decision is available at http://www.bundeskartellamt.de/. *See also* Giuseppe Colangelo & Mariateresa Maggiolino, *Antitrust Über Alles: Whither Competition Law after Facebook?*, 42 World Competition 372-373 (2019). It is contested that the GCA was applying a national rule on unilateral conduct that was stricter than Article 102 TFEU. *See*, in this sense, Wouter Wils, *The Obligation for the Competition Authorities of the EU Member States to Apply EU Antitrust Law and the Facebook Decision of the Bundeskartellamt*, Concurrences Review 58 (2019).
13. *See* Case C-174/08 *NCC Construction Danmark A/S v. Skatteministeriet*, 29.10.2009, ECLI: EU:C:2009:669, para. 24, emphasis added. The principle is based on the need for the uniform application of EU law and the principle of equality.
14. An example of such type of reference can be found, for instance, in Article 2(2) of Council Framework Decision 2002/584/JHA of 13 June 2002 on the European arrest warrant and the surrender procedures between Member States, OJ L 190, 1872002, pp. 1-20; *see also* Case C-303/05 *Advocaten voor de Wereld VZW v. Leden van de Ministerraad* 3.5.2007, ECLI: EU:C:2007:261, paras 51-52.
15. *See* Lúcio Tomé Feiteira (2016), p. 63.
16. *Ibid.*
17. These are concepts with an 'independent meaning of legal terms which is distinct from those established in domestic legal orders'. Valsamis Mitsilegas, *Autonomous Concepts, Diversity Management and Mutual Trust in Europe's Area of Criminal Justice*, 57 Common Market Law Review 46 (2020).
18. *See*, for instance, Case 113/80 *Commission v. Ireland*, 17.6.1981, ECLI:EU:C:1981:139, para. 7.
19. Interestingly, the issue has not been raised in pending proceedings before the ECJ concerning the *Facebook* decision of the GCA. *See* Opinion of AG Rantos in Case C-252/21 *Meta Platforms and Others (Conditions générales d'utilisation d'un réseau social)*, 20.9.2022 ECLI:EU:C:2022:704.

is whether Article 3(2) intends to safeguard Member States' power to apply national laws against abuse of economic dependence, prohibiting resale below cost or at a loss, etc., or whether Article 3(2) simply wants to allow the Member States to develop a stricter application of national competition law in relation to unilateral conduct.

The problem here stems from an ambiguity in the text of Article 3(2). The title of Article 3 and the first part of Article 3(2) uses the narrower concept of 'national competition law(s)'. The second part of Article 3(2) uses the broader concept of 'national laws'.

Several interpretive indicia support that the Article 3(2) exception applies only to national competition laws.[20] First, the title of Article 3 refers to the relationship between Articles 101 and 102 TFEU and 'national competition laws'. Second, Recital 8 of Regulation 1/2003 explicitly references stricter national *competition* laws on unilateral conduct.[21]

Whichever answer is right, the difficulty remains, in part, rather formalistic. To take a concrete example, a national law against abuse of economic dependence may be called a 'competition law' in one Member State and something else in another. In France, legal academics refer to laws against abuse of economic dependence as the '*petit droit de la concurrence*'. In Belgium, legal academics consider the same rules to belong to unfair trading laws. If form conditions the application of the Article 3(2) exception, discrepancies amongst Member States are predictable.

The better answer, therefore, consists in considering that Article 3(2) applies to all 'national competition laws', including statutes that do not come labelled as 'competition law'. The key then is to determine when a national rule can be considered a national competition rule. The ECN + Directive defines national competition rules as provisions of national law that 'predominantly pursue the same objective as Articles 101 and 102 TFEU'.[22] To determine whether a national rule predominantly pursues the same (or different) objective as Article 101 and 102 TFEU becomes, as such, key to both the interpretation of Article 3(2) and (3).

2.1.3 To Predominantly Pursue an Objective Different from Articles 101 and 102 TFEU

The question of what constitutes an objective 'predominantly different' from Articles 101 and 102 TFEU is harder. Since the early years of EU competition law, a substantial

20. *See*, in this sense, Eddy De Smijter & Alisa Sinclair, *The Relationship Between EU Competition Law and National Competition Law*, in: *Faull & Nikpay: The EU Law of Competition* (Jonathan Faull, Ali Nikpay, & Deirdre Taylor eds, 2014), p. 109.
21. Recitals may help clarify the content of an act. Koen Lenaerts & Piet Van Nuffel, *European Union Law* (Robert Bray & Nathan Cambien eds, 2011), p. 814. At the same time, the preamble to an EU act has no binding legal force. It cannot, in particular, be relied on either as a ground for derogating from the actual provisions of the act in question or interpreting those provisions in a manner clearly contrary to their wording. *See*, for instance, Case C-136/04 *Deutsches Milch-Kontor*, 24.11.2005, ECLI:EU:C:2005:716, para. 32.
22. *See* Article 2(1)(6) of Directive 2019/1 of the European Parliament and of the Council of 11 December 2018 to empower the competition authorities of the Member States to be more effective enforcers and to ensure the proper functioning of the internal market, OJ L 11, 14.1.2019, pp. 3-33.

debate over the objectives of Articles 101 and 102 TFEU has taken place.[23] To this day, the debate is still unresolved. As often, legal scholarship has tended to obfuscate more than clarify the issue of the concrete objectives of Articles 101 and 102 TFEU.

A close reading of the statutory text throws light on the purposes of Article 101 and 102 TFEU. Recital 9 of Regulation 1/2003 states that 'Articles [101 and 102 TFEU] have as their objective the protection of competition on the market'. Additionally, when exemplifying the type of rules that predominantly pursue an objective different from that pursued by Articles 101 and 102 TFEU, Recital 9 finds that '[s]uch legislation pursues a specific objective, irrespective of the actual or presumed effects of such acts on competition on the market'.

Accordingly, the difference between a rule that predominantly pursues the same objective as Articles 101 and 102 TFEU and one that does not hinge on the following question: is the primary purpose of the law to *protect competition on the market*? Words matter here. 'Protect' does not mean 'promote'. And the reference to 'competition on the market' invites us to think more of protecting competitors, compared to the protection of other business units like customers or suppliers.

If the answer is yes, the rule predominantly pursues the same objective as Articles 101 and 102 TFEU. National rules concerning resale below cost fall within this category. If the answer is no, the rule pursues a function distinct from Articles 101 and 102 TFEU. National rules on unfair trading practices fall within this category.[24]

2.2 Examples of National Rules Regulated by Article 3(2) and (3)

Most national rules that benefit from the Article 3 exceptions set forth in Article 3 do not refer expressly to this provision.[25] The preamble to Regulation 1/2003 and a Staff Working Paper from the Commission provide some authoritative illustrations.[26]

23. For a recent literature review and empirical analysis of the evolution of the goals of EU competition law *see* Konstantinos Stylianou & Marios Iacovides, *The Goals of EU Competition Law: A Comprehensive Empirical Investigation*, Legal Studies (2022).
24. More recently, the case law added further clarification. In *bpost*, the ECJ drew a line between the objective of promoting competition followed by sector-specific regulation and the objective of protecting competition from private and public distortions pursued by Articles 101 and 102 TFEU. *See* Case C-117/20 *bpost*, 22.3.2022, ECLI:EU:C:2022:202. The ECJ was called to determine whether the principle of *non bis in idem* precluded an undertaking from being sanctioned for abuse of dominance where, on the same facts, it had already been sanctioned for breach of sectoral rules on postal services. The ECJ found that the two sets of rules pursued distinct objectives. For the ECJ, the sectoral rules pursue the objective of liberalising the internal market for postal services. By contrast, Articles 101 and 102 TFEU pursue the objective of ensuring that competition is not distorted in that market. It remains to be clarified whether, for the ECJ, the rules on liberalisation pursue an objective different from those pursued by Articles 101 and 102 TFEU *predominantly*. *See bpost*, paras. 45-46. Also, whether this type of rule could be qualified as national rules, to begin with, as they result from the transpositions of directives. On this point, *see* Eddy De Smijter & Alisa Sinclair (2014), pp. 111-112.
25. There are some outliers, as the *Facebook* decision of the GCA demonstrates in para. 914.
26. *See* Commission Staff Working Paper accompanying the Communication from the Commission to the European Parliament and Council - Report on the functioning of Regulation 1/2003 - COM(2009)206 final, (2009).

Additionally, authors have contributed to this exercise by providing additional evidence of national rules falling within the scope of the exceptions provided for in Article 3.

2.2.1 *Stricter National Laws Which Prohibit or Sanction Unilateral Conduct Engaged in by Undertakings*

The word 'stricter' in Article 3(2) is a comparative adjective. The object of comparison is Article 102 TFEU. Thus, the national rules regulated by Article 3(2) can be construed as rules that, compared to Article 102 TFEU, provide a stricter definition of abuse, a more stringent approach to market power or tougher sanctions.[27]

Within this category, one finds three types of laws:

(1) laws concerning economic dependence and similar situations which aim, for example, at '[regulating] disparities of bargaining power in distribution relationships' without a requirement of dominance;[28]
(2) laws on resale below cost or at a loss, which draw inspiration from predatory pricing rules without a requirement of dominance;
(3) laws that declare abusive practices which are not deemed abusive under Article 102 TFEU, like an abrupt termination of a contractual relationship, without a requirement of indispensability.

New examples of such rules have mushroomed in the digital sector. For example, Germany introduced a section 19a) to its competition act, intended to deal specifically with new forms of abusive conduct by firms of 'paramount significance for competition across markets'.[29] Similarly, new rules prohibiting the abuse of economic dependence have recently entered into force in Belgium,[30] a development that was welcomed by the Belgium Minister of Economic Affairs for its potential application to e-commerce platforms.[31]

2.2.2 *Provisions of National Law That Predominantly Pursue an Objective Different from That Pursued by Articles 101 and 102 TFEU*

The universe of rules that can be included in the category of laws that predominantly pursue an objective different from that pursued by Articles 101 and 102 TFEU is bigger

27. *See* Lúcio Tomé Feiteira (2016), p. 65.
28. *See* Commission Staff Working Paper accompanying the Communication from the Commission to the European Parliament and Council – Report on the functioning of Regulation 1/2003 – COM(2009) 206 final, (2009), para. 162.
29. An English translation of the German Competition Act is available at https://www.bundeskartellamt.de/.
30. *See* Arrêté Royal, of 31 July 2020, Modifiant les livres Ier et IV du Code de droit économique en ce qui concerne les abus de dépendance économique. Interestingly, no express reference to Article 3(2) of Regulation 1/2003 is found in the recitals of this statute.
31. *See* Marc Wiggers, Thomas Verstraeten & Robin Struijlaart, *New Rules Prohibiting the Abuse of Economic Dependence Entered into Force in Belgium on 22 August 2020: What Does This Mean for the Digital Sector?*, Kluwer Competition Law Blog (2020).

than that of stricter rules on unilateral conduct. For this reason, no aprioristic categorisation is available for the rules falling in the situation covered in Article 3(3). Recital 9 of the preamble to Regulation 1/2003 refers to 'legislation that prohibits or imposes sanctions on acts of unfair trading practice, be they unilateral or contractual'.[32] However, most laws in the Member States' legal systems will either exclusively or predominantly pursue an objective different from that pursued by Articles 101 and 102 TFEU.

3 ARTICLE 3 OF REGULATION 1/2003 AND THE DOCTRINE OF PRE-EMPTION

There is a debate on the effect of Article 3 in cases of conflict between EU competition law and national rules. The debate boils down to differing views about the application of the principle of primacy of EU law. Some authors - we may call them the literalists - claim that the text of Regulation 1/2003 'leaves the primacy rule untouched' when trade between Member States is affected.[33] Article 3(2) states that nothing 'in [Regulation 1/2003]' precludes Member States from adopting and applying stricter national rules on unilateral conduct. It does not say that Articles 101 and 102 TFEU do not apply. Similarly, Article 3(3) only exempts merger laws and provisions of national law that predominantly pursue an objective different from that pursued by Articles 101 and 102 TFEU from the application of Article 3(1) and (2). Additionally, Article 3(3) begins by stating that its application is '[w]ithout prejudice to general principles and other provisions of [EU] law', which includes the principle of primacy.[34]

Other commentators - we may call them the constructivists - disagree. In their opinion, the Article 3 exceptions insulate national rules from the primacy principle in regard to Articles 101 and 102 TFEU.[35] The argument builds on Article 103 TFEU, which contemplates the possibility of secondary legislation to determine the relationship between national laws and EU competition law.[36] Therefore, EU law embodies a

32. These rules 'prohibit undertakings from imposing on their trading partners, obtaining or attempting to obtain from them terms and conditions that are unjustified, disproportionate or without consideration'. *See* Recital 9 of the preamble of Regulation 1/2003. This is the only type of rule referred to in Recital 9 as an example of national rules that predominantly pursue an objective different from that pursued by Articles 101 and 102 TFEU.
33. *See*, in this sense, Eddy De Smijter & Alisa Sinclair (2014), p. 108. Other authors refer, more ambiguously, to Article 3(2) as 'implying' the application of the principle of primacy or to Article 3 as 'an expression' of this principle, *see*, in this sense, David J. Gerber & Paolo Cassinis, *The 'Modernisation' of European Community Competition Law: Achieving Consistency in Enforcement – Part I*, 27 European Competition Law Review 13 (2006); and Felix Müller, *The New Council Regulation (EC) No. 1/2003 on the Implementation of the Rules on Competition*, 5 German Law Journal 721 (2004), p. 731.
34. *See*, in this sense, Laurence Idot, *Le nouveau système communautaire de mise en œuvre des Articles 81 et 82 CE (Règlement 1/2003 et projets de textes d'application)*, Cahiers de Droit Européen 89 (2003), p. 304.
35. *See*, in this sense, Marek Szydlo, *Leeway of Member States in Shaping the Notion of an Undertaking in Competition Law*, 33 World Competition 549 (2010), pp. 557-559.
36. *See*, in this sense, Chris Townley & Alexander H. Türk, *The Constitutional Limits of EU Competition Law: United in Diversity*, 64 The Antitrust Bulletin 235 (2019), p. 282. Against, *see*

competition law system that tolerates possible modulations to the primacy of Articles 101 and 102 TFEU.

One way out of this discussion consists in approaching the issue from a different descriptive route. Instead of looking at Article 3 through the lenses of primacy, we now consider its 'twin doctrine': pre-emption.[37]

3.1 The Doctrine of Pre-emption

The doctrine of pre-emption is a federal theory of normative conflict developed in United States (US) constitutional law.[38] The idea underpinning pre-emption is that, acting in accordance with the federal constitution, the federal lawmaker is generally free to determine to what extent it wishes to pre-empt state law.[39] Pre-emption is not interested in whether EU law can evict national law - this is taken for granted.[40] Pre-emption is interested in understanding when national law is evicted - this cannot be conjectured a priori.[41]

For the purposes of the analysis of Article 3, the doctrine of pre-emption brings an important insight: a conflict between a national rule and Articles 101 and 102 TFEU does not necessarily mean that the EU rules will win. Primacy is contingent on pre-emption, and the extent of pre-emption depends on the model of pre-emption chosen by the EU legislature.

The ECJ case law embodies several categories of pre-emption.[42] Arena identifies three main categories.[43] Under *rule pre-emption*, the ECJ verifies whether the national rule contradicts the substantive content of the EU rule. Under *obstacle pre-emption*, the assessment is more abstract. The ECJ verifies whether the national rule hinders the attainment of the objectives of the EU rule. Finally, under *field pre-emption*, the ECJ will only verify whether the EU legislature has exercised a 'jurisdictional veto' by determining that no national rule can apply if EU law applies.

In short, pre-emption determines when primacy operates. This doctrine describes, thus, how normative conflict between federal and state rules is not always

---

Mariana Tavares, *A Constitutional Analysis of Multijurisdictional Conflicts in the EU Legal Order Confirms That Diversity Is Possible in EU Competition Law*, Thesis, King's College London, 2018, p. 55.

37. *See* Amedeo Arena (2018).
38. For a constitutional history of the doctrine of pre-emption in US law, *see* Stephen A Gardbaumt, *The Nature of Preemption*, 79 Cornell Law Review 785-807 (1994). In EU law, this theory has been imported by authors such as Schütze to explain the ECJ's case law on the principle of primacy. *See* the seminal article Robert Schütze (2006).
39. *See*, in this sense, Robert Schütze, *European Constitutional Law* (2021), p. 216.
40. As Hoke put it, primacy does not determine 'what constitutes a conflict between state and federal law; it merely serves as a traffic cop, mandating a federal law's survival instead of a state's law'. *See* S Candice Hoke, *Preemption Pathologies and Civil Republican Values*, 71 Boston University Law Review 755 (1991).
41. *See* Robert Schütze (2006), pp. 1023-1024.
42. As Arena explains, each category of pre-emption corresponds to the 'analytical paradigm the ECJ employs to ascertain whether the national norm is incompatible with the EU norm'. *See* Amedeo Arena (2018), p. 327.
43. *See ibid.*

decided in 'all or nothing' logic. The federal constitution can determine different modalities of pre-emption for different types of rules. Further, the federal constitution can empower the federal legislature to establish certain pre-emption arrangements for certain areas of law. This insight that has been missing in discussions over the interpretation of Article 3 is now looked at.

3.2 EU Competition Law and Pre-emption

The EU treaties provide for a default constitutional model of *field pre-emption* with respect to competition rules (i), while at the same time empowering the EU legislature to define its own model of pre-emption for the same rules (ii).

3.2.1 Constitutional Pre-emption

Since the Lisbon Treaty, *field pre-emption* has constituted the default model for establishing the competition rules necessary for the functioning of the internal market. The Lisbon Treaty introduced Article 3(1)(b) TFEU, which defines as an area of exclusive competence of the EU 'the establishing of the competition rules necessary for the functioning of the internal market'. And according to Article 2(1) TFEU, Member States can only adopt binding acts if so empowered by the EU within the scope of exclusive competences of the EU. In the absence of an EU act empowering Member States to adopt competition rules, primacy will displace most rules within the field of application of Articles 101 and 102 TFEU.

The logical consequence to draw from the Lisbon Treaty is that Member States cannot adopt national competition laws without a prior empowering EU act. An obvious difficulty with this reading is that most Member States had, and still have, after the Lisbon Treaty, enacted national competition laws. So, can national competition laws ever exist under the Lisbon Treaty? There is little doubt that the answer is yes. Regulation 1/2003 premises the existence of national competition laws on more than one occasion. Regulation 1/2003 thus appears to supply the empowering act that allows Member States to adopt national competition laws.[44]

3.2.2 Legislative Pre-emption

Empowerment of Member States competition laws by the EU is made possible by Article 103 TFEU. Under Article 103 TFEU, the Council can adopt '[t]he appropriate

44. Of course, Regulation 1/2003 predates the Lisbon reform, which introduced the competence rules in Articles 2(1) and 3(1)(b) TFEU. Trying to read this regulation in light of a posterior treaty reform amounts to a form of 'legal contortion', as Monti put it. *See* Giorgio Monti, *New Directions in EC Competition Law, in* European Union Law for the Twenty-First Century: Rethinking the New Legal Order (Takis Tridimas & Paolisa Nebbia eds, 2004), p. 179. Yet, according to the case law, secondary law – such as Regulation 1/2003 – must be interpreted, so far as possible, in a manner which is compatible with primary law – such as Articles 2(1) and 3(1)(b) TFEU. *See*, for instance, Case C-518/16 *ZPT AD*, 28.2.2018, ECLI:EU:C:2018:126, para. 29.

regulations or directives to give effect to the principles set out in Articles 101 and 102 [TFEU]'.

Further, Article 103 TFEU states that such regulations or directives shall be designed in particular to 'determine the relationship between national laws and the provisions contained in [Articles 101 to 106 TFEU] or adopted pursuant to [Article 103]'.

Article 103 TFEU constitutes, as such, a tool of pre-emption design, allowing the Council to decide the extent to which national rules are displaced by Articles 101 and 102 TFEU.[45] The originality of Article 103 TFEU is that it allows the Council to adjust the pre-emptive capacity of treaty provisions, Articles 101 and 102 TFEU. It is more frequent, in EU law, to witness a similar arrangement in regard to secondary law provisions.[46]

Article 103 TFEU constitutes the legal basis of Regulation 1/2003. And the EU legislature used it to establish a legislative model of pre-emption, regulating the extent to which EU competition rules will displace national competition rules.

3.3. Choice of Model of Pre-emption in EU Competition Law

3.3.1 From a Judicial Model of Rule Pre-emption

Pre-emption tells us when there is normative conflict and, thus, when EU competition rules will prevail and when they will not. Until the entry into force of Regulation 1/2003, the model of pre-emption that prevailed was one of *rule pre-emption*.[47] The ECJ

45. One limitation of Article 103 TFEU as a legal base for a legislative model of rule pre-emption relates to the principle of conferral. Pursuant to the principle of conferral, the EU can act only within the limits of the competences conferred upon it by the Member States in the treaties to attain the objectives set out therein. *See* Article 5(2) Treaty on the European Union (TEU). Article 103 TFEU only allows the Council to determine the relationship between national rules and EU competition rules. This excludes other EU rules, such as free movement provisions. Indeed, under the principle of primacy, stricter national rules on unilateral conduct may be disapplied in case of conflict with a provision of EU law other than Articles 101 and 102 TFEU. The application of the Czech Significant Market Power Act provides an example of this. Some have described this national law as discriminatory against foreign retailers, as these economic operators are more easily covered by the personal scope defined by the notion of significant market power. *See* Doris Hildebrand, *Article 3 (2) in fine: Time for review*, Concurrences Review (2015). Consequently, such national rules may conflict with free movement provisions and, for this reason, be displaced according to the principle of primacy.
46. In this respect, other legal bases fulfil a similar function as Article 103 TFEU. In the case of minimum harmonisation measures, Member States can introduce measures that go against the uniform application of the EU rule without primacy displacing those national rules. In fact, the approach of the EU legislature in Article 3 with respect to Article 102 TFEU resembles one of minimum harmonisation. Article 102 TFEU is, in this sense, the minimum liability threshold. Member States cannot hinder the uniform application of this treaty provision by introducing more lenient rules, but they may do so with respect to stricter rules.
47. Other national rules that do not qualify as national competition rules would (and continue to), through the application of the principle of sincere cooperation, occasionally be subject by the ECJ to a framework of *obstacle pre-emption*. In this sense, *see* Amadeo Arena (2018), p. 339. Some of these cases concerned national rules with anti-competitive effects that were liable to deprive Articles 101 and 102 TFEU of their *substantive* effectiveness. *See*, for instance, Case

confirmed this model in a line of cases that followed *Walt Wilhelm*. In a rule pre-emption model, the relationship between EU competition law and national law is considered on a case-by-case basis in the presence of a clear normative conflict. In several cases, the ECJ clarified, for instance, that the application of national competition rules could not lead to the prohibition of conduct benefiting from an Article 101(3) TFEU exemption granted in an individual decision or recognised in a regulation.[48]

3.3.2 *To a Legislative Model of Field Pre-emption*

The Commission's proposal in the procedure for the adoption of Regulation 1/2003 broke away from the judicial model of rule pre-emption. The Commission advanced a legislative model of *field pre-emption*. Articles 101 and 102 TFEU would apply to 'the exclusion of national competition laws'. The Commission proposed that any national competition rule covering conduct caught within the field of application of the EU competition rules would automatically be set aside in accordance with the principle of primacy. As such, no concrete or abstract assessment of normative conflict would have to be conducted. The difference, in other words, lies in the fact that no conflict between the national and EU competition rules must occur in a particular case for primacy to operate and displace national competition rules.

3.3.3 *To a Legislative Model of Rule Pre-emption*

The Council rejected the Commission's model of field pre-emption. Member States were, however, divided on which national rules should be pre-empted in case of parallel application of national and EU competition law. They also did not want to leave the resolution of conflict cases entirely to the ECJ, as had been the case under the judicial model of rule pre-emption of the past.

In the end, the Member States opted to reaffirm a model of *rule pre-emption*, codifying it through a specific legislative framework.[49] The selected design of rule pre-emption does not, however, correspond to the one that had prevailed since *Walt Wilhelm*.[50] In a departure from the prevailing model of judicial pre-emption, the Council specified in the text of Regulation 1/2003 situations that constitute conflict between national law and Articles 101 and 102 TFEU. Unfortunately, the text of

---

13-77 *INNO v. ATAB*, 16.11.1977, EU:C:1977:185 and, generally, Rene Joliet, *National Anti-competitive Legislation and Community Law European Community Law*, 12 Fordham International Law Journal 163 (1988). Other cases concerned rules, such as rules on limitation periods, liable to deprive Articles 101 and 102 TFEU of their *procedural* effectiveness. *See*, for instance, Joined Cases C-295/04 to C-298/04 *Manfredi*, 13.7.2006, ECLI:EU:C:2006:461.

48. *See*, e.g., Joined Cases 253/78 and 1 to 3/79 *Procureur de la République and others v. Bruno Giry and Guerlain SA* and others, 10.7.1980, EU:C:1980:188, para. 17.
49. This was something that the ECJ foresaw and accepted as early as *Walt Wilhelm*. *See supra* n. 6.
50. In fact, in the absence of the exceptions in Article 3, Article 3(1), alone could be construed, by the ECJ, as favouring a broader scope of rule pre-emption, where more types of national rules, such as stricter rules on unilateral conduct, could be found to conflict with Articles 101 and 102 TFEU.

Regulation 1/2003 does not engage in a very explicit form of codification. The following situations appear, directly or indirectly, to be considered conflict cases in the statute:

- [Adoption or application of] national competition rules that prohibit agreements, decisions by associations of undertakings or concerted practices within the meaning of Article 101(1) TFEU which may affect trade between Member States but which do not restrict competition within the meaning of Article 101(1) TFEU;
- [Adoption or application of] national competition rules that prohibit agreements, decisions by associations of undertakings or concerted practices within the meaning of Article 101(1) TFEU, which may affect trade between Member States but fulfil the conditions of Article 101(3) of the TFEU;
- [Adoption or application of] national competition rules that prohibit agreements, decisions by associations of undertakings or concerted practices within the meaning of Article 101(1) TFEU which may affect trade between Member States but which are exempted by a regulation for the application of Article 101(3) TFEU;
- [Adoption or application of] national competition rules on unilateral conduct engaged in by undertakings, that are more lenient that Article 102 TFEU.

By contrast, Article 3(2) reputes the following situation as not conflicting with Articles 101 and 102 TFEU:

- [Adoption or application of] national competition rules on unilateral conduct engaged in by undertakings, that are stricter than Article 102 TFEU.

Last, situations of conflict with other national rules, including those that predominantly pursue an objective different from that pursued by Articles 101 and 102 TFEU, are to be dealt with under the previous judicial arrangement on a case-by-case basis.[51]

One significant feature of Article 3 is that the ECJ is no longer the only institution setting the boundaries of the rule pre-emption model that regulates the relationship between national competition rules and Articles 101 and 102 TFEU since the Rome Treaty. The Council, acting as a federal lawmaker, also has a say.

3.4 Extent of Legislative Rule Pre-emption

In a literalist interpretation, the extent of legislative pre-emption cannot go beyond the text of Regulation 1/2003. Or put differently, the exception in Article 3(2) might be limited to situations of application of Articles 101 and 102 TFEU arising under

51. As these rules are not 'competition rules necessary for the functioning of the internal market', they are not caught by the residual constitutional model of field pre-emption under Articles 2(1) and 3(1)(b) TFEU. Further, as will be explained in the next subsections, these rules are only subject to a limited procedural exception under Article 3(3).

Regulation 1/2003.[52] For example, Article 3(2) operates when the Commission adopts an inapplicability decision under Article 10 of Regulation 1/2003, finding that a conduct does not amount to an abuse of dominance under Article 102 TFEU. In such a case, stricter national rules on unilateral conduct can apply. Assume, by contrast, that the ECJ reaches the same conclusion but in a referral under Article 267 TFEU. Here, the exception in Article 3(2) would not operate to safeguard the application of the stricter national rule on unilateral conduct.

Is a literalist reading of legislative rule pre-emption correct? We believe the main criticism of a literalist construction is to turn a blind eye to established principles of interpretation that must be considered when applying EU secondary law.

First, the text of Article 3 itself says that the exceptions in Article 3(3) are 'without prejudice to general principles and other provisions of [EU] law'. No similar statement is made in regard to the exception in Article 3(2). The omission allows the inference that the lawmaker intended to limit the application of some of the general principles of EU law, such as primacy, in Article 3(2).

Besides, preparatory works (or *travaux préparatoires*) go against such literal reading. Fundamental differences exist between the Commission's proposal and the final text of Regulation 1/2003. The Commission wanted to exclude the application of 'national competition laws' without any verification of conflict with EU competition law. Rejecting field pre-emption, the Council adopted a model of rule pre-emption, drafted through the use of exceptions. It is settled case law that the Council's reading prevails.[53]

Finally, secondary law must be interpreted in a way that does not render it meaningless.[54] An interpretation of Article 3(2) that would limit its application to certain procedural contexts would limit its effectiveness considerably. That interpretation would be at odds with the legislative compromise reached with the adoption of Regulation 1/2003. The concerns of the Member States that pushed for the exceptions were not procedural but substantive. Study of the legislative record – in what has become known as the Belgian compromise – shows that '[s]ome Member States were indeed keen to preserve some of their specificities in condemning, for instance, abuses of "economic dependence" or of "essential facilities"'.[55]

---

52. According to the text of Article 3(2) 'Member States shall not *under this Regulation* be precluded from adopting and applying on their territory stricter national laws which prohibit or sanction unilateral conduct engaged in by undertakings' (emphasis added).
53. Preparatory works gain interpretive weight when combined with a *a contrario* argument. *See*, for instance, Case C-17/96 *Badische Erfrischungs-Getränke GmbH & Co KG v. Land Baden-Württemberg*, 17.7.1997, ECLI:EU:C:1997:381 paras 16-17 and, generally, Koen Lenaerts & José A. Gutierrez-Fons, *Les Méthodes d'Interprétation de la Cour de Justice de l'Union Européenne* (2020), p. 52. As such, where the Council deviates from the Commission's proposal, the resulting act should not be interpreted contrary to the position of the final decision-maker.
54. *See*, for instance, Case C-439/08 *VEBIC*, 07.12.2010, ECLI:EU:C:2010:739.
55. *See* Koen Lenaerts & Damien Gerard, *Decentralisation of EC Competition Law Enforcement: Judges in the Frontline*, 27 World Competition 313 (2004), note 38.

3.5 Why Article 3(3) Contains Only a Limited Procedural Exception

Labouring under an erroneous reading of Article 3(3), one could conclude that Member States are always permitted to adopt and apply national rules that predominantly pursue an objective different from Articles 101 and 102 TFEU.

This is not the model of pre-emption set forth in Regulation 1/2003. Contrary to the situation under Article 3(2), where the Council established by decree that there is no conflict between Articles 101 and 102 TFEU and stricter national rules on unilateral conduct, the Council did not safeguard national rules that predominantly pursue an objective different from that pursued by Articles 101 and 102 TFEU. These rules can still be found in conflict with EU competition rules and consequently, be disapplied by virtue of the principle of primacy.

Many interpretive indicia favour this reading of Article 3. The main one is the text of Article 3. The exception embodied in Article 3(3) says that Article 3(1) and (2) do not apply. It does not say that Articles 101 and 102 TFEU do not apply. This literal argument which proved insufficient for the interpretation of the Article 3(2) exception, finds support in further elements of interpretation when it comes to Article 3(3).

A study of the historical context further endorses this interpretation. The concerns of the Member States that pushed for the Article 3 exceptions related, in essence, to the possibility of maintaining in force or adopting stricter national rules on unilateral conduct.[56] Also, an alternative legislative model of rule pre-emption safeguarding laws that pursue predominantly different objectives would insulate too large a universe of national rules from the primacy of Articles 101 and 102 TFEU. This would potentially overturn an established body of case law concerning the principle of sincere cooperation.[57]

This means that, with respect to national rules that predominantly pursue an objective different from Articles 101 and 102 TFEU, Article 3(3) only maintains a limited procedural exception. Indeed, when it comes to such rules, Member States are not obliged to consider the possible application in tandem with Article 101 and 102 TFEU in every case - and as the case may be, to apply both laws in a convergent manner. Article 3(3) thus provides a limited procedural exception to the obligations of parallel application and convergence of national and EU competition rules set forth in Article 3(1) and (2).

But conflicts remain possible. Taking the example of national rules on unfair trading practices, if these rules hindered the effective and uniform application of Articles 101 and 102 TFEU, primacy would require their disapplication. Indeed, by contrast with Article 3(2), the text of Article 3(3) states that its exceptions are '[w]ithout prejudice to general principles and other provisions of [EU] law', which would include the principle of primacy.

---

56. *See ibid.*
57. For examples of this case law, *see* the examples in *supra* n. 46.

4 CONCLUSION

Article 3 of Regulation 1/2003 is a great example of legalese. This chapter has shown that some clarity of thought over the purpose and effect of Article 3 can be attained by recourse to the power of the constitutional law doctrine of pre-emption. Through a pre-emption lens, the law is clearer.

What do we know? Member States can maintain the application of stricter national competition laws on unilateral conduct in cases in which Articles 101 and 102 TFEU apply. And Member States can maintain the application of national laws pursuing predominantly different objectives in cases in which Articles 101 and 102 TFEU apply, within the limits of general principles of the EU law. With respect to the primacy of Articles 101 and 102 TFEU, Article 3(2) sets forth an unconditional exception. Article 3(3) provides a conditional one.

A policy debate has emerged about the Article 3 exceptions. If national law can prohibit business conduct permitted under EU law, the internal market will suffer fragmentation. As Cseres notes, there will be no level playing field providing for a single standard of assessment allowing undertakings 'to design EU-wide business strategies without having to check them against all the relevant national sets of competition rules'.[58] Rather, 'businesses wishing to engage in cross-border trade [have] to adapt their strategy and conduct based on the rules in force in different national territories'.[59]

The *Facebook* decision of the GCA illustrates the problem.[60] The national authority applied national competition law in a way that could be considered stricter than Article 102 TFEU.[61] A resurgence of nationalism and unilateralism in the field of competition law cannot be discarded. At the same time, the fragmentation of the internal market resulting from the application of Article 3 can be rationalised as the consequence of a process of experimentalist governance in EU law.[62] The idea is interesting, but it fails in so far as Regulation 1/2003 was never conceived as an experimentalist architecture, as can be seen from the lack of mechanisms and processes for feedback collection, benchmarking, etc.[63]

58. *See* Katalin Cseres, '*Comparing Laws in the Enforcement of EU and national Competition Laws*', 3 European Journal of Legal Studies 7 (2010), p. 15.
59. *See The Impact of National Rules on Unilateral Conduct that Diverge from Article 102 of the Treaty on the Functioning of the European Union (TFEU)* (2012), report commissioned by the Commission to the College of Europe and the Centre for European Policy Studies, on file with the authors.
60. *See Facebook. See also* Giuseppe Colangelo & Mariateresa Maggiolino (2019), pp. 372-373.
61. *See supra* n. 12.
62. For an account of the *Facebook* decision of the *Bundeskartellamt* in the context of experimentalist governance, *see* Yane Svetiev, *Experimentalist Competition Law and the Regulation of Markets* (2020), pp. 45-46.
63. On experimentalism as a type of governance in EU competition law, *see generally* Yane Svetiev, *Experimentalist Competition Law and the Regulation of Markets* (2020) and Giorgio Monti & Bernardo Rangoni, *Competition Policy in Action: Regulating Tech Markets with Hierarchy and Experimentalism*, 60 Journal of Common Market Studies 1106 (2022).

Whichever interpretation is right, the policy debate must take place on a firm descriptive footing. With this paper, we have tried to set the record straight. We leave to other contributions the role of evaluating the normative costs and benefits of a more or less expansive usage of the Article 3 exceptions.

CHAPTER 8

Experimentalist Governance in EU Antitrust: Possibilities and Limitations

Giorgio Monti[*]

1 INTRODUCTION

Modern European Union (EU) antitrust enforcement is based, in the main, on a hierarchical mode of governance. It may be seen in two contexts. First, when considering the relationship between the Commission and national competition authorities (NCAs): NCAs are expected to apply EU competition law in line with the policy orientations set by the Commission.[1] Just as national courts become EU courts when adjudicating on matters pertaining to EU law, so NCAs become EU enforcement bodies when applying Articles 101 and 102 Treaty on the Functioning of the European Union (TFEU). Second, when considering the role of remedies to be imposed on undertakings that infringe competition law, the Commission or NCAs can either direct undertakings to behave in a given manner or allow undertakings to design their own path to compliance which is either accepted or rejected by the Commission. The features of hierarchical governance are the following: (1) rules are set centrally; (2) local implementation is monitored by the centre; (3) revision of the rules occurs prospectively, when the Commission changes its policy orientation or new legislation is introduced.

In contrast, an experimentalist mode of governance contains the following characteristics: (1) the EU regulator sets out some general principles, (2) Member States or private parties are afforded discretion in the implementation of these general principles, (3) there is a review of their implementation experiences, which (4)

* This chapter is based on a presentation at the College of Europe on 25 March 2022. I am grateful for the comments of participants.

1. Case C-344/98 *Masterfoods Ltd v. HB Ice Cream Ltd.* paras 46 and 49.

regularly feeds into EU-level revisions of the general principles. The strength of this system is the capacity for learning which is afforded by the creation of a continuous feedback loop so that the rules at (1) are improved regularly as experience is gained from different experiences gathered when rules are implemented.[2]

Obviously some learning from experience is also possible in a hierarchical mode, as we will see in this chapter. The difference is that in an experimentalist mode, learning is built-in as a regular occurrence and revisions occur more quickly based on lessons learned.

This chapter considers the possibility of using an experimentalist mode of governance in the application of EU antitrust law. It is structured in the following way. First, an attempt is made to find examples of experimentalist governance in the relationship between the Commission and NCAs (section 2). Second, consideration is given to how experimentalism could be built into the design of remedies (section 3). In both discussions, it is shown that there are a number of current policy challenges where experimentalism might provide a useful mechanism for sharpening enforcement. However, we observe no trace of experimentalism applied in action in the way we have defined experimentalist governance above. Some examples come close, suggesting that the legal order is open to facilitate experimentation. In section 4 it is argued that there are a number of factors that indicate why this mode of governance is not widespread. Nevertheless, there may be new opportunities for developing experimentalism as a result of the coming into force of the Digital Markets Act (DMA). Furthermore, another dynamic might exist to stimulate the development of competition policy that is neither based on hierarchy nor on experimentalism: NCAs exercising policy leadership.

2 CAN WE FIND TRACES OF EXPERIMENTALIST GOVERNANCE IN EU COMPETITION LAW?

2.1 Experimentalism by the Commission

It might be argued that experimentalist governance has been facilitated by the operation of the European Competition Network (ECN).[3] It is widely recognised that while originally the ECN appeared to be just a network to facilitate the allocation of antitrust cases and ancillary processes for information sharing, it has developed into a policy network where NCAs discuss a range of contemporary challenges.[4] For example, the EU Merger Working Group was established to identify best practices in the

2. C.F. Sabel and J. Zeitlin, 'Learning from Difference: The New Architecture of Experimentalist Governance in the EU' (2008) 14 European Law Journal 271, C.F. Sabel and J. Zeitlin (eds), *Experimentalist Governance in the European Union: Towards a New Architecture* (Oxford, Oxford University Press, 2010).
3. Joint Statement of the Council and the Commission on the Functioning of the Network of Competition Authorities (2002, 15435/02 ADD 1).
4. W. Sauter, *Coherence in EU Competition Law* (Oxford, Oxford University Press, 2016) pp. 148-149. According to some scholars, this is a natural evolution of transnational networks. *See* A.-M. Slaughter, *A New World Order* (Princeton, NJ, Princeton University Press, 2004).

substantive and procedural assessment of mergers.[5] One might see the ECN as the place where reflections on different experiences are collected and a superior policy is designed for all NCAs to follow. In particular, it is recognised that cooperation is based 'on the basis of equality, respect and solidarity' and that the Commission 'has the ultimate *but not the sole* responsibility for developing policy and safeguarding efficiency and consistency'.[6] Such statements seem to give NCAs a role in shaping competition policy.

However, the legal structure for competition law enforcement found in Regulation 1/2003 places some barriers to experimentalism.[7] Article 3, for example, provides that when applying EU competition law, NCAs may not apply stricter national competition law unless the rules apply to unilateral conduct. Other national legislation that may prevent conduct that is otherwise authorised under Articles 101 or 102 TFEU may also be enforced, subject however to such rules not hindering the internal market. Conversely the European Court of Justice's (ECJ) case law provides that if conduct is prohibited by Articles 101 and 102, Member States may not authorise such conduct in the public interest save in limited circumstances.[8] The general approach is that national laws should not diverge from EU competition policy. The exceptions are designed to allow Member States to be different but there is no provision in the regulation by which these differences can lead to a rethinking of the scope of EU competition law.

Moreover, when NCAs apply EU competition law they have a duty to keep the Commission and NCAs informed about the process of the case. This gives the Commission the option to nudge NCAs into a particular interpretation of EU competition law and this happens under the sword of Damocles: pursuant to Article 11(6) the Commission can decide to relieve the NCA of a case and investigate this itself. This has happened in two instances where one might have expected that the NCA could have pioneered an innovative approach: the e-books case was started by the Office of Fair Trading (OFT) before it moved to the Commission.[9] The Spanish competition authority stopped its proceedings against Aspen when the Commission decided to investigate concerns about excessive pricing.[10] Granted, in both cases an EU-wide remedy was preferable given that the practices in question had an EU-wide effect.[11]

5. *See* the documents at: https://competition-policy.ec.europa.eu/mergers/national-competition-authorities/eu-merger-working-group_en.
6. ECN joint statement, *supra* n. 3 paras 7 and 9 respectively (emphasis added). Observe how this seems to run counter to the approach taken by the ECJ in *Masterfoods* (*supra* n. 1).
7. Regulation 1/2003, on the implementation of the rules on competition laid down in Articles 81 and 82 of the Treaty [2003] OJ L1/1.
8. Case C-198/01, *Consorzio Industrie Fiammiferi (CIF) v. Autorità Garante della Concorrenza e del Mercato* EU:C:2003:430; Case C-35/99, *Arduino* EU:C:2002:97.
9. Case COMP/39.847/E-Books (25 July 2013). A laconic press release by the OFT indicated that the case was no longer an enforcement priority because the Commission was well-placed to act (Office of Fair Trading, closed Competition Act 1998 case, 1 December 2011).
10. Case AT.40394 – Aspen (10 February 2021). For the closure, *see* Laboratorios Aspen, Resolución del Consejo (Expte. S/DC/0601/17), 20 July 2017.
11. This raises a different issue, which is why the EU insisted on NCAs applying EU competition law when they are only able to enforce the rules within their own jurisdiction. For discussion *see* Case C-151/20, *Bundeswettbewerbsbehörde v. Nordzucker AG*, EU:C:2021:681, Opinion of AG Bobek paras 72-87. This also supports the view that the Commission just wanted to control NCAs because they are now obliged to apply EU competition law under the supervision of the

When looking at specific policy fields, the absence of experimentalism is also found. For example the ECN discussed the design of leniency policies but tracing the process which led to the ECN publishing best practices suggests that the purpose of the exercise was to align national leniency policies to the EU standard. In 2009 an exercise was carried out to measure the degree of convergence among national leniency policies, leaving little space for appreciating differences.[12] Furthermore, the ECN+ Directive now codifies the Commission's leniency policy and requires Member States to transpose it into national law.[13] This episode, discussed in more detail elsewhere, shows that the ECN was used as a site to coordinate enforcement but not as a site for experimentalist governance.[14] Granted, the 2012 version of the Model Leniency Programme did provide that it would be reviewed based on the experience gained by ECN members.[15] However, it is impossible to discern an example where one NCA applied the leniency programme in a different manner, the results of such divergence were assessed, and the policy revised based on that experience.[16] Conversely, we find statements from NCAs indicating that they would rewrite their leniency policies in light of the new programme.[17] The mode of governance remained hierarchical.

When turning to substantive law, the assessment of price parity clauses by online platforms like booking.com seemed to provide an excellent basis for experimentalism. In brief, the majority of NCAs took the view that narrow price parity clauses would not restrict competition, but the German NCA took the view that even narrow price parity clauses were contrary to EU competition law. After these decisions, some Member States intervened to ban the use of price parity clauses by online hotel platforms.[18] This created a natural experiment where one could observe the impact of competition in jurisdictions where narrow price parity clauses were allowed and those where these were banned. An early study led to inconclusive results.[19] A more recent study suggested that eliminating wide price parity clauses serves to reduce prices but that banning narrow price parity clauses does not seem to yield greater pro-competitive

Commission even if at the end of the day they could have just applied national competition law and achieved the same result since most national laws replicate Articles 101 and 102 TFEU.

12. ECN Model Leniency Programme: Report on the Assessment of the State of Convergence (2006).
13. Directive 2019/1 to empower the competition authorities of the Member States to be more effective enforcers and to ensure the proper functioning of the internal market [2019] OJ L 11/3, Chapter VI.
14. Bernardo Rangoni and Giorgio Monti, 'Competition Policy in Action: Regulating Tech Markets with Hierarchy and Experimentalism' (2021) Journal of Common Market Studies, https://doi.org/10.1111/jcms.13304. For a more optimistic reading, *see* Y. Svetiev, *Experimentalist Competition Law and the Regulation of Markets* (London, Bloomsbury, 2020).
15. ECN Model Leniency Programme, As revised in November 2012, https://competition-policy.ec.europa.eu/system/files/2021-07/mlp_revised_2012_en.pdf.
16. For a different view, *see* Svetiev (*supra* n. 14), pp. 39-41. It is true that the Commission observes differences in national leniency policies, but it is not clear that there has been an assessment whether any of the national divergences were seen as worth being uploaded into the ECN's policy.
17. 'The Model Leniency Program may result in small adjustments to the NMa's leniency program.' Dutch NCA, Press Release 22 November 2012.
18. Market study on the distribution of hotel accommodation in the EU COMP/2020/OP/002 (2022), pp. 22-24.
19. Report on the monitoring exercise carried out in the online hotel booking sector by EU competition authorities in 2016.

effects.[20] Conversely, another study of a sample of hotels and their practices suggests that the most common form of price differentiation is when hotels offer a lower price on their website as compared to the prices set in an online travel agency like booking.com.[21] This suggests that banning all price parity clauses can be helpful in allowing hotels to reduce prices. It also tallies with a study written in support of the review of the EU's Vertical Block Exemption Regulation (VBER) which found that 'narrow MFN clauses limit competition in the hotel booking sector, and result in higher prices for consumers'.[22] It is perhaps also worth noting that prohibitions of price parity clauses have little deterrent effect. In Austria and Belgium laws ban price parity clauses and yet '23 % of Austrian and 28 % of Belgian independent hotels reported that their OTA contracts contained parity clauses, in line with the average for all the study countries (27 %)'.[23]

The result of these empirical assessments gives the Commission the tools to explore what the superior policy is: should one follow the German NCA and ban all price parity clauses or should one follow the views of other NCAs that only wide price parity clauses are a problem? Or is the evidence such that further experimentation is warranted? It is not clear the extent to which the evidence presented in these studies had an impact on the EU policy. Under the new version of the VBER 'the benefit of this Regulation should not apply to retail parity obligations causing buyers of online intermediation services not to offer, sell or resell goods or services to end users under more favourable conditions via competing online intermediation services'.[24] Thus narrow price parity clauses are exempted. In the Guidelines that accompany the VBER it is suggested that the benefit of the VBER may be withdrawn when narrow parity clauses are used in concentrated markets,[25] but there is limited experience on the criteria to be used by the Commission or an NCA on the amount of evidence required to justify a withdrawal of the exemption. Not all the studies point in the direction of this policy choice, however.

In sum, this episode reveals that the Commission observed national divergences and that it encouraged studies to explore the impact of these divergent policies on competition in order to assist it in designing a new policy. It is not entirely clear however whether the policy choice taken by the Commission is in line with the economic studies. Conversely, one might see the statements in the VBER and the Guidelines as an attempt to reconcile the position of a large number of NCAs, for which

20. S. Ennis, M. Ivaldi and V. Lagos, 'Price Parity Clauses for Hotel Room Booking: Empirical Evidence from Regulatory Change' (2020) https://www.tse-fr.eu/sites/default/files/TSE/documents/doc/wp/2020/wp_tse_1106.pdf.
21. Market study on the distribution of hotel accommodation in the EU COMP/2020/OP/002 (2022), Executive Summary, p. v. This accounts for practices of 31 % of the sample, which is lower than the findings of the earlier study where this practice was found in 40 % of the sample.
22. Support studies for the evaluation of the VBER, Support study and study on consumer purchasing behaviour in Europe: final report (2020), p. 113.
23. *Supra* n. 21, p. viii.
24. Regulation 2022/720 on the application of Article 101(3) of the Treaty on the Functioning of the European Union to categories of vertical agreements and concerted practices [2022] OJ L134/4, recital 16 and *see* Article 5(1)(d).
25. Guidelines on vertical restraints [2022] OJ C248/1, paras 369-371.

narrow price parity clauses seem generally acceptable, and that of the German NCA and German courts which have condemned narrow price parity clauses set by hotel platforms but in a concentrated market.[26] In this light, the VBER reflects the policy line of the majority of NCAs and the qualification in the Guidelines supports the position taken in Germany.

One might be more optimistic about the input of NCAs in the review process of the VBER, however. After all, 20 NCAs provided feedback to the Commission, based on their experience of handling vertical restraints in national law. Some of the NCAs were able to draw on their enforcement experience to take a stance on certain issues, for example there is some experience with resale price maintenance and NCAs took the view that their black listing continued to be warranted as the cases handled at national level revealed little evidence of possible countervailing effects to warrant exemption.[27] However, while NCAs have had a say in the reform, it is difficult to see an example where the Commission's policy is informed by divergences among NCAs and the Commission choosing one approach as opposed to another on the basis of an assessment of the market effects of different regulatory choices. Conversely, NCAs request that the Commission set a clearer policy line on a number of issues.[28]

In sum, in these examples it is not clear whether the Commission has utilised national level enforcement experiences to inform the review of the rules. In the context of vertical restraints, the most that can be said is that the enforcement experiences of NCAs with regard to vertical restraints in the digital economy informed the scope of the review exercise.

2.2 NCAs as Laboratories?

One can find traces of the ideas of experimentalist governance going quite far back. In a dissenting judgment reviewing the legality of state laws set during the Great Depression, Justice Brandeis posited that '[t]here must be power in the states and the nation to remould, through experimentation, our economic practices and institutions to meet changing social and economic needs .... It is one of the happy incidents of the federal system that a single courageous state may, if its citizens choose, serve as a laboratory; and try novel social and economic experiments without risk to the rest of the country'.[29] In this section we suggest that some NCAs (and possibly some legislators) are eager to have the opportunity to explore alternative policy choices. This can facilitate a process whereby experiences drawn from the national level can feed into a rethinking of the EU rules.

26. BGH, 18 May 2021 – KVR 54/20, DE:BGH:2021:180521BKVR54.20.0.
27. Valuation support study on the EU competition rules applicable to vertical agreements in the VBER and the Guidelines (2020), pp. 88-89.
28. Summary of the replies of the national competition authorities of the European Competition Network provided during the targeted consultation for the impact assessment of the review of Regulation (EU) No. 330/2010 (available at: https://competition-policy.ec.europa.eu/system/files/2021-06/VBER_IA_summary_contributions_from_NCAs.pdf).
29. *New State Ice Co. v. Liebmann*, 285 U.S. 262, 311 (1932). The Supreme Court was called to examine whether a state law was unlawful for requiring a license to manufacture ice.

The most clear example of this are the endeavours by the Greek and Dutch NCAs to facilitate cooperation among undertakings who promise to deliver greater environmental sustainability. The Dutch have been committed to adopting a divergent approach for some time. Originally the Commission displayed some hostility with the Dutch NCA.[30] However, once the Commission embraced a green agenda, it has shown a willingness to adapt its policy to facilitate collaboration among firms too. Even though there is some convergence, the Dutch NCA continues to push for a more liberal approach under Article 101(3) TFEU. In particular, the main divergence is in the interpretation of the requirement that consumers should obtain a fair share of the positive effects of an agreement. According to the Commission's interpretation, consumers should be fully compensated for the restriction of competition.[31] Conversely, according to the Dutch NCA if the undertakings enter into what it calls an environmental damage agreement, a different approach should be taken. An environmental damage agreement is one where the parties try reduce negative environmental externalities. If this agreement helps to comply with an international or national environmental standard, or it helps realise a concrete policy goal, then there is no need for consumers to be fully compensated. The rationale, according to the Dutch NCA, is 'because their demand for the products in question essentially creates the problem for which society needs to find solutions. Moreover, they enjoy the same benefits as the rest of society'.[32]

To illustrate: suppose all makers of shampoo change their production process so there is less pollution but the price of shampoo goes up. The Commission would ask how much the consumer is willing to pay for the reduction in pollution: if the consumer is willing to pay as sum greater than or equal to the price increase of the shampoo then the consumer is fully compensated (e.g., suppose the consumers say that they are happy to pay EUR 2 more for shampoo if they knew there were fewer emissions during the manufacturing process: if the agreement raises the price of shampoo by EUR 1 then the consumer is fully compensated for the price increase). According to the Dutch NCA there is no need to perform this calculation when the agreement reduces pollution because we should not be concerned about the small welfare loss of the consumer since it is their demand for shampoo that had caused the negative externality in the first place. Returning to our shampoo example, the Dutch NCA would exempt the agreement if it was clear that it was likely to reduce pollution even if consumers are not willing to pay EUR 1 for that benefit.

This is a relatively minor difference between the two approaches and it may be beneficial to allow the Dutch NCA to implement this and review in a few years whether this more lenient approach serves to create incentives to invest in sustainability initiatives that work, and that these effects are more pronounced than in jurisdictions which take a more restrictive approach. However, for this to be a site of experimentalist

30. Monti and Mulder 'Escaping the Clutches of EU Competition Law: Pathways to Assess Private Sustainability Initiatives' (2017) 42 European Law Review 635.
31. Guidelines on the application of Article 81(3) of the Treaty [2004] OJ C101/97, para. 85.
32. Dutch NCA, Second draft version: Guidelines on Sustainability Agreements – Opportunities within competition law (2021), para. 48.

governance we need to ensure that the Dutch NCA is very clear about the policy choices it makes with its decisions and that it supervises the conduct of the undertaking to identify the effects that the agreement has in resolving the market failure. At the time of writing the Dutch NCA has issued a set of press releases indicating that it is favourably disposed to certain horizontal agreements.[33] These are not informative and do not allow for a sufficiently robust peer review of the outcomes of the exemption. This review is an essential element of experimentalist governance for it allows one to evaluate the extent to which the Dutch experiment is worth replicating.

Another NCA which is eager to support such agreements is the Greek. Here the innovation is procedural rather than substantive. Drawing on an approach found in the regulation of financial markets, a sustainability sandbox has been created.[34] The approach is to allow some firms to cooperate under the regular supervision of the competition authority and assessing the competition risks as well as the potential of the agreement to deliver on environmental sustainability during the period when the agreement is implemented in the sandbox. This allows the undertakings to explore possible forms of collaboration while shielded from antitrust liability.[35] The sandbox was launched in October 2022 and it is too soon to assess how it will operate but it promises a clear procedure by which the likely impact of collaboration is assessed. This facilitates experimentalist governance as the results of this approach will be visible to the agency and it will allow it to determine how to proceed with the application of antitrust law. This approach also facilitates peer review to determine two things: first whether there are valuable cooperation agreements that should be exempted and second whether the sandbox as a regulatory tool can function effectively in the enforcement of competition law.

3 EXPERIMENTALISM IN ENFORCEMENT

When an infringement is found, undertakings are required to stop infringing the law. In a cartel case, what this means is clear for the parties: stop meeting to agree on prices and output. However, for a number of other forms of conduct, the borderline between legality and illegality is less clear. For example when Michelin was accused to have offered rebates that were contrary to Article 102 TFEU, the undertaking discussed what sort of discounts could be offered to dealers with the Commission and the two came to an understanding about what would be lawful during the time that the Commission was determining the abuse of dominance.[36] In some cases the Commission prescribes the conduct that firms should engage in to avoid infringing competition law, but even here at times the details are to be set by the parties. For example in *Magill* the

33. For example, ACM: Shell and TotalEnergies can collaborate in the storage of CO_2 in empty North Sea gas fields (Press Release 27 June 2022).
34. D. Ahern, 'Regulatory Law, Regulatory Friction and Regulatory Transition as FinTech Disenablers: Calibrating an EU Response to the Regulatory Sandbox Phenomenon' (2021) 22 European Business Organization Law Review 395.
35. Hellenic Competition Commission, Press Release – Creation of the Sandbox for sustainable development and competition 22 June 2022.
36. Case COMP/E-2/36.041/PO, *Michelin* [2002] OJ L143/1 para. 350.

Commission required that the dominant undertakings should supply advance weekly programme listings and allow their reproduction so that rival weekly TV listings could be compiled. Royalties should be reasonable and include other conditions seen as necessary to ensure comprehensive high-quality comprehensive coverage of their programmes. To ensure that these terms were consistent with Article 102 TFEU the parties were requested to submit proposals to the Commission for approval.[37] These approaches are not experimentalist: the parties are told what conduct to adopt and some room for designing compliance is left open to them, but it is for the Commission to approve the choices of the undertaking.

More recently, the Commission's policy has been to leave the undertakings greater latitude to determine how to comply with a prohibition decision. This is motivated by the importance to afford undertakings with maximum freedom to redesign their conduct or their products.[38] This can be seen in two decisions against Google.[39] Consider for example the remedy in *Android*. Recall that the Commission considered that the conduct foreclosed market access to competing search engine. The Commission left it to the undertaking to implement measures to bring the infringement to an end within 90 days of the decision. The undertaking was expected to notify the Commission of its planned measures in advance so that the Commission is able to make a preliminary assessment that the measures bring the infringement to an end. Furthermore, the undertaking was required to keep the Commission informed every six months for a period of five years. This power to supervise Google's conduct was justified because of the variety of measures that Google may adopt to comply.[40] Implied in this is that the Commission can provide informal advice to Google as to whether planned steps would comply with Article 102 TFEU. This created room for experimentation as to the design of an adequate remedy.

At first, Google introduced a choice screen so that a buyer of a new smartphone could select a search engine of its choice: Google Search would no longer be the default. In order to determine which competing search engines should be displayed in the choice screen, Google set up an auction system. This led to concerns because the consumers would have limited choice and search engines without financial power, who wished to attract users because of their privacy-friendly or sustainability policies (Duck Duck Go and Ecosia respectively) considered that the auction system placed them at a competitive disadvantage.[41] In response, Google changed its policy, removing the auction system and increasing the number of search engines in the choice

---

37. Case IV/31.851, *Magill TV Guide/ITP, BBC and RTE* [1989] OJ L78/43, Article 2. The remedy was confirmed on appeal: Joined Cases C-241/91 P and C-242/91 P, *RTE and ITP v. Commission*, EU:C:1995:98, paras 90-94.
38. V. Bottka, L. Repa and E. Rousseva, 'Ordinary Procedure: From Initiation of Proceedings to the Adoption of a Final Decision' in E. Rousseva (ed.) *EU Antitrust Procedure* (Oxford, Oxford University Press, 2020).
39. with respect to Google Shopping decision, *see* Svetiev (*supra* n. 14) Ch. 3 and Rangoni and Monti (*supra* n. 14).
40. Case AT.40099, Google Android (18 July 2018) paras 1404-1407.
41. N. Lomas, 'Google's "No Choice" Screen on Android Isn't Working, Says Ecosia Querying the EU's Approach to Antitrust Enforcement', Tech Crunch, 30 July 2020.

screen.[42] This new policy (which came into force on 1 September 2021, three years after the decision) seems to have been approved by the Commission. A rose-tinted view of this process suggests that the undertaking explored a compliance option with the Commission and revised this after it was observed that the measures were not effective: experimentalism was at play. However, it is a matter of regret that this experimentation is carried out in relative secrecy: no official Commission communications are available, and no market test was carried out. This lack of transparency places a barrier to understanding how far this approach was the paragon of experimentation or a setting where the undertaking tried an ineffective remedy and delayed the application of a worthwhile remedy until the risks of non-compliance became too great to bear. Svetiev has made a similar point about the procedure for remedy design, in Google Shopping, emphasising the importance that remedies are to be jointly designed under an experimentalist framework. Moreover, he suggests that a truly experimentalist design might have to be one where Google tries different designs in different jurisdictions. For example, in the Android case one might envisage choice screen of four search engines for some users, while others would be able to elect from a significantly longer list of search engines in the choice screen: studying consumer responses would allow the undertaking and the Commission to identify the most suitable remedy.[43]

A second, more convincing example of experimentalism in remedy design, is the use of review clauses in merger decisions where the parties offer commitments. The review clause provides that the remedy which has originally been agreed could be modified having regard to changes in the market.[44] This can serve as a sunset clause for commitments that are no longer necessary to avoid the arm to competition. A good illustration of the operation of this clause is found in *Deutsche Lufthansa AG v. Commission*.[45] The alliance between Lufthansa and Swiss was authorised subject to commitments on two routes where there was a concern that the merger would impede competition. The commitments were in the form of slot divestitures and a price undertaking to ensure low prices on those routes. Lufthansa invoked the review clause indicating that the conditions on the two routes had changed and there was now competition in the relevant routes, with the General Court finding that the parties should be released from their commitments in one of the two routes. This episode is interesting because it also reveals that the Commission's policy in reviewing airline alliances evolved as it gained more experience and it tried remedies to control prices, which are normally not accepted. In a situation where the correct assessment of the competitive effects of alliances are unclear, an experimentalist position is helpful in tailoring the remedy to the changes in the market.

Observe, however, that this form of experimentalism is rather limited. First it is clear from the Commission's guidelines that it expects to review commitments rarely. This is compounded by the fact that it is only behavioural commitments that are going

42. An up-to date policy is available at: https://www.android.com/choicescreen/.
43. Svetiev *supra* n. 14, p. 77.
44. Commission notice on remedies acceptable under Council Regulation 139/2004 and under Commission Regulation 802/2004 [2008] OJ C267/1, paras 71-76.
45. Case T-712/16, *Deutsche Lufthansa AG v. European Commission*, EU:T:2018:269.

to be renegotiated or removed, and these are agreed upon infrequently – structural remedies are preferred and there is no review clause that allows a merged entity to buy back assets it has sold off as a condition for merger clearance.[46] Second, it is not clear how frequently merger remedies are renegotiated ex post and the evidentiary burden on the undertaking is quite high, judging from the litigation in *Lufthansa*. Third, experimentalism is one way only: the parties may ask for fewer remedies, but the Commission cannot demand greater commitments. Thus Type 1 errors can be corrected, but not Type 2 errors. There is good justification for this: if the Commission has authorised a transaction on certain terms it cannot later go back and add further conditions. Nevertheless, this is one instance where remedies are altered based on a review of the facts after the decision and where a better understanding of markets allows for the removal of regulatory obligations.

Finally, it is worth observing that there is a fresh opportunity to utilise this approach when enforcing the DMA. This regulation asks that gatekeepers demonstrate compliance with the obligations imposed on them by the DMA. It envisages the possibility of a regulatory dialogue with the Commission and involving third parties and a process where it is possible for compliance measures to be modified as gatekeepers, the Commission and third parties learn what the effects of compliance are.[47] It remains to be seen the extent to which the Commission and the designated gatekeepers will use these opportunities to secure compliance. If it is utilised then, this is an excellent setting where we could see experimentalism in action: gatekeepers can design compliance in consultation with business users, test different modalities for facilitating access, and then learn from these and apply the most effective means of compliance which facilitate. Conversely, the Commission can observe how far gatekeepers' compliance is needed to make markets more contestable and fair which may allow it to decide to remove some obligations if these are not working well.

4 WHAT ACCOUNTS FOR THE MODEST PRESENCE OF EXPERIMENTALISM?

In earlier sections it has been demonstrated that it is difficult to see any real experimentalist governance in action. One reason for the reluctance to experiment is the importance placed by the Commission and NCAs on the value of legal certainty. In the recent revision of the policy on vertical restraints for example, a regular refrain is that 'harmonised rules contribute to ensuring that businesses operating across the EU benefit from a level playing field, which in turn can contribute to the proper functioning of and to enhancing the European Single Market'.[48] In summarising the input that NCAs gave to the review of existing policy in vertical restraints, we find similar

46. The undertaking can always enter into another concentration, which the Commission would review.
47. Regulation 2022/1925 on contestable and fair markets in the digital sector and amending Directives (EU) 2019/1937 and (EU) 2020/1828 (Digital Markets Act) [2022] OJ L 265/1. *See* in particular Articles 8 (duty to demonstrate compliance) and 11 (compliance reports).
48. European Commission, Evaluation of the Vertical Block Exemption Regulation SWD(2020) 173 final p. 59. *See also* Regulation 1/2003, recital 8.

sentiment: even in fields where NCAs have considerable experience, like in cases about resale price maintenance, 'most NCAs considered that it would be helpful if the revised [guidelines] included more guidance on which practices amount to [resale price maintenance] RPM and on the conditions under which efficiencies can be argued for the use of RPM and the evidence needed for this purpose'.[49] Generalising: there is limited demand for experimentalist governance by the parties best placed to put it into operation.

There is also a supply-side barrier: the costs of monitoring the effect of different policies. Consider again the discussion about price parity clauses in hotels: several extensive studies have been carried out and yet it is hard to discern a clear message from these to inform policy. Furthermore, the cost incurred in funding such studies takes resources away from enforcement and NCAs might find it more valuable to keep doing cases rather than study what they do, not least because it is enforcement action which proves the success of an agency's performance in the eyes of the politicians whose job it is to determine the funding of NCAs. However, investing in optimising enforcement should be high on the agenda of any competition authority.[50] Nevertheless, even if agencies are willing to trade off some enforcement action in favour of examining its policies, experimentalism requires a systematic ex post assessment by multiple actors which may not be something we can expect with current budgets.

Finally, another factor that hampers the emergence of experimentalism is the role of national and EU courts. In the field of selective distribution for example, there has been some discussion about how far platform bans could be justified. The context of this discussion can be traced back to the first revision of the VBER in 2010. At that time, with online shopping emerging as a new channel, the Commission was eager to promote online distribution. However, from the perspective of makers of branded goods, being required to allow online sales was seen as an unfair burden because they preferred to sell their goods in brick and mortar store as a means of protecting their brand. The subsequent emergence of large platforms like Amazon made sellers of branded goods recoil just like in the days before the Internet they were reluctant to see their luxurious products displayed in supermarkets like Leclerc.[51] The legal question was the extent to which a distribution agreement which forbade buyers from selling via online platforms constituted a restriction of competition. The German NCA took the view that platform bans were anti-competitive but one court in France took the view that platform bans were not. The Commission also noted that in this setting there were 'different interpretations of the applicable EU competition rules in recent years'.[52] We thus have a space for experimentalist governance: which approach is best from a

49. Summary of the replies of the national competition authorities of the European Competition Network provided during the targeted consultation for the impact assessment of the review of Regulation (EU) No. 330/2010 (2021) p. 5 (available at: https://competition-policy.ec.europa.eu/system/files/2021-06/VBER_IA_summary_contributions_from_NCAs.pdf).
50. W.E. Kovacic, H.M. Hollman and P. Grant 'How Does Your Competition Agency Measure Up?' (2011) 7(1) European Competition Journal 25.
51. Case T-88/92, *Groupement d'achat Édouard Leclerc v. Commission* EU:T:1996:192.
52. European Commission, 'EU competition rules and marketplace bans: Where do we stand after the Coty judgment?' Competition Policy Brief 2018-01, April 2018, p. 1.

competition law perspective? Allowing platform bans or prohibiting them? The possibility for this discussion, however, was settled by the ECJ in *Coty* when a German court sought clarification of what the law was. The Court held that, at least insofar as luxury products were concerned, a platform ban does not mean that the selective distribution agreement infringes Article 101(1) TFEU.[53] The ECJ thus harmonised the law and prevented any further divergences by NCAs. Generalising from this episode, we can observe that once courts get involved, they have to provide an answer as to the legality of a given practice, and the result of this stifles further experimentation. It is unlikely that courts can be a place where competing policy approaches can be compared.

5 CONCLUSION: EXPERIMENTALIST GOVERNANCE AND ITS ALTERNATIVES

It is important to distinguish experimentalism as defined in the literature and in this chapter from evidence that the Commission learns from past enforcement practices more generally. For example in 2005 DG Competition carried out a study of remedies imposed in a set of merger decisions. The survey considered whether, judged ex post, the remedies had been successful. It found that there were some instances where the remedies did not resolve the competition problem.[54] In response, amendments were made to the merger remedies notice to avoid these defects.[55] This is not experimentalism because it is not as if the Commission tried different remedies in similar cases and compared results. It simply assessed policy and identified problems. Of course, this exercise is to be praised because it reveals that the Commission is eager to learn from its enforcement practices, but it is not learning through experimentation. This kind of learning may not necessarily require a granular analysis of decisions. For example, a number of economic studies have indicated that a fairly lax merger regime during the past twenty years has contributed to a degree of economic concentration that is likely to have anti-competitive effects.[56] These studies indicate a general trajectory for reform: more aggressive merger enforcement.

Moreover, what seems to emerge from the practices of some NCAs is another policy approach, which we might term 'intellectual leadership'.[57] The efforts of the Dutch and Greek NCAs to adopt a policy to accommodate agreements that have a positive effect on environmental sustainability, or the German NCA's case against Facebook mixing abuse of dominance with data protection law can be read as examples of agencies trying to push the EU's competition policy agenda. The recent reform of German antitrust, which widens the agency's power to act against tech giants is viewed by its Chairman as an example of the German legislator taking an 'international pioneer

53. C-230/16, *Coty Germany GmbH v. Parfümerie Akzente GmbH* EU:C:2017:941.
54. DG COMP, European Commission *Merger Remedies Study, Public Version* (October 2005).
55. *Supra* n. 44.
56. J. Kwoka, *Controlling Mergers and Market Power* (Boston, MA, Competition Policy International, 2020).
57. *See also* Svetiev, *supra* n. 14, p. 42.

role'.[58] These initiatives are not experimentalist as the agencies are not able, at the present time, to reveal policy successes. In fact, many of the sustainability initiatives considered by the Dutch NCA between 2010 and 2015 were instances where the NCA found that the agreements did not achieve a good enough amount of sustainability benefits.[59] Nevertheless the choice to draft a guideline document is an attempt to influence the direction of EU competition policy.

This chapter does not advocate experimentalist governance in EU competition law. While it seems to have clear advantages, the purpose of this chapter was to try and find out whether this has been applied at all. As has been shown with a number of case studies, it is not clear that the process of experimentalist governance as envisaged in the literature has been implemented fully. Nevertheless, some traces of this approach may be seen and it is clear that there are the legal and institutional means to use this framework to implement and improve the application of EU competition law. Some Member States and NCAs appear to prefer using their experience to shape policy. While in 2000 the ECJ in *Masterfoods* was right to insist that the Commission should be shaping EU policy, the emergence of experienced and well-resourced NCAs during the last 20 years suggests that they too have a key role to play in shaping EU competition policy.

58. German NCA Press Release, Amendment of the German Act against Restraints of Competition (19.1.2021).
59. Monti and Mulder, *supra* n. 30.

CHAPTER 9

Is the Effects-Based Approach Too Cumbersome?: Taking Stock of Recent Practice and Case Law on Article 102 TFEU

*Fernando Castillo de la Torre**

1 INTRODUCTION

In the late 1990s, the Commission started embracing the idea of reducing what some perceived as an over-reliance on so-called form-based analysis of lawfulness of conduct, in favour of a more detailed assessment of the conduct's effects. It invested a great deal of time and resources towards creating a new framework of analysis for Articles 101 and 102 of the Treaty on the Functioning of the European Union (TFEU) cases. The idea of 'effects-based' analysis, or the 'more economic approach', became popular and was first reflected in several changes in block exemptions. The approach, its evolution and its consequences, have been the subject of numerous publications[1] and this contribution focuses on its application to Article 102 TFEU in the light, in particular, of recent developments in the case law of European Union (EU) Courts. I will focus on the practical and conceptual challenges that the 'effects-based' approach has created, and how the Commission and EU Courts have dealt with them.

---

* I would like to express sincere thanks to Giuseppe Conte, Anthony Dawes, Eric Gippini Fournier, Pablo Ibáñez Colomo, Massimiliano Kadar, Justin Lindeboom, Ekaterina Rousseva and Cristina Sjödin whose comments helped improve this chapter. All errors are mine. The views expressed are purely personal and can under no circumstance be attributed to the European Commission.

1. Bourgeois, J.H.J. and Waelbroeck. D., *Ten Years of Effects Based Approach in EU Competition Law*, Bruylant, 2013; Witt, A., *The More Economic Approach to EU Antitrust Law*, Hart Publishing, 2018; Ibáñez Colomo, P., 'Beyond the "More Economics-Based Approach": A Legal Perspective on Article 102 TFEU Case Law', *Common Market Law Review* 53:709 (2016); Witt, A., 'The European Court of Justice and the More Economic Approach to EU Competition Law: Is the Tide Turning?', *The Antitrust Bulletin*, 64(2):172-213 (2019).

In my view, the 'effects-based', more economic, approach meant probably different things to different people. Yet, a common theme was questioning how certain types of practices were examined in the past. Some favoured the absence of sharp rules, deciding on the basis of all relevant considerations of the individual case, the analysis being driven primarily by the purpose that the rule was meant to achieve (under this view, it is often consumer welfare). Yet, there is a crucial distinction between taking into account the purpose in creating the rule and taking into account the purpose in applying the rule. For example, as regards consumer welfare, the *SEN* judgment has confirmed (in case someone really needed such confirmation)[2] that the decision-maker does not have to prove the loss of consumer welfare, but it is sufficient for a competition authority to prove that that practice is capable of impairing the effective competition structure of the relevant market, without it being necessary for that authority to prove that that practice may also cause direct harm to consumers.[3]

Others, while presenting 'form' and 'effects' as a dichotomy, disagreed with how to determine the categories of conduct that were to be considered unlawful. Considering that the existing categories could lead to results which were wrong, likely to be wrong, or arbitrary, this approach was often premised on a chronic epistemological doubt that could mainly be dispelled using a certain set of economic tools. They proposed a different type of formalisation,[4] through tests which were primarily shaped by economic knowledge and tools (but also, in many cases, by a certain view of the purpose of competition law).

2 THE GUIDANCE ON ENFORCEMENT PRIORITIES

The main by-product of the 'effects-based', more economic, approach as regards Article 102 TFEU was the 'Guidance on the Commission's enforcement priorities in applying Article [102 TFEU] to abusive exclusionary conduct by dominant undertakings'[5] (in short 'the Guidance' or 'the Guidance on Enforcement Priorities'). The Guidance on Enforcement Priorities was adopted in December 2008 and represented the result of a long reflection process, which included a Discussion Paper published in December 2005[6] and a public consultation that yielded more than one hundred written comments. The Guidance sought to address what some at the time perceived as a disconnect between the Commission's practice and the state of the law under merger control and Article 101 TFEU on the one hand, and Article 102 TFEU on the other. In

2. This is something already clear in prior case law, *see* C-280/08 P, *Deutsche Telekom v. Commission*, EU:C:2010:604, para. 177; C-52/09, *TeliaSonera*, EU:C:2011:83, para. 24. *See also*, as regards Article 101 TFEU, C-286/13 P, *Dole Food v. Commission*, EU:C:2015:184, paras 123 and 125, and C-8/08, *T-Mobile Netherlands and Others*, EU:C:2009:343, paras 36, 38 and 39.
3. C-377/20, *Servizio Elettrico Nazionale*, EU:C:2022:379, paras 40-48.
4. As Lindeboom opines, 'if the content of competition law is largely based on economic knowledge, and current economic knowledge consists mostly of formal assumptions and models, the content of competition law is likely to consist largely of formalistic rules as well' (Lindeboom, J., 'Formalism in Competition Law', *Journal of Competition Law & Economics*, 18(4):1-49, p. 31 (2022)).
5. OJ 2009 C 45, p. 7.
6. https://ec.europa.eu/competition/antitrust/art82/discpaper2005.pdf.

particular, the Commission's and the Court's approach towards exclusionary conduct was seen at the time as being largely based on a formalistic (some said 'legalistic') framework of assessment and *per se* prohibitions (a term never endorsed, let alone used, by the EU Courts).

The Guidance made clear that it was not intended to constitute a statement of the law and was without prejudice to the interpretation of Article 102 TFEU by the EU Courts.[7] Priority setting is by definition something that is liable to change over time and the Guidance was to be read in that light. At the same time, it set out a framework of assessment for setting priorities that was more demanding than what the case law required at the time to prove an infringement. The Guidance did constitute a conscious attempt by the Commission to steer the enforcement of Article 102 TFEU (although not necessarily the law as such) towards a more economic and effects-based approach.

The Commission was also explicit in stating that it saw the Guidance as an exercise aimed at providing 'greater clarity and predictability',[8] i.e., to increase legal certainty. With hindsight, this is quite interesting since, due to the different value attributed to the Guidance in subsequent judgments[9] and to the fact that later case law has deviated from the Guidance on significant points, its continued existence as drafted at the time does not really contribute, today, to 'greater clarity and predictability'.

Over the last 15 years, the Commission has generally engaged in a more detailed and thorough analysis of anti-competitive effects than previously. Yet, in some cases the analysis, while far more detailed than what was done previously, was still perceived by some to fall short of what was 'required' by the Guidance, even in terms of 'enforcement priorities'. In certain cases, the Commission used mainly quantitative analysis, but qualitative demonstrations continued to be prominent in other cases. In *Qualcomm (exclusivity payments)* the Commission did not consider it necessary to carry out an as-efficient-competitor test (AEC test) on its own motion and in the light of the quantitative and qualitative evidence already gathered. However, it analysed and rebutted the AEC test submitted by Qualcomm.[10] It was not surprising that some applicants typically argued before the EU Courts that the Commission had not followed its own Guidance. While some judgments considered the argument ineffective, as the

7. *See* para. 3 of the Guidance.
8. Guidance, point 2.
9. On the value of the Guidance, some case law tends to stress that it does not concern the substantive law, but just the priorities of the Commission, and therefore it is irrelevant for examining the lawfulness of a decision (C-23/14, *Post Danmark (II)*, EU:C:2015:651, paras 52, 57-58, and T-827/14, *Deustche Telekom v. Commission*, EU:T:2018:930, paras 113-114). On the contrary, in *Intel RENV* the General Court also recalled that the Commission's failure to determine the share of the market covered by the practice at issue was contrary to the Commission's own guidelines on the analysis of cases falling within the scope of Article 102 TFEU, and in particular contrary to para. 20 of the Guidance (T-286/09 RENV, *Intel Corporation v. Commission*, EU:T:2022:19, para. 499) (there is an appeal pending, *Commission v. Intel*, C-240/22 P).
10. Commission Decision C(2018) 240 final of 24 January 2018 relating to proceedings under Article 102 [TFEU] and Article 54 of the [EEA Agreement] (Case AT.40220 – Qualcomm (Exclusivity payments). The decision was annulled, on other grounds, see T-235/18, *Qualcomm v Commission*, EU:T:2022:358.

Guidance was not meant to deal with substantive law, other judgments, in different ways, have considered that the Guidance was relevant for the assessment.[11]

The changes in the enforcement of Article 102 TFEU have been echoed also at the level of the EU Courts in different ways. Overall, as we will see below, the EU Courts have moved away in part from a 'traditional' so-called formalistic approach (although I think the allegation of formalism regarding older case law is probably exaggerated) and now tend to require a closer examination of 'potential effects' or 'capability to produce effects'. This is, as we will see, not so new, since such 'capability' was also present in case law prior to the Guidance, as well as the need to consider all relevant elements. In my view, it is the 'intensity' of the duties which already existed that has evolved, as well as the introduction of certain elements of 'efficiency' into the picture.

Some issues have emerged in relation to the application of the priorities in the Guidance, which have the potential of hampering the application of Article 102 TFEU. In certain cases, the EU Courts may have been too demanding as regards the evidentiary requirements associated with the 'effects-based' approach. Embracing an approach favoured by the Commission has, ironically, probably led to an increase of annulments of Commission decisions. At the same time, there are several instances where the EU Courts have taken a position that contradicts the one adopted by the Guidance or where the EU Courts have simply developed the case law in a different direction or in more detail, compared to the Guidance. For example, the Guidance proposed to apply the *Bronner* criteria well beyond the situation of outright refusals to supply,[12] in the understanding that other types of conduct could be the functional equivalent of a refusal to supply, but this approach has been dismissed by the EU Courts,[13] which have given relevance to the 'means' used to achieve certain effects (element absent in the Guidance, as indicated above).

11. *See supra* n. 9.
12. According to the Guidance, such constructive refusal can take the form of 'unduly delaying or otherwise degrading the supply of the product or involve the imposition of unreasonable conditions in return for the supply' (para. 79).
13. In the Guidance, margin squeeze abuses are considered a specific type of refusal to supply (*see* section IV.D of the Guidance 'Refusal to supply and margin squeeze'), and the conditions that must be met in order to establish that a refusal to supply is abusive – the so-called *Bronner* conditions – must also be met for a margin squeeze to be found abusive. However, in *TeliaSonera* in particular, the Court held that margin squeeze is 'an independent form of abuse distinct from that of refusal to supply' to which the criteria established in the *Bronner* case do not apply, in particular the essential nature of the inputs (C-52/09, *TeliaSonera Sverige*, EU:C:2011:83, paras 55-56; T-336/07, *Telefónica and Telefónica de España v. Commission*, EU:T:2012:172, paras 180-182, and in appeal C-295/12 P, *Telefónica v. Commission*, EU:C:2014:2062, paras 75 and 96; C-165/19 P, *Slovak Telekom v. Commission*, EU:C:2021:139, para. 52). In *Google Shopping*, the General Court reiterated that the indispensability condition of *Bronner* applies only to outright refusals to supply, not to other abusive conduct concerning access conditions when access has already been given (T-612/17, *Google and Alphabet v. Commission (Google Shopping)*, EU:T:2021:763, paras 230-234; there is an appeal pending, C-48/22 P).

3 THE CONDITIONS REGARDING 'MEANS' AND 'EFFECTS'

The task of distinguishing between legitimate competition and exclusionary conduct is inherently difficult, since they are often similar in appearance.[14] The Guidance only briefly mentioned the notion of 'competition on the merits' and neither defined, nor developed it.[15] Lack of interest in this notion may be conceptually related, in my view, to the idea that distinguishing 'good' or 'bad' ways to compete may imply evaluative judgments, whereas, for some proponents of a more economic approach, what matters primarily is outcomes and if an inefficient competitor is forced to leave the market, the decision-maker may not have to worry too much about the means.[16] It is fashionable to say that the expression 'competition on the merits' has no content or is not useful because one man's competition on the merits or 'normal competition' is another man's 'unfair' or 'abnormal' competition. I am not so sure that the phrase is an empty standard. Surely, deciding what is competition on the merits and what is not is not always easy. However, the case law subsequent to the Guidance has reiterated and highlighted competition on the merits as an essential element of an abuse and it has provided some indications on how to define it (*see* section 9 below). In my view, it is an important notion to which not enough attention had been paid recently.

The recent judgment in *SEN* refers to two conditions, that the judgment suggests are cumulative, that must be met for an exclusionary practice by a dominant undertaking to be characterised as abusive. The first one concerns the effects, in that the practice at issue must be 'capable of producing an exclusionary effect'. The second one concerns the means used, in that the practice must be 'based on the use of means other than those which come within the scope of competition on the merits'.[17] Although the relevance of these enquiries in establishing the existence of an abuse could already be derived from settled case law,[18] the Court's confirmation is useful for the sake of clarity.[19]

---

14. O'Donoghue, R., and Padilla, J., *The Law and Economics of Article 102 TFEU*, Third Edition, Hart Publishing, 2020, 265.
15. *See* para. 6 of the Guidance.
16. Under this approach, the conditions appear to merge. *See, e.g.*, Peeperkorn, L., 'Conditional Pricing and the AEC Test: A Happy Marriage or an Awkward Couple?', *Concurrences*, n. 2-2019, pp. 40-53, at 41: 'the Court equates competition on the merits with conduct that does not harm consumers'.
17. C-377/20, *Servizio Elettrico Nazionale*, EU:C:2022:379, para. 103. According to para. 103, these two conditions are applicable in the case of 'a practice which is lawful outside the context of competition law'. This reflects the wording of the first question, which specifically referred to such type of practice. However, in light of the grounds underlying para. 103, there is no reason why these two conditions would not apply across the board, i.e., irrespective of whether the practice is lawful or not outside competition law and without first needing to examine if that is the case. Indeed, the Court itself emphasises that '[i]t is settled case-law that the definition of "abuse" for the purposes of Article 102 TFEU is based on an objective assessment of the conduct in question. The illegality of abusive conduct under that provision is unrelated to the characterisation of that conduct in other areas of law' (para. 67).
18. C-377/20, *Servizio Elettrico Nazionale*, EU:C:2022:379, para. 68, which refers *inter alia* to 85/76, *Hoffmann-La Roche v. Commission*, EU:C:1979:36, para. 91. *See also* C-457/10 P, *AstraZeneca v. Commission*, EU:C:2012:770, para. 130. *See also* the OECD Paper on 'Competition on the merits' (DAF/COMP(2005)27), in particular, the Commission's contribution, making a clear difference between the two conditions (p. 223). The debate on this point has not been facilitated by the use

Nowhere in its reply to the third question, concerning the capability of producing effects, does the Court refer in *SEN* to the efficiency of competitors affected by the exclusionary effects. This suggests that, for the first condition (capability of producing effects) to be satisfied, it is not necessary to systematically establish that the hypothetical competitors that would be affected by the conduct at issue are as efficient as the dominant undertaking. The Court's answer to the first question[20] suggests that the efficiency of hypothetical competitors is, at least for certain types of conduct, an issue that pertains to the condition for a finding of abuse regarding the use of means not based on competition on the merits (*see* on this notion section 9 below)[21] rather than to the condition regarding the capability of exclusionary effects.[22] While, admittedly, some judgments on pricing abuses do mention the efficiency of competitors in the context of the capability to restrict competition, as will be explained below one can interpret that the potential foreclosure of an as-efficient competitor is just one proxy for identifying conduct that is not based on competition on the merits. Yet, it's not because an as-efficient competitor is not foreclosed that, for other types of abuse in particular, the conduct becomes competition on the merits.

This also implies, more generally, that if the dominant undertaking uses means of competition which are *not* 'on the merits', the efficiency of rivals (or a hypothetical competitor) should in principle be irrelevant, and the conduct is prohibited by Article 102 TFEU, if it has at least potential exclusionary effects (on competitors which would try to compete on the merits, not just on the 'as-efficient' ones). The general

of certain, in my view incorrect, expressions in the English versions of the first judgments. *Hoffman-La Roche* (85/76, *Hoffmann-La Roche v. Commission*, EU:C:1979:36) refers to 'normal competition on the basis of transactions of commercial operators', while the French version uses the word '*prestation*' and the German '*Leistung*' (instead of 'transactions') which have a different meaning, closer to 'performance' (which is the expression used in C-209/10, *Post Danmark*, EU:C:2012:172, para. 24). *Akzo* refers to 'competition on the basis of quality' when the French versions refers to the 'merits' (C-62/86 *Akzo v. Commission*, EU:C:1991:286, para. 70). Not totally reliable English versions are unfortunately a constant problem in analysing the case law of EU courts, *see infra* nn. 36, 69, 70, 74, and 76.

19. This clarification is also in line with the approach followed in T-612/17, *Google and Alphabet v. Commission (Google Shopping)*, EU:T:2021:763, para. 195. This is all the more so as the Court of Justice in *SEN* does not follow Advocate General Rantos' Opinion, according to which those two conditions should be analysed as part of one and the same analysis aimed at determining whether a given practice is abusive (Opinion of delivered on 9 December 2021 in C-377/20, *Servizio Elettrico Nazionale and Others*, EU:C:2021:998, paras 47-50).
20. C-377/20, *Servizio Elettrico Nazionale*, EU:C:2022:379, paras 78-82.
21. The different criteria to define 'competition on the merits' or 'normal competition' discussed in the OECD Paper on 'Competition on the merits' (DAF/COMP(2005)27), *supra* n. 18, often refer to efficiency considerations (those of the dominant undertaking but also of the competitors). On the different tests now debated in EU competition law, *see* O'Donoghue/Padilla, *supra* n. 14, 279-294.
22. Some statements in the Court's reply to the first question seem to point to a different direction, in that they refer to the need for a practice to be capable of foreclosing *as efficient competitors* (C-377/20, *Servizio Elettrico Nazionale*, EU:C:2022:379, paras 71, 76). However, this does not call into question the large number of instances where the judgment refers to capability of restrictive effects without further qualification as to the efficiency of competitors (*ibid.*, paras 50, 61, 69, 72, 76 (second sentence), 93, 103). Similarly, when describing what the *Autorità Garante della Concorrenza e del Mercato* (AGCM, the Italian competition authority) should have done to discharge its burden of proof in relation to exclusionary effects, the Court makes no mention of as efficient competitors (*see* para. 98).

observation in *Post Danmark I*, *Intel* and *SEN* that Article 102 TFEU generally cannot be relied on by less efficient undertakings as a shelter from 'competition on the merits' by the dominant undertaking does not mean that every finding of an infringement of abuse is contingent on demonstrating that the conduct was capable of foreclosing an equally efficient competitor. The 'general principle' is simply that 'competition on the merits may, by definition, lead to the departure from the market or the marginalisation of competitors that are less efficient and so less attractive to consumers from the point of view of, among other things, price, choice, quality or innovation'. It is not the role of Article 102 TFEU to 'seek to ensure that competitors less efficient than the undertaking with the dominant position should remain on the market' (what many call nowadays the 'AEC principle').[23] The fallacy is the extrapolation of that dictum to assert that conduct (any conduct) cannot constitute an abuse *unless* it forecloses an equally efficient competitor. The condition requiring the dominant undertaking to use means of competition 'on the merits' is very often omitted.[24]

The judgment in *Unilever* confirms this approach. Paragraphs 39 and 57 make it abundantly clear that when a dominant undertaking uses means other than those which come within the scope of 'normal' competition, that is to say, competition on the merits, there is no need to take into account the efficiency of hypothetical or actual competitors. Actually, those paragraphs may even be interpreted as considering that the conditions of 'means' and 'effects' are not cumulative.[25]

4 SUBSTANTIVE LEGAL STANDARDS VERSUS STANDARD OF PROOF

In the context of assessing the anti-competitive effects, there is often no 'true account of facts' in the 'traditional' sense (of course the conduct as such must be proven to the requisite standard) but mainly estimates, based on objective elements and evidence, of the link between the conduct and a certain effect, about which one may be more or less confident. Often, the effects cannot be anticipated with any degree of certainty by just having a look at the conduct,[26] without an examination of contextual, exogenous, elements.[27]

23. C-209/10, *Post Danmark*, EU:C:2012:172, para. 21.
24. *See*, *inter alia*, Gaudin, G. and Mantzari, D., '*Google Shopping* and the As-Efficient-Competitor Test: Taking Stock and Looking Ahead', *Journal of European Competition Law & Practice*, Vol. 13(2):125-135 (March 2022), https://doi.org/10.1093/jeclap/lpac006. The AEC principle is presented as applicable 'across the board', but, while the authors accept that it 'does not mean that only conduct that would exclude as-efficient competitors is abusive' (at 126), no clear weight is apparently given to the reference in the case law to the condition related to 'competition on the merits' as limiting the scope of that 'principle'.
25. C-680/20, *Unilever Italia Mkt. Operations*, EU:C:2023:33, paras 39 and 57. The latter clearly states that 'the use by a undertaking in a dominant position of resources other than those governing competition on the merits may be sufficient, in certain circumstances, to establish the existence of such an abuse'.
26. In *Intel*, the Court of Justice refers to the 'intrinsic capacity' of the conduct to produce effects (C-413/14 P, *Intel v. Commission*, EU:C:2017:632, para. 140). This qualification is again present in *Google Android* (T-604/18, *Google and Alphabet v. Commission* (*Google Android*), EU:T:2022:541, paras 640-641). It is unclear if the Court of Justice by adding 'intrinsic' intends

Achieving certainty on the effects of the conduct and the causal link between such effects and the conduct is difficult, and impossible for certain type of situations. Several tools can come into play to soften the rigour of such principle. One tool is setting the substantive legal standard in ways that do not require such certainty, but something lower such as the 'capability' or likelihood of the conduct to produce effects, or the 'realistic' or probable nature of such effects. Another tool is to set a lower standard of proof.

In other words, the substantive legal standard itself can be already designed in terms that facilitate the administration of the burden of proof. These more relaxed demands on exogenous elements of the conduct may be detected even with regard to factual issues which are clearly constituent elements of the infringement, such as the requirement of effect on trade between Member States under Articles 101 and 102 TFEU.[28] The fact that effect on intra-Community trade needs to be only 'potential' has been justified by the difficulties of proving actual effect 'to a sufficient legal standard'.[29] A similar approach applies to whether the conduct is capable of producing an effect on competition. The substantive legal test already excludes any requirement of certainty regarding the impact of a practice and the causal link between them. The examination is not whether B (an observable 'fact') was caused by A, but simply whether A *may* cause B (in the sense of 'is able to', irrespective of whether B actually happened or not).

Requiring only 'potential' effects on competition instead of 'actual' effects on competition and the meaning of 'effect' are legal questions going to the definition of an infringement and, as such, are not questions of standard of proof.[30] The distinction between the substantive legal test and the standard of proof may not be so relevant

---

to add an element of qualification to the 'capability' analysis, in the sense that contextual elements may be less relevant or simply that what happens afterwards (if there are actual effects) is not relevant (there is an appeal pending, C-738/22 P).

27. To be clear, in practice such contextual analysis may not be needed, for clear-cut cases, but not because effects do not depend on context, but rather because it is difficult to imagine a context in which the conduct does not have at least potential effects. Such absence of contextual analysis by the decision-maker is anchored on experience and logical inference, but it does not mean that the conduct by itself reveals enough about the effects it will bring about.
28. The capability of a conduct to affect trade between Member States, that is to say, its potential effect, is sufficient and it is not necessary to demonstrate an actual effect on trade (C-215/96 and C-216/96, *Bagnasco and Others*, EU:C:1999:12 para. 48; T-259/02-T-264/02 and T-271/02, *Raiffeisen Zentralbank Österreich and Others v. Commission*, EU:T:2006:396, para. 166).
29. T-25/95, T-26/95, T-30/95 to T-32/95, T-34/95 to T-39/95, T-42/95 to T-46/95, T-48/95, T-50/95 to T-65/95, T-68/95 to T-71/95, T-87/95, T-88/95, T-103/95 and T-104/95, *Cimenteries CBR and Others v. Commission*, EU:T:2000:77, para. 3376; T-395/94, *Atlantic Container v. Commission*, EU:T:2002:49, para. 90. The substantive test for 'effect on trade' is itself a relatively low standard formulated in lenient, probabilistic terms, by the case law: 'it must be possible to foresee with a sufficient degree of probability on the basis of a set of objective factors of law or fact that it may have an influence, direct or indirect, actual or potential, on the pattern of trade between Member States' (5/69, *Völk v. Vervaecke*, EU:C:1969:35, para. 5; 209/78-215/78 and 218/78, *Van Landewyck and Others v. Commission*, EU:C:1980:248, para. 171; T-24/93-T-26/93 and T-28/93, *Compagnie Maritime Belge and others v. Commission*, EU:T:1996:139, para. 201; T-254/12, *Kühne & Nagel International and Others v. Commission*, EU:T:2016:113, para. 56 and 62-102.
30. The Court of Justice has widely interpreted when an issue is one of law. *See*, for Article 102 TFEU, C-413/14 P, *Intel v. Commission*, EU:C:2017:632, where the argument that the analysis of effects raised an inadmissible point (para. 124) was simply ignored. The definition of the

when decisions are adopted and reviewed at EU level, but becomes crucial for decisions by national competition authorities (NCAs) (and generally national litigation). Whereas the substantive legal test is a uniform one and must be applied at both EU and national level, the standard of proof is determined by national law.[31] Recital 5 of Regulation No. 1/2003 provides that this regulation affects 'neither national rules on the standard of proof nor obligations of competition authorities and courts of the Member States to ascertain the relevant facts of a case, provided that such rules and obligations are compatible with general principles of Community law'. This differentiation in the levels of enforcement is important, as the EU legal order has its own rules on these issues, and the evaluation of evidence is governed by its 'own' principle of autonomy, meaning that only Union law governs the submission of evidence in procedures before the Commission and EU Courts.[32]

Yet, the legal and evidentiary thresholds are often conflated.[33] It is conceptually possible to have a legal test of 'capability' to restrict competition combined with proof 'beyond reasonable doubt' (of that capability),[34] and a legal test of exclusion of all effective competition which must be proven according to a 'balance of probabilities' standard. The 'lower' substantive legal threshold does not imply a 'lower' standard of proof in the same way as a 'higher' substantive legal threshold (elimination of all competition) does not imply 'certainty'. Admittedly, a 'low' substantive test will facilitate proof of the infringement, but it does not mean that the 'standard of proof' is low. Of course, the stricter the substantive legal test, the more difficult it will be to discharge the burden of proof, but mainly because the substantive conditions, in themselves, are difficult to be met. Vice versa, the stricter the standard of proof, the more difficult it will be to prove in specific cases the constituent elements of the substantive legal test, whatever they may be. Accordingly, the presumption of innocence and the principle of *in dubio pro reo* does not mandate a standard of 'actual effects', since the standard of effects required for conduct to be abusive is an issue of substantive law.

To be fair, part of the confusion is due to the fact that both the legal test and the standard of proof have often been presented in probabilistic terms. Besides, the case

'threshold' for the effects is seen as an issue of law, governed by EU law, in *Post Danmark II*, for example (C-23/14, *Post Danmark (II)*, EU:C:2015:651).

31. Castillo de la Torre, F. and Gippini-Fournier, E., *Evidence, Proof and Judicial Review in EU Competition Law*, Edward Elgar Publishing, 2017, paras 1.020-1.023.
32. Lenaerts, K., 'Some Thoughts on Evidence and Procedure in European Community Competition Law', *Fordham International Law Journal* 30(5):1463-1495, 1465 (2006).
33. It is not uncommon to read that requiring 'actual effects' implies a higher 'standard of proof'. In the same vein, it is said that the (substantive legal) standard of 'elimination of all effective competition' in *Bronner* implies a higher standard of proof. *See, e.g.*, Ibáñez Colomo, P., 'Anticompetitive Effects in EU Competition Law', *Journal of Competition Law & Economics*, 17 (2): 309-363 (2021). While he notes a confusion between the legal test and the standard of proof (at 359) he also states, at 348 that 'a threshold of certainty (or quasi-certainty) applies to conduct subject to a 'enhanced effects' test'.
34. This does not mean that the presumption of innocence is irrelevant in this context. It means that it is applied over a different subject: the doubt is about the capability or likelihood of the conduct producing an effect. In other words, the benefit of the doubt administers the risk of probability error, not of factual error.

law of the Court of Justice itself is not always clear on this distinction. Some judgments refer to the 'probability' that certain conduct gives rise to (actual or) 'potential' effects.[35] One could argue that the 'potential effect' refers in those judgment to the substantive test, whereas the adjective 'probable' refers to the standard of proof.

The 'probable' nature of a 'potential' effect is in itself a qualification that some may consider open to challenge today. Later judgments appear to require more than just a 'probable' potential effect and appear to consider that any doubt on such potential effect benefits the undertaking concerned (*see* section 6 below). Another complicating factor may be that, ultimately, every step in the analysis is simply probabilistic. While most judgments tend to use qualitative expressions to describe the link between the practice and its effect,[36] one can argue that the 'capacity' to produce an effect relates to an increase in the probability of certain observable effect happening.[37] But then the decision-maker assesses the probability of a probability (second-order probability), which does not make a lot of practical sense.[38]

Another complicating factor is that some of those judgments are rendered in preliminary references, where, as explained above, the standard of proof is set out by national law (Recital 5 of Regulation No. 1/2003). It is surprising how the Court of

35. In *TeliaSonera*, the Court of Justice refers to 'potential effects' that are 'probable' (C-52/09, *TeliaSonera Sverige*, EU:C:2011:83, paras 71-73). The substantive test for 'effect on trade' is: 'it must be possible to foresee with a sufficient degree of probability on the basis of a set of objective factors of law or fact that it may have an influence, direct or indirect, actual or potential, on the pattern of trade between Member States' (*see* case law in *supra* n. 29).
36. In *Post Danmark II* the Court of Justice uses the expressions of 'capable' of having an (exclusionary) effect in some paragraphs (C-23/14, *Post Danmark (II)*, EU:C:2015:651, paras 38, 50, 68), whereas it qualifies as 'likely' the relevant effect in other paragraphs (paras 67, 69), or as 'probable' (para. 74). Yet, the French version uses '*susceptible de*' for 'likely', and the language appears to be less probabilistic. The *Intel* judgment consistently uses the expression 'capable of' (C-413/14 P, *Intel v. Commission*, EU:C:2017:632, paras 138, 141, 132 and 143), despite Intel insistently arguing on the basis of the substantive test being 'likely' effects. Counterfactuals in the context of Article 101 TFEU, when explicitly mentioned, are said to be 'realistic' (C-307/18, *Generics UK and Others*, EU:C:2020:52, paras 120-121) which evokes an assessment that is more qualitative than probabilistic.
37. If a course of conduct makes a consequence more likely, then there are potential effects. This is, however, only a 'comparative' type of analysis, which does not assess in absolute terms 'how likely' the consequence is. For example, if the *ex ante* probability was 5% and the conduct increases the probability of the consequences occurring to 10% or 20%, is that enough to consider that there are potential effects? One could argue that the reference in some judgments to a 'sufficient degree of probability' and the exclusion of merely 'hypothetical effects' means that the occurrence of the event must be sufficiently probable. Yet it is unclear if such threshold is to be 50% or higher, so that it is only if the increase in probability renders the consequences more likely than not that the relevant legal standard is met. The exclusion of merely hypothetical effects (*see, inter alia*, C-680/20, *Unilever Italia*, EU:C:2023:33, para. 42: 'beyond mere hypothesis') suggests that the probability may be much lower than 50%. Another issue is to which notion does the adjective 'potential' refer. The case law on potential effects (or capability to produce effects) focuses sometimes on the existence of potential competition, so that the existence of the obstacle to effective access must be actually proven, but it is enough if the competition excluded is merely potential. In other words, here 'potential' refers to the 'competitor'. Another view is to consider that the word 'potential' does not only refer to the competitor, but to the effect as such, so that it is enough if there is evidence that the conduct increases the probability of certain observable obstacle happening.
38. The existence of such second-order probability is often disputed in probability theory and in any event its practical application by decision-makers lacks cognitive realism.

Justice, while formally leaving to the national court the task of assessing the evidence, is increasingly prescriptive in the process of submission and assessment of that evidence. In *SEN* the Court of Justice gives extensive guidance on how to proceed in the assessment of the evidence in the particular case at hand.[39] In *Unilever* the Court of Justice describes the types of evidence that the decision-maker must collect to prove sufficiently a case, and provides some guidance on the evidential 'dynamics' between the undertaking and the Commission.[40] While one could argue that some guidance on evidence reflects the application of principles such as the presumption of innocence or the right to be heard, which must also apply when national authorities implement EU law, one can also legitimately wonder if the Court of Justice is sometimes not going beyond the interpretation of EU law and entering into factual matters where some divergence may still exist at national level.[41]

A further complicating factor, of a different kind, is that there is still no concrete definition of principle of what anti-competitive exclusionary effects really are.[42]

39. C-377/20, *Servizio Elettrico Nazionale*, EU:C:2022:379, paras 87-103.
40. C-680/20, *Unilever Italia Mkt. Operations*, EU:C:2023:33, paras 42, 44 or 59.
41. At the risk of stating the obvious, the intensity of judicial review does not have to be at national level the same as one as at EU level either. The EU strikes its own balance to make appropriate use of concepts of discretion that fit best to its own legal framework, and decision-making processes. It is because such balance may be different from that prevailing in some Member States that it is not always appropriate to draw conclusions from the case law in the EU Courts as regards the degree of judicial review that must be exercised at national level. While judicial review at national level must comply with the right to effective judicial protection enshrined in Article 47 of the Charter, the intensity of judicial review which one can see nowadays in certain judgments of the General Court goes, in my view, beyond what is required by Article 6 ECtHR. More recently, the criteria to assess whether 'full jurisdiction' has been exercised have been set out in quite detail by the ECtHR in its Grand Chamber judgment in *Ramos Nunes De Carvalho e Sá* (ECtHR, Judgment of 6 November 2018, *Ramos Nunes De Carvalho e Sá v. Portugal* (CE:ECHR:2018:1106JUD005539113). The ECtHR has held, building in several precedents, that the requirement that a court should have 'full jurisdiction' is met where it has exercised 'sufficient jurisdiction' or provided 'sufficient review' in the proceedings before it. This reflects the fact that 'it is often the case in relation to administrative law appeals in the Member States of the Council of Europe that the extent of judicial review over the facts of a case is limited and that it is characteristic of review proceedings that the competent authorities review the previous proceedings rather than taking factual decisions'. It added that 'it is not the role of Article 6, in principle, to guarantee access to a court which can substitute its own assessment or opinion for that of the administrative authorities. In this regard, the Court has placed particular emphasis on the respect which must be accorded to decisions taken by the administrative authorities on grounds of expediency and which often involve specialised areas of law' (*ibid.*, paras 176 to 178). The exact extent of the review carried out by the competent court in *Menarini* as regards decisions imposing fines for breaches of competition law (ECtHR, judgment of 27 September 2011, *Menarini Diagnostics v. Italy*, CE:ECHR:2011:0927JUD004350908) is not very clear from the judgment, but it is similar to, if not more limited than, the review exercised by EU Courts (Castillo de la Torre/Gippini Fournier, *supra* n. 31, para. 6.062).
42. The *de minimis* doctrine plays no role in Article 102 TFEU. The Court of Justice has ruled that it is not appropriate fixing an appreciability (*de minimis*) threshold for the purposes of determining whether there is an abuse of a dominant position (C-23/14, *Post Danmark (II)*, EU:C:2015:651, paras 72 and 73; C-525/16, *MEO*, EU:C:2018:270, para. 29). Since the structure of competition on the market has already been weakened by the presence of the dominant undertaking, any further weakening of the structure of competition may constitute an abuse of a dominant position. An anti-competitive practice 'is, by its very nature, liable to give rise to not insignificant restrictions of competition, or even of eliminating competition on the market on which the undertaking concerned operates'.

Generally speaking, the test is whether the conduct 'has the effect of hindering the maintenance of the degree of competition still existing in the market or the growth of that competition'.[43] Different judgments refer to foreclosure, to hindering the ability of competitors to operate in the relevant market,[44] to marginalisation of competitors,[45] or to a 'significant' competitive advantage.[46] It is not controversial that the analysis is not limited to prices and the conduct may impact the various parameters of competition, such as price, production, innovation, variety or quality of goods or services. The judgment in *Google Android* tries, for the first time, to give a more general definition of 'exclusionary effects': 'exclusionary effects characterise situations in which effective access of actual or potential competitors to markets or to their components is hampered or eliminated as a result of the conduct of the dominant undertaking, thus allowing that undertaking negatively to influence, to its own advantage and to the detriment of consumers, the various parameters of competition, such as price, production, innovation, variety or quality of goods or services.'[47]

5 DO STANDARDS CHANGE WHEN ASSESSMENT IS 'RETROSPECTIVE'?

A recent topic of discussion is whether the substantive legal test or the standard of proof change if the conduct at issue has been implemented in the past. One author calls this 'the time variable' and submits that when the analysis is retrospective, actual

43. C-377/20, *Servizio Elettrico Nazionale*, EU:C:2022:379, para. 44, with further references.
44. C-52/09, *TeliaSonera Sverige*, EU:C:2011:83, para. 67.
45. C-377/20, *Servizio Elettrico Nazionale*, EU:C:2022:379, paras 45, 73 ; C-413/14 P, *Intel v. Commission*, EU:C:2017:632, para. 134; T-235/18, *Qualcomm v. Commission*, EU:T:2022:358, para. 351.
46. C-377/20, *Servizio Elettrico Nazionale*, EU:C:2022:379, paras 88 (competitive advantage) and 100, 102 (comparative advantage). It has been suggested that 'competitive disadvantage' is not enough, but there must be an impact 'on efficient firms' ability and incentive to compete' (Ibáñez Colomo, *supra* n. 33, 311); he also refers to the 'reduction of competitive constraints' (p. 349). While I would tend to agree with the relevance of impact on 'ability and incentives' to compete, the efficiency of competitors is not something that is generally required as a matter of law, but may be relevant for certain types of abuse (*see* section 9 below). The judgment in *Google Android* shows that a competitive advantage may not be enough, *see* T-604/18, *Google and Alphabet v. Commission* (*Google Android*), EU:T:2022:541, para. 564: 'As to the alleged conflating of competitive advantage and anticompetitive foreclosure, it must be pointed out that this complaint is based on a misreading of the contested decision, from which it is apparent that it establishes, first, the existence of an advantage linked to the MADA pre-installation conditions that cannot be offset by competitors, and, second, the anticompetitive effects of that advantage.' *See also MEO*, as regards the concept of 'competitive disadvantage', for the purposes of subpara. (c) of the second paragraph of Article 102 TFEU. The Court stressed that a finding of such a 'competitive disadvantage' does not require proof of actual quantifiable deterioration in the competitive situation, but must be based on an analysis of all the relevant circumstances of the case leading to the conclusion that that behaviour has an effect on the costs, profits or any other relevant interest of one or more of those partners, so that that conduct is such as to affect that situation. It is only if the behaviour of the undertaking in a dominant position tends, having regard to the whole of the circumstances of the case, to lead to a distortion of competition between those business partners that the discrimination between trade partners which are in a competitive relationship may be regarded as abusive (C-525/16, *MEO*, EU:C:2018:270).
47. T-604/18, *Google and Alphabet v. Commission* (*Google Android*), EU:T:2022:541, para. 281.

effects must be considered.[48] However, it is settled case law that the fact that anti-competitive effects failed to materialise is not necessarily conclusive.[49] It is perfectly possible that a conduct that is 'capable' of restricting competition ultimately does not achieve its aim. This is because the success of the conduct may depend on a number of variables, not always in the hands of the dominant undertaking.[50] Where it is established that behaviour is objectively of such a nature as to restrict competition, the question whether it is abusive in nature cannot depend on the contingencies of the reactions of third parties.[51]

The *Servier*[52] and *Krka*[53] judgments on Article 101 TFEU are relevant in this context. The General Court found that the approach of the Commission, in examining effects of the conduct on competition, was not to consider relevant facts after the agreement was concluded.[54] For the Commission, Krka would have continued to be a

48. '[T]he analysis of potential effects is relevant where the analysis is prospective in nature. Thus, it may come into play in ... two circumstances ... : where the practice has not yet been implemented and where the practice has already bee implemented at the time of the adoption of the decision and the analysis considers the future evolution of the relevant market' (Ibáñez Colomo, *supra* n. 33, 324); 'Anticompetitive effects would not exist, for instance, where the contemporary evolution of the market reveals that the practice has not precluded entry' (*ibid.*, 341).
49. T-201/04, *Microsoft v. Commission*, EU:T:2007:289, paras 560-564. The purpose of Article 102 TFEU is to penalise abuse by one or more undertakings of a dominant position within the internal market or in a substantial part of it, irrespective of whether such practice has proved successful (C-538/18 P and C-539/18 P, *České dráhy v. Commission*, EU:C:2020:53, para. 70 and the case law cited). *Post Danmark (I)* suggested that later events could be relevant, even if it left the final factual analysis to the referring court: C-209/10, *Post Danmark*, EU:C:2012:172, para. 39: 'it is worth noting that it appears from the documents before the Court that Forbruger-Kontakt managed to maintain its distribution network despite losing the volume of mail related to the three customers involved and managed, in 2007, to win back the Coop group's custom and, since then, that of the Spar group'.
50. As the General Court ruled in *AstraZeneca*, 'in order to achieve its aim, conduct aimed at excluding competitors frequently requires cooperation from third parties, whether from public authorities or market players, since, in practice, such conduct is rarely capable of having a direct effect on the competitive position of competitors' (T-321/05, *AstraZeneca v. Commission*, EU:T:2010:266, para. 377).
51. T-321/05, *AstraZeneca v. Commission*, EU:T:2010:266, para. 360. This reluctance of the General Court to exclude capability or causation on account of external factors or reactions of others is also visible in *SEN*. Advocate General Rantos considered that if competitors had the means to obtain the contact details, exclusion would not be caused by the conduct of the dominant undertaking. *See SEN* Advocate General Opinion, *supra* n. 19, paras 78-79 : 'it seems to me that it could be concluded that any potential risk of foreclosure of the relevant market was due not to Enel's actions but to the negligence of its competitors, which did not act competitively in order to capture customers of the protected market'. The Court of Justice rejects that approach, at para. 102. The Court of Justice states that the finding that conduct was 'capable of impairing effective, undistorted competition' cannot be called into question by 'the actions that competitor undertakings potentially took or could have taken, such as purchasing files from third parties containing information on customers in the protected market, in order to limit the harmful consequences of that practice' (C-377/20, *Servizio Elettrico Nazionale*, EU:C:2022:379, para. 102).
52. T-691/14, *Servier and Others v. Commission*, EU:T:2018:922, paras 1075-1234 (there are two appeals pending, C-176/19 P, *Commission v. Servier and Others*, and C-201/19 P, *Servier and Others v. Commission*).
53. T-684/14, *Krka v. Commission*, EU:T:2018:918.
54. T-691/14, *Servier and Others v. Commission*, EU:T:2018:922, paras 1084, 1089, 1092.

'competition threat' in the absence of the agreement,[55] and at the time of the agreement it was 'likely' that other sources of potential competition would be eliminated in a future agreement.[56]

The General Court concluded that past case law on potential effects concerned Commission decisions that 'did not penalise past conduct constituting a restriction by effect, but rather prevented the occurrence of such conduct by envisaging the effects that the measures in question could have if they were applied'.[57] For the General Court it appeared paradoxical, where the clauses of an agreement have been implemented and their impact on competition can be measured by taking into account the relevant factual developments, including those subsequent to the conclusion of the agreement, which took place before the Commission issued its decision, to allow the Commission to demonstrate merely the anti-competitive effects that such clauses are likely to have without taking those developments into account.[58] For the Court, 'demonstrating that an agreement has anti-competitive effects requires that the Commission, in the light of the need to be realistic that arises from the case law of the Court of Justice, take into account, in the context of the comparison (the counter-factual), all the relevant factual developments, including those subsequent to the conclusion of the agreement, which took place before it adopts its decision'.[59] The Court concludes that the Commission must prove 'the sufficiently realistic and probable nature of the restrictive effects' of the agreements in question.[60] The General Court found several shortcomings in the decision. The General Court carried out a sort of counterfactual analysis which examined the actual events as they occurred in the course of and further to the implementation of the agreement, and not only in the absence of it, and also concluded that it had not been established that, in the absence of an agreement, Krka would probably have entered at risk the markets of the 18 to 20 Member States in question, in particular the markets of France, the Netherlands and the United Kingdom.[61]

I think that the General Court may be conflating two different issues. On the one hand, there is the issue whether what actually happened (after the conduct is implemented) is or may be relevant for the assessment. I am of the view that what happens afterwards cannot be simply ignored. Admittedly, the mere fact that the effect

55. *Ibid.*, paras 1096-1100.
56. *Ibid.*, para. 1101.
57. *Ibid.*, paras 1107-1120. For the General Court there was 'no previous case-law, concerning agreements, decisions and concerted practices, in which the Court of Justice or the General Court has accepted that the Commission may rely only on the potential effects of the measure at issue in order to find that an infringement has been committed and impose a fine on the infringers on the basis of that finding' (para. 1121).
58. *Ibid.*, para. 1123. For the General Court if it were possible for the Commission to rely, in relation to agreements which have been implemented, solely on the effects that they are likely to have, in order to demonstrate that they had an anti-competitive effect, the distinction between restrictions of competition by object and by effect, established by Article 101(1) TFEU, would lose its relevance.
59. *Ibid.*, para. 1130. In order to stress that comparison must be 'realistic', the General Court refers to 56/65, *LTM*, EU:C:1966:38 and C-382/12 P, *MasterCard and Others v. Commission*, EU:C:2014:2201, para. 166.
60. T-691/14, *Servier and Others v. Commission*, EU:T:2018:922, para. 1139.
61. *Ibid.*, paras 1160 and 1192 to 1213.

does not materialise is not, in itself, evidence of the lack of capability to produce the effect. However, subsequent events (which by definition are not yet known when the analysis is solely prospective) may cast light on whether the conduct was capable to produce such effects or not in the first place.[62] On the other hand, the substantive legal test should not vary depending on when the analysis is carried out. The mere fact that, a few years after the events, the decision-maker may have more information at its disposal does not change the substantive legal standard. The anti-competitive nature of the conduct 'must be evaluated at the time when those acts were committed'.[63] It is a legal imperative to be able to anticipate if your conduct falls within the prohibition when, or before, you engage in the conduct, not later, depending on what happens. This is why in predatory pricing or margin squeeze, it is the costs of the dominant undertaking that are determinative. In the same vein, any possible counterfactual analysis must be conducted at the time when the agreement is concluded or the unilateral conduct is implemented.

The judgment in *Generics* does not set out any difference in the tests just because they are applied retrospectively.[64] This is what the Court of Justice has also decided in *SEN*. The analysis of the capability to produce effects focused on the relevance of evidence of lack of actual restrictive effects, as that was the question raised by the referring court. After referring to settled case law whereby the finding of an abuse does not require proof of actual restrictive effects,[65] the Court of Justice relies *a contrario* on point 20 of the Guidance on Enforcement Priorities[66] to hold that the 'opposite situation that a certain course of conduct has not produced actual anti-competitive effects cannot rule out the possibility that that conduct was in fact capable of doing so when it was implemented, even if a long period of time has passed since that conduct took place. Such absence of effect could stem from other causes and be due to, inter alia, changes that occurred on the relevant market since that conduct began or to the fact that the

62. E-15/10, *Posten Norge v. ESA*, [2012] EFTA Ct. Rep. 246, para. 192: '[w]hile the Court agrees with the applicant that, in some cases, the persistent lack of actual negative effects on competition may cast doubt on a finding by ESA that a certain conduct is liable to restrict competition, the Court considers that the claims of the applicant in this particular case are not convincing'.
63. C-457/10 P, *AstraZeneca v. Commission*, EU:C:2012:770, para. 110. The *ex post* analysis does not change the standard of proof either. In an *ex post* analysis there can typically be a larger amount of potential relevant information and data. To the extent that the weight of the evidence may depend on a somewhat ideal amount of evidence that is potentially available, one could argue that the extent of the enquiry cannot be limited to the evidence that was available to the undertaking at the time of the conduct, or related to that point in time only. Therefore, the evidential enquiry should not exclude *ex post* facts. As a result, the *ex ante* evidence may have less weight, but taking into account *ex post* events does not change the standard of proof, even if it may de facto make it more difficult to satisfy it.
64. C-307/18, *Generics UK and Others*, EU:C:2020:52, paras 154 and 170, already confirming that capability to restrict competition is the correct legal standard, even in circumstances where the dominant undertaking's conduct had been implemented in the past.
65. C-377/20, *Servizio Elettrico Nazionale*, EU:C:2022:379, para. 53.
66. Guidance, para. 20, 6th point ('if the conduct has been in place for a sufficient period of time, the market performance of the dominant undertaking and its competitors may provide direct evidence of anti-competitive foreclosure').

undertaking in a dominant position was unable to complete the strategy underpinning that conduct'.[67]

The Court further holds that, while the evidence produced by a dominant undertaking attesting to the lack of actual effects 'cannot be regarded as sufficient of itself to preclude the application of Article 102 TFEU',[68] this 'may constitute evidence[69] that the conduct in question was not capable of producing the alleged exclusionary effects'. However, the Court adds that this evidence[70] must 'be supplemented, by the undertaking concerned, by items of evidence intended to show that that absence of actual effects was indeed the consequence of the fact that that conduct was unable to produce such effects'.[71] Accordingly, evidence of lack of concrete effects 'may' count as evidence of lack of capability to produce exclusionary effects but it is not sufficient in itself to exclude such capability. The Court applies this principle to the case at hand by stating that the fact that Enel Energia SpA (EE) obtained, by means of the use of the Servizio Elettrico Nazionale SpA (SEN) lists, just 0.002% of the customers in the protected market, cannot suffice in itself to show that the practice was not capable of producing an exclusionary effect.[72]

In practice, the above suggests that, although a competition authority must examine the evidence of lack of actual effects submitted by a dominant undertaking, it might be able to dismiss it relatively easily, absent self-standing evidence submitted by the dominant undertaking that the conduct is incapable of producing restrictive effects. There is no indication that the substantive legal test changes just because the examination takes place ex post.

Yet, it is interesting that, just a few months later, the Court of Justice in *Unilever* uses a stricter tone. Whereas prior case law requires the 'capacity' to restrict competition, sometimes qualified as 'intrinsic capacity',[73] the Court of Justice requires for the first time in *Unilever* what is called in French '*capacité effective*' to restrict competition and in English 'actual capacity' ('is actually capable of producing such effects').[74] It is

67. C-377/20, *Servizio Elettrico Nazionale*, EU:C:2022:379, para. 54. The Court's explicit recognition that the lack of actual effects of a conduct does not rule out its capability of producing effects contrasts with the approach suggested by Advocate General Rantos, who relied on point 20 of the Guidance on Enforcement Priorities to hold that the absence of actual effects could make it reasonable to assume that the practice was not even theoretically capable of harming competitors (*SEN* Advocate General Opinion, *supra* n. 19, para. 119).
68. C-377/20, *Servizio Elettrico Nazionale*, EU:C:2022:379, para. 55.
69. In the French version of the judgment, '*un indice*'.
70. In the French version of the judgment, '*début de preuve*'. The Italian version of the judgment, in line with the French one, uses the terms '*indizio*' and '*principio di prova*'.
71. C-377/20, *Servizio Elettrico Nazionale*, EU:C:2022:379, para. 56.
72. *Ibid.*, para. 57. The Court further holds that, to discharge its burden in relation to effects, the AGCM was simply required to 'show, in the decision at issue, supported by evidence such as behavioural studies, that the procedure used by SEN in order to collect its customers' consent to the transfer of their information was indeed such as to favour the lists intended to be transferred to EE' (*ibid.*, para. 98). It does not seem to require a further analysis, e.g., of the extent to which such favouring would lead to the departure from the market or the marginalisation of EE's competitors.
73. *See supra* n. 26.
74. C-680/20, *Unilever Italia Mkt. Operations*, EU:C:2023:33, paras 42 and 52. It is unclear if the Court of Justice sees this qualification as the mirror image of its settled case law that the conduct

unclear what has happened between May 2022 and January 2023 for the Court of Justice to seemingly 'upgrade' the substantive legal test (or even what appears to be the standard of proof, or at least the 'quality' of the evidence, when it requires 'tangible evidence'). The Court of Justice further stresses that 'a competition authority may rely on the guidance from economic sciences, confirmed by empirical or behavioural studies, the taking into consideration of that guidance cannot, however, be sufficient'. It adds that 'factors specific to the circumstances of the case ... must be taken into account when determining whether, in the light of that guidance, the conduct at issue must be regarded as having had, at least during part of the period during which it was implemented, the ability to produce exclusionary effects on the market concerned'.[75] Probably the somewhat stronger language is linked to the clear statement that the undertaking will benefit from any (reasonable, I suppose) doubt (*see* section 6 below), and in order to rule out that the standard is set 'too low'. In other words, the capacity (or 'ability') must exist, and not be just theoretical (or dependent on certain specific circumstances which are '*peu probable*' to arise, using the language of another paragraph).[76] To what extent the new formulation represents a real change or just a nuance of the language in *Intel* ('intrinsic capacity') or in *Generics UK* (on 'realistic' developments)[77] remains to be seen.

The subsequent judgment in *Google Android* shows the debate is not over.[78] Unlike *Google Shopping*, that stresses that actual effects are not required, only at least potential effects,[79] *Google Android* suggests that in a case of tying, in certain circumstances, the Commission is 'required' to carry out a 'close examination of the actual effects or further analysis', in a context where download was easy and in principle consumers could theoretically offset the anticompetitive effects of preinstallation.[80] This approach is based on several reasons. First, on a certain reading of *Microsoft*,[81] where the Commission did not 'merely assume' the capability to restrict competition, but also examined 'actual effects'.[82] Second, the General Court considers that even if the Commission referred in its decision to the 'capacity to restrict competition', it

must restrict 'effective competition' (*see ibid.*, paras 44 or 55). The same adjective in French, i.e., '*effective*' is translated as 'effective' or 'actual' in the English version depending on the context.

75. C-680/20, *Unilever Italia Mkt. Operations*, EU:C:2023:33, para. 44.
76. *Ibid.*, para. 43. The English version uses an expression that appears to have a slightly different meaning. It may not be the same to say that something is 'not likely to arise' and to say that it is '*peu probable*', which can be rather translated as 'unlikely' or having a 'low likelihood'. These nuances may matter when it comes to proving an infringement.
77. C-307/18, *Generics UK and Others*, EU:C:2020:52, paras 120-122.
78. T-604/18, *Google and Alphabet v. Commission* (*Google Android*), EU:T:2022:541. The recent *Qualcomm* judgment can also be seen as part of this trend. In that case, the General Court effectively disregarded evidence related to the potential effects of Qualcomm's conduct and decided to focus on the actual effects at stake (T-235/18, *Qualcomm v. Commission*, EU:T:2022:358).
79. T-612/17, *Google and Alphabet v. Commission (Google Shopping)*, EU:T:2021:763, paras 378, 440-442.
80. T-604/18, *Google and Alphabet v. Commission* (*Google Android*), EU:T:2022:541, para. 295.
81. T-201/04, *Microsoft v. Commission*, EU:T:2007:289.
82. T-604/18, *Google and Alphabet v. Commission* (*Google Android*), EU:T:2022:541, paras 286-288.

established that the exclusionary effects 'were real'.[83] The General Court concluded that the Commission 'correctly found ... that close examination of the actual effects or further analysis, according to the terminology used in the past in that regard, was required before it could be concluded that the tying in question was harmful to competition'.[84]

The General Court further explained why it considered that this was the right approach: '[s]uch an examination, first, serves to reduce the risk that penalties may be imposed for conduct which is not actually detrimental to competition on the merits and, second, further to clarify the gravity of the conduct in question, which will facilitate determination of the appropriate level of any penalty'.[85] The General Court makes a difference between examination of future effects of a conduct and the effects of a conduct implemented in the past, and suggests that it should be more demanding in the latter situation. The General Court explains that, in the instant case, it was not 'a question of the Commission carrying out a prospective analysis which would be based on effects that will arise in the light of assumptions that cannot yet be verified in practice, as might be the case in other circumstances'.[86] It added that 'where conduct has covered a number of years, the Commission may establish a restriction of competition by finding that those practices have eliminated or hampered sources of competition which would otherwise have taken place or developed. It is not, therefore, disputed that the actual and concrete effects of the practices at issue, effects which have arisen in the past, are to be assessed both in the light of the actual competition which the dominant undertaking had to face and in the light of the potential competition that could not arise because of the exclusionary practices'.[87] The General Court considered that in the present case 'the Commission has characterised the restriction of competition on the basis of the effects which the implementation of the practices at issue have had over a significant period of time, effects which may be observed and which enable the Commission to determine the nature and scope of the ensuing anticompetitive foreclosure, and the Court to review those findings'.[88]

Yet, this judgment may show the debate may be semantic. The analysis of 'actual and concrete effects' also covers obstacles to sources of 'potential competition', and the analysis of other parts of the conduct, such as the Anti-Fragmentation Agreements (AFAs), shows that the General Court is not as demanding as Google requested it to be

83. *Ibid.*, paras 291-294. 'the Commission endeavoured to characterise a restriction of competition not only as "potential" or "possible" but also as "actual" or "concrete" with regard to some of its aspects' (para. 293). There is a tendency to assess the legality of the Commission's own analysis on the basis of what the Commission claimed to have proven. If it claimed to have proven actual effects, the General Court will check if that is the case. In my view, the mere fact that in a decision the Commission may have focused on demonstrating 'actual' effects should not affect the threshold against which judicial review is carried out. If the Commission does not provide enough evidence of actual effects but the evidence is good enough to prove, at least, potential effects, a decision should not be annulled. In any event, the decision clearly states that it showed potential effects, in line with the applicable legal standard.
84. *Ibid.*, para. 295.
85. *Ibid.*
86. *Ibid.*, para. 297.
87. *Ibid.*, para. 298.
88. *Ibid.*, para. 299.

when it comes to demonstrating the competition (including innovation) that would have arisen in the absence of the practice (*see* section 10 below).

6 BENEFIT OF THE DOUBT IN 'BY EFFECT' CASES

EU Courts have become more explicit about the application of the benefit of the doubt in the analysis of the capability of the conduct to produce effects.[89] This aspect has appeared in recent case law in two ways. The first is the classical one where there is an analysis of whether the conduct is 'capable' of producing (exclusionary) effects, and the doubt concerns the capability of the conduct to produce the effect. The second is developed when there are observable facts about the evolution of competitors or parameters of competition (such as prices, decrease in quality or marginalisation of competitors) which are consistent with a finding of effects and the issue is whether such evolutions can be attributed to the conduct, i.e., in other words, the causal link is contested (*see* section 7).

The application of somewhat stricter standards is illustrated by *Slovak Telekom*.[90] The General Court considered that the presumption of innocence applied, that any doubt benefited the applicant[91] and concluded that the Commission had not demonstrated in the contested decision that the applicant's pricing practice, during the period between 12 August and 31 December 2005, resulted in such exclusionary effects.[92] It considered that the Commission did not demonstrate exclusionary effects in that period, and 'such a demonstration was required particularly given the presence of positive margins'.[93]

The *Intel RENV* judgment has also applied a 'reasonable doubt' test on some points. Section III.B of that judgment is exclusively concerned with the review of the AEC test carried out in the decision, in which context Section III.B.3 sets out the judgment's approach to the standard of proof. In setting out the standard of proof to be applied in reviewing the AEC test, a peculiar aspect of the judgment is that it begins, at paragraph 165, by describing cases where the Commission relies on 'the supposition that the facts established cannot be explained other than by the existence of anticompetitive behaviour', which allows undertakings to provide a plausible (non-infringing) alternative explanation for the facts, which will suffice to rebut the Commission's findings. The General Court later rejected the decision's assessment of Dell's contestable share on the finding that 'the assumption of a 7.1% contestable share was not the

89. Prior case law appeared to stick to require more something like a 'reasonable probability', *see* Castillo de la Torre/Gippini Fournier, *supra* n. 31, paras 2.044-2.052. *See also* case law in *supra* n. 35.
90. T-851/14, *Slovak Telekom v. Commission*, EU:T:2018:929.
91. *Ibid.*, para. 267.
92. *Ibid.*, para. 259. The General Court recalled that case law has indeed held that, if a margin is positive, 'it is not ruled out that the Commission can, in the context of the examination of the exclusionary effect of a pricing practice, demonstrate that the application of that practice was, by reason, for example, of reduced profitability, likely to have the consequence that it would be at least more difficult for the operators concerned to trade on the market concerned'.
93. *Ibid.*, para. 260.

only conceivable assumption',[94] and that there remained 'a doubt as to the definitive percentage of the contestable share for Dell and, more particularly as to that contestable share having to be set at 7.1 %'.[95]

The *Google Android* judgment tells a somewhat similar story. While the General Court acknowledged, once again, that the AEC test is not mandatory, but simply 'useful', it added that 'where, as in this instance, the AEC test is applied, it must be conducted rigorously'.[96] The General Court recalled the presumption of innocence and the benefit of the doubt at the beginning[97] and explicitly applied the benefit of the doubt when it annulled the Commission's findings on portfolio-based Revenue Share Agreements (RSAs), in particular as regards the AEC test.[98] The General Court concluded that 'in the present case, the Commission did not fulfil its obligation to analyse the intrinsic capacity of the fourth abuse, that relating to the portfolio-based RSAs ..., to foreclose competitors at least as efficient as the dominant undertaking. The Court remains doubtful as to the capacity of the payments at issue to restrict competition and, in particular, to produce the foreclosure effects alleged'.[99]

In *Qualcomm*, the General Court found that a number of factual elements gave rise 'to doubts as to the ability of Intel's chipsets, or those of other competitors of the applicant, to comply with Apple's technical and scheduling requirements for the models allegedly concerned and, where relevant, for the other iPad models which Apple intended to launch over that period'.[100] It followed that the Commission's assessment of the actual anti-competitive effects of the payments concerned was not carried out in the light of all the relevant evidence which had to be taken into consideration.[101]

Finally, in *Unilever*, the Court of Justice unambiguously rules that in the context of the demonstration of the capacity to restrict competition, the existence of doubt must benefit the undertaking which engages in such a practice.[102] While the doubt concerns the 'capacity' of the conduct to restrict competition (so it is not a doubt about whether the conduct will actually achieve the effect to restrict competition), the qualifiers added in this judgment ('effective' or 'actual' capacity) show that not any theoretical possibility will do, and that the decision-maker must take into account the specific circumstances, not just rely on general assumptions.

On this point, it may be somewhat surprising that the Court of Justice relies on *Woodpulp*. In that case the doubt concerned the very existence of the conduct (collusion), and whether it could be inferred from observable market developments. In *Woodpulp* the Court of Justice concluded that parallel conduct cannot be regarded as furnishing proof of concertation unless concertation constitutes the only plausible

94. T-286/09 RENV, *Intel v. Commission*, EU:T:2022:19, para. 244.
95. *Ibid.*, para. 239, similarly, referring to such 'doubt', paras 234, 244, 254-256.
96. T-604/18, *Google and Alphabet v. Commission* (*Google Android*), EU:T:2022:541, paras 643-644.
97. *Ibid.*, paras 78 and 80, and *see also*, paras 363 and 500.
98. *See, ibid.*, paras752 (as regards costs), 770 and 772-773 (as regards the contestable share of search queries) and the conclusion at 779.
99. *Ibid.*, para. 1017.
100. T-235/18, *Qualcomm v. Commission*, EU:T:2022:358, paras 359, 467 and 476.
101. *Ibid.*, paras 477-481.
102. C-680/20, *Unilever Italia Mkt. Operations*, EU:C:2023:33, para. 42.

explanation for such conduct.[103] When the analysis concerns contextual elements which influence whether the conduct (proven to the required standard) is capable of restricting competition, we are not examining the conduct, but the context. To the extent that an 'alternative plausible explanation' has been advanced in some cases to exclude causation, its relevance has been rejected by the Court of Justice (*see* section 7 below).

Moreover, some of these judgments, or at least some passages thereof, tend to deal with complex assessments as they would with traditional issues of 'hard fact'. The evolution is visible if we compare certain judgments. In a case of margin squeeze where price and cost information was missing for the few last months, and the Commission had found an abuse in the second half of 2006 based on the available data for mid-2006, the Court of Justice did not find that this constituted an impermissible reversal of the burden of proof.[104] *Intel* tells a different story. The AEC test for Hewlett-Packard (HP) was calculated for the whole period on the basis of data of some quarters only, the same ones the Commission claimed Intel itself had used, or at least not contested, in the administrative procedure[105] presumably because they were deemed sufficiently representative. When this was criticised by Intel, seemingly for the first time before the General Court, the Commission attempted to demonstrate that the outcome would not change even using the data of the other periods as well (and that the method used by the Commission in the decision was even favourable to Intel) but that demonstration was considered inadmissible.[106] Examining if information on rebates over additional periods would alter the outcome for the whole period was dealt with as if the Commission was trying to prove that an undertaking's conduct had lasted longer by providing inculpatory evidence that it had attended an additional meeting, for example.

One may wonder if, in some cases, the demands of the General Court may not go beyond what is reasonable. The AEC test does not rely on 'suppositions about conduct derived from observed facts',[107] but on the application of an econometric model to assessments of the input values for that model. The AEC test is in essence an evaluative exercise where, in particular as regards the contestable share, it relies on assumptions for which, *by definition*, there is no certain and definitive answer, only a best or reasonable estimate.[108] That being so, applying an evidential standard where it is sufficient to create a doubt on the assessment, or a fortiori, merely to suggest that

103. C-89/85, C-104/85, C-114/85, C-116/85, C-117/85 and C-125/85 to C-129/85, *Ahlström Osakeyhtiö and Others v. Commission*, EU:C:1993:120.
104. C-295/12 P, *Telefónica v. Commission*, EU:C:2014:2062, paras 220-221.
105. T-286/09 RENV, *Intel v. Commission*, EU:T:2022:19, paras 295, 302.
106. *Ibid.*, paras 316-317.
107. *Ibid.*, para. 165.
108. *See* the Opinion of Advocate General Kokott in C-23/14, *Post Danmark II*, EU:C:2015:343, paras 66-67 where she observed that, '[t]he methodology applied can ... prompt considerable differences of opinion. What is more, the data available for use as a basis for such analyses are not always reliable ... it is wrong to suppose that the issue of price-based exclusionary conduct can be managed simply and in such a way as to ensure legal certainty by applying some form of mathematical formula based on nothing more than the price and cost components of the businesses of the undertakings concerned. As I have already said, corporate data is not uncommonly open to different interpretations'.

another result would be 'conceivable', means that any assessment made in the context of an econometric model is probably bound to be annulled. An approach framed in terms of 'presumption of innocence' which leads to applying a standard of 'proof beyond reasonable doubt' may be understandable in relation to primary facts, but it may not always be fully appropriate when the evidential dispute concerns estimates, economic hypotheses and assumptions.

It is unclear how the future case law will solve the tension between the generalisation of the benefit of the doubt and the settled case law on complex economic assessments. In application of the case law on 'complex economic assessments' the EU judicature must, among other things, not only establish whether the evidence put forward is factually accurate, reliable and consistent, but must also determine whether that evidence contains all the relevant data that must be taken into consideration in appraising a complex situation and whether it is capable of substantiating the conclusions drawn from it.[109] When the General Court faces a complex economic assessment the possibilities for review somewhat shift and are 'modulated', but do not disappear. The threefold test in paragraph 39 of *Tetra Laval* tries to capture three different aspects of the assessment.[110] The test refers first to the quality of the evidence relied upon by the deciding authority and requires the EU Courts to review the existence of 'factually accurate, reliable, and consistent' evidence. Second, the test captures elements of 'completeness', somewhat more quantitative, when it mentions that the evidence shall contain 'all the information that must be taken into account in order to assess a complex situation' (*see* section 8 below). Third, the assessment whether that evidence is 'capable of substantiating the conclusions drawn' from it is more 'relational' in nature, but the case law has not provided that the conclusion must be drawn from that evidence beyond any reasonable doubt, but only that the evidence must be 'capable of substantiating' the conclusion, which is more a plausibility test. The test allows a finding that is justified by the factual record, while not excluding that another reasonable person could draw a different conclusion on the basis of the same facts.[111] We will come back to this issue in section 11.

109. C-12/03 P, *Commission v. Tetra Laval*, EU:C:2005:87, para. 39; C-386/10 P, *Chalkor v. Commission*, EU:C:2011:815, para. 54; T-201/04, *Microsoft v. Commission*, EU:T:2007:289, paras 87-89.

110. Nehl, H.P., 'Judicial Review of Complex Socio-economic, Technical, and Scientific Assessments in the European Union', in Mendes, J. (ed.), *EU Executive Discretion and the Limits of Law*, Oxford University Press, 2019, pp. 157, 182.

111. As one Advocate General has put it: 'A "complex" assessment is, to my mind, only one where the relevant factual background *cannot* be established *objectively* or with *absolute certainty*, since reasonable and well-informed persons could, at least to some extent, disagree on the outcome of the fact-finding exercise or the legal qualification of the facts. That may be the case where the institution in question is required, for example, to make use of some models or assumptions in order to infer, from a set of simple facts, certain complex facts, or to make some value-judgments to qualify the facts and/or determine the ensuing legal consequences' (Opinion of Advocate General Emiliou in C-389/21, *European Central Bank v. Crédit Lyonnais*, EU:C:2022:844, para. 50, with further references) (emphasis in the original).

7 COUNTERFACTUALS

Even when there is evidence that competitors are becoming marginalised in a market, and even if the authority must only prove the capacity of the conduct to produce exclusionary effects, dominant undertakings often rely on an array of arguments to claim that everything is fine. One frequent argument, which is evidential in nature, is to claim that there is no causal link between the conduct and the effects observed. Either there are other 'plausible' explanations for the observable effects or, in a 'but for' world, the effects would have happened anyway (the 'counterfactual').

It has been argued that the counterfactual must also take into account the ex ante dimension, so that the ex post restraints cannot be dissociated from the ex ante gains resulting from it (so they may not exist in the absence of the former).[112] In reality, such ex ante analysis exists in EU law as well, since the Court of Justice has accepted that efficiencies and in general benefits for consumer can be put in the balance with the restrictive effects on competition.[113] Yet, if it is simply an objective justification the burden to show how the ex post and ex ante dimensions are associated falls with the undertaking.[114] This is important since, under certain versions of the counterfactual, the efficiency considerations would be part of the counterfactual and, therefore, of the proof of effects and causation that is part and parcel of the burden of proof for the Commission.

The Court of Justice ruled decades ago that to assess the effects of an agreement or concerted practice with regard to Article 101 TFEU, competition should be assessed within the actual context in which it would occur *in the absence of the agreement in dispute.*[115] Logically, in the context of Article 101 TFEU the alternative conduct to be assessed is easily identifiable: the counterfactual is the absence of agreement or the absence of one clause of the agreement (whether such counterfactual is realistic or not is conceptually a different issue). Such general statement has never been made, as such, in the context of Article 102 TFEU. This does not mean that such methodological approach is irrelevant there. The Guidance on Enforcement Priorities indicates that the Commission's assessment 'will usually be made' by comparing the actual market situation with the 'appropriate counterfactual', i.e., the situation in the 'simple absence' of the conduct or 'another realistic alternative scenario'. The concept of 'counterfactual analysis' in the Guidance can be subject to different interpretations.

On the one hand, in line what the analysis under Article 101 TFEU, one could argue that a counterfactual analysis simply means to assess the capability of unilateral conduct to produce exclusionary effects against a baseline scenario where the conduct does not materialise. This approach appears to be explicitly or implicitly used in

112. Ibáñez Colomo, *supra* n. 33, 331. An *ex ante* approach to the counterfactual 'does not merely assume that the pro-competitive gains resulting from a practice (or transaction) would have existed' (*ibid.*, 315, and also 331, 357).
113. C-377/20, *Servizio Elettrico Nazionale*, EU:C:2022:379, para. 86.
114. *Ibid.*, para. 84 and C-209/10, *Post Danmark*, EU:C:2012:172, para. 42.
115. C-382/12 P, *MasterCard and Others v. Commission*, EU:C:2014:2201, para. 161; C-307/18, *Generics UK and Others*, EU:C:2020:52, para. 118. This case law goes back to 56/65, *Société Technique Minière*, EU:C:1966:39.

practice. While this position is at times contrasted with the statement that there is 'no need for a counterfactual analysis in Article 102', the debate is semantic to some extent. The analysis of capability to restrict competition is not done in a vacuum. It needs to be carried out against some form of baseline scenario, which can be very simple (normally, the mere absence of the conduct).

On the other hand, when a counterfactual analysis was discussed in a few recent court cases, such as *Google Shopping* or *Google Android*, it was in a context where applicants have argued that a counterfactual analysis necessarily implies a complex assessment of what the world would have looked like in the absence of the conduct (and all the different facts, reactions and events allegedly associated with the behaviour in question). Under this interpretation, a counterfactual analysis would require a comparison of the 'real life' scenario where the conduct is in place with a hypothetical scenario where not only the conduct, but also variables associated with the conduct would have not materialised.[116] This approach would consider it simplistic to rely on the baseline counterfactual scenario consisting of the situation 'without the conduct', since the dominant undertaking may claim that its conduct would have been different in other respects, so the counterfactual cannot simply be what happened 'minus the conduct'.

Counterfactuals by their nature are not facts. They are difficult to 'prove' with any degree of certainty, for they require the fact finder to speculate what would have happened if the undertaking had not done what it actually did. If combined with a benefit of the doubt, it would be simply impossible to prove an infringement. Although the word 'counterfactual' is often used in the merger context, merger control by definition involves a binary comparison between two different future scenarios (with or without a merger), both prospective. Such comparative analysis is by definition inherent in the analysis of mergers, and both elements of the comparison are placed at the same cognitive level. However, under Article 102 TFEU, the Commission would be retrospectively comparing conduct that actually happened (that must be proven to the required standard) with one or more other forms of conduct that did not take place and whose effects the Commission could not assess, given that they never took place. The decision-maker cannot 'prove' something that did not happen, but may, at most, develop an explanation of what could have (realistically) happened. However, since any realistic scenario is, by definition, never certain and it is therefore subject to doubt, the undertaking cannot claim that it did not commit an infringement by merely raising a 'doubt' about whether or not an alternative course of events would have occurred. This probably explains why the case law sometimes deals with this issue, in particular when the conduct is claimed to be associated with competitive benefits, as one of objective justification. This pragmatic approach allows for an examination of the

116. For instance, Google argued in AT.40099 – *Google Android* that the Commission ought to have analysed how all the several markets affected by the infringement would have evolved in the absence of Google's behaviour, e.g., in terms of entry and market shares evolution. In particular, Google argued that the Commission would have needed to compare the real-world situation of the market in the presence of the restrictions with a hypothetical world where Google would not have developed Android, given that it could not put in place the restrictions (*see* Decision of 18 July 2018, recitals 993-999 and 1146-1154, for example).

allegations of the dominant undertaking, but under an evidential regime which is actually administrable.[117]

The case law supports the view that elaborate counterfactuals of the type recently proposed by certain applicants are not required.[118]

The benefit of the doubt was recalled in *AstraZeneca* in the context of a discussion regarding the causal link between observed market developments (decrease of parallel trade) and the conduct at issue. This judgment is sometimes mentioned as support for the use of counterfactual analysis under Article 102 TFEU. The Court of Justice held that 'a presumption of a causal link ... is incompatible with the principle that doubt must operate to the advantage of the addressee of the decision finding the infringement'.[119] Yet, this statement must be placed in its context. A careful reading of the judgment at first instance confirms that neither the General Court nor the Court of Justice required a counterfactual when reviewing the Commission's assessment of AstraZeneca's conduct in Denmark, Norway and Sweden. Very simply, this is because there was no evidence that the parallel trade licence had been withdrawn in two countries, and therefore, necessarily, it had not been proven that any decrease in parallel trade resulted from AstraZeneca's conduct.[120]

In *AstraZeneca*, the General Court also found, in another part of the judgment, that conduct remains an abuse even if the dominant undertaking could hypothetically have engaged in other conduct (even lawful one) that would also have been capable of restricting competition. The mere existence of such hypothetical alternative conduct does not mean that the conduct actually implemented by the dominant undertaking was incapable of restricting competition.[121]

117. Examining an alleged *ex ante* scenario as one of objective justification, *see* T-604/18, *Google and Alphabet v. Commission* (*Google Android*), EU:T:2022:541, paras 599-617.
118. Generally speaking, there is not a single way to prove causation in EU law. Actually, there is not just one single concept of causation in law. Without getting into an elaborate discussion of the state of the debate about causation in legal theory, the 'but for' approach is not the only possible way to assess causation in all contexts, and it is not suitable in a number of circumstances (being under-inclusive or over-inclusive).
119. C-457/10 P, *AstraZeneca v. Commission*, EU:C:2012:770, para. 199.
120. As regards Denmark, the Commission had relied on the fact that parallel trade had decreased. However, the General Court considered that there was no evidence that the Danish authority had withdrawn the parallel trade licence (T-321/05, *AstraZeneca v. Commission*, EU:T:2010:266, paras 840 and 847) and that such a withdrawal would have been 'possibly in violation of European Union law' (para. 843). Moreover, as para. 852 of the General Court judgment confirms, the General Court considered that the Commission had failed to demonstrate that the Danish authority was likely to withdraw (or actually withdrew) the parallel trade licence as a result of AstraZeneca's conduct. Since there was no evidence that the parallel trade licence had been withdrawn, any decrease in parallel trade could not be the result of AstraZeneca's conduct. Regarding Norway, paras 856-861 of the General Court's judgment applied the same reasoning. The Norwegian authority did not withdraw the parallel trade licence after AstraZeneca's conduct. Regarding Sweden, paras 862-863 of the General Court judgment found that the Commission had demonstrated that AstraZeneca's conduct was capable of restricting competition because the Swedish authority withdrew the parallel trade licence.
121. T-321/05, *AstraZeneca v. Commission*, EU:T:2010:266. Before the General Court, AstraZeneca had claimed that its conduct was incapable of restricting competition because it had at its disposal other means to create obstacles to the introduction on the market of generic products. Paragraph 836 of the General Court's judgment dismissed the claim, observing that the fact that

The Court of Justice rejected in *Deutsche Telekom* a claim that the General Court had failed to examine the existence of a causal link because the development of market shares of competitors could allegedly have been explained by other reasons.[122] It did the same in *Telefónica*. In a case where the Commission stated (in the context of the fine) to have found 'actual effects', the General Court considered enough for the Commission to produce 'sufficient specific, credible and adequate indicia to establish that Telefónica's conduct had actual exclusionary effects on the market'.[123] Neither the General Court nor the Court of Justice, on appeal, considered that a 'but for' analysis was necessary. Actually, the challenge of the General Court's assessment of 'actual effects' (including causation) was considered inadmissible on appeal, as it concerned findings of fact.[124]

Generics UK mentioned the counterfactual assessment in an analysis 'by effects' under Article 101 TFEU (not when it is done 'by object'). However, the *Generics UK* judgment makes it clear that the 'counterfactual' relates first of all to the *conduct* of the undertaking, not to the effects on the market, or to how the market would operate or be structured: 'the sole purpose of the counter-factual is to establish the realistic possibilities with respect to that manufacturer's conduct in the absence of the agreement at issue'. Accordingly, 'in order to establish the existence of appreciable potential or real effects on competition of settlement agreements such as those at issue in the main proceedings, the referring court does not have to find either that the manufacturer of generic medicines who is a party to that agreement would probably have been successful in the patent proceedings, or that the parties to that agreement would probably have concluded a less restrictive settlement agreement'. Therefore a 'realistic' counterfactual is all that can be requested, not a 'probable' one.[125] Interestingly, *Generics UK* does not mention a counterfactual analysis in the context of Article 102 TFEU.

Moving back to Article 102 TFEU cases, the case law does not stand for the proposition that the Commission is obliged to 'recreate' what the different alternative conducts would be (and their effects) in all cases, in order to ascertain a causal link between the conduct and the situation in the market.[126] At least on that front, the case

AstraZeneca could have prevented the entry of generic products in other ways, which were arguably lawful, in no way made AstraZeneca's actual conduct incapable of restricting competition.

122. *See*, C-280/08 P, *Deutsche Telekom v. Commission*, EU:C:2010:603, para. 257.
123. T-336/07, *Telefónica v. Commission*, EU:T:2012:172, paras 394-402, and in particular para. 402.
124. C-295/12 P, *Telefónica v. Commission*, EU:C:2014:2062, paras 175-176. *See*, for Telefónica's argument, point 63 of the Advocate General Opinion, EU:C:2013:619. The Advocate General considered that 'specific, credible and adequate evidence' was enough, and there was no need of a 'but for' test (para. 64).
125. C-307/18, *Generics UK and Others*, EU:C:2020:52, paras 120-122.
126. O'Donoghue and Padilla acknowledge as much when, after examining national and EU case law, they say that 'there is no clear authority that the counterfactual is an essential under Article 102 TFEU'. They consider that 'some consideration of the counterfactual is necessary under Article 101 TFEU', and plead for some consistency in the application of Article 102 TFEU (O'Donoghue/Padilla, *supra* n. 14, 320-321). But their nuanced words ('some consideration of the counterfactual') are far away from claims that typically are made nowadays by some applicants.

law so far appears to be sufficiently realistic. When the expression 'counterfactual' is mentioned, it is in the 'simpler' version described above. In *Baltic Rail*, at one point the General Court examines what would have happened if the track had not been removed and finds that the removal 'aggravated the situation existing at the time of the suspension of traffic'.[127]

In *Google Shopping*, in the context of the examination of the causal link between the conduct and the impact on traffic to competing comparison shopping services (CSSs), the General Court showed openness to examine information that may 'cast doubt' on the link between the conduct and observable market developments.[128] Yet, it considered that the causal link was proven on the basis of the body of evidence,[129] and confirmed that the decrease of traffic to competing CSSs was attributable to the conduct. The General Court dismissed the specific counterfactual proposed by Google, because it only concerned part of the conduct, but also in a more principled manner:

> identifying a credible counterfactual scenario in order to analyse the effects on a market of what are assumed to be anticompetitive practices, that is to say, identifying the events that would have occurred in the absence of the practices that are being examined and identifying the situation that would have resulted, may, in a situation such as that of the present case, be an arbitrary or even impossible exercise if that counterfactual scenario does not really exist for a market that originally had similar characteristics to the market or markets in which those practices were implemented. In principle, in the case of existing competitive relationships, not just possible or potential competition, a credible counterfactual scenario must reflect an actual situation that is initially similar but whose development is not affected by all of the practices at issue. In comparing such a counterfactual scenario with the situation observed on the market to which those practices relate, the actual effects of those practices can normally be established, by isolating them from changes that are attributable to other reasons. In that respect, a counterfactual scenario, which compares two actual developments in such a situation, can be distinguished from an assessment of potential effects which, although it must be realistic, effectively describes a probable situation.
>
> Therefore, in the context of the allocation of the burden of proof ..., for the purpose of demonstrating an infringement of Article 102 TFEU, particularly as regards the effects of practices on competition, the Commission cannot be required, either spontaneously or in response to a counterfactual analysis put forward by the undertaking being challenged, systematically to establish a counterfactual scenario in the sense referred to above, contrary to Google's contention. That would, moreover, oblige it to demonstrate that the conduct at issue had actual effects, which ... is not required in the case of an abuse of a dominant position, where it is sufficient to establish that there are potential effects.

127. T-814/17, *Lietuvos geležinkeliai v. Commission*, EU:T:2020:545, para. 227.
128. T-612/17, *Google and Alphabet v. Commission (Google Shopping)*, EU:T:2021:763, para. 382.
129. *Ibid.*, paras 382-394. More specifically, it held at para. 382: 'in order to establish the actual or potential effects of practices which it examines, the Commission may in particular rely on other information obtained by observation of the actual evolution of the market or markets concerned by the practices. If a correlation is observed between those practices and the modification of competition on those markets, additional information, which may include for example the assessments of market participants, their suppliers, their customers, professional or consumer associations, may be capable of demonstrating the causal link between those practices and the evolution of the market. It may in some circumstances be for the undertaking concerned to put forward relevant information that may cast doubt on that causality'.

> In order to challenge the Commission's assessment of the potential effects of a practice on the market, or of its actual effects if these are determined by the Commission, the relevant undertaking can certainly put forward a counterfactual analysis. However, that analysis must then enable the effects of the impugned practice as a whole to be established, rather than the partial effects.[130]

The General Court did not rule out that a counterfactual analysis of the type put forward by Google may be a useful tool in certain cases. Rather, the General Court merely stated that the Commission is not 'systematically' required to conduct such an analysis,[131] and that Google's specific version of the counterfactual should be rejected.[132] The General Court ruled that, faced with the evidence that the Commission had adduced, it was for Google to provide some counter-evidence or explanation. This is in line with case law of the Court of Justice, that 'even if the burden of proof rests, ..., either on the Commission or on the undertaking concerned, the evidence on which a party relies may be of such a kind as to require the other party to provide an explanation or justification, failing which it is permissible to conclude that the rules on the burden of proof have been satisfied'.[133] In that case, the evidence on which the Commission relied was of such a kind as to require the other party to provide an explanation or justification, failing which it is permissible to conclude that the rules on the burden of proof have been satisfied.

The General Court also makes the point that, while the conduct at issue in that case may not have been the sole cause of the impact on traffic, the conduct did contribute to the impact (without finding that it was necessarily the only cause).[134] This is important as applicants often develop arguments around the idea that the Commission must prove that the conduct was the only, or at least, the main, cause of the effects. In reality, it should be enough to prove that the conduct contributes to the emergence of anti-competitive effects by increasing their probability, and therefore contributes to their materialisation.

Finally, it must be recalled that in *Google (Shopping)* the General Court rejected the use of the counterfactual mainly because the version proposed by Google was a partial one: comparing only certain elements of the conduct. However, certain forms of conduct may contain several elements and the analysis of their impact must in principle relate to the combination of the different elements,[135] not to each element in isolation, irrespective of whether each element in isolation is unlawful or not. There is no obligation on the Commission to deconstruct an overall conduct into components

130. T-612/17, *Google and Alphabet v. Commission (Google Shopping)*, EU:T:2021:763, paras 377-379.
131. *Ibid.*, para. 378.
132. *Ibid.*, paras 379-394.
133. *Ibid.*, para. 133. Referring to C-413/08 P, *Lafarge v. Commission*, EU:C:2010:346, paras 29 and 30 and the case law cited. This approach has been applied in many judgments, C-591/16 P, *Lundbeck v. Commission*, EU:C:2021:243, para. 79; C-623/15 P, *Toshiba v. Commission*, EU:C:2017:21, paras 51-52.
134. T-612/17, *Google and Alphabet v. Commission (Google Shopping)*, EU:T:2021:763, para. 412.
135. *See*, by analogy, regarding jurisdiction under public international law, C-413/14 P, *Intel v. Commission*, EU:C:2017:632, para. 50; and regarding effect on interstate trade, C-125/07 P, C-133/07 P, C-135/07 P and C-137/07 P, *Erste Group Bank and Others v. Commission*, EU:C:2009:576, paras 54-59.

and examine the (often hypothetical) individual impact of each component. On the one hand, certain forms of conduct may consist of individual elements that are also, in themselves, infringements of Article 102 TFEU. On the other hand, the different elements of certain other forms of conduct may not necessarily each constitute an infringement. Whichever the scenario, this does not mean that each individual element becomes a valid counterfactual.[136]

The *SEN* judgment is also interesting in this respect, as it appears to reject a narrow view of causation. On the one hand, the case was partly based on biases observable in consumers. This was part of the 'context' of the conduct, and the authority would have to prove the existence of such bias 'by evidence such as behavioural studies'.[137] The Court of Justice held that, if such bias was proven, 'the existence of such bias would preclude the finding that the difference in the quantity of information contained in the lists intended for EE and in the lists intended for competitors is due to the fact that the companies in the ENEL Group performed better on the free market or due to the attractiveness of the ENEL brand. The very existence of that bias would, by definition, make it impossible to determine whether there were objective causes for the difference in the consents given. Consequently, given that, in that scenario, that bias would stem from SEN's conduct, that company should be responsible for the difference in the number of customers in the lists intended for EE and those intended for EE's competitors'.[138] In other words, in examining causation the Court of Justice did not require or suggest conducting a counterfactual analysis, as the conduct made it 'impossible' to ascertain the 'objective causes' for the differences in the lists.[139] This reluctance to exclude causation is also visible in the way the Court of Justice deals with the possible reaction of competitors. Advocate General Rantos considered that if competitors had the means to obtain the contact details of customers, exclusion would not be caused by the conduct of the dominant undertaking.[140] The

136. As the General Court explains, comparing scenarios in which only one of the practices that form part of the conduct varies, would lead to the impact on traffic of the other parts of the conduct being neutralised, as they remain unchanged in both scenarios for each of the comparisons made (T-612/17, *Google and Alphabet v. Commission (Google Shopping)*, EU:T:2021:763, para. 374). Any infringing conduct may be composed of several elements. If the Commission were obliged to compare the impact of the infringing conduct with that of more limited allegedly non-infringing conduct, it would be obliged to examine if each element, in isolation, or in a different combination, would also infringe Article 102 TFEU. Ultimately, this would require the Commission to carry out an analysis not just of the conduct actually implemented, but also of alternative forms of conduct, including 'partial' ones, in isolation, even if such conduct, in isolation, may not have existed in reality. This would add an unjustified additional layer of complexity.
137. C-377/20, *Servizio Elettrico Nazionale*, EU:C:2022:379, para. 98.
138. *Ibid.*, para. 99.
139. If the bias exists, and the dominant undertaking exploits it, the effects stem from the conduct, and not from the bias. The uncertainty that derives from the conduct should not benefit its author. To put it differently, the special responsibility of a dominant undertaking also implies not to exploit such biases to its own advantage, as that would not constitute competition on the merits.
140. *SEN* Advocate General Opinion, *supra* n. 19, paras 78-79: 'it seems to me that it could be concluded that any potential risk of foreclosure of the relevant market was due not to Enel's actions but to the negligence of its competitors, which did not act competitively in order to capture customers of the protected market'.

Court of Justice rejects that approach, at paragraph 102.[141] The *Unilever* judgment, while stressing the quality that evidence should have for finding that the conduct has the capacity to restrict competition, does not mention any need for a counterfactual analysis.

In *Google Android*, the General Court also rejected the need to conduct a complex counterfactual analysis. For the General Court, having sufficiently demonstrated the existence of the restrictions at issue and of their effects on competition, the Commission was not also required (contrary to the views taken by Google) 'to carry out a counterfactual analysis to evaluate the hypothetical consequences that might have been observed, in the absence of the second abuse, on the markets for Android app stores, for general search services, on which that abuse was identified, and for licensable operating systems, on which Google also holds a dominant position'.[142]

8 COMPLETENESS AND CONTEXT: THE EXAMINATION OF ALL RELEVANT FACTS, ASPECTS AND DATA

The principle that context and all the relevant circumstances must be examined is not, as such, new.[143] Context may weaken or strengthen the capability to restrict competition of conduct. What is relatively new is the scope and intensity of this duty and its influence on judicial review of Commission decisions. A few recent cases illustrate this trend.

In *Post Danmark II*, the Court observed that the assessment of whether a rebate scheme is capable of restricting competition must be carried out in the light of *all relevant circumstances*, including the rules and criteria governing the grant of the rebates, the number of customers concerned and the characteristics of the market on which the dominant undertaking operates.[144] The analysis of coverage and the AEC test in that judgment also shows how contingent the analysis can be.[145]

141. The Court of Justice considers that its conclusion cannot be put into question by 'the actions that competitor undertakings potentially took or could have taken, such as purchasing files from third parties containing information on customers in the protected market, in order to limit the harmful consequences of that practice' (C-377/20, *Servizio Elettrico Nazionale*, EU:C:2022:379, para. 102).
142. T-604/18, *Google and Alphabet v. Commission* (*Google Android*), EU:T:2022:541, paras 892-893.
143. 56/65, *Société Technique Minière*, EU:C:1966:39, p. 249. The context may consist of elements which relate to the legal framework, the market context, or the conduct of others or of the dominant undertaking itself.
144. C-23/14, *Post Danmark (II)*, EU:C:2015:651, para. 68. *See also MEO*, as regards the concept of 'competitive disadvantage', for the purposes of subpara. (c) of the second paragraph of Article 102 TFEU (*supra* n. 46).
145. The Court of Justice examined the relevance of whether the rebate scheme applied to a majority of customers or not and held that there was no need to ascertain this point. At the same time, 'the fact that a rebate scheme, such as that at issue in the main proceedings, covers the majority of customers on the market may constitute a useful indication as to the extent of that practice and its impact on the market, which may bear out the likelihood of an anticompetitive exclusionary effect' (C-23/14, *Post Danmark (II)*, EU:C:2015:651, paras 43-46). In other words, this verification is not a precondition (thus, no legal rule), but the fact that it is complied with

The *Intel* judgments are also illustrative on this point. At first instance, the General Court attached no importance to the AEC test carried out by the Commission and, accordingly, did not address Intel's criticisms of that test.[146] On appeal, the Court of Justice set aside the judgment of the General Court. After recalling its own case law on loyalty rebates, it added that that 'case-law must be further clarified' in the case where the undertaking concerned submits, during the administrative procedure, on the basis of supporting evidence, that its conduct was not capable of restricting competition and, in particular, of producing the alleged foreclosure effects. In that case, the Commission is not only required to analyse, first, the extent of the undertaking's dominant position on the relevant market and, second, the share of the market covered by the challenged practice, as well as the conditions and arrangements for granting the rebates in question, their duration and their amount; it is also required to assess the possible existence of a strategy aiming to exclude competitors that are at least as efficient as the dominant undertaking from the market.[147] The Court of Justice considered that the analysis of the capacity to foreclose is also relevant in assessing whether a system of rebates which, in principle, falls within the scope of the prohibition laid down in Article 102 TFEU, may be objectively justified.[148] Consequently, the Court of Justice concluded that the General Court wrongly failed to take into consideration the dominant undertaking's line of argument seeking to expose alleged errors committed by the Commission in the AEC test.

The General Court's second judgment in *Intel RENV* appears to take a broader view of the duty of the Commission when the undertaking produces evidence trying to contest the capability to produce effects of a practice.[149] Despite the fact that the General Court refers to a 'presumption' of infringement,[150] there is very little in the

is an indication of the existence of abuse (so this fact may be relevant). The same happened a bit later in the judgment, when discussing the AEC test (*ibid.*, paras 56-61).

146. T-286/09, *Intel v. Commission*, EU:T:2014:547, paras 151 and 166.
147. C-413/14 P, *Intel v. Commission*, EU:C:2017:632, paras 138-139.
148. That balancing of the favourable and unfavourable effects of the practice in question on competition can be carried out in the Commission's decision only after an analysis of the intrinsic capacity of that practice to foreclose competitors which are at least as efficient as the dominant undertaking. If, in a decision finding a rebate scheme abusive, the Commission carries out such an analysis, the General Court must examine all of the dominant undertaking's arguments seeking to call into question the validity of the Commission's findings concerning the foreclosure capability of the rebate concerned (*see* paras 133-147). In the case, the Court pointed out that, while the Commission emphasised, in the decision at issue, that the rebates at issue were by their very nature capable of restricting competition such that an analysis of all the circumstances of the case and, in particular, an AEC test were not necessary in order to find an abuse of a dominant position, it nevertheless carried out an in-depth examination of those circumstances, setting out a very detailed analysis of the AEC test, which led it to conclude that an as efficient competitor would have had to offer prices which would not have been viable and that, accordingly, the rebate scheme at issue was capable of having foreclosure effects on such a competitor. It followed that, in the decision at issue, the AEC test played an important role in the Commission's assessment of whether the rebate scheme at issue was capable of having foreclosure effects on as efficient competitors. In those circumstances, the General Court was required to examine all of the dominant undertaking's arguments concerning that test.
149. T-286/09 RENV, *Intel Corporation v. Commission*, EU:T:2022:19.
150. '[W]hat is involved is, in that regard, a mere presumption and not a per se infringement of Article 102 TFEU, which would relieve the Commission in all cases of the obligation to conduct an effects analysis' (*ibid.*, paras 124, 522).

judgment about the evidence produced by Intel during the administrative procedure to rebut such a 'presumption', and it appears that the Commission bears the full burden of examining every single relevant element, without in reality being able anymore to rely on a presumption to prove its case. The judgment in *Google Android*, while using somewhat different language, also suggests that if the undertaking disputes that the practice restricts competition, the burden of proof borne by the Commission may not be alleviated in any way, without any clear indication of a qualitative threshold applying to the evidence adduced to rebut the presumption.[151] Yet, the General Court showed in *Google Android* that it does not accept allegations contesting the capability to restrict competition based on 'theoretical competition assumptions' as opposed to those based on 'practical reality'.[152]

The annulment in *Qualcomm* was based on the fact that the Commission's analysis 'was not carried out in the light of all the relevant factual circumstances and which is, on that ground, unlawful'.[153]

In *SEN*, the Court found that '[g]iven that the abusive nature of a practice does not depend on the form it takes or took, but presupposes that that practice is or was capable of restricting competition and, more specifically, of producing, on implementation, the alleged exclusionary effects, that condition must be assessed having regard to all the relevant facts'.[154] While the second part of the sentence is not novel,[155] it is for the first time that the Court of Justice expressly rejects that 'form' is determinative as such (although in reality the Court of Justice had never said the opposite before either). In addition, in replying to the third question,[156] the Court provides guidance on the analysis of exclusionary effects to be carried out by the relevant competition authority, including on how to treat evidence of lack of actual effects (*see* section 5 above).

The Court, relying on *Intel*,[157] holds in *SEN* that 'where a dominant undertaking submits, during the administrative procedure and with supporting evidence, that its conduct was not capable of restricting competition, the competition authority concerned is required to examine whether, in the particular circumstances, the conduct in question was indeed capable of doing so'.[158] The Court adds, that, in accordance with the right to be heard, competition authorities are obliged 'to hear the undertaking concerned, which means that they must pay due attention to the observations thus submitted by that undertaking, examining carefully and impartially all the relevant aspects of the individual case, and, in particular, the evidence submitted by that

151. T-604/18, *Google and Alphabet v. Commission* (*Google Android*), EU:T:2022:541, para. 795.
152. *Ibid.*, paras 427-428 (*see also* paras 451, 464 and 556).
153. T-235/18, *Qualcomm v. Commission*, EU:T:2022:358, para. 417.
154. C-377/20, *Servizio Elettrico Nazionale*, EU:C:2022:379, para. 72.
155. C-165/19 P, *Slovak Telekom v. Commission*, EU:C:2021:239, para. 42; C-549/10 P, *Tomra v. Commission*, EU:C:2012:221, para. 18.
156. The third question asked whether the evidence adduced by a dominant undertaking – seeking to show that its conduct did not actually produce restrictive effects despite its abstract ability to do so – should be considered relevant, and, if so, whether a competition authority is required to examine that evidence in depth. *See* C-377/20, *Servizio Elettrico Nazionale*, EU:C:2022:379, para. 49.
157. C-413/14 P, *Intel v. Commission*, EU:C:2017:632, paras 138 and 140.
158. C-377/20, *Servizio Elettrico Nazionale*, EU:C:2022:379, para. 51.

undertaking'.[159] As such, these statements are not novel, but stress the importance of procedural guarantees applicable in competition law proceedings.[160] Yet, the specific reference to these principles in this context may be interpreted by some to raise the burden on competition authorities for those types of exclusionary abuses in relation to which the case law so far did not require a specific demonstration of the capability of restricting competition for a finding of abuse.[161] However, paragraphs 51-52 do not provide a clear indication as to the degree of detail of the analysis to be carried out.[162] The degree of detail could therefore vary depending on the case at issue. As explained in section 5 above, in *SEN* the Court of Justice did not finally appear to set the bar very high for the national competition authority.

It seems to me that, as regards conduct for which there is at least a 'mere presumption' (to take the language of *Intel RENV*),[163] it is only where the undertaking provides evidence during the administrative procedure, trying to demonstrate that its conduct was not capable of restricting competition in the specific case, that the Commission must look into this evidence and subject it to a detailed examination. As is clear from the judgment in *SEN*, the Court of Justice does not consider an undertaking's mere claim of an absence of actual exclusionary effects as, in itself, sufficient to rebut the presumption of capability to foreclose,[164] the undertaking concerned must provide a specific and detailed submission. Such submissions cannot rely on 'theoretical competition assumptions' but on 'practical reality', as the General Court stressed in *Google Android*.

In other words, the submissions put forward by the undertaking concerned during the administrative procedure set out the scope of the Commission's examination obligation. If the sufficiently detailed arguments put forward by the undertaking concerned during the administrative procedure relate to one or more factors, it is for the Commission to examine whether the presumption of capability to foreclose is, as an exception, rebutted on the grounds which have been specifically mentioned. If the

159. *Ibid.*, para. 52.
160. The need for competition authorities to carefully and impartially examine the arguments and evidence submitted by the investigated undertaking is a general 'procedural guarantee' (*see* C-525/04 P, *Spain v. Commission*, EU:C:2007:698, para. 58; C-405/07 P, *Netherlands v. Commission*, EU:C:2008:613, para. 57), which also stems from the principle of good administration (C-505/09 P, *Commission v. Estonia*, EU:C:2012:179, para. 95; T-616/18, *Polskie Górnictwo Naftowe i Gazownictwo v. Commission*, EU:T:2022:43, para. 118 ; T-799/17, *Scania v. Commission*, EU:T:2022:48, para. 146). In preliminary references only the right to be heard is mentioned (C-377/20, *Servizio Elettrico Nazionale*, EU:C:2022:379, para. 52; C-680/20, *Unilever Italia Mkt. Operations*, EU:C:2023:33, para. 54), probably because Article 41 of the Charter is addressed not to the Member States but solely to the institutions, bodies, offices and agencies of the European Union (C-496/18 and C-497/18, *Hungeod and Others* EU:C:2020:240, para. 63; C-225/19 and C-226/19, *R.N.N.S. and K.A.*, EU:C:2020:951, para. 33).
161. Arguably for predatory pricing (*see, e.g.*, C-62/86, *Akzo v. Commission*, EU:C:1991:286, paras 71-72 and T-340/03, *France Télécom v. Commission*, EU:T:2007:22, paras 195-196) and exclusive purchasing obligations (85/76, *Hoffmann-La Roche v. Commission*, EU:C:1979:36, para. 89).
162. In particular, the Court does not require the analysis of the evidence submitted by the dominant undertaking to be 'in depth', contrary to the suggestion by the referring court (C-377/20, *Servizio Elettrico Nazionale*, EU:C:2022:379, para. 49).
163. *See supra* n. 150.
164. C-377/20, *Servizio Elettrico Nazionale*, EU:C:2022:379, para. 56.

Commission concludes that that is not the case, the presumption remains that the rebates are capable of foreclosure. However, the authorities should not be required, irrespective of the submissions made by the undertaking concerned during the administrative procedure, to provide details of criteria which are not of primary relevance to the overall decision.

Finally, the Court of Justice in *Unilever* stresses even more the relevance that specific circumstances of the case may have. Assumptions based on experience or economics about what the effects a certain conduct may typically have are not enough, and the decision-maker must also examine all the relevant surrounding circumstances.[165] The completeness of the enquiry is presented in such terms that, for some more complex cases, one could well have the perception that the task of proving a case will be a daunting one. While still labelling the substantive test as one of 'capacity' to produce effects, the scope of the factual enquiry may end up being close to one having to prove actual effects (*see* section 5 above).

More interestingly, the Court of Justice, in the context of the examination of exclusivity clauses,[166] defines the scope of the duty of the decision-maker when confronted with the submission, in the course of the procedure, of evidence (notably an economic study) capable of demonstrating the inability to produce restrictive effects. There is an obligation to 'examine' that evidence, and the competition authority cannot exclude the relevance of that study without setting out the reasons why it considers that the study does not contribute to demonstrating that the practices in question were incapable of restricting competition.[167] The duty of the competition authority appears to be first of all 'procedural', in that it must examine the evidence and explain why it does not prove what it intends to prove (i.e., the lack of capacity to restrict competition). If the file already contains evidence, and experience and economics provide certain assumptions, which are relied upon by the authority, there is no automatic 'shift' in the evidential burden of proof, in the sense that, when faced with the newly produced evidence, some 'additional' counter-evidence is always needed.

To the extent that the Court of Justice makes a link between these procedural duties and the possible existence of objective justifications or efficiencies,[168] it is important to bear in mind that the burden of proof regarding the latter is on the undertaking. As regards efficiencies 'it is for the dominant undertaking to show that the efficiency gains likely to result from the conduct under consideration counteract any likely negative effects on competition and consumer welfare in the affected markets, that those gains have been, or are likely to be, brought about as a result of that conduct, that such conduct is necessary for the achievement of those gains in efficiency and that it does not eliminate effective competition, by removing all or most existing sources of actual or potential competition'.[169] In *Generics UK*, the Court of Justice added that 'consequently that undertaking has to do more than put forward vague, general and

165. C-680/20, *Unilever Italia Mkt. Operations*, EU:C:2023:33, paras 43-44.
166. It is therefore unclear to what extent this may apply in full to other practices.
167. C-680/20, *Unilever Italia Mkt. Operations*, EU:C:2023:33, para. 55.
168. *Ibid.*, paras 49-50.
169. C-209/10, *Post Danmark*, EU:C:2012:172, para. 42. *See also* C-307/18, *Generics (UK) and Others*, EU:C:2020:52, para. 166; C-377/20, *Servizio Elettrico Nazionale*, EU:C:2022:379, para.

theoretical arguments on that point or rely exclusively on its own commercial interests'.[170]

A second dimension of the completeness paradigm tends, on the contrary, to stress formalism. The Court of Justice has already stated that, whilst, in areas giving rise to complex economic assessments, the Commission has a margin of discretion with regard to economic matters, that does not mean that the EU judicature must refrain from reviewing the Commission's interpretation of information of an economic nature. The EU judicature must, among other things, not only establish whether the evidence put forward is factually accurate, reliable and consistent, but must also determine whether that evidence contains all the relevant data that must be taken into consideration in appraising a complex situation and whether it is capable of substantiating the conclusions drawn from it.[171] These complex analyses may increasingly imply the application of economic models, which are in turn based on assumptions, but also on the collection of all relevant data. In this sense, completeness in this context is related to the increasing (economic) formalisation of the enforcement of competition law. If an

---

86. With somewhat different words, the test had already been mentioned in C-95/04 P, *British Airways v. Commission*, EU:C:2007:166, para. 86.

170. C-307/18, *Generics (UK) and Others*, EU:C:2020:52, para. 166 *in fine*. In *Generics*, the Court of Justice also deals with allegations of pro-competitive effects in the context of restrictions 'by object'. The Court observes that, 'where the parties to that agreement rely on its pro-competitive effects, those effects must, as elements of the context of that agreement, be duly taken into account for the purpose of its characterisation as a 'restriction by object', ..., in so far as they are capable of calling into question the overall assessment of whether the concerted practice concerned revealed a sufficient degree of harm to competition and, consequently, of whether it should be characterised as a 'restriction by object' (C-307/18, *Generics (UK) and Others*, EU:C:2020:52, para. 103). The pro-competitive effects must be 'demonstrated and relevant', and 'specifically related to the agreement concerned' (*ibid.*, paras 105, 107). The mere existence of such pro-competitive effects (let alone simple 'claims') cannot as such preclude characterisation as a 'restriction by object' (*ibid.*, para. 106). What is relevant is whether such effects are 'demonstrated, relevant and specifically related to the agreement concerned', but also 'sufficiently significant', so that they justify a reasonable doubt as to whether the settlement agreement concerned caused a sufficient degree of harm to competition, and, therefore, as to its anti-competitive object (*ibid.*, para. 107. Reference to a 'reasonable doubt' also appears in para. 110). This test has been already applied in *HSBC*. The Court of Justice set aside the first instance judgment for having erred in law in holding that, with the exception of restrictions ancillary to a main operation, it is only in the context of the assessment of Article 101(3) TFEU that any pro-competitive effects can be taken into account (C-883/19 P, *HSBC Holdings and Others v. Commission*, EU:C:2023:11, paras 139-141). However, when deciding on the action for annulment, it dismissed HSBC's argument that the exchanges made it possible to offer prices which were more favourable to customers of the banks concerned, as it did not give rise to any reasonable doubt as to the harmful nature of those exchanges with regard to competition on the market concerned (*ibid.*, paras 198-205). Despite this reference to 'reasonable doubt', this is not a low threshold, and applicants have generally been unable to meet it. *See* C-586/16 P, *Sun Pharmaceutical and Ranbaxy v. Commission*, EU:C:2021:241, paras 82-83; C-591/16 P, *Lundbeck v. Commission*, EU:C:2021:243, para. 137 (a mere unsubstantiated assertion concerning the pro-competitive effects of the agreements at issue is insufficient to rebut their characterisation as 'restrictions by object'); C-883/19 P, *HSBC Holdings and Others v. Commission*, EU:C:2023:11, paras 198-205.

171. C-12/03 P, *Commission v. Tetra Laval*, EU:C:2005:87, para. 39; C-386/10 P, *Chalkor v. Commission*, EU:C:2011:815, para. 54; T-201/04, *Microsoft v. Commission*, EU:T:2007:289, paras 87-89.

AEC test is conducted, the General Court has ruled in *Google Android* that it must be 'rigorously conducted'.[172]

Both trends may be having a distinct impact on the very definition of an infringement. Since Articles 101 and 102 TFEU are relatively vague,[173] the definition of the infringements has historically relied on its refinement through case law. When the characterisation of the facts relied on relatively abstract categories, the definition of what was relevant or irrelevant was relatively straightforward. The contextualisation of the examination of the lawfulness of the conduct, however, introduces elements which make any decision on whether something is relevant or irrelevant much harder, since the Courts insist that the circumstances of the individual case must all be considered. It will be rare for the factual circumstances to be identical from one case to another. Even if the conduct follows a pattern already examined in the past, the structure of the market at issue and its dynamics may be different. While there are still types of conduct that will be normally considered infringements, without need for much examination of the context, the Commission may risk annulment if it does not make at least a cursory examination of that context. All in all, this trend risks leading to a situation where prior case law is not considered to contain normative statements about how the conduct should be legally qualified, but at most a background assumption, or a factual premise, that alleviates the burden of proof of the Commission, but does not do away with the examination of each and every case specific allegation and evidence that might support a different result. The problem with that approach is that legal certainty suffers, since everything may be relevant, while nothing appears to be dispositive.

In summary, the case law shows a tendency to do partly away with previous case law which appeared to contain the scope of the enquiry to certain facts, while leaving, at most, some 'defences' to the undertaking. This tendency is visible in cases of dominance as well as for certain types of agreements outside the cartel area. While under traditional case law the fact that conduct with certain features was characterised as unlawful was considered to contain a normative statement, in that it defined the features in question as being those that the Commission needs to prove for the conduct to be considered unlawful, recent case law is showing an increased willingness to deal with such definitions in the prior case law as simple factual 'premises' of the decision-maker, based on past experiences and economic consensus. Such 'premises' would be just background knowledge without any normative value because each specific case is to be examined afresh in the light of all circumstances. One may wonder

172. *See Google Android, supra* n. 96.

173. *See* T-167/08, *Microsoft v. Commission*, EU:T:2012:323, para. 91: 'the use of imprecise legal concepts within a provision does not prevent liability being established as against a person who contravenes it. As the Commission points out, if it were otherwise, an infringement of Article 101 or 102 TFEU – which are themselves drawn up using imprecise legal concepts, such as distortion of competition or 'abuse' of a dominant position – could not give rise to a fine without the prior adoption of a decision establishing the infringement'. In *Towercast*, the Court of Justice has ruled that 'Article 102 TFEU is sufficiently clear, precise and unconditional, with the result that there is no need for a rule of secondary law expressly prescribing or authorising its application by the national authorities and courts' (C-449/21, *Towercast*, EU:C:2023:207, para. 51).

how this 'contextualisation' can be easily reconciled with legal certainty and the need to define in advance the prohibition.

9 COMPETITION ON THE MERITS AND EFFICIENCY

As explained above, the general observation in *Post Danmark I*, *Intel* and *SEN* that Article 102 TFEU generally cannot be relied on by less efficient undertakings as a shelter from 'competition on the merits' does not mean that every finding of abuse is contingent on demonstrating that the conduct was capable of foreclosing or marginalising an equally efficient competitor as the dominant undertaking.[174] *Unilever* could not be clearer on this point.[175] Very often efficiency, as one of the ultimate goals of competition law, is conflated with the relative efficiency of the dominant undertaking and its competitors (actual or potential), as if this needed to be assessed and demonstrated in all cases.[176]

It is not surprising that the discussion of efficiency of competitors first appeared in pricing abuses. There is nothing in the level of a price that can be regarded as abusive in itself. Indeed, in principle, a lower price may be a sign of superior efficiency, and that imposes some caution both on the legal test and the assessment of the evidence.[177] An additional specific filter is therefore necessary to examine the abusiveness of price-related conduct.

By contrast, other filters have often been used when assessing the abusiveness of non-price-based types of conduct. Surely, deciding what is competition on the merits and what is not is not always an easy question. But it does not mean that there are no signposts along the road. Our signposts are in the case law. Allowing customers or consumers to make choices on the basis of the merits of product or services is often a crucial element, and *Microsoft* contains some of the most developed language on

174. In *Compagnie Maritime Belge*, the Court of Justice did not require the Commission to show that the only remaining independent competitor targeted by the price-based conduct was as efficient as the members of the liner conference (C-395/96 P and C-396/96 P, EU:C:2000:132); in *AstraZeneca*, the Court did not require the Commission to show that AstraZeneca's competitors on the market for proton pump inhibitors were as efficient as AstraZeneca (C-457/10 P, *AstraZeneca v. Commission*, EU:C:2012:770); and *Generics (UK)*, further confirms that not every finding of abuse depends on whether the conduct was capable of foreclosing an equally efficient competitor (C-307/18, EU:C:2020:52). For example, in *Tetra Pak*, a tying case, the Court of Justice did not require the Commission to show that other manufacturers of non-aseptic cartons were as efficient as Tetra Pak (C-333/94 P, EU:C:1996:436). This is probably because tying cannot probably be considered, almost by definition, as competition on the merits, since precisely not giving customers a choice to obtain the tying product without the tied product means that the tied product is not acquired because it is better (*see also infra* n. 178).
175. C-680/20, *Unilever Italia Mkt. Operations*, EU:C:2023:33, paras 39 and 57. The latter clearly states that 'the use by a undertaking in a dominant position of resources other than those governing competition on the merits may be sufficient, in certain circumstances, to establish the existence of such an abuse'.
176. Similarly, while consumer welfare may be one of the ultimate goals of Article 102 TFEU, this does not imply that an effect on consumer welfare must be assessed and demonstrated in each individual case.
177. *See* Castillo de la Torre/Gippini Fournier, *supra* n. 31, paras 2.061-2.064.

'competition on the merits'.[178] The applicable filters may be contextual,[179] and may also include whether the conduct is based on obvious economic or objective reasons, whether it is not standard practice in a certain sector,[180] or whether there is any justification for the conduct other than to harm competitors.

Even for certain forms of price-based conduct, the Court of Justice has previously considered them abusive where the intent or the strategy of the dominant undertaking was to exclude competitors,[181] without suggesting that such intent or strategy should be limited to intent to exclude equally efficient competitors. This confirms that less

178. T-201/04, *Microsoft v. Commission*, EU:T:2007:289, paras 407, 1046, 1048, 1069-1070. The General Court concludes that the Commission was correct to make certain findings, including, in particular, that because of bundling, Microsoft's competitors are a priori at a disadvantage even if their products are inherently better than Windows Media Player, that Microsoft interferes with the normal competitive process as a consequence of unfettered competition on the merits and that Microsoft shields itself from effective competition from vendors of potentially more efficient media players which could challenge its position (para. 1088). As can be seen, the language of 'product quality' and 'efficiency' is clearly relevant to the issue of 'competition on the merits'. Indeed, the central focus of consumer choice in the General Court's analysis of Article 102 TFEU cases can be seen in the remedy prescribed in Article 6(a) of the contested decision which, as the General Court pointed out, 'allows consumers to exercise their choice on the basis of the merits of the products' (para. 1143).
179. For example, in *AstraZeneca*, the Union Courts did not hold that the de-registration of a medicinal product generally falls outside of the scope of competition on the merits. Rather, the EU Courts held that the de-registration fell outside of the scope of competition on the merits in the specific circumstances of that case (T-321/05, *AstraZeneca v. Commission*, EU:T:2010:266, pars 804-812, confirmed on appeal in C-457/10 P, *AstraZeneca v. Commission*, EU:C:2012:770, paras 129-134). In C-170/13, *Huawei Technologies*, EU:C:2015:477, bringing an action for infringement seeking an injunction prohibiting the infringement of a patent was considered abusive or not depending on very specific contextual circumstances (paras 48-53). *See also* O'Donoghue/Padilla, *supra* n. 14, 267, lamenting this contextual character of notions such as 'competition on the merits', because a practice may be regarded as not constituting competition on the merits, 'in one situation, but not in others'.
180. The fact that something may be standard practice in a sector is not decisive, but the fact that it is not may well be. In Case T-65/98, *Van den Bergh Foods v. Commission*, EU:T:2003:281, the General Court recalled the criterion regarding 'competition on the merits' (para. 157) and found that the conduct was abusive largely on the basis of the context despite the argument that exclusivity constituted 'a standard practice on the relevant market' (para. 159). The Commission submitted that the exclusivity clause in question interfered with retailers' freedom to choose suppliers on the basis of the merits of the products which they offer (para. 148) and was at variance with conditions of normal competition for consumable items (para. 152). If we assume that the General Court agreed with the Commission when it referred to 'harm to consumers', it would seem that the freedom of consumers to choose would be a component of 'competition on the merits', and conduct which is directed at preventing consumers from choosing which product wins their favour in the marketplace does not constitute 'competition on the merits'. The Court of Justice upheld the judgment and recalled that Article 102 prohibits 'recourse to methods different from those which condition normal competition' (C-552/03 P, *Unilever Bestfoods v. Commission*, EU:C:2006:607, para. 129). In other words, the qualification of competition as 'normal' is not dependent only on how often the practice is deployed in a specific sector. Although some authors consider that it may be inconsistent to define an abuse as 'novel' while also considering that the conduct is not 'normal competition' (O'Donoghue/Padilla, *supra* n. 14, 266) this may conflate the type of conduct with the lack of precedents.
181. C-62/86, *Akzo v. Commission*, EU:C:1991:286, para. 72; C-202/07 P, *France Télécom v. Commission*, EU:C:2009:214, para. 108; C-52/09, *TeliaSonera Sverige*, EU:C:2011:83, paras 41 and 45; C-549/10 P, *Tomra v. Commission*, EU:C:2012:221, paras 19-20; and C-23/14, *Post Danmark (II)*, EU:C:2015:651, paras 59-60.

efficient competitors are also protected by Article 102 TFEU against certain forms of competition by dominant undertakings which are *not* on the merits.

In *Google Shopping*, the General Court considered that the AEC test was irrelevant in non-price abuses: 'the use of the as-efficient-competitor test is warranted in the case of pricing practices (predatory pricing or a margin squeeze, for example), in order, in essence, to assess whether a competitor that is as efficient as the dominant undertaking allegedly responsible for those pricing practices, and which, in order not to be driven immediately from the market, would charge its customers the same prices as those charged by that undertaking, would have to do so at a loss and accentuating that loss, causing it to leave the market in the longer term .... In the present case, the practices at issue are not pricing practices'.[182] Furthermore, 'assuming it is possible for a competition authority such as the Commission to compare the actual efficiency of several undertakings by studying in depth the various parameters of their business, such an exercise could produce objective results only if the conditions of competition were not in fact distorted by anticompetitive behaviour. Consequently, such an exercise could not in itself serve to determine whether such conduct had been established'.[183]

Google Shopping is interesting as it stresses that the AEC test is a specific method which examines a 'hypothetical' competitor, and it is not about examining whether the actual competitors in the market are efficient or not. *Google Android* prominently makes the same point.[184] At times, the discussion refers to an 'AEC principle' (or AEC assessment), whereby it is the analysis of the actual (or potential) competitors which is relevant, beyond cases of price-based conduct. This implies an examination of the (actual) efficiency of such competitors, as regards all types of abuses. Leaving aside that such principle appears to be based on an incorrect interpretation of the case law (*see* section 3 above), *Google Shopping* already indicates how difficult such assessment can be in practice.[185] In my view, the competition authority (or the dominant undertaking, for that matter) cannot be realistically expected to examine systematically how efficient competitors were or are, in the different dimensions that efficiency may have. As *Unilever* stresses, such efficiency is also about capacity to innovate and

182. T-612/17, *Google and Alphabet v. Commission (Google Shopping)*, EU:T:2021:763, para. 538. It added that, 'in principle, the "as-efficient competitor" is a hypothetical competitor, which is therefore presumed to charge its customers the same prices as the dominant undertaking, but is faced with the same costs as the dominant undertaking bears or makes its competitors bear if it sells them an input for the end product .... The use of the as-efficient-competitor test is intended to show that even a competitor as efficient as the undertaking that established the pricing practice at issue would be unable to withstand it in the long term by adopting the same pricing, since it would not be able to rely on the power conferred by the dominant position. That competitor is not therefore in principle an actual competitor whose actual efficiency would be assessed, ... The use of that test, which involves comparing prices and costs, did not therefore make sense in the present case, since the competition issue identified was not one of pricing'.
183. *Ibid.*, paras 538-540. Also stressing the idea that the conduct itself has made it impossible to carry out an 'objective' assessment, *see* C-377/20, *Servizio Elettrico Nazionale*, EU:C:2022:379, para. 99.
184. T-604/18, *Google and Alphabet v. Commission* (*Google Android*), EU:T:2022:541, paras 644-645, 770-772.
185. T-612/17, *Google and Alphabet v. Commission (Google Shopping)*, EU:T:2021:763, para. 540.

quality.[186] It is also irrelevant in most cases: if, in non-pricing abuses, the Commission finds that the conduct does not constitute competition on the merits, any analysis of the efficiency of competitors (actual, or hypothetical) should be in principle irrelevant.[187]

The Court of Justice has provided in *SEN* some guidance on the concept of means 'not based on competition on the merits' in reply to the first question.[188] In contrast with *Google Shopping*, the issue of efficiency is presented as part of this condition (*see* section 3 above). The Court sets out some general considerations on the concept of means not based on competition on the merits but falls short of providing a clear and comprehensive definition. It refers in this regard, in line with previous case law, to 'means different from those governing normal competition in goods or services on the basis of the transactions of commercial operators'.[189] On the contrary, according to the Court, an undertaking competes on its own merits when it relies on 'its skills and abilities in particular'.[190]

Interestingly, the Court appears to give more guidance at paragraph 85 by stating that 'the concept of competition on the merits covers, in principle, a competitive situation in which consumers benefit from lower prices, better quality and a wider choice of new or improved goods and services' and, as a result, 'conduct which has the effect of broadening consumer choice by putting new goods on the market or by increasing the quantity or quality of the goods already on offer must, inter alia, be considered to come within the scope of competition on the merits'. However, the latter statement is made in relation to the possibility to invoke the interests of consumers as an *objective justification* to escape a finding of abuse.[191]

The Court of Justice draws a close link between the use of means not based on competition on the merits and the potential foreclosure of competitors that are as efficient as the dominant undertaking.[192] The underlying assumption seems to be that, if a practice implemented by a dominant undertaking threatens the survival of a hypothetical as-efficient competitor (where efficiency is to be measured not only by reference to price, but also to choice, quality or innovation),[193] that practice is unlikely

186. C-680/20, *Unilever Italia Mkt. Operations*, EU:C:2023:33, para. 39.
187. In *Google Shopping* the General Court examined the argument in the context of the capability of the practice to restrict competition (because the argument was raised in that context) and it could have also rejected it by simply referring to the fact that once the allegation that Google was competing on the merits has been rejected in previous section of the judgment, there was no need to examine whether competitors were efficient or not.
188. The first question requested guidance as to the criteria for distinguishing the means or resources which come within the scope of normal competition from those which come within the scope of distorted competition. *See* C-377/20, *Servizio Elettrico Nazionale*, EU:C:2022:379, para. 65.
189. C-377/20, *Servizio Elettrico Nazionale*, EU:C:2022:379, para. 68. On the fact that reference to 'transactions' is probably an incorrect translation *see supra* n. 17.
190. *Ibid.*, para. 73.
191. It does not refer as such to the analysis whether the hypothetical (or actual) competitor is as efficient, but whether the conduct is in the interest of the consumer and it is therefore 'objectively justified' (*ibid.*, para. 84, *in fine*).
192. *Ibid.*, paras 71-76. Such a link could already be derived from previous case law. *See, e.g.*, C-52/09, *TeliaSonera Sverige*, EU:C:2011:83, para. 43.
193. *See* C-377/20, *Servizio Elettrico Nazionale*, EU:C:2022:379, para. 73 (and also para. 85), referring to C-413/14 P, *Intel v. Commission*, EU:C:2017:632, §§133-134.

to be based on competition on the merits. In other words, the Court seems to consider the potential foreclosure of an as efficient competitor as a possible proxy for identifying conduct that is not based on competition on the merits. However, this does not mean, *a contrario*, that the condition of competition not based on the merits can only be established by demonstrating that a given practice could foreclose hypothetical as efficient competitors (and indeed, the Court does not say so), or that if equally efficient competitors are not foreclosed, the conduct is by definition lawful.[194]

The Court of Justice describes two types of conduct that are not based on competition on the merits,[195] and, at that stage of its reasoning, the Court does not positively give examples of conduct that can be considered competition on the merits. These types of conduct are not presented as being exhaustive. In other words, there is no clear indication that conduct that does not fall into either of these categories should automatically be regarded as being competition on the merits.

The first type of conduct that is not based on competition on the merits relates to '[a]ny practice the implementation of which holds no economic interest for a dominant undertaking, except that of eliminating competitors so as to enable it subsequently to raise its prices by taking advantage of its monopolistic position'.[196] As an example of conduct falling within the first category, the Court of Justice only refers to *AKZO*, which related to the application of prices below average variable costs.[197] By referring to that precedent, the Court identifies what appears to be one recurring feature of conduct that has been found to be outside competition on the merits in past case law, that is to say the fact of not being (purely) driven by economic considerations (or possibly by other objective justifications), but rather by the underlying objective to restrict competition. Indeed, besides *AKZO*, this feature follows from the wording used in other cases such as, for instance, *Hoffman-La Roche* (exclusive purchasing obligations),[198] *Post Danmark II* (fidelity/target rebates),[199] *TeliaSonera Sverige* (margin squeeze)[200] and *AstraZeneca* (provision of misleading information to authorities and de-registration of market authorisations).[201]

194. This is confirmed by the fact that neither of the two scenarios laid down at paras 77-78 as examples of conduct that is not based on competition on the merits requires such a demonstration.
195. C-377/20, *Servizio Elettrico Nazionale*, EU:C:2022:379, paras 77-83.
196. *Ibid.*, para. 77.
197. C-62/86, *AKZO v. Commission*, EU:C:1991:286, para. 71.
198. 85/76, *Hoffmann-La Roche v. Commission*, EU:C:1979:36, para. 90.
199. Opinion of Advocate General Kokott in C-23/14, *Post Danmark*, EU:C:2015:343, para. 29, where the Advocate General considered that, to establish whether certain rebates are abusive, '[t]he decisive criterion is ... whether, in providing an advantage not based on any economic supply justifying it, the rebates seek to remove or restrict the buyer's freedom to choose his sources of supply, to bar competitors from access to the market, or to strengthen the dominant position by distorting competition'.
200. C-52/09, *TeliaSonera Sverige*, EU:C:2011:83, para. 88, where the Court clarified that the pricing practice in question was abusive because, 'in the absence of any other economic and objective justification, such conduct [could] be explained only by the dominant undertaking's intention to prevent the development of competition in the downstream market and to strengthen its position, or even to acquire a dominant position, in that market by using means other than reliance on its own merits'.
201. C-457/10 P, *AstraZeneca v. Commission*, EU:C:2012:770, para. 130, where the Court noted that 'conduct ... consisting in the deregistration, without objective justification ... of the [market authorisations for certain products], by which AZ intended ... to hinder the introduction of

The second type of conduct that is not based on competition on the merits relates to 'a practice that a hypothetical competitor – which, although it is as efficient, does not occupy a dominant position on the market in question – is unable to adopt, because that practice relies on the use of resources or means inherent to the holding of such a position'.[202] This scenario, which appears to describe a more prescriptive category of practices, will be referred to below as the 'non-replicability test'. While it is settled case law that a causal link between dominance and the abuse is not necessary for a finding of abuse,[203] this scenario does not appear to be incompatible with that case law, insofar as the replicability is only one of the possible criteria to identify conduct not based on competition on the merits. It is not because a practice is 'replicable' that it constitutes competition on the merits.

According to the Court of Justice, this non-replicability approach follows from the case law on both price and non-price related exclusionary practices.[204] As regards pricing practices, the Court refers to the AEC test as applied *inter alia* in *TeliaSonera Sverige*.[205] The Court considers that a pricing practice is not based on competition on the merits if a hypothetical as efficient competitor would be unable to charge the same prices as the dominant undertaking while continuing to viably compete in the market (i.e., without incurring losses or making an insufficient profit margin).[206]

As regards non-pricing practices, at paragraph 83 the Court only refers to the *Bronner* case law concerning a dominant undertaking's refusal to grant access to an essential facility. However, this case law cannot easily be squared with a criterion based on the non-replicability of the dominant undertaking's practice. Indeed, *Bronner* related to the non-replicability (or, more precisely, the indispensability) of the input supplied by the dominant undertaking, not of that undertaking's practice.[207]

Leaving aside the possible inconsistencies between the non-replicability test and the *Bronner* case law, the Court's presentation of that case law at paragraph 80-83 is, on a closer look, relatively cautious and it would not be appropriate to read too much in it. First, with respect to pricing practices, although the Court states that 'those practices must be assessed, as a general rule, using the "as-efficient competitor" test',[208] it then clarifies that 'that test is merely one of the ways to show that an undertaking in a dominant position has used means other than those that come within the scope of "normal" competition'.[209] Second, with respect to non-pricing practices

generic products and parallel imports does not come within the scope of competition on the merits'. *See also* para. 93 of the same judgment.

202. C-377/20, *Servizio Elettrico Nazionale*, EU:C:2022:379, para. 78. The following paragraph refers to this criterion as 'the material or rational impossibility for [an as efficient competitor] to imitate the practice in question'.
203. *See, e.g.*, C-6/72, *Europemballage Corporation and Continental Can Company v. Commission*, EU:C:1973:22, para. 27.
204. C-377/20, *Servizio Elettrico Nazionale*, EU:C:2022:379, para. 79.
205. C-52/09, *TeliaSonera Sverige*, EU:C:2011:83, paras 41-43.
206. C-377/20, *Servizio Elettrico Nazionale*, EU:C:2022:379, paras 80-82.
207. C-7/97, *Bronner*, EU:C:1998:569, paras 44-46.
208. C-377/20, *Servizio Elettrico Nazionale*, EU:C:2022:379, para. 80.
209. *Ibid.*, para. 81, referring to C-23/14, *Post Danmark*, EU:C:2015:651, para. 57. This is also in line with T-286/09 RENV, *Intel Corporation v. Commission*, EU:T:2022:19, para. 126. It is to be noted that the Court explicitly mentions initially 'loyalty rebates' within the list of pricing

generally, the Court (rightly) does not state that replicability of the dominant undertaking's input or of its practice precludes a finding of abuse.[210] Unlike Advocate General Rantos,[211] it does not even state that a refusal to supply involving an input that can be replicated by competitors of the dominant undertaking necessarily constitutes competition on the merits,[212] and it does not refer to bundling and tying as additional practices in relation to which the replicability of the conduct would be relevant for the purposes of finding an abuse.[213]

In sum, as follows from the above, the Court takes the non-replicability of the dominant undertaking's conduct as an indication that such conduct falls outside the scope of competition on the merits. By contrast, the Court (rightly) does not draw the opposite conclusion from the replicability of the dominant undertaking's conduct.

When turning to the facts of the main case,[214] the Court begins by stating that the practice at issue did not relate to SEN's refusal to allow competitors of EE to access an essential facility, but to 'SEN's decision to transfer, for consideration, certain commercial information which it held concerning its customers, including their contact information in particular, to EE, in an unfavourable and therefore discriminatory way in respect of EE's competitors on the free market, even though SEN was in a dominant position on the protected market'.[215] The Court then applies the second of the two above-mentioned scenarios, namely the non-replicability test. In doing so, it seems to adopt a strict interpretation of the 'use of resources or means inherent to the holding of [the dominant] position', which tends to facilitate a finding of abuse. Indeed, it refers to the use by SEN of a structure capable of providing large amounts of customer contact details in the protected market, which is available to SEN on account of its former monopoly and which, for that reason, is not available to its competitors.[216] However, it refuses to assess whether the same or similar customer contact details could be

practices which must be assessed 'as a general rule', by means of the AEC test (para. 80). In doing so, the Court seems to blur any distinction between, on the one hand, (i) margin squeeze and predatory pricing, in relation to which demonstrating that the dominant undertaking fails the AEC test is inherently necessary for a finding of abuse (as the fact that prices are below costs is a necessary precondition for margin squeeze or predatory pricing to be abusive); and, on the other hand, (ii) other pricing practices, such as fidelity rebates, for which such a demonstration is neither necessary nor decisive. In particular, paras 80-81 may not be fully consistent with *Post Danmark II*, where the Court acknowledged that distinction (*see* C-23/14, *Post Danmark*, EU:C:2015:651, paras 55-57).

210. As regards replicability of the input, such a statement would have been incompatible with the case law whereby indispensability of the input is not decisive for practices other than refusal of access (*see, e.g.*, C-165/19 P, *Slovak Telekom v. Commission*, EU:C:2021:239, para. 50). Likewise, as regards replicability of the practice, such a statement would have been incompatible with case law whereby, because of a dominant undertaking's special responsibility not to distort competition, a given conduct can be acceptable if adopted by a non-dominant undertaking, while being abusive if adopted by a dominant undertaking (*see, e.g.*, T-191/98, *Atlantic Container Line and Others v. Commission*, EU:T:2003:245, paras 1124 and 1460).
211. *See SEN* Advocate General Opinion, *supra* n. 19, para. 71, second sentence.
212. C-377/20, *Servizio Elettrico Nazionale*, EU:C:2022:379, para. 83.
213. *See SEN* Advocate General opinion, *supra* n. 19, para. 71, third sentence (referring to the Guidance, paras 54 and 61, which in turn refer to the replicability of 'the bundle').
214. *See* C-377/20, *Servizio Elettrico Nazionale*, EU:C:2022:379, paras 87-102.
215. *Ibid.*, para. 89.
216. *Ibid.*, paras 92 and 101.

obtained by competitors through other means, as argued by SEN (while even hinting at paragraph 102 to the fact that this may be possible).[217] In other words, the Court seems to use as reference for the replicability test the exact conduct of the dominant undertaking through the use of its own resources, regardless of the replicability of the input involved in the conduct.[218] Unsurprisingly, in these circumstances, the Court concludes that SEN's behaviour 'would necessarily be incapable of being adopted by a hypothetical as-efficient competitor'.[219]

10 RECALIBRATING: 'INNOVATION, CHOICE AND QUALITY', THE 'NOT (YET) AS EFFICIENT COMPETITOR', AND THE FATE OF THE AEC TEST

While using means not based on competition on the merits is prohibited, if the means have actual or potential exclusionary effects, regardless of an analysis of the efficiency of actual or hypothetical competitors, case law has also specifically recognised that in certain instances, competition may also come from undertakings that are less efficient than the dominant firm (or a 'not-(yet)-as efficient competitor').

That may be the case in particular in markets where the emergence of as-efficient-competitors may not be possible because of the 'structure of the market'.[220] Thus, the competitive constraint they exert may also warrant protection under Article 102 TFEU. While the Guidance's recurring references to as efficient competitors seem to imply that cases where the competitive constraint exerted by a 'not-(yet)-as-efficient' competitor may deserve protection are somewhat exceptional, experience shows that cases where the protection may be warranted are actually more common, especially in markets presenting specific characteristics.[221] In *TeliaSonera* the Court of Justice stressed that '[p]articularly in a rapidly growing market, Article 102 TFEU requires action as quickly as possible, to prevent the formation and consolidation in that market of a competitive structure distorted by the abusive strategy of an undertaking which has a dominant position on that market or on a closely linked neighbouring market, in other words it requires action before the anti-competitive effects of that strategy are realised'.[222]

217. *See supra* n. 141.
218. This is also in contrast to Advocate General Rantos' Opinion, who considered that if competitors had the means to obtain the contact details, exclusion would not be caused by the conduct of the dominant undertaking (*see supra* n. 140).
219. C-377/20, *Servizio Elettrico Nazionale*, EU:C:2022:379, para. 101.
220. C-23/14, *Post Danmark (II)*, EU:C:2015:651, paras 59-60. The Guidance on Enforcement Priorities does recognise this possibility in the context pricing abuses, but limits it to 'certain circumstances' (Guidance, point 24), suggesting a narrower approach.
221. In markets where barriers to entry and expansion are very high, such as in the presence of significant economies of scale or network effects which lead to the emergence of (super-) dominant firms, market entrants cannot be expected to achieve the same or even a similar cost structure as the incumbent. In these markets, entrants typically offer certain specific features that can be attractive to customers, in the hope to gain enough demand to reach a minimum efficient scale. Abuses in these markets typically take place at this early stage, to deprive entrants from any realistic prospect of expansion or even long-term survival.
222. C-52/09, *TeliaSonera Sverige*, EU:C:2011:83, para. 108.

In their recent case law EU Courts have been open to uphold findings not exclusively based on quantitative analyses and 'as efficient competitor' approaches. EU Courts have confirmed that as a matter of law, the Commission does not have a legal obligation to run a price-cost AEC test to prove the existence of a price-based exclusionary abuse, and particularly concerning rebates. In *Post Danmark II*, the Court of Justice made it clear that 'it is not possible to infer from Article [102 TFEU] or the case-law of the Court that there is a legal obligation requiring a finding to the effect that a rebate scheme operated by a dominant undertaking is abusive to be based always on the as-efficient-competitor test. Nevertheless, that conclusion ought not to have the effect of excluding, on principle, recourse to the as-efficient-competitor test in cases involving a rebate scheme for the purposes of examining its compatibility with Article [102 TFEU]'. Therefore, the AEC test is, in the words of the Court of Justice, 'one tool amongst others' for the purposes of assessing whether there is an abuse of a dominant position in the context of a rebate scheme.[223] This is clearly confirmed in *Unilever*.[224] The judgment rules out the obligation to carry out such test in pricing abuses, while extending its potential relevance beyond pricing abuses to conduct whose consequences can be 'quantified'.[225]

In *Google Android*, the General Court recalled that the AEC test 'constitutes a possible framework for analysing exclusionary effects in relation to a given case and the exclusionary effects alleged. However, it is only one of several factors that may be applied in order to establish, by means of qualitative or quantitative evidence, whether anticompetitive foreclosure exists for the purposes of Article 102 TFEU.' However, it added that 'where, as in this instance, the AEC test is applied, it must be conducted rigorously'.[226] While the issue was discussed in the *Qualcomm* case, the General Court eventually ended up annulling the Commission decision on other grounds, without ruling on this point.[227]

223. C-23/14, *Post Danmark (II)*, EU:C:2015:651, paras 56-61. *See also* C-413/14 P, *Intel v. Commission*, EU:C:2017:632, paras 142-144.
224. C-680/20, *Unilever Italia Mkt. Operations*, EU:C:2023:33, paras 57-58. Also in C-377/20, *Servizio Elettrico Nazionale*, EU:C:2022:379, paras 80-82.
225. C-680/20, *Unilever Italia Mkt. Operations*, EU:C:2023:33, para. 59.
226. The General Court stated that, in that regard, in order to determine whether a competitor which hypothetically is at least as efficient would be likely to be foreclosed by the contested practice, the Commission must examine economic data relating to cost and sales prices, and in particular whether the dominant undertaking is engaging in below-cost pricing. This requires, however, that sufficiently reliable data be available. Where they are, the Commission is required to use information on the costs of the dominant undertaking itself. The Commission has investigative powers to obtain the necessary data. Further, if reliable information on those costs is not available, the Commission may decide to use the cost data of competitors or other comparable reliable data (T-604/18, *Google and Alphabet v. Commission* (*Google Android*), EU:T:2022:541, paras 643-644).
227. The Commission did not apply an AEC test in the *Qualcomm (Exclusivity payments)* case. Qualcomm argued that the Commission was obliged to run its own AEC test in light of the Guidance. The Commission disputed such argument, pointing *inter alia* to the fact that the case was prioritised due to other reasons. The General Court in its judgment insists that the analysis must examine 'the foreclosure capacity of at least as-efficient competitors' (T-235/18, *Qualcomm v. Commission*, EU:T:2022:358, para. 424), and notes that that the decision 'did not rely on an economic model, such as an as-efficient competitor test, in order to conclude that the payments concerned were capable of having anticompetitive effects and, in Section 11.5 of the

Moreover, other parameters of competition such as 'choice, quality or innovation' are important.[228] The Court of Justice recalls in *Unilever* the limits of the AEC test as that method takes into consideration only price competition.[229] *Google Android* gives specific examples of the importance that non-price elements may have. The General Court stresses the impact on innovation that the foreclosure of non-compatible Android forks by means of the AFAs had.[230] The Commission found in the contested decision that, by preventing the development of different variants of the OS, the practice of excluding non-compatible Android forks that was established in the AFAs had thereby hindered opportunities for innovation and deprived users of functionalities distinct from those offered by Android-compatible forks or additional to them. The Commission 'was not required, for the purpose of establishing that that finding was well founded, to define more precisely which functionalities could have been introduced had the practice at issue not been adopted'. Google did not dispute that the markets in question are characterised by rapid innovation, to which forks with characteristics differing from those of compatible forks would have been able to contribute.[231] In markets characterised by innovation, obstacles to entry may have an impact on innovation and may therefore constitute a restriction of competition.

On the contrary, after having considered that the Commission had committed errors in essential aspects of the competitive analysis of the portfolio-based RSAs, namely the assessment of their coverage and the application of the AEC test, it could not be concluded that the portfolio-based RSAs are abusive just on the basis of the twofold finding of a restriction of innovation or of an interest on the part of original equipment manufacturers (OEMs) and mobile network operators (MNOs) in pre-installing several general search service apps if those RSAs did not exist.[232] But even in that context, the General Court was open to examine foreclosure 'by means of qualitative or quantitative evidence'.[233] It was also open to consider that the abuse could have been found 'even if notwithstanding a share of the relevant markets covered by the contested practice that is not significant, the segment covered by that practice or even just the OEMs and MNOs concerned in this case were of such strategic importance that the foreclosure effect attributable to that practice was capable of excluding Google's rival general search services from the relevant markets', but found that the Commission did not argue the case in those terms.[234]

contested decision, the Commission merely stated that the critical margin analysis presented by the applicant did not undermine its conclusions' (para. 426).

228. C-377/20, *Servizio Elettrico Nazionale*, EU:C:2022:379, paras 45 and 48.
229. C-680/20, *Unilever Italia Mkt. Operations*, EU:C:2023:33, para. 57.
230. T-604/18, *Google and Alphabet v. Commission* (*Google Android*), EU:T:2022:541, para. 892 : 'That conduct deprived potential or existing competitors of Google of any market, strengthened Google's dominant position on the markets for general search services and deterred innovation. Moreover, Google has neither demonstrated that the exclusion of non-compatible Android forks resulting from the AFAs met a legitimate objective nor established that that exclusion produced pro-competitive effects attributable to that undertaking.'
231. *Ibid.*, para. 862.
232. *Ibid.*, paras 800-801.
233. *Ibid.*, para. 643.
234. *Ibid.*, paras 696-697. The Court cannot, either of its own motion or at the request of the administrative authority, add further reasons to those used by the administrative authority in

In other parts, the General Court also stresses the importance of choice: 'the needs of consumers are not necessarily met by what is qualitatively the best solution, assuming that Google might claim that its services represent such a solution, given that variables other than technical quality, such as the protection of privacy or the account taken of specific linguistic features of search queries, also play a role'.[235] In its findings, the General Court considers that the practices at issue 'were detrimental to the interest of consumers in having more than one source for obtaining information on the internet' and 'restricted the development of search services directed at those segments of consumers that attached particular value to, inter alia, the protection of privacy or specific linguistic features within the EEA'. It added that 'such interests were not only consistent with competition on the merits, in that they encouraged innovation for the benefit of consumers, but were also necessary in order to ensure plurality in a democratic society'.[236]

Bearing these more qualitative elements in mind, as well as the need to carry out an overall assessment of a number of factors, the crucial role of the 'correctness' of the AEC test in some judgments betrays the role of the test. The presence of errors in the AEC test in a decision does not mean that the undertaking *passed* the AEC test, but only that the decision did not prove that the undertaking *failed* the AEC test. Moreover, whereas *failing* the test can be strong evidence of abuse in the context of all relevant circumstances of the case, *passing* it does not mean that the conduct is necessarily lawful. If the *Intel* judgment of the Court of Justice had agreed that passing the AEC test was decisive, it would not have enumerated all the criteria for analysis in paragraph 139, before it addressed the relevance of the AEC test. Typically, in the context of rebates cases, even if the undertaking does pass the AEC test, given the nature of the AEC test generally applied in Commission decisions, this is only one consideration to be taken into account in the overall assessment of whether the rebates were capable of foreclosure.

Moreover, experience with the AEC test has shown that its importance should not be overstated. In cases where intervention would be necessary to protect effective competition from not-(yet)-as-efficient competitors, the application of an AEC principle (let alone the AEC test) may not be warranted. More in general, the test can only reflect quantitative and not qualitative parameters. If the application of the AEC test must comply with the very demanding standards set out in *Intel RENV* or *Google Android* (*see* section 6 above), it may turn out to be virtually impossible for the Commission to rely on the AEC test in order to assess the capability to foreclose. If the EU Courts are too demanding on how the AEC test is conducted, they may be providing arguments

that decision (T-691/14, *Servier and Others v. Commission*, EU:T:2018:922, para. 1379, with further references). Moreover, as recently put, 'the participation of an undertaking in an infringement of the competition rules must ... be assessed by reference solely to the evidence gathered by the Commission in that decision. The only relevant question is therefore whether that participation is or is not proved in the light of that evidence' (T-344/17, *Latam Airlines and Lan Cargo v. Commission*, EU:T:2022:185, para. 484).

235. T-604/18, *Google and Alphabet v. Commission* (*Google Android*), EU:T:2022:541, paras 577-578.

236. *Ibid.*, para. 1028.

not to use it, since at the same time case law clearly says that conducting such test is not necessary to prove capability to produce exclusionary effects.

At a more conceptual level, it is also important to bear in mind, in the 'form versus effects' dichotomy, that the fact that the General Court requires the AEC test to be conducted 'rigorously' evokes the importance of doing things 'by the book', and therefore stresses the formal nature of the test. It is an example of legal formalism as it prevents decision-makers from deciding on the basis of all considerations that are relevant to the purpose of protecting competition,[237] unless of course one were to consider that protecting only equally efficient competitors is itself the relevant purpose of the law. The introduction of qualitative elements allows the decision-maker to take into account other considerations, including the degree to which competitive pressure is reduced by less efficient competitors.

11 JUDICIAL REVIEW IN THE ERA OF 'EFFECTS-BASED', MORE ECONOMIC, APPROACH

Examining how 'cumbersome' the effects-based, more economic approach, is would not be complete without having at least a brief look at the issue of judicial review. The Court of Justice has reacted to concerns about lack of review of complex assessments by developing a type of 'process-oriented' review paradigm, based on the criteria for judicial review outlined in *Tetra Laval*,[238] as explained above. However, some recent judgments appear to go beyond such standard, which is not even mentioned or paraphrased in the critical parts of the analyses.[239] Applying the 'process-oriented' review paradigm, the EU Courts rarely disagree openly with the Commission's substantive assessment (although they occasionally do). Instead, errors in assessment are increasingly framed in procedural terms. Rather than finding that the Commission's assessment is erroneous, judgments find instead that the Commission did not 'sufficiently' or 'appropriately' consider one (allegedly) relevant element or find a deficiency in the process of applying an economic test or model. The procedural clothing serves to shield the court from the criticism that it is interfering with the decision-maker's discretion.

The scope of this 'process-oriented' review has been magnified by the ever-increasing demand to consider 'all relevant' circumstances, aspects, information and data, that we have seen above. A certain view of the 'effects-based' approach deploys a different sort of formalism, based on models and extensive collection of data and this is combined with a trend towards an 'all-things-considered' approach, where every individual, often contextual, circumstance of each case may become relevant and must

237. Lindeboom, *supra* n. 4, at 35.
238. C-12/03 P, *Commission v. Tetra Laval*, EU:C:2005:87, para. 39; C-386/10 P, *Chalkor v. Commission*, EU:C:2011:815, para. 54; T-201/04, *Microsoft v. Commission*, EU:T:2007:289, paras 87-89.
239. T-286/09 RENV, *Intel Corporation v. Commission*, EU:T:2022:19. *See also*, outside Article 102 TFEU, T-399/16, *Commission v. CK Telecoms*, EU:T:2020:217.

be considered (section 8 above). Under both approaches some procedural and evidential standards constrain decision-making but their parallel implementation creates tensions because, in my view, they may not always be conceptually compatible.

Of course, not 'anything' can be 'relevant'. There are multiple examples of cases where EU Courts considered that the Commission was right in not examining a certain aspect or a study, or explicitly rejected the relevance of it without having a thorough look at it.[240] In other cases, while some relevant element was not examined and the Commission's analysis may have presented certain gaps, the overall body of evidence was solid enough for the gaps not to lead to the annulment of the decision, since typically the EU Courts will conduct an overall assessment of the available evidence.[241] There are indications that for certain types of conduct the context can be subject to a more summary analysis, in the understanding that the circumstances under which context may influence the outcome will be exceptional.[242] However, other recent cases appear to be more formalistic, in that absence of analysis of an element creates the basis for finding errors irrespective of the demonstration that such deficiency had an impact on the finding in question.[243]

In practice, the 'relevance' is increasingly focused on the individual situation at hand. In such case, it is not always clear what may turn out to be relevant or not, unless it is first at least examined by the decision-maker, and there is an attempt to gather the relevant evidence on that point. If certain aspects are not examined since, in accordance with past cases, they are irrelevant, the risk is that the Courts will consider that

240. For example, in *Google Android*, the question, debated by the parties, of the extent to which the relative competitive pressure exerted by Android-compatible forks and by other licensable OSs is more or less significant by comparison with the competitive pressure exerted on Google by non-compatible Android forks was considered irrelevant. It was sufficient, for the purpose of characterising a restriction of competition, to establish that the non-compatible Android forks would have been competitors of Android in the market for licensable OSs, which Google did not dispute (T-604/18, *Google and Alphabet v. Commission* (*Google Android*), EU:T:2022:541, para. 844).

241. For example, in *AstraZeneca*, even if the Commission was criticised for not examining certain elements, the General Court did not find them to be material for the outcome, showing that the Commission's findings were supported by sufficient evidence (T-321/05, EU:T:2010:266, paras 177-182, 188-191).

242. For example, for 'particularly serious' horizontal restrictions of competition, the Court of Justice has held that 'the analysis of the economic and legal context of which the practice forms part may … be limited to what is strictly necessary in order to establish the existence of a restriction of competition by object' (C-373/14 P, *Toshiba v. Commission*, EU:C:2016:26, para. 29; C-469/15 P, *FSL Holdings and Others v. Commission*, EU:C:2017:308, para. 107; T-433/16, *Pometon v. Commission*, EU:T:2019:201, para. 279 ; T-240/17, *Campine v. Commission*, EU:T:2019:778, paras 309-310). In *Servier*, the General Court held 'that, depending on the context and the unlawful conduct in question, the threshold for a finding of potential competition may vary' (T-691/14, *Servier and Others v. Commission*, EU:T:2018:922, para. 320).

243. In *Google Android*, in the context of the examination of the AEC test, the Commission maintained that the question of costs was irrelevant. This argument is considered ineffective by the General Court (without much explanation) since Google referred to a substantially lower percentage than that used by the Commission in the contested decision, no further investigation was initiated by the Commission and no detailed reasons relating thereto were given in the contested decision, so that the General Court had 'doubts as to the correctness and validity of the AEC test carried out by the Commission' (T-604/18, *Google and Alphabet v. Commission* (*Google Android*), EU:T:2022:541, paras 737, 751-752).

an individual examination is always necessary, especially when the undertaking makes certain types of allegations. The Court may not engage into an examination of the impact of the lack of analysis of certain elements, by having a look at the strength of the elements which were proven or remained uncontested and may annul the decision not because any error is found as such, but because one aspect of the case was not examined. The Commission may also 'pay a price' for examining something which it is not, as such, legally required to examine. As the recent *Intel* saga shows, the risk is that the Courts may consider that, since the Commission has examined the point, it must be because it is somehow relevant, so by examining a given element the Commission is also shaping how the law is to be interpreted in the future.

Logically, the EU Courts must rely on a standard of review that nudges the Commission towards collecting all relevant available information. However, while an incomplete examination makes a finding less resistant to possible challenges, it is not because an examination is incomplete that a finding is necessarily erroneous. In my view, defining 'relevance' and dealing with incompleteness are important issues which deserve further reflection. It is often the 'relevance' of the information that is crucial in the review nowadays, but 'relevance' is situated in a 'grey zone' overlapping the administration's factual appraisals as well as the procedural and substantive legality.[244] In litigation, one possible view, in line with the 'process-oriented' nature of the review, is that it is for the applicant to demonstrate that the elements or data not considered could plausibly alter the outcome of the analysis, on the basis of a concrete examination of such potential impact and the strength of other elements effectively considered. Another possible view is that as soon as one element, considered relevant ex ante, is not examined, the burden has not been discharged or there can be a 'doubt' about the correctness of the assessment that fatally affects the finding. While this second view appears to stress the substantive nature of the problem, it is in reality more formalistic. If taken too far it risks turning the dynamics of litigation on its head and creating a procedural 'tunnel vision'.

The risk is that judicial review is transformed into a 'ticking boxes' exercise, i.e., the review of a long list of elements of the 'assessment process', where judges may lose sight of the substance of the case, and form and process unduly prevail over substance. The somewhat 'mechanical' application of paragraph 139 of the *Intel* judgment[245] visible in *Intel RENV* and *Qualcomm*,[246] where each of the five elements mentioned must be 'sufficiently' considered regardless of the strength of the evidence on other aspects (which may not even be examined) is a case in point. In my view, considering all the elements of a case implies assessing also the overall strength of the case as presented and how likely it is that allegedly omitted aspects, if any, may plausibly alter

244. Nehl, *supra* n. 110, 177. The author refers to current case law as relying on a 'relevance paradigm'. In certain cases, the 'relevance' of a given aspect may be, in itself, something that may relate to the 'legal characterisation of facts'. Outside competition law, this was at the center of the judgment in C-691/15 P, *Commission v. Bilbaina de Alquitranes*, EU:C:2017:882, paras 47, 49.

245. C-413/14 P, *Intel v. Commission*, EU:C:2017:632.

246. T-286/09 RENV, *Intel Corporation v. Commission*, EU:T:2022:19 ; T-235/18, *Qualcomm v. Commission*, EU:T:2022:358.

the outcome. It is not just about checking that the boxes in a list have been 'sufficiently' ticked. I find it hard to assess if the examination of any given element is 'sufficient' without looking at the strength of other elements of the case. As explained above, I think that, when the case law has created some (rebuttable) presumption, the submissions put forward by the undertaking concerned during the administrative procedure, contesting the capability to restrict competition, will in turn define the scope of the Commission's duties.

Moreover, the focus on 'finding errors' (often with a magnifying glass) that logically permeates judicial review may lead the EU Courts not to have the full picture of the case and create a 'tunnel vision'. Because it is the decision that is reviewed, the focus is on whether the decision observes the law, not whether the conduct of the undertakings does. In particular, some judgments convey a reluctance to 'reassess' what remains of the case and evidence, after finding an error, as the court could be exceeding its competence by doing so. I think this is partly incorrect. To be clear, the fact that the applicant defines the subject matter of the case and a decision can only be annulled on the basis of submissions made by the applicant, does not mean that the EU Courts are bound to ignore in their assessment other aspects or evidence of the case. The EU Courts must examine, as part of their judicial function and without relying on new grounds, if the uncontested (or judicially upheld) points and evidence in the decision may still sustain the substantive finding in question.

All these trends have a major impact in a context where the Court of Justice has accepted that an applicant can provide new evidence during the court proceedings, not previously submitted during the administrative proceedings,[247] while, by contrast, the Commission must prove in principle its case on the basis of the arguments and evidence in the decision (and on which the undertaking has been heard). The General Court in *Intel RENV* considered (at several passages) that it was inadmissible for the Commission to submit new calculations and economic reports in rebuttal of expert reports submitted by Intel for the first time in the court proceedings.[248] Some other past judgments have taken a more permissible approach.[249] In my opinion, there is a difference between introducing new facts or grounds in the debate,[250] and being allowed to properly substantiate why the new elements (arguments and evidence) provided by the applicant are either not probative or do not have an impact on the outcome. Dealing with elements of complex assessments as issues of 'hard fact' will tend to blur that difference. While the Commission cannot fundamentally catch up on a deficient enquiry, it must be able to show that the element or data omitted is not relevant or, even if it is relevant, the omission does not affect the outcome.

247. C-603/13 P, *Galp v. Commission*, EU:C:2016:38, para. 72.
248. T-286/09 RENV, *Intel Corporation v. Commission*, EU:T:2022:19, paras 235-236, 252-253, 316-317 and 443-444; interestingly, in the first judgment the General Court appeared to have ruled the opposite (T-286/09, *Intel v. Commission*, EU:T:2014:547, para. 1197).
249. C-286/13 P, *Dole Food v. Commission*, EU:C:2015:184, para. 38; T-395/94, *Atlantic Container v. Commission*, EU:T:2002:49, paras 252-254 ; T-168/01, *GlaxoSmithKline v. Commission*, EU:T:2006:265, para. 58; T-705/14, *Unichem v. Commission*, EU:T:2018:915, para. 241.
250. Something not allowed, C-628/10P and C-14/11 P, *Alliance One v.* Commission, EU:C:2012:479, paras 76-79.

12 CONCLUSION

In the 2000s, the decentralisation of the enforcement of EU competition law was meant to free Commission resources in order to adopt even more decisions. However, in parallel, the 'effects-based', 'more economic', approach, when applied to specific cases, was probably going in the opposite direction. It implied an increase in the resources devoted to each case, for, at least for certain types of cases, the assessment had to take into account larger amounts of factors and data, and it implied the examination of issues which were not always considered relevant in the past. The expected outcome could well be fewer decisions overall, as the different layers of the analysis were meant to avoid 'false positives' that, according to some, the previous 'formalistic' approach was potentially delivering.

Over the years it is an observable fact that the amount of time and resources devoted to each Article 102 TFEU case has greatly increased, while the overall number of decisions (all types of cases, both Articles 101 and 102 TFEU) does not appear to have increased, at least significantly. This is so even if the Commission did not apply an extreme version of the 'more economic' approach some were advocating, but a more pragmatic or realistic one. Actually, many undertakings complained about it, when challenging the legality of decisions in court.

The case law so far has sent mixed messages and the interpretation of each judgment (even each passage) may not always be univocal so that judgments could be like inkblots in a Rorschach test, on which each practitioner or academic may be seeing different things. The situation is certainly not ideal for those who have to take decisions on whether there is an infringement or not.

Some judgments of the General Court review the legality of decisions against a standard of 'actual effects' (not just potential effects) and set a high evidentiary standard of 'beyond reasonable doubt' also for some complex elements of the analysis. While some judgments of the Court of Justice, like *SEN*, do not appear to materially increase the evidentiary burden on competition authorities in the enforcement of Article 102 TFEU, just a few months later the very same chamber has delivered a judgment that requires 'case specific', 'tangible' evidence of 'actual capacity' to produce effects, while at the same time seemingly excluding such requirements in certain cases by stating that the use by an undertaking in a dominant position of resources other than those governing competition on the merits may be sufficient, in certain circumstances, to establish the existence of such an abuse. Moreover, the case law has ultimately downplayed the relevance of the AEC test, has so far not required complex 'counterfactuals' of the type put forward by some 'dominant' applicants, and is becoming sensitive to the importance of examining the impact of the course of conduct on non-price parameters such as choice and innovation. Yet, overall, the slogan of 'competition, not competitors' that is often used to justify inaction may be having an impact.

The current emphasis on the completeness of the enquiry, clothed in the language of fundamental rights, assumes a background of systemic epistemological doubt about the ability of decision-makers to distinguish between conduct that undermines competition and conduct that promotes it. 'Raising the evidentiary bar' across the board, as a reflection of this systemic epistemological doubt, in the absence of evidence that the conduct is really pro-competitive, is probably leading to chronic under-enforcement, in a situation where only a handful of cases can realistically be pursued, due to limited resources, and at least a fraction of the decisions will be probably annulled, for reasons of procedure or substance (courts may not be perceived as doing their job if the authority wins all cases). The current focus on the 'means' (the comeback of the condition of means based on 'competition on the merits') and the articulation of some 'efficiencies' as a 'defence', may certainly limit this risk. However, one cannot avoid the impression that some judges (and academics) may harbour unrealistic expectations about how much reliable data the Commission (or any competition authority, for that matter) can obtain during the administrative procedure, or how much certainty economic analysis can generally provide. Ultimately, applying a 'certainty' standard to economic analysis may move competition enforcement away from an effects-based approach, or at least from one based on quantitative types of analysis.

The proof of anti-competitive effects is, at least for some types of practices, increasingly taking the form of a dialectic process, where the Commission is, first, required to adduce sufficient proof that the conduct is capable of producing (at least potential) anti-competitive effects, and may rely on certain, relatively 'light', rebuttable presumptions or assumptions, but the dominant undertaking may adduce evidence to the contrary that must be systematically assessed.[251] The Commission must examine all these allegations, carefully and impartially. This is, of course, in line with traditional shifts in the evidential burden of proof which are visible in other areas of competition law. However, it is still unclear how much the Commission must engage with the allegations of the dominant undertaking, whether in such cases it must prove all the elements of the abuse without relying on any inference (or prior experience) that would lighten such burden, or whether the duties on the competition authority are mainly procedural and relate more to stating reasons in case of rejection of the evidence.

One could argue that it was the Commission who imposed upon itself certain very demanding constraints. The EU Courts, when annulling certain decisions, may be said to be simply echoing an approach (if not the letter) that the Commission itself initiated. Some may even say that the change in enforcement has been successful as it has been at least partly embraced in the case law, even at the price of having some Commission decisions annulled. However, the Commission in its Guidance on Enforcement Priorities only set out priorities, and it was never its intention to set out substantive requirements. If EU Courts considered that, after all, the Commission did not demonstrate in a given case that it was right to give it priority, this does not make the final decision unlawful. EU Courts must apply the law, not aspirational enforcement standards which in some cases went beyond the case law. In any event, even as a matter of priorities, there are areas in which the enforcement experience has shown

251. For an explanation of how this may happen in different scenarios, Di Giovanni Bezzi, R., 'Anticompetitive Effects and Allocation of the Burden of Proof in Article 102 Cases: Lessons from the Google Shopping Case', *Journal of European Competition Law & Practice*, Vol. 13 n. 2, 112-124, at 122-124- (2022).

that the Guidance itself, rather than the EU Courts, adopted a position that turned out to be overly restrictive. This is not in itself surprising: at the time of adoption of the Guidance, the Commission lacked enforcement experience with regard to several areas. Yet, if there was in some respects no prior practice on which the Guidance was built, it was not the intention to apply such Guidance rigorously, and the Commission has spent much of the last years defending in court that the Guidance was not relevant for assessing the legality of any of its decisions, some may legitimately wonder why the Commission decided to adopt such Guidance in the first place. If some of the recent annulments are due to judges 'embracing' much of the 'more economic' approach that the Guidance was meant to embody, a realistic counterfactual is that the Commission would have been more successful in court if the Guidance had not been adopted.

The objective consequence of some of the trends described, including the attitude of EU Courts in judicial review, is that the administrative enquiry becomes more burdensome, as the Commission must deliver decisions which must resist the challenge even on the basis of evidence not adduced during the administrative procedure. Somewhat surprisingly, the Court of Justice is systematically applying standards developed in the context of the review of Commission decisions also to national competition authorities, even if recitals of Regulation 1/2003 make it clear that there is still scope for some differences at national level on evidential matters, and, quite obviously, the Guidance on Enforcement Priorities does not apply to national authorities, which determine their priorities quite autonomously. At EU level, some may have expected in the 2000s that the complexity introduced by the more economic approach would be followed up by cautious judicial review at the time when the 'manifest error' was still the prevailing standard of review. However, the label of 'complex economic assessment' is disappearing and the complexity of cases just increases the angles of attack.

The decision-maker, both the Commission and the NCAs, must examine a potentially increasing number of additional elements, facts and evidence, and the application of any formal economic test must be 'rigorously' done. Some judgments appear to accept more qualitative assessments, but it is unclear if this trend will be confirmed. While a majority of Commission decisions still 'survive' – at least so far – an enhanced degree of judicial scrutiny, these trends objectively imply more complex investigations and, critically, many more resources. When additional resources are allocated to certain cases, some other cases inevitably end up not being investigated.

CHAPTER 10

The Consumer Welfare Standard: A 'Problem' to Fix in EU Competition Law?

Assimakis Komninos[*]

1 INTRODUCTION

Consumer welfare is currently under attack, especially in the United States (US). Of course, it is not clear what one means by this notion. Is it a general guiding principle, more akin to policy, or a legal/economic test that should decide cases?[1] There is no doubt that in the US consumer welfare has been both. But in Europe, it is more the former than the latter.

The European approach towards the concept remains somewhat awkward. Although it never really acquired in Europe the quasi-religious status it had in the US, it was nevertheless embraced – not without some resistance and incidents, initially by the Commission and subsequently by the European Union (EU) Courts, as a form of disciplining principle that goes hand in hand with the so-called new economic approach that was introduced in the late 1990s in response to the criticisms against the overly formalistic approach of EU competition law enforcement.

It is now with some bemusement that the Europeans observe the heated discussions in the US. Is Europe embracing a wrong dogma that has fallen out of favour in its birthplace? And is the latest embracement of consumer welfare by the EU Courts an anachronism? In this contribution, I develop three main theses:

* The views expressed here are strictly personal. This a slightly updated and expanded version of my contribution '"Consumer Welfare" and the EU Courts: An Unexpected Refuge for a Persecuted Concept?' that appears in: Oles Andriychuk (ed.) *Antitrust and the Bounds of Power: 25 Years On* (Hart Publishing, 2023).

1. *See* G.J. Werden, 'Back to School: What the Chicago School and New Brandeis School Get Right', available at SSRN: https://ssrn.com/abstract=3247116.

First, the EU case law has historically given more emphasis to competition as process rather than to competition as outcome and EU competition law has never been about just short-term price effects. Instead, other parameters of competition, such as quality, innovation, choice and the single market imperative have always remained important. The mantra has been the safeguarding of an 'effective competitive structure'.

Second, the increasing references to consumer welfare, which is a relatively recent phenomenon, have to be seen in the context of the EU case law becoming less formalistic and more attuned to economics, and to developing clear theories of harm which are based on effects as opposed to form. In other words, consumer welfare encapsulates and personifies the methodological shift to economic analysis. This cannot be but a positive development.

Third, the EU case law has seen consumer welfare as more of an abstract objective or guiding principle, as opposed to an operational standard or test. It serves only to distinguish the mere exclusion of rivals (which may be pro-competitive) from distortion of competition that leads to consumer harm. At the same time, the term 'consumer' encompasses not only end users but also intermediaries.

Having discussed these three theses, I conclude that, in Europe, there has never been a 'tyranny' of the consumer welfare concept. On the contrary, consumer welfare has been a very welcome overarching principle that has brought discipline and intellectual rigour to competition enforcement. Even if it were possible for the European Commission and the EU Courts to somehow 'abandon' consumer welfare, which it is not, since EU competition law as interpreted by the EU Courts amounts to primary law that can be changed only through an amendment of the Treaty, it would be a retrogression to disavow it and would not be to the benefit of the quality of competition enforcement in Europe.

2 THE FIRST REFERENCES TO CONSUMER WELFARE: A COMMISSION-INSPIRED DEVELOPMENT

It is not the purpose of this chapter to explain the concept of the consumer welfare standard.[2] In the US, it is seen as a 'standard', in the sense that it can guide the

2. The US literature is voluminous. For a few introductory works from a European angle, *see* S. Albæk, 'Consumer Welfare in EU Competition Policy', in: C. Heide-Jorgensen et al. (eds) *Aims and Values in Competition Law* (DJØF Publishing, 2013) 67ff; O. Andriychuk, 'Rediscovering the Spirit of Competition: On the Normative Value of the Competition Process', 6 *European Competition Journal* 575 (2010); D.R. Biggar and A. Heimler, 'Is Protecting Sunk Investments an Economic Rationale for Antitrust Law?', 4 September 2019, available at SSRN: https://ssrn.com/abstract=3935776; V. Daskalova, 'Consumer Welfare in EU Competition Law: What Is It (Not) About?', 11 *Competition Law Review* 133 (2015); F. Marty, 'Is the Consumer Welfare Obsolete? A European Union Competition Law Perspective', GREDEG Working Paper No 2020-13; H. Schweitzer, 'The Role of Consumer Welfare in EU Competition Law', in: Drexl (Ed.), *Technology and Competition, Contributions in Honour of Hanns Ullrich* (Larcier, 2009).

application of the antitrust laws to specific cases. The consumer welfare standard gives emphasis to consumers' surplus and focuses on the buyers' side. Total welfare, on the contrary, encompasses the sum of producers' and consumers' surplus and focuses on deadweight loss and on the effects of the conduct in question on the volume of sales rather than on prices. Traditionally, a total welfare approach has been considered as possibly generating under-enforcement risks. Other standards or objectives have also been proposed, such as consumer sovereignty, freedom of choice, protection of 'smallness' from 'bigness', etc.

In Europe, however, the competition rules have traditionally been seen in a functionalist way, as part of the EU economic constitution designed to protect economic freedom and the competitive process. The Ordoliberalist theories of the Freiburg School have been particularly influential, and the focus is on economic efficiency and 'performance competition' (*Leistungswettbewerb*), which the EU Courts refer to as 'normal competition' or 'competition on the merits'.[3] Under this approach, the competition rules protect rational commercial conduct consistent with the profit-maximising strategy of a non-dominant company, based on superior efficiency.[4] In addition, the EU competition rules have historically been seen through their single market imperative and this explains the long line of cases on parallel trade and market-partitioning, which has always been considered as a European oddity by US antitrust experts.

It was only at the end of the 1990s that consumer welfare started to be mentioned in EU competition policy papers and guidelines. There is no doubt that the European Commission played an important role in spearheading this development. The Commission was responding to criticism - usually waged by the bar where US-trained lawyers were particularly influential, that its competition law enforcement was too formalistic.[5]

The first reference to the concept of consumer welfare can be traced back to the Commission's 1996 Green Paper on vertical restraints,[6] which is generally considered the policy document that introduced the 'new economic approach' drive in EU competition law. The first references are rather timid and mention consumer welfare

3. The terminology used by the EU Courts has not always been consistent and the English version may be less successful than the French one. Compare Case 85/76, *Hoffmann-La Roche & Co. AG v. Commission*, ECLI:EU:C:1979:36, para. 91 ('normal competition in products or services on the basis of the transactions of commercial operators' - 'une compétition normale des produits ou services sur la base des prestations des opérateurs économiques'); Case T-65/89, *BPB Industries Plc and British Gypsum Ltd v. Commission*, ECLI:EU:T:1993:31, para. 113 ('competition on the merits' - 'concurrence fondée sur l'efficacité'); Case T-228/97, *Irish Sugar plc v. Commission*, ECLI:EU:T:1999:246, para. 111 ('normal competition in products or services on the basis of the transactions of commercial operators' - 'une compétition normale des produits ou services sur la base des prestations des opérateurs économiques'); Case C-413/14 P, *Intel Corp. Inc. v. Commission*, ECLI:EU:C:2017:632, para. 134 ('competition on the merits' - 'concurrence par les mérites').
4. *See, e.g.*, R. Nazzini, *The Foundations of European Union Competition Law: The Objective and Principles of Article 102* (OUP, 2011), p. 171.
5. *See, e.g.*, the seminal article by B.E. Hawk, 'System Failure: Vertical Restraints and EC Competition Law', 32 *Common Market Law Review* 973 (1995).
6. European Commission, Green Paper on Vertical Restraints in EC Competition Policy COM(96), Brussels (22 January 1997).

together with 'the structure of competition'.[7] In paragraph 180, the Commission also stated:

> In assessing possible restrictive practices, the notion that the competitive structure of markets must not suffer should always be the foremost consideration. In its decisions, the Commission has consistently demonstrated a willingness to consider economic factors such as efficiency and consumer welfare.

Consumer welfare had a more central role in the Commission's Article 101(3) Guidelines, a centrepiece in its modernisation package of 2004.[8] In paragraphs 13 and 33, the Commission stressed that the objective of the competition rules and of Article 101 Treaty on the Functioning of the European Union (TFEU) in particular is 'to protect competition on the market as a means of enhancing consumer welfare and of ensuring an efficient allocation of resources'. The same approach was followed in the Commission's 2004 Horizontal Merger Guidelines[9] and Technology Transfer Guidelines,[10] which included references to consumer welfare.

It is with the 2009 Guidance Paper on exclusionary abuses[11] that consumer welfare was given a prominent role, from a policy point of view, in Article 102 TFEU. Paragraph 19 of the Guidance Paper, which refers to the general framework of analysis, is quite explicit:

> The aim of the Commission's enforcement activity in relation to exclusionary conduct is to ensure that dominant undertakings do not impair effective competition by foreclosing their competitors in an anti-competitive way, thus having an adverse impact on consumer welfare, whether in the form of higher price levels than would have otherwise prevailed or in some other form such as limiting quality or reducing consumer choice. In this document the term 'anti-competitive foreclosure' is used to describe a situation where effective access of actual or potential competitors to supplies or markets is hampered or eliminated as a result of the conduct of the dominant undertaking whereby the dominant undertaking is likely to be in a position to profitably increase prices to the detriment of consumers.

The Guidance Paper's references to consumer welfare are closely linked with the fundamental distinction between pro-competitive and anti-competitive foreclosure of competitors.[12] The criticism that Article 102 TFEU enforcement was too formalistic was based precisely on the point that it tended to protect competitors without regard to the interests of consumers.[13]

7. *Ibid.*, para. 25.
8. Communication from the Commission, Guidelines on the application of Article 81(3) of the Treaty, OJ [2004] C 101/97.
9. Guidelines on the assessment of horizontal mergers under the Council Regulation on the control of concentrations between undertakings, OJ [2004] C 31/3, para. 61.
10. Commission Notice, Guidelines on the application of Article 81 of the EC Treaty to technology transfer agreements, OJ [2004] C 101/2, paras 5, 7.
11. Communication from the Commission – Guidance on the Commission's enforcement priorities in applying Article 82 of the EC Treaty to abusive exclusionary conduct by dominant undertakings, OJ [2009] C 45/7.
12. *Ibid.*, para. 6.
13. *See* Report by the Economic Advisory Group for Competition Policy ('EAGCP') on 'An Economic Approach to Article 82', available at: https://competition-policy.ec.europa.eu/chief-competition-economist/eagcp_en.

Since these early policy pronouncements, consumer welfare has now established itself as a prominent objective mentioned in all basic Commission policy documents.[14] However, the Commission's embracement of consumer welfare should not be seen as an espousal of the technical characteristics of the US 'standard', with its main focus on price, but rather as a guiding principle that brings economic rationale and discipline into enforcement. The Commission also clarifies that its concept of 'consumer' is a broad one and encompasses intermediaries[15] and that, apart from price, other elements, such as quality, innovation and choice are constituent elements of competition.[16]

3 EU CASE LAW: NO LOVE AT FIRST SIGHT

The reception of the consumer welfare objective in the case law of the EU Courts has had a different history, which is not difficult to understand, bearing in mind the courts' conservative nature and their different task vis-à-vis the Commission: the EU Courts will only interpret the law as such and will review the legality of Commission decisions; they cannot introduce policy changes. Only the Commission and the enforcement agencies can design and implement policy changes.

Initially, from the 1960s to the 1990s, there were no references to consumer welfare in the case law. When the question of the objective of the competition rules arose, the EU Courts did not refer to consumer welfare or indeed to the protection of consumers as such, although the word 'consumers' appears both in primary law – Article 101(3) TFEU ('allowing consumers a fair share of the resulting benefit') – and

14. *See, e.g.*, Communication from the Commission – Guidelines on the applicability of Article 101 of the Treaty on the Functioning of the European Union to horizontal co-operation agreements, OJ [2011] C 11/1, para. 52 and numerous references to benefits to 'consumers'; Guidelines on Vertical Restraints, OJ [2010] C 130/1, para. 7; Communication from the Commission – Guidelines on the application of Article 101 of the Treaty on the Functioning of the European Union to technology transfer agreements, OJ [2014] C 89/3, para. 5. These texts sometimes use language that does not include the word 'welfare' but there is no doubt that they mean to refer to the consumer welfare objective.
15. *See, e.g.*, Communication from the Commission – Guidance on the Commission's enforcement priorities in applying Article 82 of the EC Treaty to abusive exclusionary conduct by dominant undertakings, OJ [2009] C 45/7, para. 19 *in fine*, fn. 15 ('The concept of "consumers" encompasses all direct or indirect users of the products affected by the conduct, including intermediate producers that use the products as an input, as well as distributors and final consumers both of the immediate product and of products provided by intermediate producers. Where intermediate users are actual or potential competitors of the dominant undertaking, the assessment focuses on the effects of the conduct on users further downstream'); Guidelines on the assessment of horizontal mergers under the Council Regulation on the control of concentrations between undertakings, OJ [2004] C 31/3, fn. 55 and para. 84; Guidelines on the assessment of non-horizontal mergers under the Council Regulation on the control of concentrations between undertakings, OJ [2008] C 265/6, para. 16.
16. *See, e.g.*, Communication from the Commission, Guidelines on the application of Article 81(3) of the Treaty, OJ [2004] C 101/97, para. 16; Communication from the Commission – Guidance on the Commission's enforcement priorities in applying Article 82 of the EC Treaty to abusive exclusionary conduct by dominant undertakings, OJ [2009] C 45/7, paras 5, 6, 11, 19; Guidelines on the assessment of horizontal mergers under the Council Regulation on the control of concentrations between undertakings, OJ [2004] C 31/3, para. 8.

in secondary law – the EU Merger Regulation.[17] Instead, the EU Courts saw the competition rules in a functionalist way and always in conjunction with the single market imperative. With particular reference to Article 102 TFEU, the mantra was that it 'is aimed not only at practices which may cause prejudice to consumers directly, but also at those which are detrimental to them through their impact on an effective competition structure'.[18] In the words of AG Kokott in *British Airways*:

> The starting-point here must be the protective purpose of Article 82 EC. The provision forms part of a system designed to protect competition within the internal market from distortions (Article 3(1)(g) EC). Accordingly, Article 82 EC, like the other competition rules of the Treaty, is not designed only or primarily to protect the immediate interests of individual competitors or consumers, but to protect the *structure of the market* and thus *competition as such (as an institution)*, which has already been weakened by the presence of the dominant undertaking on the market. In this way, consumers are also indirectly protected. Because where competition as such is damaged, disadvantages for consumers are also to be feared.[19]

We had to wait until 1999 for the first reference to consumer welfare in an Advocate General (AG) Opinion in a very unlikely case that had little to do with substantive competition law questions. This was the *Eco Swiss* case, which concerned arbitration and EU competition law. AG Saggio was referring to the importance of the competition rules in the Treaty and stressed that 'while they govern the conduct of individuals, also pursue objectives of a general nature such as the smooth functioning of the common market and the well-being of consumers'.[20] It may not be coincidence that the first judicial pronouncement on consumer welfare is almost cotemporaneous with the first ever use of the term in a Commission policy document, the 1996 Green Paper on vertical restraints.

From the 2000s onwards, the term started to be used quite often in AG Opinions, especially by those AGs that seemed more open to the new economic approach. The trend started with AG Jacobs in *Syfait*[21] and continued with AG Trstenjak in *Irish*

17. Council Regulation 139/2004 of 20 January 2004 on the control of concentrations between undertakings, OJ [2004] L 24/1, Art. 2(1)(b) and Recital 29. The reference to 'consumers' in Art. 2(1)(b) was already included in the first Merger Regulation (Council Regulation 4064/89 of 21 December 1989 on the control of concentrations between undertakings, OJ [1989] L 395/1).
18. *See, e.g.*, Case 6/72, *Europemballage Corporation and Continental Can Company Inc. v. Commission*, ECLI:EU:C:1973:22, para. 26; Case C-95/04 P, *British Airways plc v. Commission*, ECLI:EU:C:2007:166, para. 106; Case C-52/09, *TeliaSonera*, ECLI:EU:C:2011:83, paras 22, 108; Case C-307/18, *Generics (UK)*, ECLI:EU:C:2020:52, para. 147.
19. Case C-95/04 P, *British Airways plc v. Commission*, Opinion of AG Kokott, ECLI:EU:C:2006:133, para. 68 (emphasis in the original).
20. Case C-126/97, *Eco Swiss*, Opinion of AG Saggio, ECLI:EU:C:1999:97, para. 42. The reference to 'well-being of consumers' as opposed to 'consumer welfare' is a translation glitch from the French 'bien-être des consommateurs', which obviously refers to consumer welfare. This is a common problem in judgments and opinions that refer to consumer welfare.
21. Case C-53/03, *Syfait*, Opinion AG Jacobs, ECLI:EU:C:2004:673, paras 91-92. AG Jacobs referred to consumer welfare in the course of his argumentation that too restrictive an approach vis-à-vis the imposition of some limitations to parallel trade would disincentivise pharmaceutical companies to offer their products in low-priced countries. In his words, '[t]he levels of output and consumer welfare generated by some pharmaceutical products would therefore fall within

Beef,[22] AG Wahl in *Treuhand*,[23] *AKKA/LAA*,[24] *Skanska*[25] and *MEO*,[26] and AG Bobek in

---

the Community. Similarly, the regulatory negotiation of prices in low-price Member States would almost certainly become more difficult. There would be considerable pressure for prices to rise in those States if they were to be generalised, by process of parallel trade, across the Community. Such price rises as were agreed would again reduce output and consumer welfare in the States where they occurred'.

22. Case C-209/07, *Beef Industry Development Society*, Opinion of AG Trstenjak, ECLI:EU:C:2008:467. AG Trstenjak stressed that 'Article 81 EC protects competition in particular in regard to its function of forming a single market with conditions akin to an internal market and its function of supplying consumers as well as possible' and referred in fn. 16 of her Opinion to 'consumer welfare'. At paras 56-57 of her Opinion, she made a distinction between the first and second paragraphs of Article 101 TFEU: 'different aspects of consumer welfare are taken into account under Article 81(1) EC and under Article 81(3) EC. Under Article 81(1) EC, agreements which restrict competition between market participants and thus its function of supplying consumers optimally with a product at the lowest possible price or with innovative products are prohibited in principle. Such agreements directly affect consumer welfare and as such are prohibited in principle. Nevertheless, Article 81(3) EC recognises that agreements which restrict competition between market participants result in particular in a reduction in production costs, and the reduction in production costs can contribute indirectly to consumer welfare.'
23. Case C-194/14 P, *AC-Treuhand AG v. Commission*, Opinion of AG Wahl, ECLI:EU:C:2015:350, para. 1: 'The rules applicable to undertakings under Articles 81 EC and 82 EC (now Articles 101 TFEU and 102 TFEU) are intended to prohibit restrictions on free competition. The identification of a restriction of competition presupposes that it has been established, following an economic analysis, that, by its conduct, the undertaking in question has fully or partially ceased to constitute a constraint – the defining feature of effective competition – for the other operators on the market or markets concerned, to the detriment, ultimately, of economic efficiency and consumer welfare.' *See also* para. 45: 'The overall objective of the competition rules is to ensure that the effects of freedom of competition, which are the counterpart of the opening up of markets, are not distorted by measures, in the broadest sense of that term, which have the consequence of favouring or putting at a disadvantage certain undertakings and, ultimately, operate to the detriment of consumers.'
24. Case C-177/16, *AKKA/LAA*, Opinion of AG Wahl, ECLI:EU:C:2017:286, para. 101: 'At the outset, let us start by recalling the economic rationale of the unfair pricing abuse: when a dominant undertaking applies prices above competitive levels, there is an inefficient allocation of resources and consumer welfare is reduced (part of the welfare is transferred to the dominant company, whereas part is simply lost). Accordingly, from a theoretical point of view, any deviation from the competitive price in a regulated market might justify an intervention of the competition authorities. Indeed, any difference between the benchmark price and the actual price implies a certain loss in consumer welfare that would not have been there had the market been competitive.' *See also* para. 105.
25. Case C-724/17, *Skanska*, Opinion of AG Wahl, ECLI:EU:C:2019:100, para. 50: 'Fundamentally, however, the real harm caused by illegal restrictions of competition is the dead weight loss resulting from such restrictions, that is to say a loss of economic efficiency caused by the anticompetitive conduct in question. This means that the harm identified in actions for damages based on an infringement of competition law is in reality a proxy for the economic inefficiencies resulting from the infringement and the corollary loss to society as a whole in terms of reduced consumer welfare.'
26. Case C-525/16, *MEO*, ECLI:EU:C:2017:1020, paras 61, 62, 64: 'On a general note, it is important to bear in mind that discrimination, including discrimination in the charging of prices, is not in itself problematic from the point of view of competition law. The reason for that is that price discrimination is not always harmful to competition. On the contrary, as is evidenced in particular by the (vain) official attempts made in the United States to repeal the provision in the Robinson-Patman Act of 1936 which prohibits such discrimination, purely and simply prohibiting price discrimination may prove injurious to economic efficiency and the well-being of consumers. Indeed, it is well established that a practice of discrimination, and a differential pricing practice in particular, is ambivalent in terms of its effects on competition. Such a practice may have the consequence of increasing economic efficiency and thus the well-being of

Budapest Bank.[27] In particular AG Wahl's Opinions were quite rich in their references to consumer welfare and were also linking that concept to the more economic approach in the analysis of pro- and anti-competitive conduct. AG Wahl never considered that consumer welfare should be an operational test to deal with competition law infringements, but clearly thought that it was a guiding principle that ought to influence also the legal tests.

The use of the term in an EU Court judgment took more time and was rather traumatic at the beginning. It was the then Court of First Instance (CFI) that first relied in the 2000s on consumer welfare as an objective of competition law. This first happened in *Österreichische Postsparkasse*, a procedural case, where the CFI put emphasis on the interests of 'final consumers':

> It should be pointed out in this respect that the ultimate purpose of the rules that seek to ensure that competition is not distorted in the internal market is to increase the well-being of consumers. That purpose can be seen in particular from the wording of Article 81 EC. Whilst the prohibition laid down in Article 81(1) EC may be declared inapplicable in the case of cartels which contribute to improving the production or distribution of the goods in question or to promoting technical or economic progress, that possibility, for which provision is made in Article 81(3) EC, is inter alia subject to the condition that a fair share of the resulting benefit is allowed for users of those products. Competition law and competition policy therefore have an undeniable impact on the specific economic interests of final customers who purchase goods or services. Recognition that such customers – who show that they have suffered economic damage as a result of an agreement or conduct liable to restrict or distort competition – have a legitimate interest in seeking from the Commission a declaration that Articles 81 EC and 82 EC have been infringed contributes to the attainment of the objectives of competition law.[28]

Contemporaneously with *Österreichische Postsparkasse*, the CFI also rendered its judgment in the *Spanish Glaxo* case, where the above principles were cited and

consumers. These are goals which, to my mind, should not be overlooked in the application of the rules of competition law, and they are, in any event, quite distinct from considerations of fairness. As the Court has repeatedly held, the rules of competition law are designed to safeguard competition, not to protect competitors ... even where an undertaking is charged higher prices than those applied to other undertakings and, as a result, suffers (or considers that it suffers) discrimination, the conduct in question will be caught by Article 102 TFEU only if it is established that it is likely to restrict competition and diminish the well-being of consumers.' Again, the reference to 'well-being of consumers' as opposed to 'consumer welfare' is a translation glitch.

27. Case C-228/18, *Budapest Bank*, Opinion of AG Bobek, ECLI:EU:C:2019:678, para. 40: 'As the Court has emphasised in recent case-law, the concept of a restriction of competition 'by object' must be interpreted restrictively, and can be applied only to certain types of coordination between undertakings which reveal a sufficient degree of harm to competition and for which it is thus unnecessary examine their effects. That approach is justified by the fact that certain types of coordination between undertakings can be regarded, by their very nature, as being harmful to the proper functioning of normal competition since they normally produce inefficient economic outcomes and reduce consumer welfare.'
28. Joined Cases T-213/01 and T-214/01, *Österreichische Postsparkasse AG and Bank für Arbeit und Wirtschaft AG v. Commission*, ECLI:EU:T:2006:151, para. 115. Again, the reference to 'well-being of consumers' instead of 'consumer welfare' is a translation glitch.

developed further. The CFI referred on numerous occasions to the 'welfare of final consumers'. In particular:

> 118. In effect, the objective assigned to Article 81(1) EC, which constitutes a fundamental provision indispensable for the achievement of the missions entrusted to the Community, in particular for the functioning of the internal market, is to prevent undertakings, by restricting competition between themselves or with third parties, from reducing the welfare of the final consumer of the products in question. At the hearing, in fact, the Commission emphasised on a number of occasions that it was from that perspective that it had carried out its examination in the present case, initially concluding that the General Sales Conditions clearly restricted the welfare of consumers, then considering whether that restriction would be offset by increased efficiency which would itself benefit consumers.
>
> 119. Consequently, the application of Article 81(1) EC to the present case cannot depend solely on the fact that the agreement in question is intended to limit parallel trade in medicines or to partition the common market, which leads to the conclusion that it affects trade between Member States, but also requires an analysis designed to determine whether it has as its object or effect the prevention, restriction or distortion of competition on the relevant market, to the detriment of the final consumer
>
> ...
>
> 121. While it has been accepted since then that parallel trade must be given a certain protection, it is therefore not as such but, as the Court of Justice held, in so far as it favours the development of trade, on the one hand, and the strengthening of competition, on the other hand, that is to say, in this second respect, in so far as it gives final consumers the advantages of effective competition in terms of supply or price. Consequently, while it is accepted that an agreement intended to limit parallel trade must in principle be considered to have as its object the restriction of competition, that applies in so far as the agreement may be presumed to deprive final consumers of those advantages.
>
> 122. However, if account is taken of the legal and economic context in which GSK's General Sales Conditions are applied, it cannot be presumed that those conditions deprive the final consumers of medicines of such advantages. In effect, the wholesalers, whose function, as the Court of Justice has held, is to ensure that the retail trade receives supplies with the benefit of competition between producers, are economic agents operating at an intermediate stage of the value chain and may keep the advantage in terms of price which parallel trade may entail, in which case that advantage will not be passed on to the final consumers.
>
> ...
>
> 171. ... as the objective of the Community competition rules is to prevent undertakings, by restricting competition between themselves or with third parties, from reducing the welfare of the final consumer of the products in question (paragraph 118 above), it is still necessary to demonstrate that the limitation in question restricts competition, to the detriment of the final consumer. Incidentally, the Commission itself explained, at the hearing, that the limitation of the freedom of action of the Spanish wholesalers was difficult to envisage in isolation and constituted only the starting-point of its examination.
>
> 172. Consequently, GSK is correct to maintain that, after relying on the effect of Clause 4 of the General Sales Conditions on the freedom of action of the Spanish

> wholesalers, the Commission was still required to demonstrate how that provision had the effect of restricting competition to the detriment of the final consumer.[29]

However, the Court of Justice, on appeal, severely criticised the CFI's zeal, in particular because of the latter's emphasis on the welfare of 'final' consumers and substituted the reasoning of the CFI judgment with text that echoed the traditional conservative approach. The Court of Justice, in particular, held that the CFI erred in its findings that the objective of the competition rules was to protect the 'final' consumers. In particular:

> 62. With respect to the Court of First Instance's statement that, while it is accepted that an agreement intended to limit parallel trade must in principle be considered to have as its object the restriction of competition, that applies in so far as it may be presumed to deprive final consumers of the advantages of effective competition in terms of supply or price, the Court notes that neither the wording of Article 81(1) EC nor the case-law lend support to such a position.
>
> 63. First of all, there is nothing in that provision to indicate that only those agreements which deprive consumers of certain advantages may have an anti-competitive object. Secondly, it must be borne in mind that the Court has held that, like other competition rules laid down in the Treaty, Article 81 EC aims to protect not only the interests of competitors or of consumers, but also the structure of the market and, in so doing, competition as such. Consequently, for a finding that an agreement has an anti-competitive object, it is not necessary that final consumers be deprived of the advantages of effective competition in terms of supply or price.
>
> 64. It follows that, by requiring proof that the agreement entails disadvantages for final consumers as a prerequisite for a finding of anti-competitive object and by not finding that that agreement had such an object, the Court of First Instance committed an error of law.[30]

The words of the Court of Justice were quite harsh. They need to be seen as more targeted against the CFI's excessive zeal to focus on 'final' consumers rather than against the concept of consumer welfare. Still, this whole incident must have proved a rather traumatic experience for the CFI, which did not mention consumer welfare again until the Court of Justice itself started to refer to that concept.

4 EU CASE LAW: FALLING IN LOVE

After a silence following the *Spanish Glaxo* incident, the Court of Justice gave the first indications that it was now more willing to follow its AG Opinions and refer approvingly to consumer welfare, while discussing the objectives of the competition rules. This happened in *Post Danmark I*, a Grand Chamber judgment that is credited as being

29. Case T-168/01, *GlaxoSmithKline Services Unlimited v. Commission*, ECLI:EU:T:2006:265. *See also* references in paras 134, 135, 147, 185, 190 and 194. This is probably the first and last judgment ever with so many references to 'final consumers'.
30. Joined Cases C-501/06 P, C-513/06 P, C-515/06 P and C-519/06 P, *GlaxoSmithKline Services Unlimited v. Commission, Commission v. GlaxoSmithKline Services Unlimited, European Association of Euro Pharmaceutical Companies (EAEPC) v. Commission* and *Asociación de exportadores españoles de productos farmacéuticos (Aseprofar) v. Commission*, ECLI:EU:C:2009:610.

the first judgment that showed an openness towards the new economic approach in Article 102 TFEU and a positive stance vis-à-vis the Commission's 2009 Guidance Paper. This first reference was relatively timid. The Court referred to 'negative effects on competition and consumer welfare'[31] and also stressed the importance of consumer harm resulting from competition law violations.[32] These quotes were again repeated in *Post Danmark II*,[33] which followed a few years later.

In the meantime, the Court of Justice's case law became less formalistic and more attuned to economics both in Articles 101 and 102 TFEU. In Article 101 TFEU cases such as *Cartes Bancaires*, *Maxima Latvija* and *Budapest Bank*, where the Court adopted a more restrictive meaning of what constitutes an anti-competitive 'object', it also spoke of the anti-competitive consequences of conduct that 'leads to falls in production and price increases, resulting in poor allocation of resources to the detriment, in particular, of consumers'.[34] Similar economically minded language has appeared in cases such as *Sumal* and *Paccar*, where the Court has stressed the benefits of private enforcement in cartel cases and has drawn attention to damages actions 'not only ... providing a remedy for the direct damage alleged to have been suffered by the [cartel victims], but also the indirect harm done to the structure and operation of the market, which was not able to reach full economic efficacy, in particular as regards benefits to the consumers concerned'.[35]

The area where perhaps the most important shift took place is Article 102 TFEU. In the post-*Intel*[36] world an effects-based approach is now the default position.[37] As soon as the Union's highest judge started using the 'prohibited' term, the General Court felt at ease to restart citing consumer welfare albeit within the confines of the Court of Justice's terminology. Thus, in *Google Shopping*,[38] the General Court used the terms 'negative effects on competition and consumer welfare', faithfully copying the Court of Justice's pronouncements.

However, it is at the Court of Justice level where the most recent pronouncements indicate a rather enthusiastic embracement of consumer welfare as a leading or indeed 'the ultimate' objective of the competition rules. Thus, AG Pitruzzella in his *SABAM* Opinion went as far as stating that '[u]ltimately, therefore, it is consumer welfare – the

31. Case C-209/10, *Post Danmark I*, ECLI:EU:C:2012:172, para. 41.
32. *Ibid.*, paras 20, 24.
33. Case C-23/14, *Post Danmark II*, ECLI:EU:C:2015:651, paras 49, 69.
34. Case C-67/13 P, *Groupement des cartes bancaires (CB) v. Commission*, ECLI:EU:C:2014:2204, para. 51; Case C-345/14, *Maxima Latvija*, ECLI:EU:C:2015:784, para. 19; Case C-227/14 P, *LG Display Co. Ltd and LG Display Taiwan Co. Ltd v. Commission*, ECLI:EU:C:2015:258, para. 62; Case C-228/18, *Budapest Bank*, ECLI:EU:C:2020:265, para. 36; Case C-307/18, *Generics (UK)*, ECLI:EU:C:2020:52, para. 64.
35. Case C-882/19, *Sumal*, ECLI:EU:C:2021:800, para. 36; Case C-163/21, *Paccar*, ECLI:EU:C:2022:863, para. 56. In reality, the Court of Justice refers here to the deadweight loss of cartels.
36. Case C-413/14 P, *Intel Corp. Inc. v. Commission* ECLI:EU:C:2017:632.
37. *See* A. Komninos, '*Intel*: The ECJ Finally Speaks – Time to Listen!', 4(2) *Competition Law & Policy Debate* 42 (2018).
38. Case T-612/17, *Google LLC and Alphabet, Inc. v. Commission*, ECLI:EU:T:2021:763, paras 553, 568, 572.

main (and some would say the only) objective of competition law – that suffers', while speaking of excessive pricing abuses. He went on to say:

> [T]he Commission, the national competition authorities and the national courts, when applying the concept of excessive prices, are faced with a Procrustean dilemma. On the one hand, there is the risk of antitrust over-enforcement based on false positives, which ultimately erode efficiency and consumer welfare. On the other, there is the risk of under-enforcement due to false negatives, which, in addition to eroding consumer welfare, may have, as mentioned in the previous point, wider negative repercussions.[39]

Perhaps the most detailed analysis on the role of consumer welfare is found in the recent AG Rantos Opinion in *Servizio Elettrico Nazionale*. The case at issue related to conduct by the former electricity state monopoly in Italy. After the liberalisation of the electricity market, generation and sale were opened to competition, whereas transmission and distribution were still operated under a monopoly system. The former state monopoly – Enel – was structurally separated in three companies: Enel Energia (EE), electricity supplier for the deregulated market; Servizio Elettrico Nazionale (SEN), supplier of the 'enhanced protection service'; and e-distribuzione, concessionaire for electricity distribution activities. The Italian Competition Authority condemned the Enel Group for illegally using commercially sensitive information by operators to transfer customers from SEN to EE, in view of the announced market change. In particular, SEN obtained the consent of users to receive commercial proposals in a discriminatory manner, involving a request for initial authorisation for the processing of personal data by companies within the Enel Group and a second request in favour of third-party operators. The customers usually gave the initial consent, believing that this was necessary for managing the existing relationship with their supplier, while they usually refused the second consent, intended for other operators. Consent for third-party operators was only given in 30% of cases. The Italian authority considered this a 'sui generis abuse' and imposed fines on EE, SEN and the parent undertaking.

The case was an academic's paradise and a judge's nightmare. In this preliminary reference case, the referring court, the Italian *Consiglio di Stato*, addressed some very abstract and theoretical questions to the Court of Justice that touched upon the basic objective of Article 102 TFEU. One of the specific questions asked was whether:

> the purpose of the concept of abuse [is] to maximise the well-being of consumers, with the court being responsible for determining whether that well-being has been (or could be) reduced, or does the concept of an infringement of competition law have the function of preserving in itself the competitive structure of the market, in order to avoid the creation of economic power groupings that are, in any case, considered harmful for the community.

In proposing a response to that question, AG Rantos took a bold and principled position: protecting the structure of competition cannot be an objective alternative to

39. Case C-372/19, *SABAM*, Opinion of AG Pitruzzella, ECLI:EU:C:2020:598, paras 22, 27.

consumer welfare.[40] In his view, protecting consumer welfare is a more central objective than the preservation of a competitive structure, although it would be unwise to view the two objectives as unconnected to each other. Indeed:

> Article 102 TFEU aims at the end of the day at maximising consumer welfare, in particular through the protection of the competitive structure of the market. Therefore, that protection may well constitute an objective pursued by Article 102 TFEU, not autonomously but only if in a specific case is integrated in the ultimate rationale of the (direct or indirect) protection of the consumers.[41]

AG Rantos added that effects on the structure of competition on a specific market can be considered a good 'proxy' of the effects that a certain exclusionary practice may have on consumer welfare. But an effect on the structure of competition does not necessarily mean a reduction of consumer welfare.[42]

The Court of Justice, in its judgment did not go as far as AG Rantos but included for the first time an express acknowledgement that consumer welfare is the ultimate objective of Article 102 TFEU:

> It follows that, as observed in essence by the Advocate General in point 100 of his Opinion, the well-being of both intermediary and final consumers must be regarded as the ultimate objective warranting the intervention of competition law in order to penalise abuse of a dominant position within the internal market or a substantial part of that market.[43]

This is a more far-reaching statement than the previous references of the Court of Justice to the objective of the competition rules being the 'protection of competition and consumer welfare'. The Court of Justice did retain its long-standing position that an authority only needs to show harm to the structure of competition, not harm to consumers as such,[44] but the protection of an 'effective competitive structure' is seen more as a proxy for that broader ultimate objective.[45] Thus, it can be seen as subservient to consumer welfare. At the same time, the Court's words make clear that consumer welfare is not seen in a technical sense that can have a direct bearing on which legal/operational tests need to be followed to find an abuse of dominance. The

40. Case C-377/20, *Servizio Elettrico Nazionale*, Opinion of AG Rantos, ECLI:EU:C:2021:998, paras 94-95. Unfortunately, the English text of the Opinion is not reflecting the nuances of the French text. Again, the reference to the 'well-being of consumers' instead of 'consumer welfare' is the result of a translation glitch.
41. *Ibid.*, para. 100.
42. *Ibid.*, para. 106.
43. Case C-377/20, *Servizio Elettrico Nazionale*, ECLI:EU:C:2022:379, para. 46. As above, the reference to the 'well-being of consumers' instead of 'consumer welfare' is the result of a translation glitch.
44. *Ibid.*, para. 47: 'Therefore, a competition authority discharges its burden of proof if it shows that a practice of an undertaking in a dominant position could impair, by using resources or means other than those governing normal competition, an effective competition structure, without it being necessary for that authority to prove that that practice may also cause direct harm to consumers.'
45. Paragraph 47 is linked with the broader pronouncement of para. 46 with the word 'therefore' ('*des lors*' in French), which means that the standing of consumer welfare as 'ultimate objective' of competition law is not put in question by the references to 'effective competition structure'.

Court of Justice also clarifies that the concept of 'consumer' encompasses final consumers but also intermediaries. In other words, this amounts to a development though not a reversal of the *Spanish Glaxo* case law.[46]

5 CONCLUSIONS

This contribution has demonstrated that there has been no 'tyranny' of the consumer welfare standard in EU competition law. Protection of an 'effective competitive structure' has always been, and remains, a valid objective and is seen as a good proxy of the broader consumer welfare principle, which is the 'ultimate objective' of the competition rules but does not amount to an operational-technical test that can be applied to specific cases. At the same time, the EU case law makes it clear that consumer welfare is not just about prices but also pertains to quality, innovation and choice.[47]

An 'ideological' approach that advocates the repudiation of consumer welfare, echoing the current state of affairs in the US, would not be in conformity with the more recent case law of the Court of Justice and its repeated and enthusiastic references to that objective behind the competition rules. Indeed, we can consider this as an *acquis* of EU competition law. Bearing in mind that the EU case law relates to the interpretation of primary Union law (Articles 101 and 102 TFEU), only a change of the Treaty would make a departure from that *acquis* possible.

46. The inclusion of intermediaries into the concept of 'consumers' is also in line with the Commission guidelines and policy papers. *See* above.
47. Case C-413/14 P, *Intel Corp. Inc. v. Commission*, ECLI:EU:C:2017:632, para. 134: 'not every exclusionary effect is necessarily detrimental to competition. Competition on the merits may, by definition, lead to the departure from the market or the marginalisation of competitors that are less efficient and so less attractive to consumers from the point of view of, among other things, price, choice, quality or innovation'.

CHAPTER 11

The Role of the EU Courts in Competition Cases: A View from the Bar

Alfonso Lamadrid de Pablo

1 INTRODUCTION

The Global Competition Law Centre has invited me to comment on the role of the European Union (EU) Courts from the point of view of a private practitioner who is a frequent user of the General Court (GC) and the Court of Justice (CJ).[1] The views developed in these pages are therefore necessarily subjective and non-academic in nature; they are inevitably informed and deformed by my personal experience, mainly challenging European Commission ("Commission") decisions on behalf of clients (and, in a few cases, defending decisions on the Commission's behalf).

Practising lawyers involved in litigation tend to take an ex-post and relatively simple approach to the review of the Courts' performance in competition cases: if we win a case, then the merit is on us, and the Court only did what it was required to do; if we lose, then it is the Court's fault for failing to adequately play its role. Other stakeholders, including in academia and in the media, often assess the performance of the Courts in a quantitative manner, associating effective or thorough judicial review with the number of annulments or with other observable metrics (e.g., number of cases decided, amount of fines annulled or average duration of proceedings). But these, too, are very superficial ways of measuring performance.

In my view, one cannot assess the work of the EU Courts without inquiring first about the role that one may reasonably expect them to play in competition cases. It is

1. This written contribution develops the points made in my intervention at the GCLC's annual conference in Bruges on March 26, 2022 at a panel that also featured Marc van der Woude (President of the GC) and Judge Ingeborg Simonsson (Stockholm City Court). I provided my views about the role and performance of judges, and I was relieved that they did not provide their views about the role and performance of lawyers.

only once we have identified this benchmark that we can properly discuss the Court's performance and identify possible challenges.

Following this logic, section 2 discusses the role that one can expect the EU Courts to play in the field of competition law; section 3 seeks to evaluate the Court's performance against that benchmark; section 4 identifies new generation challenges.

2 THE ROLE OF THE EU COURTS IN THE FIELD OF COMPETITION LAW

There have been various, and very valuable, attempts to conceptualize the role of the EU Courts and the hallmarks of effective judicial review in competition cases.[2] For the purposes of this contribution, the following pages will discuss what I regard as their three core missions, namely (i) preserving the rule of law and the legitimacy of the EU enforcement system; (ii) contributing to a stable, consistent and predictable legal framework, and (iii) balancing the need for effective enforcement with the need for constraints to administrative discretion.

2.1 Preserving the Rule of Law and the Legitimacy of the EU Enforcement System

Competition law is not only about policy or economics or outcomes; it is primarily law, and it is a field of the law where undertakings are subject to penalties that are *quasi-criminal* in nature.[3]

In this context, the first and arguably most important role of the EU Courts is to ensure that the interpretation and enforcement of the competition rules are in line with fundamental rights and general principles of law that also apply in other domains. There are fundamental rights and principles, like the principle of presumption of innocence or the rules on the burden of proof, that cannot be bypassed or sacrificed in the altar of expediency because they are core rule of law requirements.[4] These principles, rights, and constraints are what make public enforcement sound, effective and legitimate. In the peculiar context of the EU administrative enforcement system, moreover, full review of all questions of fact and law by the EU Courts is necessary to ensure compliance with basic due process requirements.[5]

---

2. Pablo Ibáñez Colomo, *Law, Policy, Expertise: Hallmarks of Effective Judicial Review in EU Competition Law* (September 5, 2022), https://papers.ssrn.com/sol3/papers.cfm?abstract_id=4210327.
3. Case C-546/18, *FN and Others v. Übernahmekommission*, 9.9.2021, EU:C:2021:711, para. 46 and case law cited therein.
4. As observed by the current President of the GC, "where the contested conduct of the public authorities is repressive in nature, it is hard to conceive, at least in free democratic societies, that citizens and firms can be condemned on the basis of estimates, approximations or guesses, even if they are informed ones. Uncertainty must then be balanced against the requirements of the presumption of innocence […]. [T]his balance is struck by relying on legal concepts, such as the burden of proof"; Marc van der Woude, *Judicial Control in Complex Economic Matters*, Journal of European Competition Law and Practice Volume 10, Issue 7, 415-423 (2019).
5. *See, e.g.*, case of A. *Menarini Diagnostics SRL v. Italy*, ECHR:2011:0927JUD004350908 and case C-510/11P, *Kone*, 24.10.2013, EU:C:2013:696, para. 22.

2.2 Contributing to a Stable, Consistent and Predictable Legal Framework

The rule of law also requires legal certainty; to play by the rulebook, one needs to know what the rules are. This is a major concern for private practitioners and for our clients. As much as we might enjoy the dynamic nature of competition law and the case-by-case discussion, we need to build on a common and stable analytical framework that we can anticipate.

This is particularly important in a context where companies are required to self-assess their conduct and can be subject to multi-billion-euro fines and to very intrusive remedies. This is also a concern for the Commission, a repeat player that needs to base its decisions on a clear and established analytical framework.[6] It is of course desirable for the law to move and evolve but, in this area, wide pendulum swings do not benefit anyone, certainly not the public interest.

When it comes to predictability, it is remarkable that after many decades of EU competition law enforcement we continue to debate questions such as, what is a restriction of competition?;[7] do we need always need to consider a realistic and likely counterfactual?;[8] what is the meaning of "anticompetitive effects" and of "foreclosure"?;[9] does the as-efficient competitor principle apply across the board to the assessment of all unilateral practices or does it only apply to pricing cases?;[10] or what is a significant impediment to effective competition absent dominance?.[11] These are not minor questions, but the very matters that need to be established, as the bottom line, in any given case.

Against this background, and because Articles 101 and 102, like the merger rules, "are drawn up using imprecise legal concepts,"[12] a key role of the Courts is to provide guidance about meaning of these and other concepts and, importantly, about the methodology to inquire about them.

At the same time, however, we also need to be realistic. We lawyers expect the Courts to state what the law is, but we often fail to realize that the Courts do not always enjoy this possibility. Courts are subject to their own constraints: they are generally called upon to decide on specific cases, based on arguments raised by the parties, and they cannot substitute their own assessment for that of the institution at issue, but only

6. On the relevance of the Commission's role as a repeat player in competition litigation *see, generally*, Pablo Ibáñez Colomo, *The Shaping of EU Competition Law* (Cambridge University Press 2018).
7. Pablo Ibáñez Colomo & Alfonso Lamadrid de Pablo, *On the Notion of Restriction of Competition: What We Know and What We Don't Know We Know*, Damien Gerard, Massimo Merola and Bernd Meyring (eds.), *The Notion of Restriction of Competition: Revisiting the Foundations of Antitrust Enforcement in Europe* (Bruylant 2017).
8. Case T-612/17, *Google and Alphabet v. Commission*, 10.11.2021, EU:T:2021:763, para. 378.
9. Pablo Ibáñez Colomo, *Anticompetitive Effects in EU Competition Law*, Journal of Competition Law & Economics, Volume 17, Issue 2, 309-363 (2021).
10. Assimakis Komninos, *Practical Thoughts of a 'Consumer' of the EU Courts' Judicial Review 'Services'*, EU Law Live (October 5, 2022), https://eulawlive.com/competition-corner/practical-thoughts-of-a-consumer-of-the-eu-courts-judicial-review-services-by-assimakis-komninos/#.
11. Case C-376/20 P, *Commission v. CK Telecoms UK Investments* (pending).
12. Case T-167/08, *Microsoft v. European Commission*, 27.6.2012, EU:T:2012:323, para. 91.

review the legality of a given act. Admittedly, the CJ does enjoy more freedom in the context of preliminary rulings but, even then, it is somewhat constrained by the questions and the factual framework provided by the referring Court.

2.3 Balancing the Need for Effective Enforcement with Effective Constrains to Administrative Discretion

Courts do not only need to protect general principles of law and fundamental rights and lay down a stable and predictable framework, they also have the complex duty of doing this while not getting in the way of effective enforcement and of the way of protecting a system of "free and undistorted competition" as foreseen in the Treaties. The application of the law must not be arbitrary, discretional and based on mere hypothesis, but constraints to administrative action need to be reasonable.

In my view, the standard of judicial review applied by the EU Courts already factors in this trade off. The Commission enjoys no discretion to establish the law or the facts, but it does enjoy discretion as to priorities and policy choices,[13] and it has, traditionally, enjoyed a generous margin of appreciation when it comes to complex economic assessments.[14] What is interesting in this regard, however, is not what Courts say (i.e., how the standard of review is formulated), but what the Courts actually do.[15] This is discussed below.

3 THE PERFORMANCE OF THE EU COURTS IN THE FIELD OF COMPETITION LAW

3.1 Have the EU Courts Preserved the Rule of Law and the Legitimacy of the EU Competition Enforcement System?

A historical complaint from the bar is that the Courts have been excessively deferential to the Commission.[16] Over the years, prominent practitioners even argued that the

13. The Commission may nonetheless, by adopting rules of conduct designed to produce external effects, such as guidelines, impose a limit on the exercise of its discretion; those rules may produce legal effects and bind the Commission, as departing from them would breach general principles of law, such as equal treatment of the protection of legitimate expectations. *See, e.g.*, joined cases C-189/02 P, C-202/02 P, C-205/02 P, C-208/02 P and C-213/02 P, *Dansk Rorindustri*, 28.6.2005, EU:C:2005:408, paras. 209-211, case C-167/04, *JCB Service v. Commission*, 21.9.2006, EU:C:2006:594, paras. 207-208, or case C-226/11, *Expedia*, 13.12.2012, EU:C:2012:795, para. 28.
14. *See* Marc van der Woude, *Judicial Control in Complex Economic Matters*, Journal of European Competition Law and Practice Volume 10, Issue 7, 415-423 (2019); Marc Jaeger, *The Standard of Review in Competition Cases Involving Complex Economic Assessments: Towards the Marginalisation of the Marginal Review?*, Journal of European Competition Law & Practice, Volume 2, Issue 4, 295-314 (2011).
15. *See also* Fernando Castillo de la Torre & Eric Gippini Fournier, *Evidence, Proof and Judicial Review in EU Competition Law* (Elgar Competition Law and Practice 2017), p. 299.
16. *See, e.g.*, Damien Geradin & Nicolas Petit, *Judicial Review in European Union Competition Law: A Quantitative and Qualitative Assessment*, TILEC Discussion Paper No. 2011-008 (2010), also available at http://papers.ssrn.com/sol3/papers.cfm?abstract_id=1698342.

standard of marginal judicial review could compromise the very legality of the institutional set up under which the Commission both investigates and decides cases.[17]

In my view, however, the Courts have generally been up to the task. This does not have to do with numbers or with the outcome of cases, but rather with the scope and the intensity of the Court's scrutiny. Over the years, the EU Courts have (i) recalibrated the standard of judicial review, marginalizing marginal review;[18] (ii) placed a renewed emphasis on the right allocation of the burden of proof[19] and the presumption of innocence;[20] and (iii) they have been acutely aware of the need to protect fundamental rights, including rights of defence.[21]

The recent intensification of judicial review is particularly important at a time when the role of the law in competition law enforcement has diminished significantly. Indeed, recent enforcement has privileged cooperation procedures (including commitments, leniency, cartel settlements and cooperation in non-cartel cases)[22] which, in turn, has reduced the role of the law in administrative enforcement, and has also largely reduced the number of direct actions in competition cases reaching the EU Courts.[23] This move away from legal standards, and the shift from the analysis of

17. *See*, for instance, Ian S. Forrester, *Due Process in EC Competition Cases: A Distinguished Institution with Flawed Procedures*, European Law Review, Volume 34, Issue 6, 817-843 (2009); Ian S. Forrester, *A Bush in Need of Pruning: The Luxuriant Growth of Light Judicial Review*, in Claus-Dieter Ehlermann & Mel Marquis eds., *European Competition Law Annual 2009: Evaluation of Evidence and Its Judicial Review in Competition Cases* (Hart Publishing 2011). Ivo Van Bael, *Due Process in Competition Proceedings*, 357-363 (Kluwer 2011), and Donald Slater, Sébastien Thomas and Denis Waelbroeck, *Competition Law Proceedings Before the* [EC] *and the Right to a Fair Trial: No Need for Reform?*, The Global Competition Law Centre Working Papers Series, GCLC Working Paper 04/08 (2008).
18. Case C-272/09 P, *KME Germany and Others v. Commission*, 8.12.2011, EU:C:2011:810, para. 106 and case C-386/10 P, *Chalkor v. Commission*, 8.12.2011, EU:C:2011:815, para. 67.
19. *See, e.g.*, case C-67/13 P, *Groupement des cartes bancaires (CB) v. European Commission*, 11.9.2014, EU:C:2014:2204; and case C-413/14 P, *Intel v. Commission*, 6.9.2017, EU:C:2017:632, and, in the field of State aid, T-101/17, *Apple Distribution International v. Commission*, 27.7.2018, EU:T:2018:505, and case C-300/16 P, *Commission v. Frucona Košice Frucona*, 20.9.2017, EU:C:2017:706.
20. *See, e.g.*, case C-457/10 P, *AstraZeneca v. Commission*, 6.12.2012, EU:C:2012:770, paras. 48-49, 199; case T-180/15, *Icap and Others v. Commission*, 10.11.2017, EU:T:2017:795; and case T-286/09 RENV, *Intel Corporation v. Commission*, 26.1.2022, EU:T:2022:19, paras. 160-162, and case T-235/18, *Qualcomm Inc v. Commission*, 28.1.2021, EU:T:2022:358, para. 192.
21. *See* case C-117/20, *bpost*, 22.3.2022, EU:C:2022:202 and case C-151/20, *Nordzucker and Others*, 22.3.2022, EU:C:2022:203 (regarding the principle of *ne bis in idem*), case T-249/17, *Casino, Guichard-Perrachon and AMC v. Commission*, 5.10.2020, EU:T:2020:458 (on the right to private domicile), the Order of the President of the GC in *Facebook Ireland*, T-451/20 R, *Meta Platforms Ireland v. Commission*, 29.10.2020, EU:T:2020:515 (in relation to the right to privacy), or case T-791/19, *Sped-Pro v. Commission*, 9.2.2022, EU:T:2022:67 (in relation to the right to effective judicial protection).
22. For an overview of all competition decisions adopted since the entry into force of Regulation 1/2003, *see* Wouter P.J. Wils, *Regulation 1/2003: An Assessment after Twenty Years*, World Competition, Volume 46, Issue, 1, Annex A (2023); accessible at http://ssrn.com/author=456 087.
23. *See, e.g.*, L. Crofts, *Increase in EU Settlements Risks Sidelining Courts, Victims, Wahl Says* (Mlex 2014), citing then Advocate General Wahl's view that this trend "risks marginalizing courts and antitrust victims by reaching too many settlements with companies suspected of abusing their market clout [...]. The increasing use of 'commitments' (...) means that the policymaker is escaping judicial scrutiny"; *see also* Melchior Wathelet, *Commitment Decisions and the Paucity*

conduct and to the design of remedies has arguably reached a paroxysm with the adoption of the Digital Markets Act (DMA).[24]

The EU Courts have so far stepped up to the challenge posed by this paradigm shift, paying particular attention to the new procedural questions that these cases entail regarding, for example, the principle of presumption of innocence,[25] third parties' rights and the principle of proportionality,[26] or the need to balance an undertaking's rights of defence with other considerations.[27]

The Courts' emphasis on the need for negotiated or cooperation procedures to strictly abide to general principles of law and rights of defense is what ensures the legitimacy and soundness of this new breed of competition cases. The same will be true for the DMA; creating a regulatory system from scratch is a challenge, and the Courts will also face the challenge of keeping the law relevant and ensuring that this system is compatible with general principles of law.

3.2 Have the EU Courts Contributed to a Stable and Predictable Legal Framework?

Absolute predictability may not be a reasonable aspiration, but it is probably fair to say that, in recent years, there has been a meaningful evolution in our understanding of some key notions.

The EU Courts have provided us with a clearer framework to understand, for example, what is and what is not a restriction by object,[28] the criteria that are relevant to assess anticompetitive effects,[29] or how to assess selectivity in State aid cases.[30]

---

of Precedent, Journal of European Competition Law & Practice, Volume 6, Issue 8, 553-555 (2015) and Ryan Stones, *Commitment Decisions in EU Competition Enforcement: Policy Effectiveness v. the Formal Rule of Law*, Yearbook of European Law, 361-399 (2019).

24. Regulation (EU) No. 2022/1925 of the European Parliament and of the Council of 14 September 2022 on contestable and fair markets in the digital sector and amending Directives (EU) 2019/1937 and (EU) 2020/1828 (Digital Markets Act), OJ L 265, 12.10.2022. The DMA establishes a new regulatory framework to address certain practices, many of which were previously addressed under competition law. Under this new regulatory framework, legal principles and rules governing market definition, market power, counterfactuals, effects, pro-competitive effects, efficiencies and incentives will no longer play a role; enforcement will eminently focus on the proportionality of remedies.
25. Case T-180/15, *Icap and Others v. Commission*, 10.11.2017, EU:T:2017:795; and case C-440/19 P, *Pometon v. Commission*, 18.3.2021, EU:C:2021:214.
26. Case C-132/19 P, *Groupe Canal + v. Commission*, 9.12.2020, EU:C:2020:1007.
27. Case T-79/19 R, *Lantmännen and Lantmännen Agroetanol v. Commission*, 2.4.2019, EU:T:2019:212.
28. Case C-67/13 P, *Groupement des cartes bancaires (CB) v. European Commission*, 11.9.2014, EU:C:2014:2204, and case C-228/18, *Budapest Bank and Others*, 2.4.2020, EU:C:2020:265, and C-307/18, *Generics (UK) and Others*, 30.1.2020, EU:C:2020:52.
29. Case C-23/14, *Post Danmark*, 6.10.2015, EU:C:2015:651 and C-413/14 P, *Intel v. Commission*, 6.9.2017, EU:C:2017:632.
30. Case C-51/19 P, *World Duty Free Group and Kingdom of Spain v. European Commission*, 6.10.2021, EU:C:2021:793, and case C-53/19 P, *Banco Santander and Santusa v. Commission*, 6.10.2021, EU:C:2021:795, case C-885/19 P, *Fiat Chrysler Finance Europe v. Commission*, 8.11.2022, EU:C:2022:859.

There certainly remains room for improvement in the quest to have a more systematic and internally consistent doctrine, perhaps particularly in the field of Article 102 Treaty on the Functioning of the European Union (TFEU), where fundamental issues remain in dispute.[31] At the same time, however, one needs to be realistic, and prudent; progress is more often than not incremental; it takes place case by case; and that is, for the most part, a good thing. "Legal change may seem slow; *eppur si muove.*"[32]

3.3 Have the EU Courts Succeeded at Constraining Administrative Discretion While Enabling Effective Enforcement?

Over the years, I have often heard practitioners complain that litigating against the Commission before the EU Courts is like playing a match where one starts losing 2-0 in an away game. There was even an assumption that it was impossible to win certain cases,[33] and that there was no point in trying to litigate them. That perception may also have contributed to the surge of commitment decisions in recent years, particularly in abuse of dominance cases. Some argued, critically, that this was not a problem of judicial deference, but rather had to do with the inadequate normative legal standard applied by the EU Courts.[34]

---

31. Further clarity on those fundamental questions is, however, expected to result from the CJ's forthcoming judgments on several cases that are pending at the time of writing, including C-240/22 P, *Commission v. Intel Corporation*, case C-48/22 P, *Google and Alphabet v. Commission (Google Shopping)*, and case C-738/22 P, *Google and Alphabet v. Commission (Google Android)*. Given my direct involvement in the latter two cases, I will not engage in any substantive discussion of the questions at issue in these matters.
32. Pablo Ibáñez Colomo, *Judicial Review and Article 102 TFEU: Undue Deference to the Commission? Not So Fast*, Chillin' Competition Blog (May 11, 2018), https://chillingcompetition.com/2018/05/11/judicial-review-and-article-102-tfeu-undue-deference-to-the-commission-not-so-fast/.
33. *See, e.g.*, Christian Ahlborn & David S. Evans, *The Microsoft Judgment and Its Implications for Competition Policy Towards Dominant Firms in Europe*, Antitrust Law Journal, Volume 75, Issue 3, 887-932 (2009), also available at https://papers.ssrn.com/sol3/papers.cfm?abstract_id=1115867, p. 2 ("the Microsoft Judgment confirms a trend which has been so long standing that it almost has become a law itself: the Commission always wins Article [102] on appeal as far as points of substance are concerned. During the last 20 years, the Commission has not lost a single Article [102] on substance, while the failure rate of the Commission on points of resistance was in the region on 25%").
34. Damien Geradin & Nicolas Petit, *Judicial Review in European Union Competition Law: A Quantitative and Qualitative Assessment*, TILEC Discussion Paper No. 2011-008 (2010), also available at http://papers.ssrn.com/sol3/papers.cfm?abstract_id=1698342, p. 35: "In our opinion, the fact that undertakings challenging Article 102 TFEU decisions of the Commission almost systematically lose before the GC is not due to the fact that the Court would apply weaker standards of review to abuse of dominance cases (judgments such as Microsoft review in excruciating details the challenged Commission decision), but that the normative legal standards relied upon by the GC to assess the compatibility of dominant firm practices with Article 102 TFEU, and the way the GC applies such standards when reviewing a Commission decision, are generally inadequate. ... the legal tests developed by the Court of Justice in the field of abuse of dominance are sometimes so strict that they can almost accommodate any decision of the Commission even if it appears poorly in line with elementary economics. In other words, the problem is not one of judicial deference in the degree of control exercised by the GC with respect

Despite having been on the partially losing side on some of those Court cases (at least in the first instance, at the time of writing), and despite occasional frustration or disagreement, I have never shared that view. Some degree of deference might indeed have played a role in certain large-stake case, but my impression is that, generally, the Commission's successful track record before the EU Courts might be better explained by other factors.[35]

In recent times, the EU Courts have, generally, shown their willingness to engage in a thorough review of Commission decisions, also in the relative minority of abuse of dominance cases that have reached them. This has happened in relation to cases that the Commission won and lost. While most of the attention has focused on Commission defeats, arguably because of their exceptional nature, the EU Courts have also made a visible effort to convey an impression of greater thoroughness (both in the context of oral hearings and in the drafting of judgments) in cases where they have endorsed Commission decisions.

The EU Courts have largely responded to calls for more intense judicial review (and to the need to ensure compliance with the standards set by the European Court on Human Rights ("ECtHR") in *Menarini*[36]) by underscoring the need for the Commission to conduct a contextual assessment and satisfy its burden of proof by considering "all the relevant circumstances." The Courts have connected this more demanding review to the *Tetra Laval* standard for the review of complex economic assessment.[37] This was the message emphasized by the CJ in the landmark *Cartes Bancaires*,[38] and *Intel*[39] judgments. This was also the consistent message of a long list of State aid judgments.[40]

of abuse of dominance decisions, but one of defective rule-making in that the legal standards relied upon by the Court are out of touch with contemporary economics (and even in some cases with basic common sense)."

35. *See also* Fernando Castillo de la Torre & Eric Gippini Fournier, *Evidence, Proof and Judicial Review in EU Competition Law* (Elgar Competition Law and Practice 2017). p. 287; *see also* Heike Schweitzer, *Judicial Review in Competition Law*, Ioannis Liannos & Damien Geradin (eds.), *Handbook on European Competition Law: Enforcement and Procedure* (Edward Elgar Publishing 2013), pp. 491-538.
36. Case of *A. Menarini Diagnostics SRL v. Italy*, ECHR:2011:0927JUD004350908.
37. Case C-12/03 P, *Commission v. Tetra Laval*, EU:C:2005:87, para. 39 ("evidence must be factually accurate, reliable and consistent, contains all the information which must be taken into account in order to assess a complex situation and be capable of substantiating the conclusions drawn from it"). For a discussion on this "forgotten paragraph," *see* Marc Jaeger, *The Standard of Review in Competition Cases Involving Complex Economic Assessments: Towards the Marginalisation of the Marginal Review?*, Journal of European Competition Law & Practice, Volume 2, Issue 4, 295-314 (2011).
38. *See* case C-67/13 P, *Groupement des cartes bancaires (CB) v. European Commission*, 11.9.2014, EU:C:2014:2204.
39. Case C-413/14 P, *Intel Corporation v. Commission*, 6.9.2017, EU:C:2017:632.
40. Alfonso Lamadrid de Pablo, *EU Judicial Review: Major Antitrust Implications of Recent State Aid Cases*, Chillin' Competition Blog (March 18, 2019), https://chillingcompetition.com/2019/03/18/eu-judicial-review-major-antitrust-implications-of-recent-state-aid-cases/, and Alfonso Lamadrid de Pablo, *EU Judicial Review: Major Antitrust Implications of Recent State Aid Cases, Part 2 (Real Madrid, Case T-791/16)*, Chillin' Competition Blog (May 28, 2019), https://chillingcompetition.com/2019/05/28/eu-judicial-review-major-antitrust-implications-of-recent-state-aid-cases-part-2-real-madrid-case-t-791-16/. *See also* case T-778/16 and T-892/16, *Apple v. Commission*, 15.7.2020, EU:T:2020:338.

And this is a key point underlying the recent partial annulments *Servier*,[41] *Intel*[42] and *Google Android*[43] as well as the full annulment in *Qualcomm*.[44]

This "contextual analysis"[45] or "process-oriented" review[46] would appear to be a way for the Courts to reflect the idea that administrative enforcers can enjoy some leeway, but not an unfettered one; or rather, that this leeway comes with obligations. The Courts "rarely disagree openly with the Commission's assessment (although they occasionally do)" and, instead, verify whether the Commission's analysis had regard to all the relevant elements and circumstances.[47] Indeed, while the Courts continue to defer to the Commission's assessment on substance (at least most of the time), they condition this trust on the Commission demonstrating that it has not avoided any relevant issues and that its assessment of the relevant economic and legal context is sufficiently complete and impartial.

Following recent annulments of Commission decisions, this sort of judicial review has been criticized as "ticking boxes formalism" imposing an excessive burden on the Commission.[48] In my view, however, this sort of judicial review should rather be welcome by enforcers. The burden of conducting a complete analysis would not appear to be unreasonable, particularly when, in exchange, one can enjoy an appreciable leeway on substance. In my view, the analysis required by the Courts may indeed require greater care, but it is not liable of endangering enforcement. Provided that the Commission covers all bases, it still has a very high likelihood of winning any given case.

In my view, this kind of review is helpful when reasonable. Admittedly, not every error in a given reasoning is sufficient to invalidate an entire finding, conclusion or case. At the same time, however, there are certain elements that an enforcer must absolutely consider, the omission of which will necessarily taint its analysis. For example, as the CJ and the GC have arguably made clear, it is not possible to determine whether a given practice is capable of resulting in foreclosure without first inquiring about its coverage.[49]

---

41. Case T-691/14, *Servier and Others v. Commission*, 12.12.2018, EU:T:2018:922 (pending appeal).
42. Case T-286/09 RENV, *Intel Corporation v. Commission*, 26.1.2022, EU:T:2022:19 (pending appeal).
43. Case T-604/18, *Alphabet and Google v. Commission*, 14.9.2022, EU:T:2022:541 (pending appeal).
44. Case T-235/18, *Qualcomm Inc v. Commission*, 28.1.2021, EU:T:2022:358, paras. 477, 480, 483.
45. *See* Marc van der Woude, *Judicial Control in Complex Economic Matters*, Journal of European Competition Law and Practice, Volume 10, Issue 7, 415-423 (2019).
46. Koen Lenaerts, *The European Court of Justice and Process-Oriented Review*, College of Europe, Research Papers in Law (2012).
47. *See* Fernando Castillo de la Torre, *On Boxes and Paradoxes: Form and Substance in Judicial Review of Competition Decisions*, EU Law Live (September 29, 2022), https://eulawlive.com/competition-corner/on-boxes-and-paradoxes-form-and-substance-in-judicial-review-of-competition-decisions-by-fernando-castillo-de-la-torre/.
48. *Ibid.*
49. *See*, among others, case C-413/14 P, *Intel Corporation v. Commission*, 6.9.2017, EU:C:2017:632, para. 139; case C-23/14, *Post Danmark II*, 6.10.2015, EU:C:2015:651, paras. 38-46; case T-65/98, *Van den Bergh Foods*, 23.10.2003, EU:T:2003:281, para. 83; case C-234/89, *Delimitis*, 28.2.1991 EU:C:1991:91, para. 19; case T-286/09 RENV, *Intel Corporation v. Commission*, 26.1.2022, EU:T:2022:19, paras. 498, 499.

But this contextual review is not sufficient. The fact that a given analysis may seem complete does not necessarily mean that it is legally correct (although it is probably more likely to be correct). Similarly, more thorough judicial review is not necessarily better judicial review (although it is also more likely to produce better outcomes). For example, a seemingly rigorous analysis of foreclosure effects may not have great value if the enforcer relies on a wrong legal notion of "foreclosure."

The role of the Courts is indeed not limited to ascertaining that the Commission ticks all boxes; as discussed above, the Commission has no discretion on points of law, and it is for the Courts to verify that the Commission's application of the law (and not only the appraisal of the relevant facts or context) is correct.

4 NEW GENERATION CHALLENGES FOR THE EU COURTS

4.1 Preserving the Rule of Law and Legitimacy of the Enforcement System

Challenges to the rule of law, are unfortunately, a sign of our times, and the EU has a responsibility to uphold it, to set the global standard, and to not compromise on it, no matter the circumstances.

There may be a risk of believing that challenges to the rule of law may only originate from "the bad guys." One may, at times, feel that the law places uncomfortable constraints that ties our hands when facing certain problems. This may result in the temptation to avoid legal constraints regarded as inconvenient to the pursuit of a certain view of the public interest. That is natural; and that is why we need to remain vigilant against it.

Proposals to reverse the burden of proof in a *quasi-criminal* context,[50] disregard due process requirements, shield certain decisions from judicial review or "take antitrust away from the Courts"[51] because "they are barriers to progress"[52] are, in my view, some of the temptations that we should avoid at all costs. The law is about constraints, and constraints are uncomfortable; but those constraints are precisely "the wise restraints that make men free."[53] There are a few but vital red lines that cannot be crossed.

50. *See* Alfonso Lamadrid de Pablo, *Meeting and Shifting: The Burden of Proof*, Chillin' Competition Blog (October 31, 2019), https://chillingcompetition.com/2019/10/31/meeting-and-shifting-the-burden-of-proof-in-digital-and-beyond/.
51. Ganesh Sitaraman, *Taking Antitrust Away from the Courts*, Vanderbilt Law School Faculty Publications (September 2018), https://scholarship.law.vanderbilt.edu/cgi/viewcontent.cgi?article=2055&context=faculty-publications.
52. Ganesh Sitaraman, *Don't Trust the Courts to Fight Monopolies: They Are a Barrier to Progress*, The Guardian (October 26, 2018), https://www.theguardian.com/commentisfree/2018/oct/26/antitrust-monopolies-courts-concentration.
53. John MacArthur Maguire, LL.B. Harvard 1911, Professor of Law 1923-1957, Royall Professor of Law 1950-1957, composed this declaration, which has been used by Harvard Presidents when conferring degrees at Commencement since the late 1930s: "You are ready to aid in the shaping and application of those wise restraints that make men free." The quotation is enshrined on a plaque that hangs in the Harvard Law School Library's main stairwell.

4.2 Maintaining Predictability and Consistency in an Increasingly Fragmented Landscape

A major challenge for the future will be to offer a stable EU law framework in an increasingly decentralized but also fragmented landscape. This is particularly important at a time when much of what we knew is in dispute, when several Member States are experimenting with new theories, and when politicians are increasingly interested in competition law and in the introduction of sovereignty-related concerns.

While some degree of experimentation is acceptable, even desirable, major substantive divergences on the interpretation of the competition rules threaten the very idea of the internal market. The current enforcement system incorporates certain safeguards, but these would not appear to be working properly.[54] The EU Courts are much better placed than the Commission to address this challenge, for there may be a certain tension between an enforcers' desire to advance a certain interpretation of the law and its duty to ensure the uniform and consistent interpretation of the law.[55]

A second fundamental challenge has to do with consistency. The EU Courts have the responsibility of ensuring consistency across competition law provisions, across different types of practices, across time, between Courts (also between preliminary rulings and judgments in annulment cases) and even across Chambers of a same Court.

4.3 Contributing to a Balanced and Workable Framework: On Evidence and Speed

The discussion above has focused mostly on the law, but the outcome of cases ultimately hinges on the application of the law to a set of facts and evidence. Evidential requirements on both the Commission and private parties need to be realistic and proportionate to the information that is available to every party, depending on their means and powers of investigation at their disposal.

---

54. Alfonso Lamadrid de Pablo, *Against the Fragmentation of EU Competition Law: A Proposal for Reform EU Judicial Review: Major Antitrust Implications of Recent State Aid Cases*, Chillin' Competition Blog (May 31, 2021), https://chillingcompetition.com/2021/05/31/against-the-fragmentation-of-eu-competition-law-a-proposal-for-reform/. First, national competition authorities' obligation to apply EU law in parallel to national law when a given practice affects trade between Member States may not have been strictly complied with. Second, the obligation not to prohibit under national law conduct that would not be prohibited under EU law is diluted by the possibility for Member States to apply stricter national laws in relation to unilateral conduct pursuant to Article 3(2) of Regulation 1/2003. Third, the possibility for the Commission to comment on national draft decisions under Article 11(4) of Regulation 1/2003 has limited effects given that the Commission's feedback is generally oral, that it is always cautious and confidential, and that it may be influenced by the Commission's own policy priorities. Fourth, the possibly for the Commission to deprive national competition authorities from their competence pursuant to Article 11(6) of Regulation 1/2003 has practically not been used in the past 18 years. Fifth, to the extent that national competition authorities are not "Courts," they are prevented from referring questions to the CJ under the preliminary reference procedure (*see* C-462/19, *Anesco e.a*, 16.9.2020, EU:C:2020:715).
55. *See* Marc van der Woude, *The Preliminary Ruling Procedure: In Need of Rethinking?*, 17th GCLC Annual Conference, College of Europe (2022).

In recent years, the EU Courts have, in my view, moved the case law in the right direction. The Courts have clarified that the notion of information "available" to the Commission "includes that which seemed relevant to the assessment to be carried out in accordance with the case-law ... and which could have been obtained, upon request by the Commission, during the administrative procedure."[56] In line with the case law of the ECtHR,[57] they have also identified the circumstances in which the Commission may be required to gather evidence not available to undertakings.[58]

At the same time, the Courts have also recently clarified that it is not sufficient for undertakings to raise the mere possibility that a circumstance might affect the value of the evidence relied on by the Commission, except in cases where such proof could not be provided by the undertaking itself. Indeed, when possible, it is for the undertakings to prove the existence of that circumstance and to show how it calls into question the probative value of other evidence.[59]

Altogether, these rules result in a balanced outcome that adequately combines accuracy and administrability in line with the "proof-proximity" principle.[60]

Finally, external observers commenting on the Court's work frequently complain that it takes too long to find out what the law is; parties to Court cases often do too. My personal experience includes several sagas of cases that have lived (moving up and down the Commission, the GC and the CJ) for over 10 years. This is not ideal but, once again, criticism may often be overstated. Going through all the motions of a case, giving all parties sufficient time to develop their arguments, thoroughly reviewing them, and writing (and translating) increasingly long and detailed judgments inevitably takes time. In some cases, moreover, some delay may allow Courts to decide cases with greater distance or less pressure and, in areas of scientific uncertainty, it may give time for consensus to emerge.[61]

In recent years, in any case, the EU Courts have made a significant effort to reduce the existing backlog, cut down the average duration of cases, and ensure an efficient management of particularly burdensome cases. The reform, and effective duplication of the GC, was in part meant to alleviate this problem (perhaps contributing to other challenges, including in relation to ensuring the consistency of judgments). Remarkably, in recent years the EU Courts have even awarded damages in cases where judicial proceedings took too long.[62]

---

56. *See* case C-300/16 P, *Frucona Košice*, 20.9.2017, EU:C:2017:706, paras. 71 and 80-81. *See also* case C-579/16 P, *FIH Holding*, 6.3.2018, EU:C:2018:159, paras. 46-47.
57. *See Vidal v. Belgium [C]*, no. 12351/86, ECHR 1992, *Suominen v. Finland*, no. 37801/97, ECHR 2003.
58. *See* case T-286/09, *Intel v. Commission*, 12.6.2014, EU:T:2014:547, paras. 374-382 (set aside on other grounds).
59. *See* case T-286/09 RENV, *Intel Corporation v. Commission*, 26.1.2022, EU:T:2022:19, para. 166.
60. *See also* Cristina Volpin, *The Ball Is in Your Court: Evidential Burden of Proof and Proof-Proximity Principle in EU Competition Law*, Common Market Law Review, Volume 51, Issue 4, 1159-1185 (2014) (ISSN 0165-0750), also available at https://papers.ssrn.com/sol3/papers.cfm?abstract_id=2906724 and Andriani Kalintiri, *Evidence Standards in EU Competition Enforcement* (Hart Publishing 2020).
61. *See also* Rebecca Haw, *Delay and Its Benefits for Judicial Rulemaking Under Scientific Uncertainty*, Boston College Law Review, Volume 55 (2014).
62. *See, e.g.*, joined cases C-138/17 P and C-146/17 P, *Gascogne v. Commission*, 13.12.2018, EU:C:2018:1013.

While there may still be a certain margin for shortening the duration of proceedings and reducing the number of cases sent back to the Commission or to the GC, doing things well, and the quality of judicial review, remains more important than the speed of judicial review.[63]

5 CONCLUSION

The EU Courts face the difficult task of preserving the legitimacy of the EU competition enforcement system, ensuring the predictability, stability, and consistency of competition law, and balancing effective enforcement with the need for constraints to administrative discretion.

In recent years, the GC and the CJ have had to fulfill these missions while reviewing fewer, different and increasingly more complex competition cases. At a time when competition law is in flux and, paradoxically, as the number of competition appeals before the EU Courts continue to decrease, the role of the EU Courts is arguably more important than ever.

The Commission's remarkable litigation track record has historically drawn criticism from the bar regarding an alleged excessive deference on the part of the EU Courts. More recently, a minority of exceptional annulments and partial annulments have attracted the opposite criticism targeting alleged excessive demands on the part of the EU Courts. This may be an additional signal that judicial review is accomplishing its mission.

In a properly functioning system, administrative authorities should arguably perceive that judicial review is demanding and uncomfortable, and they should do their best to meet those standards. As a result of that perception, and of those ensuing efforts, in a properly functioning system administrative defeats should be the exception.

This contribution has sought to explain, however, that it is misleading to assess judicial review in terms of victories or defeats. The quality of judicial review is better assessed with other benchmarks, and it is determined by factors that do not always have to do with standards of review (including, among others, the pleas, evidence and arguments raised by parties, and the mechanisms for the selection of judges).

This contribution also submits that, while helpful, more thorough judicial review does not necessarily equal better judicial review. Process-oriented review may be necessary to counterbalance the Commission's margin of appreciation in relation to complex economic assessments (particularly in areas where the presumption of innocence is of relevance), but it is not sufficient.

---

63. Joined cases C-238/99 P, C-244/99 P, C-245/99 P, C-247/99 P, C-250/99 P to C-252/99 P and C-254/99 P, *Limburgse Vinyl Maatschappij and others v. Commission*, 15.10.2002, EU:C:2002:582 para. 234. "the aim of promptness—which the Commission, at the stage of the administrative procedure, and the Community judicature, at the stage of judicial proceedings, must seek to achieve—must not adversely affect the efforts made by each institution to establish fully the facts at issue, to provide the parties with every opportunity to produce evidence and submit their observations, and to reach a decision only after close consideration of the existence of infringements and of the penalties."

Beyond making sure that the Commission has reviewed "all the relevant circumstances" of a given case, the primary task of the Courts is to interpret the law, to correct errors of law, and to safeguard the rule of law and fundamental rights. The EU Courts have overall been up to the task, but they will continue to be tested by new and ever more complex cases and challenges.

CHAPTER 12

Rethinking the Preliminary Reference Procedure

Marc van der Woude[*]

1 INTRODUCTORY REMARKS

The invitation of the Global Competition Law Centre to contribute to an academic debate on the reshaping of the preliminary reference procedure took me somewhat by surprise. Since the beginning of my tenure at the General Court, I regularly receive invitations to come and speak on judicial review in competition cases brought to the General Court pursuant to Article 263 Treaty on the Functioning of the European Union (TFEU), but never to discuss the assessment of those cases under Article 267 TFEU. Indeed, the General Court does not have any competence to deal with preliminary reference procedures. Admittedly, Article 256, paragraph 3, TFEU provides that the General Court shall have jurisdiction to hear and determine such cases in the specific areas laid down by the Statute of the Court of Justice of the European Union (Statute). At this stage, however, the Statute does not define these specific areas. Activating the competence foreseen by Article 256, paragraph 3, TFEU, requires a modification of the Statute pursuant to Article 281 TFEU at the request of the Court of Justice or the Commission. No such request was filed so far.

Even so, in light of its increasing workload, the Court of Justice could possibly submit such a proposal to the legislator in a not too distant future. I suppose that the organizers of this conference share this view and that they ask themselves the question as to whether it would make sense to include competition law in the specific areas referred to in Article 256, paragraph 3, TFEU. By competition law, I refer to Articles 101 and 102 TFEU, but not to the rules relating to State aid or concentration control.

* All opinions expressed herein are personal to the author.

Before dealing with the advantages and disadvantages of granting the General Court jurisdiction to rule on preliminary references relating to Articles 101 and 102 TFEU, I will briefly recall the main features of the judicial architecture as it evolved until now.

2 THE EUROPEAN JUDICIAL ARCHITECTURE

In 2022, the Court of Justice of the European Union will celebrate its 70th anniversary. Although the Court of Justice was competent from the outset to deal with direct actions brought by Member States and private entities against decisions taken by the European Institutions, the European legal order, as we know it today, was shaped in the context of the dialogue between the Court of Justice and national courts under the preliminary reference procedure, foreseen by Article 177 of the European Economic Community (EEC) Treaty, now Article 267 TFEU. The milestone judgments in *Van Gend & Loos*[1] and *Costa v. Enel*[2] laid down the foundations of this order and confirmed its autonomy vis-à-vis national law. Despite the seminal importance of these two judgments, they were not the first preliminary reference cases the Court of Justice had to deal with. In fact, the very first case was a competition law case concerning the validity of distribution agreement under Article 101 TFEU or Article 85 EEC Treaty as that provision was known at the time.[3] This is not surprising because Article 101, paragraph 2, TFEU concerns a civil law sanction that directly affects the validity of agreements concluded between undertakings. In *Van Gend & Loos* the Court of Justice alluded to this provision as one of the examples showing that European Union (EU) law is much more than an intergovernmental matter.[4] The gradual construction of this innovative legal edifice was a matter of the Court of Justice and national courts.

As mentioned already, answering preliminary reference questions was and is a crucial task of the Court of Justice, but it is not its only task. It also ensures adequate judicial protection to States and private entities contesting legislative, regulatory and administrative acts adopted by the EU institution themselves. Here again, such judicial protection is particularly important in the field of competition law, because of the Commission's competence to impose sanctions which are akin to criminal sanctions. During the eighties, the Commission significantly increased the number of cartel investigations and the level of the fines in its fight against hard-core cartels.

This development had the blessing of the Court of Justice, which explicitly mentioned that it was for the Commission to define competition policy and determine the adequate level of fines.[5] The Community's industry, represented by organizations, such as the European Round Table of Industrialists and UNICE (the predecessor of BUSINESSEUROPE), did not oppose tougher competition law enforcement, provided

1. Case C-26/62, *Van Gend & Loos*, 5.2.1963, ECLI:EU:C:1963:1.
2. Case C-6/64, *Costa v. ENEL*, 15.7.1964, ECLI:EU:C:1964:66.
3. Case 13/61, *Geus v. Bosch*, 6.4.1962, ECLI:EU:C:1962:11.
4. *See* Opinion of AG Karl Roemer in Case C-26/62, *Van Gend & Loos*, 6.12.1962, ECLI:EU:C:1962:42.
5. Joined Cases C-100/80, C-101/80, C-102/80 and C-103/80, *Musique Diffusion française v. Commission*, 7.6.1983, ECLI:EU:C:1983:158, paras 105-109.

that it went hand in hand with effective judicial protection. In the context of the Commission's initiative to transform the common market into a truly internal market, European industry not only considered that the Court's level of review was insufficient, but also that higher fines could be justified only in the presence of judicial protection in two degrees. These discussions ultimately led to the insertion of a specific Treaty provision allowing for the creation of a Court of First Instance adjoined to the Court of Justice.[6] In 1988, the legislator adopted the decision setting up this new court, which saw the life as a child that the Court of Justice did not really want.[7]

Although staff matters were added to the initial competencies of the Court of First Instance, the General Court essentially started its activities in 1989 as a competition law court. Ever since its activities gradually expanded into other areas of Union law, a development that ultimately led the authors of Treaty to redefine the role of General Court as a truly general administrative court competent to deal with all direct actions brought by individuals against acts of the institutions of the Union. Between 2004 and 2016, the General Court also acted as an appeal court in staff cases brought against decisions adopted by the specialized Civil Service Tribunal. In the second part of the first decade of this century, the General Court started to suffer from the same problem that the Court of Justice had to face in the eighties. It was not in a position to deal with cases on time, as acknowledged by the Court of Justice in actions brought against the institution for the violation of the principle of reasonable delay.[8]

In order to overcome this problem, the legislator decided in 2015 to abolish the specialized Civil Service Tribunal and, in parallel, to double gradually the number of judges at the General Court.[9] This reform, which implied a net increase in the number of judges by 21, was achieved in 2019.[10] Obviously, this doubling exercising represented a major investment in judicial protection, an investment in which the legislator legitimately expects a return. Article 3 of Regulation 2422/2015 therefore provides that the Court of Justice should report in two ways on the reform. First, the Court of Justice had to deliver in 2020 a report dealing with the efficiency of the General Court and addressing, surprisingly ex-post, the necessity of the increase.[11] Second, the Court of Justice had to present in 2017 a report concerning the topic of this contribution, i.e., the possible changes to the distribution of competence for preliminary rulings under Article 267 TFEU.[12] That report concluded that that question was premature, as one could expect from a report on a reform process that had only started in 2016.[13]

6. The Single European Act inserted Article 168a EEC Treaty.
7. Council Decision 88/591/ECSC, EEC, Euratom of 24 October 1988 establishing a Court of First Instance of the European Communities, OJ L 319, 25.11.1988.
8. *See* Case C-50/12 P, *Kendrion v. Commission*, 26.11.2013, ECLI:EU:C:2013:771 and joined Cases C-138/17 P and C-146/17 P, *European Union v. Gascogne Sack Deutschland and Gascogne*, 13.12.2018, ECLI:EU:C:2018:1013.
9. Regulation (EU) 2422/2015 of the European Parliament and of the Council of 16 December 2015 amending Protocol No 3 on the Statute of the Court of Justice of the European Union, OJ L 341, 24.12.2015.
10. Article 1 Regulation 2422/2015.
11. Article 3(1) Regulation 2422/2015.
12. Article 3(2) Regulation 2422/2015.
13. Court of Justice, *Report submitted pursuant to Article 3(2) of Regulation (EU, Euratom) 2015/2422 of the European Parliament and of the Council amending Protocol No 3 on the Statute*

Even so, the situation since 2017 has changed considerably. The workload of the Court of Justice increased considerably both in quantitative and qualitative terms, whereas it saw its capacity shrink by one judge because of Brexit. The Court of Justice increasingly has to deal with highly complex or socially sensitive issues that are often constitutional in nature and that are mostly referred to the Grand Chamber composed of 15 judges. This is, and should be, a highly time consuming activity that causes a strain on the Court's capacity to deal with other cases. In parallel, the General Court cleared its docket. It manages to deal with cases as they come in. Against such a backdrop, one may expect the Court of Justice to reassess the expediency of a transfer of preliminary reference questions to the General Court pursuant to Article 256, paragraph 3, TFEU. Work should logically flow to where the resources are.

The Court of Justice will therefore have to determine the specific areas of Union law in which the General Court shall have jurisdiction. The Treaties do not give much guidance in that respect. There are, however, a series of practical and dogmatic considerations that could play a role. First, from a practical point of view, the number of cases to be transferred should be sufficiently important in order to alleviate the workload of the Court of Justice to a significant extent. Second, the subject matters should be clearly defined and not give rise to confusion. The referring national courts should be able to understand why a specific case ends up before the General Court rather than before the Court of Justice. Third, the areas of law should preferably not give rise to constitutional questions or other issues that could affect the unity or consistency of Union law. Indeed, in those circumstances, Article 256, paragraph 3, TFEU invites the General Court to refer the case to the Court of Justice.

The question thus arises as to whether the competition rules of Articles 101 and 102 TFEU are suitable candidates to be identified as a specific area in which the General Court should have jurisdiction to rule on preliminary reference requests within the meaning of Article 267 TFEU. As so often in legal matters, there is no unequivocal answer to that question.

3 COMPETITION LAW AS A SPECIFIC SUBJECT MATTER

The first argument, which could be put forward to support the view that Articles 101 and 102 TFEU could qualify as a specific matter, relates to the parallelism that exists between the concept of the legality of an administrative act assessed under Article 263 TFEU, on the one hand, and the validity notion referred to in Article 267 TFEU, on the other hand. Indeed, it results from standard case law that parties cannot invoke the invalidity of an act before a national court and expect that court to ask a preliminary question to that effect pursuant to Article 267 TFEU, if they had the possibility to contest the legality of that same act before the General Court under Article 263 TFEU. As reiterated by the Court of Justice in *Georgsmarienhütte*, the General Court has the

of the Court of Justice of the European Union, https://curia.europa.eu/jcms/upload/docs/application/pdf/2018-01/en_2018-01-12_08-43-52_183.pdf.

main role in controlling the legality of Union acts.[14] It would therefore make sense to entrust the General Court with the responsibility to assess the validity of Commission decisions concerning Article 101 or 102 under Article 267 TFEU. Similarly, since follow-on litigation in private damages actions is often based on Commission decisions that were challenged or could have been challenged before the General Court, it would make sense to entrust that court with the responsibility to interpret those decisions.[15]

Second, Articles 101 and 102 TFEU are two relatively short and abstract provisions, which become specific and concrete through their factual application; facts, economic concepts and theories of harm often determine the outcome of the case. It is hard to disconnect the facts from the law when applying competition rules. However, preliminary reference procedure tends to that. Indeed, 267 TFEU does not authorize the Court of Justice to establish the facts. It must rule on the basis of the facts, as presented by the referring court in the reference request. This disconnect sometimes leads to very abstract answers, which the referring courts may find difficult to apply.[16] Making the General Court answer preliminary references in competition cases may help to contain this risk, because the General Court has the experience to deal with the facts, unlike the Court of Justice that only deals with the legal side of competition cases, either in the context of Article 267 TFEU or on appeal on points of law.

Third, the Commission plays for sure a leading and coordinating role in the system of competition authorities set up by Regulation 1/2003. Even so, it is only one of the 28 competition authorities constituting the European Competition Network (ECN). This network, which is now officially identified as such by Directive 2019/1,[17] operates in a flexible and casuistic manner. Work within the network is shared pragmatically on an ad hoc basis. This holds true in particular for investigations in the digital sector in which the German, French and European authorities each took the lead on specific issues (respectively, *Facebook*,[18] *booking.com*[19] and *Google*[20]). The ECN has become a player in itself in the field of antitrust enforcement. Moreover, the ECN

14. Case C-135/16, *Georgsmarienhütte and Others*, 25.7.2018, ECLI:EU:C:2018:582.
15. Case C-882/19, *Sumal*, 6.10.2021, ECLI:EU:C:2021:800; Case C-267/20, *Volvo and DAF Trucks*, 22.6.2022, ECLI:EU:C:2022:494; Case C-199/11, *Otis and Others*, 6.11.2012, ECLI:EU:C:2012:684.
16. C-32/11, *Allianz Hungária Biztosító and Others*, 14.3.2013, ECLI:EU:C:2013:160.
17. Directive (EU) 2019/1 of the European Parliament and of the Council of 11 December 2018 to empower the competition authorities of the Member States to be more effective enforcers and to ensure the proper functioning of the internal market, OJ L 11, 14.1.2019.
18. German Federal Cartel Office, decision B6-22/16, *Facebook*, Exploitative business terms pursuant to Section 19(1) GWB for inadequate data processing.
19. Autorité de la concurrence, decision no 15-D-06, regarding practices implemented by Booking.com B.V., Booking.com France SAS and Booking.com Customer Service France SAS in the online hotel booking sector.
20. Commission Decision of 27 June 2017 relating to proceedings under Article 102 TFEU and Article 54 of the EEA Agreement (Case AT.39740 – *Google Search (Shopping)*) (notified under document number C(2017) 4444); Commission Decision of 18 July 2018 relating to a proceeding under Article 102 of the Treaty on the Functioning of the European Union and Article 54 of the EEA Agreement (Case AT.40099 – *Google Android*) (notified under document C(2018) 4761); Commission Decision of 20 March 2019 relating to a proceeding under Article 102 of the Treaty on the Functioning of the European Union and Article 54 of the EEA Agreement (Case AT.40411 – *Google Search (AdSense)*) (notified under document number C(2019) 2173).

members all apply the same substantive rules: Article 3 of Regulation 1/2003 has blurred the distinction between national and European competition law.

The more and more integrated manner in which the ECN operates, contrasts with the judicial control exercised on its members. Each jurisdiction organizes judicial protection against the decisions adopted by its competition authorities. Obviously, case allocation decisions are just preparatory in nature and possible procedural shortcomings can always be contested in the context of the appeal against the final decisions, as recalled by the Court of Justice and the General Court in the Silgan and Amazon cases.[21] Even so, the result is that judicial control is fragmented, whereas the administrative action, which is the subject matter of that control, is coordinated. This situation could be overcome to a certain extent, if the court overseeing the activities of Commission as the leading and coordinating member of ECN, could also interact, under Article 267 TFEU, with review courts, that control the national competition authorities. Conferring the General Court the competence to answer preliminary reference questions could help to restore this equilibrium.

Finally, as mentioned above, the General Court was born as a competition law court. It has developed considerable expertise in the field of competition law and is known worldwide as one of the leading courts in that area. It is therefore fair to say that the General Court has acquired sufficient authority to engage in a judicial dialogue with national courts under Article 267 TFEU. Seen from this angle, the 1989 decision to confer judicial powers to the then Court of First Instance under Article 263 TFEU, could be duplicated under Article 267 TFEU.

4 IS COMPETITION LAW SPECIFIC?

There are also arguments against a transfer of preliminary reference competence in competition law cases to the General Court. The first argument is practical in nature and concerns the number of competition law cases on the docket of the Court of Justice. This number is relatively modest and oscillates between 10 and 15 cases per year. This quantitative issue could be overcome by transferring comparable subject areas in the sphere of economic regulation, such as energy and electronic communications and banking regulation, but transferring such additional competencies may create legal problems of their own, which are beyond the scope of the present contribution.

The second argument, which could plead against a transfer of competence as regards Articles 101 and 102 TFEU, concerns the interaction between these competition rules and other legal provisions. For example, competition law enforcement may raise questions as regards the interpretation of the Charter of Fundamental Rights,[22] questions of a constitutional nature affecting the procedural autonomy of a Member

21. Case T-410/18, *Silgan Closures and Silgan Holdings v. Commission*, 15.3.2019, ECLI:EU:T:2019:166; Case C-418/19 P, *Silgan Closures and Silgan Holdings v. Commission*, 29.1.2020, ECLI:EU:C:2020:43; Case T-19/21, *Amazon.com and Others v. Commission*, 14.10.2021, ECLI:EU:T:2021:730.
22. Case C-386/10 P, *Chalkor v. Commission*, 8.12.2011, ECLI:EU:C:2011:815.

State[23] or questions concerning the Brussels Regulation on judicial competence.[24] In the light of such side effects, one can legitimate wonder whether the competition rules are sufficiently specific.

The third and probably most significant argument, which could be relied upon to oppose a transfer in the field of the competition rules concerns the fact that the Court of Justice is the appeal court for judgments adopted by the General Court. Disconnecting the preliminary reference competence from the appeal function may cause significant problems because the combination of both competencies ensures that there is only one court, the Court of Justice, having the final say on the interpretation of the law. It would be curious, to say the least, that the Court of Justice acting on appeal would interpret these rules differently in appeal procedures than the General Court under Article 267 TFEU. The uniformity of the law, that Article 267 TFEU seeks to ensure, could thus be compromised.[25]

Moreover, both in quantitative and qualitative terms, the role of the Court of Justice as a competition court in appeal procedures is very important. In terms of figures, appeal rates in competition cases are considerably higher than average and may sometimes oscillate around 50 % of the decisions taken by the General Court. This implies that the Court of Justice has to deal with a significant number of appeals in competition cases. This number corresponds to 14 on average for the past five years. In qualitative terms, the origins of the General Court should not be lost out of sight. It was the need to have a two-tier judicial protection system, which was one of the main considerations for setting up this court, as indicated above.

5 FINAL OBSERVATIONS

To conclude this brief presentation on the possibility that the General Court obtains jurisdiction under Article 267 TFEU as regards the application of the competition rules, there are arguments in favour and against this option. It is for the legislator to strike the balance between the two. Before doing so, however, the legislator could possibly await the outcome of the consultation process launched by the Commission on the revision of Regulation 1/2003.

23. Case C-439/08, *Vebic*, 7.12.2010, ECLI:EU:C:2010:739; Case C-308/19, *Whiteland Import Export*, 21.1.2021, ECLI:EU:C:2021:47.
24. Case C-451/18, *Tibor-Trans*, 29.7.2019, ECLI:EU:C:2019:635.
25. Even so, this argument would apply to all legal areas in which the Court of Justice scrutinizes judgments rendered by the General Court, hence significantly reducing the scope of subject matters that could possibly be transferred to the General Court under Article 256, paragraph 3, TFEU.

CHAPTER 13

Competition Law and the New Regulatory Landscape: What Lies Ahead?

Cani Fernández & Adriana Meijide[*]

1 INTRODUCTION

The main purpose of competition policy and - by extension - of the competition authorities enforcing it, is to ensure effective market competition. Through this, these authorities promote the proper functioning of the free market economy and guarantee consumer welfare.

However, there are other instruments of economic policy, such as regulation, that while trying to address different or broader objectives are also relevant and fundamental for the correct functioning of the market. Because of this, we must take into account the fact that competition and regulation are often interrelated and, in many cases, complement one another. This complementary interrelationship has occurred in classic regulated markets such as electricity and telecommunications, but also, more recently, with the so-called digital markets.

Conversely, the analysis performed by competition authorities traditionally focuses on those parameters that directly impact competition, such as price, quality or innovation. However, other public interests may also be relevant. Sustainability, national security and data privacy rules can affect competition and, therefore, can be incorporated into competition analyses. In fact, within the European Union (EU), competition rules have contributed to achieving greater integration of the internal market, as well as other goals included in the treaties.

* The views expressed in this chapter are those of the authors and do not reflect the official position of the CNMC.

In terms of sustainability, there has been a very heated debate on how competition law should incorporate sustainability goals into its assessment, to what extent it should do so, and whether this requires new tools.

Given this complex relationship, the objective of this chapter is twofold: on the one hand to show how competition law and regulation work together, their challenges and the benefits of their complementarity. On the other, to review where the debate between competition law and sustainability is heading.

The chapter is structured in the following way: the first section provides a brief overview of the interrelationship between competition law and regulation. It also refers to recent examples of success where the interaction was complementary, focusing on the experience of the Spanish National Markets and Competition Commission (CNMC), which is both the sectoral regulator (of telecommunications and media, energy, transport and postal services) and the Spanish Competition Authority.

The second section delves into the specific debate on competition law and sustainability. It briefly examines whether competition authorities are sufficiently equipped or require a new approach to incorporate sustainability considerations into their analyses. Additionally, it reviews recent developments on sustainability at the EU level, mainly with regard to agreements between competitors and merger control.

Ultimately, the debate surrounding competition policy and sustainability can be summarised in two main perspectives: (i) the objectives of competition law are currently insufficient and should be broadened to completely support the achievement of the sustainable development goals; or, (ii) the current competition framework is capable of contributing to the achievement of sustainability and, in any case, is complementary to other tools, making it better suited to fully addressing sustainability challenges, such as regulation.

Although the approaches of the two possibilities pose different challenges and have specific nuances, both relate to current and future manifestations of how competition law and regulation interrelate.

2 BALANCING COMPETITION LAW AND REGULATION

Regulation can be broadly defined as the imposition of rules by a government, backed by the use of penalties that are specifically intended to modify the economic behaviour of individuals and firms in the private sector.[1] Regulation can deal with several public interests, such as health, consumer protection or environmental policies, and is also a key tool for mitigating market failures.

The goal of competition law, as stated in the introduction, is much narrower than other forms of regulation as its purpose is to prevent an unjustified accumulation of market power or, when this already exists, to control it so that effective competition in the market is guaranteed. By ensuring effective competition in markets, firms are forced to operate more efficiently, offer a greater variety of products and choices and,

1. This is the definition that the Organisation for Economic Co-operation and Development (OECD) provides in its *Glossary of Industrial Organisation Economics and Competition Law* p. 73 (1993).

importantly, to offer these products and services at lower prices. All of these effects lead to increased consumer welfare and allocative efficiency.[2]

Competition laws and regulation – economic or otherwise – can easily overlap, leading to situations where they may behave as substitutes or, ideally, complements.

2.1 Why Is Competition Law Preferable?

Given the potentially complex relationships between competition law and regulation, the current consensus is that mechanisms based on market competition, including competition law and policy, are the preferred policy option for ensuring efficiency and consumer welfare. However, there are scenarios where competition law may be insufficient and other instruments, including regulation, are necessary.[3]

From an economic perspective, regulation should be considered a last resort and applied only when market failures and bottlenecks cannot be solved by markets themselves, as it can have various flaws:

> First, there is the risk of regulatory failure, i.e., when regulation intended to correct market failures or to protect the public at large fails to do so. This failure also includes situations where the costs (of all types) of regulation are greater than the associated benefits.[4] There are a variety of reasons which may lead regulation to fail, including failures in its design, failure in its implementation and, lastly, regulatory capture of the institutions enforcing it.

Failures in the analysis and the design of the regulation are often caused by the imperfect or asymmetric information available to legislators or rule makers. In some cases, the basis on which the regulation is designed provides an incomplete view of the market. In others, the information can simply be flawed. Furthermore, regulators sometimes try to implement measures that were successful in a different context; however, similar regulatory measures do not necessarily lead to the same results, as the economic, legal and social circumstances may differ.[5]

Implementation failures may be caused by the regulator's lack of proper resources or ability to enforce the regulation, or the inability to do this in a timely manner.[6] Also, well-intentioned laws may have unintended consequences in the market derived, among other things, from side effects and unforeseen changes in the market or its environment.[7]

Lastly, regulation may be motivated by private interests (such as those of industry lobbies) or the political cycle rather than general welfare considerations,

2. *See* OECD (1993), *supra* n. 1 at 23.
3. *See* OECD, *Competition Enforcement and Regulatory Alternatives, OECD Competition Committee Discussion Paper* (2021) http://oe.cd/cera.
4. *See* Jeroen Van Der Heijden, *Regulatory Failure: A Review of the International Academic Literature State of the Art in Regulatory Governance*, Research Paper (2022) *Wellington: Victoria University of Wellington/Government Regulatory Practice Initiative.*
5. *See* Robert Baldwin et al., *Understanding Regulation: Theory, Strategy and Practice* (2nd ed. Oxford University Press, 2012), pp. 69-82.
6. *See* Jeroen Van Der Heijden, *supra* n. 4.
7. *See* Robert Baldwin et al., *supra* n. 5.

leading to regulatory capture. In this scenario, private parties seek to influence regulators and policymakers to obtain regulatory measures that favour their interests and provide them with economic rents or additional surplus. In the context of sector or market regulation, the risk of capture may come from incumbent firms that are well placed to influence the regulatory processes and actively lobby policymakers and regulators. This can result in legislation benefiting the incumbent, as well as additional barriers to entry of new companies into the market, hampering competition and innovation.[8]

2.2 A Complementary Relationship

There are several scenarios where competition law coexists together with regulation and they are, indeed, complementary. We highlight two noteworthy cases: first, when they both pursue the same objective; and second, when regulatory measures with differing objectives also foster competition (directly or indirectly).[9]

A good example of the first situation are the market liberalisation processes. In these cases, there is no substantial trade-off between competition and regulation. This is because the main purpose of the regulation is to open up a monopolistic market to competition in an orderly manner, ensuring a smooth transition where operators are able to enter the market and effectively compete with the incumbent. Although the rationale of liberalisation is to achieve a deregulated market, the process is normally cumbersome and normally entails, paradoxically, new, or at least interim regulation to achieve it.[10]

In Spain, as in many other countries, this was the case with the liberalisation of the telecommunications and energy markets, and it is currently occurring in the railway transport sector with promising results.

Within the telecommunications sector, since liberalisation began, prices have dropped significantly in Spain,[11] there has been a great improvement in the infrastructure –thanks to large fibre rollouts, not only by the incumbent but also by the alternative operators – and the incumbent's market share has consistently fallen while new entrants have become relevant players thanks to very specific pro-competitive regulation.[12] Accordingly, as market competition has become more intense, the need for regulation has lessened and many obligations imposed on the incumbent have been lifted. The recent case of the wholesale access to fixed broadband markets review is paradigmatic. Since 2016, the CNMC has deregulated 696 municipalities (around 70%

8. *See* Competition and Markets Authority (CMA), *Regulation and Competition: A Review of the Evidence* (2020), section 4.
9. *See* International Competition Network (ICN), *Antitrust Enforcement in Regulated Sectors Working Group Subgroup 2: Enforcement Experience in Regulated Sectors* (2004).
10. *See* OECD (2021), *supra* n. 3, section 4.2.
11. In fact, the Study on Mobile and Fixed Broadband Prices in Europe (2021) shows that Spain has one of the most attractively priced mobile broadband offers within the EU. *See* https://digital-strategy.ec.europa.eu/en/policies/desi-connectivity.
12. For detailed information on market share evolution over the past decade *see* http://data.cnmc.es/datagraph.

of the population) by including them in the so-called Ultra-Fast Broadband Zone, where there is intense infrastructure competition based on Next Generation Access (NGA) networks. As a result, the incumbent is no longer required to provide wholesale access to its fibre network.[13]

As for the railway transport sector, it is well known that within the EU the liberalisation of this sector has been conducted through a series of 'railway packages'. The last of these, the fourth package,[14] sought to open up passenger rail transport service market, beginning in December 2020.

The CNMC has followed the process closely and actively. First, by producing a market study on the liberalisation of rail passenger transport services.[15] The study integrates the CNMC's expertise on competition law and sectoral regulation in the railway sector and refers to the particularities of the Spanish railway system. It highlights the fact that some of these could facilitate alternative operators' access to rail infrastructure, while also acknowledging the challenges and barriers that remain to achieving effective competition in the market. On the basis of its analysis, the CNMC made nine recommendations with the main goal of fostering the liberalisation process and reducing the competition restrictions identified within the market.

Second, the CNMC adopted decisions to ensure a non-discriminatory allocation of railway capacity.[16] The allocation process attracted the interest of various companies and has resulted in three operators competing in the main high-speed corridors in Spain, an unprecedented competitive result in Europe, where competition has been limited to the incumbent and a single alternative operator.[17]

Since the liberalisation began in Spain, a number of new entrants have accessed the Spanish market.[18] This has occurred in spite of the obvious problems that COVID-19 has posed for passenger travel. In fact, demand in the Madrid-Barcelona corridor, where competition is already in place, is recovering faster than in the other corridors. This has already led to better services and lower prices for consumers. Nevertheless, the sector still faces many challenges: it is key to guaranteeing an efficient and increased use of the network and to adequately allocating the spare capacity so that other operators are able to use it. Furthermore, as the liberalisation

13. For more information *see*: https://www.cnmc.es/sites/default/files/editor_contenidos/Notas%20de%20prensa/2021/20211015_NP_Mercados%20BA_CO_eng%20(1).pdf.
14. For additional information on this package *see* https://www.consilium.europa.eu/en/policies/4th-railway-package/.
15. The study is available in English here: https://www.cnmc.es/sites/default/files/2741457_2.pdf.
16. In its decision, the CNMC analysed the infrastructure manager's proposal regarding a modification of its network statement. Ultimately, and among other recommendations, the CNMC proposed that the infrastructure manager made the framework capacity statement more flexible so that potential entrants were able to develop their business model. The decision (in Spanish) is available here: https://www.cnmc.es/sites/default/files/2541816_2.pdf.
17. For an in-depth analysis regarding the allocation process in Spain *see* Iván Santos, *Estado de la liberalización de los servicios de transporte de pasajeros por ferrocarril* (2020) Boletín Económico de ICE (3127), https://doi.org/10.32796/bice.2020.3127.7084.
18. The French operator Société nationale des chemins de fer français (SNCF), under its commercial brand OUIGO and AVLO, a low-cost brand of RENFE, the Spanish incumbent. Furthermore, a third entrant, Iryo, will start operating on 26 November 2022. To date, OUIGO is operating the Madrid – Barcelona corridor and will start its operation between Madrid and Valencia on the 6 October 2022. AVLO operates the Madrid – Barcelona and Madrid – Valencia corridors.

continues and competition is fostered on additional routes, the CNMC will remain vigilant and continue to guarantee fair access to the railway infrastructure.

We may find ourselves in the opposite case, where competition law may be insufficient to maintain effective competition. This may be the case when market failures are too large to be dealt with using the standard competition law toolkit. These situations require regulation. Depending on the aggregate impact of the market failures, the intensity of the regulation will be either greater (even displacing competition law) or lesser (the regulation will create a framework where competition law is still applicable).[19]

A very recent and relevant example of the latter are digital markets, where large digital platforms have gained significant market power despite the efforts of the competition authorities. Indeed, digital markets present a combination of characteristics, such as strong network effects, significant economies of scale and scope associated in many cases with data, and services provided at very low or even at zero prices (monetarily speaking), that contribute to increased concentration. Although there are other markets where we can see some of these features, they occur simultaneously within the digital markets.[20] This has led to a situation where the market power that these platforms enjoy is persistent and very unlikely to go away.[21]

Competition law has led to several antitrust and merger investigations focused on digital markets and platforms. In particular, jurisdictions such as the EU have been particularly vigilant and tried to adapt their investigations to the digital ecosystem.

However, today it is broadly assumed that competition law alone cannot lead to competitive outcomes in markets dominated by large digital platforms and therefore specific regulation is needed to address them. That is why regulators across the world are calling for additional tools to deal with competitive challenges in the digital arena. In July 2022, the EU finally approved the Digital Markets Act (DMA), creating a new set of rules for the so-called gatekeepers that should ensure a level digital playing field.

Although national competition authorities asked for complementary enforcement powers of the DMA,[22] the European Commission (EC) will be exclusively in charge of enforcing the DMA. National competition authorities will play an important role by assisting the Commission in its investigations, for example providing information to the Commission, assisting in market investigations, inspections and interviews. There is no doubt that the experience that national competition authorities have of the digital markets will be of great use to the Commission and will allow more agile and effective

19. *See* Paul Crampton, *Striking the Right Balance Between Competition and Regulation: The Key Is Learning from Our Mistakes* (2002) APEC – OECD Co-operative Initiative on Regulatory Reform: Third Workshop.
20. *See* Chase Solán et al., *Principles of the Economic Analysis of Digital Markets* (2022) Información Comercial Española, ICE: Revista de economía, ISSN 0019-977X, Nº 925, 2022, pp. 11-26.
21. For an in-depth analysis *see* Jason Furman et al., *Unlocking Digital Competition: Report of the Digital Competition Expert Panel* (2019), HM Treasury Publications.
22. *See* European Competition Network (ECN) *Joint paper of the heads of the national competition authorities of the European Union: How national competition agencies can strengthen the DMA* (2021), https://ec.europa.eu/competition/ecn/DMA_joint_EU_NCAs_paper_21.06.2021.pdf.

investigations. Furthermore, even though the DMA constitutes an innovative framework there will be many challenges in terms of its application, but sound cooperation with National Competition Authorities (NCAs) will ease the Commission's task.

2.3 Complementarity Is Not Always Easy

Of course, the interaction between competition law and regulation is not always simple, leading to tensions in their joint implementation. The reasons for this tension may relate, among other things, to substantive and jurisdictional considerations.[23]

The main substantive concerns refer to which mechanism should apply (competition law or the regulatory measures) and, when both are applicable, how to implement them coherently. Jurisdictional concerns refer to the body that should be responsible for applying or implementing the measures in question.

The institutional design of competition and regulatory authorities can impact the mentioned considerations. Noting that there are a number of nuances depending on the jurisdiction, traditionally the regulatory bodies and the competition authorities have been kept in separate institutions. However, some jurisdictions have opted for integrated institutions. In other cases, the regulator and the competition authority are separate but some of their functions can be concurrent, i.e., the regulator enjoys some capacity to enforce competition law or the competition authority is able to regulate certain sectors.

The CNMC, as mentioned in the introduction, is an example of an integrated model. Since its creation in 2013,[24] it has combined sectoral regulation and supervision (of telecommunications and media, energy, transport and postal services) with the horizontal application of competition policy (both advocacy and enforcement).

It is true that none of the mentioned systems guarantee a perfect relationship between competition law and regulation. However, we believe that the duality of functions that integrated authorities enjoy, allows better complementarity of regulation and competition law. Furthermore, this design can reduce some of the friction and create several synergies, especially related to coherency and coordination.

In terms of coordination, the CNMC has found the creation of multidisciplinary working groups in topics such as digital markets,[25] the rail-market liberalisation, energy and sustainability to be particularly useful.[26] For example the digital markets

23. *See* OECD (2021), *supra* n. 3, section 3.1.
24. The CNMC was created in 2013 as a result of the integration of the Spanish Competition Authority and five supervision bodies, namely the National Energy Commission, Telecommunications Market Commission, National Postal Sector Commission, State Council for Audio-Visual Media, and Committee of Railway and Airport Regulation.
25. The working group comprises staff from several areas of the CNMC, but particularly experts from the Competition Advocacy Directorate, the Competition Directorate and the Directorate for Telecommunications and the Audiovisual Sector.
26. In fact, the creation of synergies among the regulatory units and the competition unit appears as one of the strategic actions of the CNMC's 2021-2022 Action Plan and as one of the pillars of the CNMC's 2021-2026 Strategic Plan. The Action Plan (in Spanish) is available here: https://www.cnmc.es/sobre-la-cnmc/plan-de-actuacion. The Strategic Plan (in Spanish) is available here: https://www.cnmc.es/sobre-la-cnmc/plan-estrategico.

group prepared the CNMC position paper on the public consultation on the Digital Services Act and the New Competition Tool. In addition, staff are continuously trained on competition law and regulatory affairs so that all directorates are aware of the developments and the priorities of each sector.

The synergies of the CNMC's integrated model are also apparent in its sectoral studies and reports on legislative and regulatory proposals, where several directorates provide their expertise on the topics subject to analysis. Recent examples of these are the study on the liberalisation of rail passenger transport services,[27] the analysis of the competitive impact of the entry of unmanned petrol station into the retail fuel markets,[28] and the legislative proposal for self-consumption in electricity.[29]

There are also various cases where the sectoral directorates have worked closely with the competition directorate, such as the monitoring of the Telefónica/DTS merger[30] or the Lyntia/Negocio Iberdrola merger.[31] The latter affected both the electricity and telecommunications sectors and illustrates how the CNMC's integrated model – the energy, telecoms and competition directorates worked together in this analysis – is optimal for assessing businesses dealing with inter-sectoral situations.

Furthermore, within the energy sector, the competition directorate recently investigated an abuse of dominant position following a number of decisions by the CNMC's Regulatory Chamber on transmission grid access.[32] This investigation reflects the cooperation efforts taken by the energy and competition directorates when supervising vertically integrated operators. Some of the regulatory conflicts, related to the access of the transmission and distribution network, can lead to potential cases of abuse of dominant position and therefore early and streamlined coordination is key to obtaining satisfactory results.

In view of the above and despite its many complexities, experience shows that competition law and regulation can be brought together and are in fact a good combination when implemented precisely. There has been major success in complex and essential markets over recent years and, hopefully, the challenge that digital markets pose will be no exception.

3 HOW IS COMPETITION ANALYSIS TAKING INTO ACCOUNT SUSTAINABILITY?

The traditional competition analysis performed by competition authorities focuses on different parameters that have a direct impact on competition, such as price, product

27. *See* subsection 1.2.
28. The study in English is available here: https://www.cnmc.es/expedientes/ecnmc00519-0.
29. The proposal is available (in Spanish) here: https://www.cnmc.es/expedientes/ipnde01115.
30. The available documents from the case file are available here: https://www.cnmc.es/expedientes/c061214 and https://www.cnmc.es/expedientes/vc061214.
31. *See* case C/1031/19 LYNTIA/NEGOCIO IBERDROLA available here: https://www.cnmc.es/expedientes/c103119.
32. *See* case S/0022/20 *Enel Green*. A press release in English is available here: https://www.cnmc.es/sites/default/files/editor_contenidos/Notas%20de%20prensa/2022/20220614_NP_S_0022_20_ENEL%20GREEN_REV_COM_en_GB_0.pdf.

quality and variety or innovation. However, certain public interests such as sustainability, national security or data privacy may also have competitive impacts and, therefore, can be incorporated into the competition analysis.

There are several definitions and studies on what sustainability means. Following the definition of the Brundtland Report, it typically refers to a specific form of development that meets the needs of the present without compromising the ability of future generations to meet their own needs.[33] Indeed, the draft chapter on sustainability agreements[34] published by the EC stems from this broad concept.

In any case, and regardless of its exact definition, it is clear that in recent years, sustainability has become a main policy issue due to one of the greatest challenges of this century, fighting climate crisis. From international organisations to governments and individuals there has been increasing concern which is very likely to expand. For that reason, governments, international organisations and non-governmental organisations are putting in place various plans. Within the EU, the EC set a strategy, called the EU Green Deal, to reach the goal of climate neutrality by 2050. In this fight, sustainability is essential.

Bearing the above in mind, the approach that competition law should adopt towards sustainability is heavily debated. On the one hand, some consider that the current competition framework, which is focused on maximising consumer welfare, leaves little room for other goals, such as sustainability, and that competition goals should move towards non-economic values.[35] On the other hand, some argue that the classic competition toolkit is sufficient for addressing sustainability goals, at least indirectly, and that, if the goal of competition were to be modified, it could undermine its effectiveness.[36]

Regardless of the academic discussion and its outcome, competition authorities should not lose sight of their main objective, which is still to protect consumer welfare. Although useful, competition policy is not the only tool available for achieving sustainability, whereas competition law continues to be the most effective tool for ensuring competitive markets that benefit consumers. Furthermore, the current framework[37] promotes competition between firms fostering innovation, which also provides consumers with more sustainable services and products.

In any case, there other ways of contributing to sustainable objectives, such as reorienting competition authorities' priorities towards sustainable development

---

33. *See* The Report of the World Commission on Environment and Development (WCED) *Our Common Future* (1987).
34. *See* Communication from the Commission – Guidelines on the applicability of Article 101 of the Treaty on the Functioning of the European Union to horizontal co-operation agreements – Draft. Chapter 9 Sustainability Agreements.
35. *See* Rutger Claasen & Anna Gerbrandy, *Rethinking European Competition Law: From a Consumer Welfare to a Capability Approach* (2016), Utrecht Law Review, Vol. 12/1, pp. 1-15, http://dx.doi.org/10.18352/ulr.321.
36. *See* Luc Peeperkorn, *Competition and Sustainability: What Can Competition Policy Do* (2020), Concurrences Vol. 2020/4.
37. Please note that we are referring, in general, to the EU framework.

projects,[38] rather than modifying the substantive analysis when dealing with anti-competitive practices or mergers.

Leaving aside the specific discussion on whether competition law should modify its goals to incorporate sustainability into its analysis, the reality is that within the EU, which currently finds itself immersed in achieving the objectives set by the EU Green Deal, sustainability is paramount and affects all public policies, including competition.

That is why competition authorities are already incorporating this parameter into their strategic plans and their competition analysis. The draft version of the guidelines on Sustainability Agreements published by the Netherlands Authority for Consumers and Markets in July 2020, followed by the EC's new chapter on sustainability agreements included in the Draft Guidelines on Horizontal Cooperation published in March 2022, and the draft guidelines on the application of sustainability-agreements published by the Austrian Federal Competition Authority on June 2022,[39] are good examples of this. In terms of annual plans, one of the main axes of the CNMC's Action Plan is to contribute to the achievement of the Sustainable Development Goals of the 2030 Agenda. The CNMC is also planning to introduce sustainability objectives as one of the cornerstones of its new multi-annual Strategic Plan.

3.1 What's Coming: The Draft Chapter on Sustainability Agreements

In March 2022, the EC published a draft of the Guidelines on horizontal cooperation agreements, which includes a new chapter on sustainability agreements (hereinafter 'the Chapter' or 'the Draft Chapter on Sustainability Agreements').[40] The Chapter provides a number of definitions and aims to clarify when a sustainability agreement would not infringe Article 101 Treaty on the Functioning of the European Union (TFEU), i.e., those agreements that genuinely relate to sustainability and are incapable of hindering competition. It also provides guidance on the agreements that may fall within the scope of the individual exemption of Article 101.3 TFEU.

The Chapter is in line with the practice of the EC regarding horizontal agreements and does not modify the traditional approach towards these agreements. However, its relevance, if approved, is twofold: on the one hand it will help national competition authorities when assessing the legality of these types of agreements. This is essential

38. *See*the CNMC position paper responding to the European Commission's call for contributions on how EU competition rules and sustainability policies can work together (2020) https://www.cnmc.es/sites/default/files/editor_contenidos/Notas%20de%20prensa/2020/SPANISH%20COMPETITION%20AUTHORITYs%20COMMENTS%20EU%20CALL%20FOR%20CONTRIBUTION%20ON%20HOW%20COMPETITION%20RULES%20AND%20SUSTAINABILITY%20POLICIES%20WORK%20TOGETHER_0.pdf.
39. However, these guidelines will only apply to internal cases where Article 101 TFEU is not invoked, i.e., when the agreement does not affect trade between Member States. For more information *see* https://www.bwb.gv.at/en/news/detail/afca-publishes-draft-guidelines-on-the-application-sustainability-agreements-asking-for-comments.
40. *See* the European Commission press release on the subject https://ec.europa.eu/commission/presscorner/detail/en/ip_22_1371. The draft of the Guidelines on horizontal cooperation agreements is available here https://competition-policy.ec.europa.eu/public-consultations/2022-hbers_en#view-the-consultation-document

for avoiding different interpretations depending on the jurisdiction, as this may disrupt the internal market. On the other hand, it provides economic operators with certainty, by allowing them to self-assess whether these agreements fall within the scope of Article 101 and clarify a number of concepts.

The Chapter introduces several definitions, including two basic concepts, namely sustainable development and sustainability agreements. Sustainable development[41] covers those activities supporting economic, environmental and social development. According to the Chapter, sustainability objectives cover a wide range of goals, from fighting climate change, to defending human rights and animal welfare, and limiting the use of natural resources, among other things. The definition provides a number of examples although they are not exhaustive.

As for sustainability agreements,[42] the definition covers 'any type of horizontal cooperation agreement that genuinely pursues one or more sustainability objectives, irrespective of the form of cooperation'.

Although these definitions of the *objectives* provide some clarification, it might be desirable to further narrow some of the aspects included in them. In particular, the reference to 'sustainability objectives' is rather broad. The current definition allows for a great variety of agreements whose analyses could be complex and rather cumbersome for national competition authorities. Furthermore, some references such as the idea of 'genuine cooperation' would force authorities to determine whether an agreement seeks that sort of cooperation, forcing them to make subjective assessments that could easily diverge from one jurisdiction to another.

Accordingly, we should not forget that, by focusing more on environmental aspects in competition analyses, competition authorities will have to adapt and adequately train their human resources. Regarding the assessment of agreements, the clearer the scope, the easier the transition will be for the officials of the authorities. Rapid and efficient adaptation by competition authorities will also determine how successful the implementation of sustainability goals is, even more in a context where competition authorities sometimes lack adequate human resources to conduct their duties.

Perhaps one of the most interesting sections of the Chapter relates to the assessment of sustainability agreements under Article 101.3.[43] This exemption applies, as with any agreement that falls under Article 101.1, if the four cumulative conditions of the provision are fulfilled: efficiency gains, indispensability, pass-on to consumers, and no elimination of competition.

The Chapter provides a detailed analysis of each of these conditions. Regarding pass-on to consumers, i.e., that consumers shall receive a fair share of the claimed benefits, non-traditional approaches for calculating the benefit of a sustainability agreement are included. This is in line with what the CNMC proposed in its December

41. *See* para. 543 of the Draft Chapter on Sustainability Agreements.
42. *See* para. 547 of the Draft Chapter on Sustainability Agreements.
43. *See* section 9.4 of the Draft Chapter on Sustainability Agreements.

2020 position paper responding to the EC's public consultation on competition policy and environmental sustainability targets.[44]

According to the Chapter, three types of benefits should be evaluated: (i) individual use value benefits, namely those resulting directly from the use of the product; (ii) individual non-use value benefits, which encompass the consumer's appreciation of the sustainable benefits of the product for others; and (iii) collective benefits, which occur irrespective of the consumers' individual appreciation of the product and can objectively benefit consumers in the relevant market if the latter are part of the larger group of beneficiaries.[45]

Furthermore, in terms of collective benefits, the Commission recognises that the efficiencies achieved by an agreement can be taken into account even if they materialise in a different, but related, relevant market, provided that the group of consumers is substantially similar. Efficiencies may also be considered when the group of consumers affected by the agreement in the relevant market also overlaps or constitutes part of the beneficiaries outside of the relevant market, as long as it compensates them for the harm suffered.

The reference to individual non-use value benefits and collective benefits constitutes a good example of the adjustment that competition law should adopt in terms of sustainability. This approach takes into account the purpose and particularities of sustainability agreements, as they can impact not only consumers but also society as a whole, while upholding the goal and purpose of competition law.

Pending the publication of the final version of the Chapter, we can only speculate as to its practical implications. In any case, the final guidelines will be a valuable tool for competition authorities, allowing them to pursue their mission of maintaining consumer welfare, and for companies who will welcome legal certainty on the matter.

3.2 What about Merger Control and Sustainability?

Lastly, although agreements concentrate much of the focus in terms of the interaction between competition and sustainability, we should not forget the implications that they may have in merger control.

Currently, public interest considerations other than competition do not form part of the substantive analysis of a merger within the EU. However, Article 21(4) of the EC Merger Regulation allows Member States, under strict conditions, to reflect other legitimate interests. In particular, Article 21(4) considers public security, plurality of the media and prudential rules as legitimate interests. Other unspecified public interests can be recognised by the Commission after notification by the Member State.

In this way, sustainability goals may fall within the public interest recognised in Article 21(4), in several ways: first, these could fall under the public security interest recognised by the Commission; second, the Commission can recognise a sustainability concern as a legitimate interest if a Member State claims this and communicates it to

44. *See* CNMC (2020), *supra* n. 38, p. 17.
45. *See* para. 601 of the Draft Chapter on Sustainability Agreements.

the Commission; lastly, Article 21(4) EU Merger Regulation could be modified to explicitly recognise sustainability goals.[46] So far, the Commission has been rather strict when implementing this provision but, if the approach were to change, any of the three possibilities could be plausible.

Conversely, there are several countries whose regime contemplates taking into account factors relating to the public interest. That is the case, for example, of Spanish legislation. Indeed, Article 10.4 of the Spanish Competition Act states that the Council of Ministers can assess mergers taking into account public interests other than competition. Among these other public interests, the provision expressly contemplates the protection of the environment. This so-called third phase, where the Council of Ministers can review and modify CNMC criteria, is limited to complex cases, namely second phase mergers that were either blocked by the CNMC or approved with remedies.

Furthermore, the effects of mergers on sustainability can be analysed and taken into account in different ways. First, sustainability plays a part when defining relevant markets.[47] Second, it can be considered within the theories of harm, from the perspective of the negative effects that the merger might cause, for example, on the environment, but also as a part of the efficiency analysis, the so-called green efficiency defence. It is true that, as with other types of efficiencies, it might be difficult for the parties involved in the transaction to justify it. However, the parties can always argue that the transaction will generate efficiencies that will outweigh the negative effects of the merger by, for example, providing more sustainable products.[48]

Along with other competition authorities, the Commission has looked into different mergers where the theories of harm include environmental concerns, such as the cases of Dow/Dupont[49] and Aurubis/Metallo.[50] Furthermore, for DEMB/ Mondelez/Charger OPCO[51] and Novelis/Aleris[52] environmental considerations played a part in defining the market.

All in all, it is obvious that competition authorities' interest in environmental issues has grown and that they are willing to cooperate, within their competences, to achieve sustainability goals. Thus, it is likely that competition authorities will give more weight, when relevant, to sustainability considerations in their merger reviews in the years to come.

4 CONCLUSION

As markets evolve, competition policy and regulation face new challenges and need to adapt to new realities. In some cases, this adaptation calls for new regulation. This is

46. *See* Hellenic Competition Commission, *Draft staff discussion paper on sustainability issues and competition law* (2020), pp. 40-41.
47. *See* OECD, *Environmental Considerations in Competition Enforcement* (2021), section 5.1.
48. *See* Nichole Rosenboom, *The Role of Sustainability in Merger Control* (2021), https://www.oxera.com/insights/agenda/articles/the-role-of-sustainability-in-merger-control/.
49. *See* case M.7932 – Dow/Dupont (2017).
50. *See* case M.9409 – Aurubis/ Metallo (2020).
51. *See* case M.7292 – DEMB/ MONDELEZ/CHARGER OPCO (2015).
52. *See* case M.9076 – NOVELIS/ALERIS (2021).

the case of the digital markets where, despite all the efforts taken by competition authorities, competition tools alone are not enough to achieve competitive markets where large digital platforms dominate them.

The approval of the DMA will create a new digital environment that will not be exempt of challenges. More than ever, complementarity between competition policy and regulation will be essential, and coordination between national competition authorities and the EC will be key. The complexities that arise when regulation and competition policy are applied at the same time are well-known, and the DMA is likely to be no exception. However, the CNMC's integrated model is proof of the many synergies that competition policy and regulation can achieve when properly designed. The complementarity of a finely tuned regulatory framework, with an efficient and strong competition policy, are the best instruments for addressing the major challenges of the digital economy.

Together with the markets and the economy, society also evolves. There are major concerns around the way we act and live will impact future generations and a growing necessity to achieve sustainable development. The debate surrounding sustainability has reached competition policy and competition authorities.

There are many ways to contribute to this challenge, and, in fact, competition authorities are already updating their analyses and taking sustainability aspects more into account; the new draft chapter on sustainability agreements is one of many examples. However, competition authorities should not lose sight of the main purpose of competition policy. If the scope of competition law were to become too broad, it could end up being undermined.

For this reason, competition authorities are likely to pay more attention to sustainable aspects and refine their assessments so that they are more oriented towards helping achieve sustainable development goals, but without altering their very nature.

CHAPTER 14

The New Normal: State Aid Policy from Financial Crisis to COVID-19 Pandemic and Beyond

Ina Lunneryd

1 WHERE DO WE COME FROM?

Over the past seven decades, State aid control has been a unique feature of the European Union (EU), firmly anchored in the Treaties. While resembling rules are now carried across both the EU-UK TCA Agreement[1] and the EU's new Foreign Subsidies regulation,[2] State aid remains a decisively EU linked concept and has been a key tool towards the realisation of the benefits of economic integration as well as the internal market. Though the rules were introduced already in the Treaty of Rome in 1957, their practical importance has in many ways seen an exponential growth, with the body of guidelines, communications and regulations increasing in both scope and numbers, in order to facilitate the practical functioning of the fundamental principles as set out in the Treaty.

As times have changed, so has the European Commission's approach to State aid policy. The fundamental principles have allowed for flexibility in a rapidly changing terrain, enabling State aid policy to keep pace with economic challenges, technological developments and new political priorities, such as the current emphasis on the European Green Deal. In times of crisis, demand has been raised for the flexibility to

1. EU-UK Trade and Cooperation Agreement between the European Union and the European Atomic Energy Community and the United Kingdom of Great Britain and Northern Ireland, Official Journal of the European Commission, 30 April 2021.
2. *See* Commission Proposal for a Regulation on Foreign Subsidies distorting the Internal Market of 5.5.2021, COM(2021) 223 final, and the provisional agreement resulting from the inter-institutional negotiation reached on 30 June 2022, COM(2021) 0223 – C9-0167/2021 – 2021/0114(COD)).

support a more pronounced role for State aid policy to enable Member States to keep struggling economies afloat. The Commission has also been held to use State aid policy to push boundaries, including in the context of its investigations into individual tax rulings. These cases brought State aid to the headlines across the globe, not least in the aftermath of the Commission's decision ordering Ireland to recover EUR 13 billion in alleged illegal State aid from Apple. The case was described as 'total political crap'[3] by Apple's CEO Tim Cook and gave Executive Vice-President Margrethe Vestager the label as the EU's 'tax lady' who 'really hates the U.S.' by then US President Donald Trump.

Taking a step back, and looking at the two most recent decades, four events stand out in shaping the State aid framework, and the two latter will be the focus of this chapter.

(1) In 2005, the Commissions published its State Aid Action Plan (SAAP), introducing a wide-ranging reform of State aid policy.[4] A key aspect of the SAAP was the focus on a more refined economic approach, bringing State aid more in line with other areas of competition law. While the use of economic tools improved, several elements for the assessment of State aid still do not require thorough economic assessment. As a notable example, the requirement in Article 107 of the Treaty on the Functioning of the European Union (TFEU) that a measure must distort competition in order to qualify as State aid does not require a relevant market to be delineated.

(2) Shortly thereafter, in 2008, the financial crisis put the Commission's State aid policy firmly in the spotlight. The crisis presented novel and significant challenges to the Commission, both in terms of the sums involved and the speed with which the market conditions evolved, requiring the Commission to rapidly adapt both in terms of assessment and procedure. As the crisis put strains on Member States' budgets, with an ailing financial sector requiring bail-outs, the Commission had to deliver a response which avoided subsidy races and threats to the integrity of the single market.

(3) In 2012, the Commission introduced a further wide-ranging overhaul of the framework, the State aid Modernisation (SAM).[5] The reform aimed to further strengthen the quality of Commission oversight and foster growth and competition, while still keeping the focus on limiting distortions that would undermine a level playing field. The reform was also linked to a perceived need for budgetary discipline as many Member States faced a familiar dilemma, with strained budgets and increased demands for public support.[6]

3. Jennifer Thompson, *'Total Political Crap': Tim Cook on the Apple Tax Verdict*, Financial Times, 1.9.2016, https://www.ft.com/content/7e4f29ae-1a22-3fa9-b059-48db56fd57ae.
4. Commission Consultation document, State Aid Action Plan – Less and better targeted state aid: a roadmap for state aid reform 2005-2009, COM(2005) 107 final, 7.6.2005.
5. Commission Communication, EU State Aid Modernisation (SAM), COM(2012) 209 final, 8.5.2012 ('SAM Communication').
6. Commission Press Release, *Speech by Vice President Joaquín Almunia, Priming Europe for Growth, European Competition Forum Brussels*, SPEECH/12/59, 2.2.2012, https://ec.europa.eu/commission/presscorner/detail/en/SPEECH_12_59.

(4) In 2020, the world faced a further crisis in the form of COVID-19, the ramifications of which we are still facing. The pandemic called for decisive action, with the Commission stressing the need for a swift and coordinated response. As during the financial crisis, the State aid rules formed a central part of the Commission's toolbox and the role of State aid policy in handling Member State's responses cannot be overestimated, with the Commission adopting decisions at an unprecedented speed and scale.

1.1 State Aid Modernisation

The Commission deemed the 2012 SAM necessary to strengthen the quality of its scrutiny. Through the SAM, the Commission also sought to ensure that State aid contributed to promoting a sound use of public resources, while ensuring a level playing field in the internal market. Indeed, in keeping with the core of State aid policy, the Commission stressed that 'the single market is Europe's best asset for generating sustainable growth' and pointed to a need for State aid policy 'in times when a few governments can spend a lot more than many others'.[7]

Among the challenges that the Commission identified in the context of the SAM, two resulted in particularly marked developments. First, the concern that the procedural framework applied equally to smaller and bigger cases and, second, the complexity of the substantive rules.[8]

1.1.1 Big on Big, and Small on Small

A key outcome of the SAM was to allow the Commission to focus its efforts on the cases most liable to distort competition and having a significant impact on the internal market. To this aim, the SAM relied heavily on Member States' self-assessment, with the centrepiece being the General Block Exemption Regulation (GBER).[9] Under the new and expanded GBER, which replaced the 2008 GBER, Member States have been able to implement State aid more quickly in clear-cut cases, without prior approval by the Commission.

The GBER has been a success story. Today, Member States notify the more complex measures, while cases that are less likely to have a negative effect on the internal market are block-exempted, ensuring tangible cuts in red tape. Block-exempted measures represented a staggering share – almost 99% – of all new aid measures in 2019.[10] And while the GBER represented a lower share of total new aid

7. SAM Communication, para. 2 and Commission Press Release SPEECH/12/59.
8. SAM Communication, para. 6.
9. Commission Regulation (EU) No 702/2014 of 25 June 2014 declaring certain categories of aid compatible with the internal market in application of Articles 107 and 108 of the TFEU, in OJ L 193, 1.7.2014, p. 1, as subsequently amended ('GBER').
10. In addition to GBER, the Block Exemption Regulations include the Agricultural Block Exemption Regulation and the Fishery Block Exemption Regulation: Commission Regulation (EU) No 702/2014 of 25 June 2014 declaring certain categories of aid in the agricultural and forestry sectors and in rural areas compatible with the internal market in application of Articles 107 and

measures in 2020, this does not suggest a reduced use of the GBER. This is instead linked to the large number of measures involving COVID-19 aid. Indeed, the absolute number of new block-exempted measures continued to increase, from 1815 measures in 2019 to 2091 measures in 2020.[11] This also serves to illustrate that Member States continued to rely on the general State aid framework to support their economies also in times of crisis.

1.1.2 A More Streamlined Approach

As part of the SAM, the Commission also sought to streamline the substantive State aid rules, thereby raising the quality and rigour of its assessments. To this aim, the Commission launched a revision of multiple instruments, including key tools such as the Rescue and Restructuring Guidelines, the Regional Aid Guidelines, the IPCEI Communication, the EEAG - now CEEAG, and the Aviation Guidelines.[12] Last but not least, the final piece of the SAM puzzle - the Notice on the notion of State aid - was published in July 2016.[13] Through the Notice, the Commission aimed to clarify the different constituent elements of aid under Article 107(1) TFEU. True to this aim, the Notice has contributed to increased legal certainty by offering a more transparent definition of aid, thereby enabling a more consistent application across the EU.

While valuable as to the definition of State aid, the Notice does not address questions relating to compatibility under Article 107(2) or (3) TFEU. To this aim, as part of the SAM package, the Commission introduced its common assessment principles in a number of guidelines (e.g., the CEEAG, the Regional Aid Guidelines and the

108 of the TFEU, in OJ L 193, 1.7.2014, p. 1, as subsequently amended; Commission Regulation (EU) No 1388/2014 of 16 December 2014 declaring certain categories of aid to undertakings active in the production, processing and marketing of fishery and aquaculture products compatible with the internal market in application of Articles 107 and 108 of the TFEU, in OJ L 369, 24.12.2014, p. 37.

11. Commission State aid Scoreboard 2021, 6.9.2022, https://competition-policy.ec.europa.eu/system/files/2022-09/state_aid_scoreboard_note_2021.pdf.
12. With regard to rescuing and restructuring aid, *see* Commission Guidelines on State aid for rescuing and restructuring non-financial undertakings in difficulty, in OJ C 249, 31.7.2014, p. 1 ('Rescue and Restructuring Guidelines'); with regard to regional aid, *see* previously Commission Guidelines on regional State aid for 2014-2020, OJ C 209, 23.7.2013, p. 1, and currently Commission Guidelines on regional State aid 2022-2027, in OJ C 153, 29.4.2021, p. 1 ('Regional aid Guidelines'); with regard to Important Projects of Common European Interest, *see* previously Commission Criteria for the analysis of the compatibility with the internal market of State aid to promote the execution of important projects of common European interest, in OJ C 188, 20.6.2014, p. 4, and currently Commission Criteria for the analysis of the compatibility with the internal market of State aid to promote the execution of important projects of common European interest, in OJ C 528, 30.12.2021, p. 10 ('IPCEI Communication'); with regard to environmental and energy aid, *see* previously Commission Guidelines on State aid for environmental protection and energy 2014-2020, in OJ C 200, 28.6.2014, p. 1 ("EEAG"), and currently Commission Guidelines on State aid for climate, environmental protection and energy 2022, in OJ C 80, 18.2.2022, p. 1 ('CEEAG'); with regard to aid to the aviation sector, *see* Commission Guidelines on State aid to airports and airlines, in OJ C 99, 4.4.2014, p. 3 ('Aviation Guidelines').
13. Commission Notice on the notion of State aid as referred to in article 107(1) of the TFEU, in OJ C 262, 19.7.2016, p. 1. ('Notice on the notion of State aid' or 'Notice').

RDI framework).[14] While not offering the benefits of one single document, such as the Notice on the Notion of State aid, the common assessment principles, similar to their predecessor the 'balancing test', have contributed to making the compatibility assessment more uniform across various types of aid. The principles have also upheld the weighing exercise, whereby it is assessed whether the market failure being solved or the policy objective being met outweigh the costs in terms of public funds and competitive distortions.

The inclusion of these principles in a number of guidelines should however not be understood as implying a general obligation on the Commission, when examining the compatibility of aid, to always weigh the beneficial effects against the adverse. While previous judgments had provided that such a weighing exercise was 'no more than an expression of the principle of proportionality and the principle that the exemptions set out in Article 107(3) TFEU must be interpreted strictly',[15] the General Court subsequently held that, contrary to what is laid down in Article 107(3)(c) TFEU, Article 107(3)(b) TFEU does not require the Commission to carry out such an exercise. Under Article 107(3)(b) TFEU a Member State seeks to remedy a serious disturbance in its economy, a fact that according to the General Court will benefit the EU in general and the internal market in particular.[16] The obligations on the Commission are therefore limited to ascertaining whether the aid is necessary, appropriate and proportionate in order to remedy such a serious disturbance.

2 WHERE ARE WE?

As detailed above, the Commission has sought a centralised vision for State aid policy. While it is ultimately for Member States to make political choices and set strategies, the Commission has pursued coordinated actions to ensure that the rules contribute to the internal market not being distorted by Member States favouring some actors to the detriment of others.[17]

This vision has not been without tests, including calls for the rules to be temporarily suspended or being labelled as 'obsolete' and 'fundamentalist'.[18] A major challenge emerged during the winter of 2020, when COVID-19 started to spread, resulting in lockdown measures being imposed across Member States. As the crisis evolved, it became evident that businesses faced liquidity problems and that public support would be required to cushion the economic crisis. The Commission was quick to point to the State aid rules in general, and two routes in particular, as means for Member States to support their economies:

14. Commission Framework for State aid for research and development and innovation, in OJ C 198, 27.6.2014, p. 1 ('RDI Framework').
15. Case T-68/15, *HH Ferries and Others v. Commission*, EU:T:2018:563, para. 211.
16. Case T-238/20, *Ryanair v. Commission (Sweden; Covid-19)*, EU:T:2021:91, para. 68.
17. SAM Communication.
18. Hugh Carnegy and Michael Stothard, *French Industry Minister Assails Brussels on State Aid for Industry*, Financial Times, 22.1.2014, https://www.ft.com/content/99515d88-8367-11e3-86c9-00144feab7de.

(1) The Commission encouraged the use of Article 107(2)(b) TFEU. This article enables Member States to compensate companies for damages suffered due to, and directly caused by, 'exceptional occurrences'. In the context of the pandemic, this covers damage caused directly by public measures, such as lockdowns, preventing companies from carrying out their activities. By contrast, Article 107(2)(b) TFEU will not cover support to address the negative impact from the general economic downturn resulting from the pandemic.

(2) A complementary route was the possibility to remedy serious disturbances to the economy under Article 107(3)(b) TFEU. Under this article, the Commission concluded that State aid was justified to remedy the crisis and ensure that the disruptions caused did not undermine the viability of companies. On this basis, a 'Temporary Framework for State aid measures to support the economy in the current COVID-19 outbreak' was adopted on 19 March 2020.[19] The rules aimed to enable Member States to use the full flexibility foreseen under State aid rules to support their economies and ensure that businesses across the EU had liquidity to keep operating.

The pandemic bore marked similarities to the financial crisis in that it presented a significant challenge to the Commission's State aid policy. During the financial crisis, unprecedented volumes of public support were required to address the systemic bank and sovereign debt crises. In view of the massive aid measures adopted by national governments to bail out their domestic credit institutions, the Commission sought to use State aid control to minimise the perils to the level playing field in the EU's banking sector. The parallels to the pandemic are manifest, as State aid again surfaced as a key tool for the Commission to assert control over Member States' actions, thereby seeking to safeguard the internal market.[20] During the pandemic, the Temporary Framework aimed to provide a roadmap for Member States, allowing for a more coordinated response than an ad hoc approach, considering in particular the scope of decisions issued.

While the Temporary Framework, by its very definition, was intended to be an interim solution, the crisis evolved and, similar to during the financial crisis, the Commission had to adjust. The Temporary Framework was amended no less than six times between 19 March 2020 and 18 November 2021. Furthermore, its consequences are likely to be long term, the same way as effects of the financial crisis contributed to shaping the development of State aid policy over the last decade. While the precise impact of the pandemic on the future of State aid control is still to be seen, it is worth a closer look, including by comparing the Commission's approach to that of the financial crisis.

---

19. Commission Temporary Framework for State aid measures to support the economy in the current COVID-19 outbreak, in OJ C 91I, 20.3.2020, p. 1, as subsequently amended ('Temporary Framework').
20. *See* Temporary Framework, Section 1.2. '*The need for close European coordination of national aid measures*'.

2.1 Keeping with Fundamental State Aid Principles

The Temporary Framework is based on familiar State aid principles, including that any aid must be appropriate, necessary and targeted.[21] While keeping with these fundamental principles, the Temporary Framework aligns them with the objectives of Article 107(3)(b) TFEU, requiring the aid to be:

- appropriate to tackle the difficulties undertakings were encountering due to the pandemic, whilst maintaining the integrity of the single market and ensuring a level playing field (minimising distortions of competition);
- necessary to ensure that the aid was proportionate and did not go beyond what was required to remedy the serious disturbance (limited to the minimum required); and
- targeted to counter the damage inflicted by the pandemic on healthy undertakings and to preserve the continuity of economic activity (to ensure viability for the beneficiaries).

A further objective underlying the Temporary Framework is avoidance of Member States resorting to beggar-thy-neighbour measures. The Commission clearly signalled such concerns when adopting the rules, stressing the importance of avoiding harmful subsidy races where governments with deeper pockets would outspend neighbours to the detriment of cohesion within the EU.[22] Similar comments were repeated a few months later, when Executive Vice-President Vestager referred to the need to 'make sure that this global symmetric crisis does not transform into an asymmetric shock to the detriment of Member States with less possibility to help their industry'.[23] To this aim, and in addition to general requirements of necessity and proportionality, the Temporary Framework includes a specific requirement that aid approved may not be conditioned on relocation of activities of the beneficiary to the Member State granting the aid.[24]

2.2 While Using Flexibility

While keeping with established State aid principles, the Commission exercised the flexibility within the rules. The Temporary Framework was swiftly adopted and, as also

21. *See, e.g.*, Temporary Framework, paras 21, 24 and 26.
22. Temporary Framework, para. 10. Similarly, Executive Vice-President Vestager stressed on 17 March 2020 that 'support for businesses in one Member State does not undermine the unity that Europe needs, especially during a crisis. Because we have to be able to rely on the European single market, to help our economy weather the outbreak, and bounce back strongly afterwards': *see* Commission Press Release, *Statement by Executive Vice-President Margrethe Vestager on a draft proposal for a State aid Temporary Framework to support the economy in the context of the COVID-19 outbreak*, STATEMENT/20/479, 17.3.2020, https://ec.europa.eu/commission/presscorner/detail/en/statement_20_479.
23. Commission Press Release, *State aid: Commission expands Temporary Framework to recapitalisation and subordinated debt measures to further support the economy in the context of the coronavirus outbreak*, IP/20/838, 8.5.2020, https://ec.europa.eu/commission/presscorner/detail/en/ip_20_838.
24. Temporary Framework, para. 16ter.

recognised by the Commission, the ability to act so quickly was in part due to the experience gained during the financial crisis.[25] In the same vein, Commission decisions were issued without delay, with the first decisions taken within 48 hours from the entry into force of the Temporary Framework.[26]

The Commission also tailored the response to the nature of the crisis, enabling wide-ranging support measures, mirroring the effects of this crisis. According to research by the European Investment Bank, more than half of EU companies received some form of state support during the pandemic.[27] By contrast, and reflecting the nature of the financial crisis, the response was substantially narrower, targeting in particular the banking sector and financial institutions. This is illustrated by 50% of all State aid granted benefiting no more than 10 financial institutions.[28] In the same vein, in multiple Member States the top three beneficiaries received more than 80% of all aid.[29]

A further important difference underlying the Commission's response to the financial crisis and the pandemic relates to burden sharing. The financial crisis raised concerns linked to moral hazard and State aid resulting in financial institutions continuing to take extensive risks, relying on future bail-outs as and when needed. To this aim, the Commission drew a distinction between banks that were 'fundamentally sound' but suffered from the effects of the (exogenous) financial crisis and 'unsound' banks experiencing endogenous problems, with the former generally requiring less restructuring and burden sharing than the latter.[30] Unsurprisingly and sensibly, there have not been corresponding requirements during the pandemic. The disruptive effect of the crisis impacted the whole economy and the Commission stressed that the exceptional nature meant that the damage inflicted could not have been foreseen.[31] The

25. *See* Commission Press Release STATEMENT/20/479. During the financial crisis, the Commission initially dealt with cases under Article 87(3)(c) and the Rescue and Restructuring Guidelines, and only subsequently were new guidelines based on Article 87(3)(b) published: *see*, i.e., Commission Communication on the application of State aid rules to measures taken in relation to financial institutions in the context of the current global financial crisis, in OJ C 270, 25.10.2008, p. 8 ('2008 Banking Communication'). Once in force, the 2008 Banking Communication was applied immediately, with approval of the UK's recapitalisation and guarantee schemes being handed down on the day of publication of the guidelines.
26. *See* Commission Press Release, *State aid: Commission approves Danish guarantee scheme for SMEs affected by Coronavirus outbreak*, IP/20/505, 21.3.2020, relating to Case SA.56708 – *Danish guarantee scheme for SMEs affected by COVID-19*, a measure which Denmark formally notified on Thursday 19 March 2020 (the day the Temporary Framework entered into force) and was approved by the Commission on Saturday 21 March 2020.
27. Martin Arnold, *State Aid Helped 56% of EU Businesses During the Pandemic*, Financial Times, 2.12.2021, https://www.ft.com/content/e87df763-2a39-47c0-a1c9-6ef3047ed80e.
28. Commission Staff Working Paper, The effects of temporary State aid rules adopted in the context of the financial and economic crisis, SEC(2011) 1126 final, 5.10.2011, p. 12.
29. Commission Staff Working Paper, SEC(2011) 1126 final, p. 12.
30. 2008 Banking Communication, paras 2, 4, 14, 33-35.
31. Temporary Framework, para. 8. *See also* Temporary Framework, para. 4: 'undertakings of all kinds may face a severe lack of liquidity. Solvent or less solvent undertakings alike may face a sudden shortage or even unavailability of liquidity. SMEs are at particular risk. This can therefore seriously affect the economic situation of many healthy undertakings and their employees in the short and medium term, while having also longer-lasting effects by endangering their survival.'

response provided for in the Temporary Framework was therefore targeted at healthy undertakings, struggling even though prepared for the risks related to the ordinary course of business. Consequently, and with limited exemptions, aid under the Temporary Framework could only be granted to undertakings that were not already 'in difficulty'[32] prior to the pandemic.

As the COVID-19 crisis evolved and companies began to face not only liquidity problems but also decreased equity, the Commission relied once more on the flexibility and amended the Temporary Framework to enable recapitalisation aid.[33] Recognising the implications of such support, the Commission stressed that recapitalisation aid would come with more strings attached, including measures to limit distortions of competition.[34] The level playing field was to be safeguarded through multiple precautions, including measures resembling remedies to preserve competition where companies with significant market power received over EUR 250 million in recapitalisation support. While there have been comments as to companies being constrained by these commitments,[35] this has not mirrored the scope of criticism from the financial crisis, where it was held that the behavioural constraints imposed risked severely restricting - rather than benefiting - competition.[36]

Lastly, the flexibility is shown by the scope of support approved. Already the financial crisis resulted in an unprecedented scale of public funding being directed at businesses and saw government support reaching over EUR 4.5 trillion. The pandemic is almost at the same scale, with approx. EUR 3.2 trillion of aid having been approved by the Commission.[37] The share of notified aid differs however materially between various Member States. Of the estimated total amount, just over half (51.7%) has been notified by Germany, followed by Italy (15.5%) and France (14.5%). At the opposite side of the spectrum, the Member States with the lowest share of notified aid are Cyprus (0.02%), Latvia (0.05%) and Bulgaria (0.06%).[38] However, if considered relative to the Member State's 2020 gross domestic product (GDP), Poland and Greece have granted

32. As defined in Article 2(18) of the GBER. *See* Temporary Framework paras 22, 25, 27, 35, 37, 39, 49, 87 and 92.
33. *See* Commission Second Amendment to the Temporary Framework for State aid measures to support the economy in the current COVID-19 outbreak, OJ C 164, 13.5.2020, p. 3, which inserted in the Temporary Framework, *inter alia*, section 3.11. '*Recapitalisation measures*'.
34. Commission Press Release IP/20/838.
35. Sarah White, *Air France-KLM Hobbled by State Aid While Rivals Pounce on Deals*, Financial Times, 1.2.2022, https://www.ft.com/content/38fbfb6a-4c40-4ae2-893f-f3a760833273.
36. *See, e.g.*, Christian Ahlborn & Daniel Piccinin, *The Application of the Principles of Restructuring Aid to Banks During the Financial Crisis*, EStAL, 1 (2010), pp. 47-64.
37. *See* the Commission's infographic of June 2022 on the Temporary Framework: https://competition-policy.ec.europa.eu/system/files/2022-06/Temporary_framwork.pdf. As noted in the Commission Staff Working Document accompanying the 2021 Report on Competition Policy, SWD(2022) 188 final, 26.8.2022, pp. 24-25, there are a number of important caveats for some measures approved under the Temporary Framework, for which it is not necessary to indicate an amount. Therefore, the amounts included are best estimates based on amounts approved in State aid decisions and other available statistics, for example, mentioned in public communications by national authorities, and in official information communicated by the national authorities.
38. *See* Commission Staff Working Document SWD(2022) 188 final, p. 25. These figures are based on data submitted to the Commission by 26 Member States in June 2021: *see* Commission Competition State Aid Brief, Issue 2/2022 - March 2022.

the largest share of support (3.8% and 3.6%, respectively). On the other side of the coin, Ireland (0.2%) and Sweden (0.2%) spent the least in relative terms.[39]

As noted, concerns have been voiced that the State aid rules would not serve to effectively protect the level playing field, but rather enable Member States with deeper pockets to strengthen their economies to the detriment of others. Against this background, it is noteworthy that, while the Temporary Framework allowed for generous amounts of aid, large parts of the approved aid have not subsequently been paid. This tendency was present also during the financial crisis, where only approximately 20% of the authorised aid was eventually paid.[40] During the pandemic, this pattern persisted with approximately 24% of the aid approved having subsequently been paid.[41] In absolute terms, France represents a fourth of the total aid paid, followed by Italy (23%), Germany (19%) and Spain (14%).[42] However, if the perspective is instead based on relative terms, Germany stands out as the Member State where the smallest share of authorised aid has been paid (8.5%), followed by Belgium (12.3%), Croatia (16.3%) and Czech Republic (19.3%).[43]

2.3 An Approach Upheld by the General Court

Akin to the Commission's swift response, the first appeals of the Commission's decisions did not stay far behind. On 1 May 2020, the first in a series of challenges focused on various COVID-19 State aid measures was launched.[44] To date, close to 50 appeals have been lodged, the vast majority by low cost airline Ryanair.[45] The General Court has generally upheld the Commission's application of Article 107(2)(b) and 107(3)(b) TFEU, and the only losses for the Commission to date have related to three instances of lack of reasoning.[46]

39. Commission State aid Scoreboard 2021.
40. Commission Staff Working Paper, SEC(2011) 1126 final, p. 38.
41. In the period until end of June 2021, of the EUR 3.01 trillion in aid approved, around EUR 729 billion was paid: *see* Commission Competition State Aid Brief, Issue 2/2022 – March 2022.
42. Commission Staff Working Document SWD(2022) 188 final, p. 25.
43. *See* Commission Competition State Aid Brief, Issue 2/2022 – March 2022, p. 5.
44. Case T-238/20, *Ryanair v. Commission (Sweden; Covid-19)*, EU:T:2021:91.
45. Next to the Irish low-cost airline, to date only five other appellants have appealed the Commission's COVID-19 State aid practice: (i) the Hungarian airline Wizz Air (Case T-142/21, *Wizz Air Hungary v. Commission (Romania – Blue Air; Covid-19)*, pending; Case T-332/21, *Wizz Air Hungary v. Commission (Romania – TAROM; Covid-19)*, pending), (ii) the German airline Condor (Case T-87/21, *Condor Flugdienst v. Commission (Germany – Lufthansa; Covid-19)*, pending), (iii) the German department store retailer Breuninger (Case T-260/21, *E. Breuninger v. Commission (Germany – Scheme; Covid-19)*, pending; Case T-525/21, *E. Breuninger v. Commission (Germany – Scheme; Covid-19)*, pending), (iv) the Dutch Bastion Hotels (Case T-102/21, *Bastion Holding and Others v. Commission (Netherlands – Scheme; Covid-19)*, pending; Case T-289/21, *Bastion Holding and Others v. Commission (Netherlands – Scheme; Covid-19)*, pending; Case T-513/21, *Bastion Holding and Others v. Commission (Netherlands – Scheme; Covid-19)*, pending) and (v) the German clothing brand Falke (Case T-306/21, *Falke v. Commission (Germany – Scheme; Covid-19)*, pending).
46. Case T-465/20, *Ryanair DAC v. Commission (Portugal – TAP; Covid-19)*, EU:T:2021:284; Case T-643/20, *Ryanair v. Commission (Netherlands – KLM; Covid-19)*, EU:T:2021:286; Case T-665/20, *Ryanair v. Commission (Germany – Condor; Covid-19)*, EU:T:2021:334.

The appeals have mainly relied upon two key legal principles: non-discrimination and the fundamental freedoms for goods and services. The General Court has provided a consistent line of reasoning in response to these pleas, including a reminder that the resources which may be allocated by Member States are finite and must address priorities.[47] The General Court confirmed that Member States are allowed to focus their support on economic sectors that are severely affected, as well certain undertakings within such sectors.[48] Indeed, there is no general right to State aid.

Further, the General Court has held that aid provided to certain air carriers involves neither a discrimination based on nationality nor an infringement of fundamental freedoms.[49] This has been confirmed both in relation to aid schemes and individual aid. In relation to the latter, the General Court noted that individual aid, by its nature introduces a difference in treatment to the exclusion of all companies that do not benefit.[50] However, the vital element to consider is whether such difference in treatment is permitted under the legal basis at stake, i.e., Article 107(2)(b) or 107(3)(b) TFEU. In essence, if the objective of the aid measure complies with the conditions laid down in the relevant article, and the conditions do not go beyond that objective, a difference in treatment can be objectively justified.[51]

As such, aid does not discriminate if aimed to compensate the damage of an exceptional occurrence or to remedy a serious disturbance in a Member State's economy, provided the support does not exceed what is necessary to that aim:

- As regards Article 107(2)(b) TFEU, the General Court goes beyond the language of the article by adding a criterion that the beneficiary is proportionately more affected by the exceptional occurrence for which damage is compensated, i.e., the COVID-19 restrictions imposed. The latter can be demonstrated for example by the beneficiary's national market share compared to its competitor(s).[52]
- For the analysis under Article 107(3)(b) TFEU, the importance of the beneficiary to the national economy is a decisive factor. For this purpose, not only market shares but also the beneficiary's social and economic weight (e.g., contribution to key economic sectors, its role as an (in)direct employer and contribution to the GDP) can be of bearing.[53]

47. Case T-238/20, *Ryanair v. Commission (Sweden; Covid-19)*, EU:T:2021:91, para. 50.
48. Case T-259/20, *Ryanair v. Commission (France; Covid-19)*, EU:T:2021:92, para. 48.
49. This was provided for already in the first two judgments, Case T-238/20, *Ryanair v. Commission (Sweden; Covid-19)*, EU:T:2021:91; Case T-259/20, *Ryanair v. Commission (France; Covid-19)*, EU:T:2021:92.
50. Case T-378/20, *Ryanair v. Commission (Denmark – SAS; Covid-19)*, EU:T:2021:194, para. 65; Case T-388/20, *Ryanair v. Commission (Finland – Finnair; Covid-19)*, EU:T:2021:196, para. 81; Case T-677/20, *Ryanair and Laudamotion v. Commission (Austria – Austrian Airlines; Covid-19)*, EU:T:2021:465, para. 58.
51. Case T-657/20, *Ryanair v. Commission (Finland – Finnair; Covid-19)*, EU:T:2022:390, para. 139; Case T-388/20, *Ryanair v. Commission (Finland – Finnair; Covid-19)*, EU:T:2021:196, para. 82; Case T-677/20, *Ryanair and Laudamotion v. Commission (Austria – Austrian Airlines; Covid-19)*, EU:T:2021:465, para. 59.
52. Case T-378/20, *Ryanair v. Commission (Denmark – SAS; Covid-19)*, EU:T:2021:194, para. 70-73; Case T-379/20, *Ryanair v. Commission (Sweden – SAS; Covid-19)*, EU:T:2021:194, para. 82-85.
53. Case T-657/20, *Ryanair v. Commission (Finland – Finnair; Covid-19)*, EU:T:2022:390, para. 39-41; Case T-388/20, *Ryanair v. Commission (Finland – Finnair; Covid-19)*, EU:T:2021:196,

An additional interesting question relates to the outer limits of these articles. While the applicant argued that the aid should not have been approved as the support only marginally relieved a serious disturbance, the General Court noted that Article 107(3)(b) TFEU does not require that the aid in question is capable, in itself, of remedying the serious disturbance in the national economy.[54] It is merely required that, once a serious disturbance has been established, the aid is suitable to help in remedying that disturbance.[55] In the same way, an aid measure approved under Article 107(2)(b) TFEU should be aimed at making good the damage resulting from an exceptional occurrence, but is not required to make good the entirety of the damage caused.[56]

In relation to assertions from the applicant that governments were using the pandemic in attempts to tilt the playing field towards national players, the Court noted that as long as justifiable, it is for the Member State concerned to set out in detail the reasons for adopting the aid at issue. The Commission is not required to positively prove that no other conceivable measure, which by definition would be hypothetical, could better achieve the intended objective.[57] A sound approach, as while Member States do sometimes make less efficient choices, this should generally not be sufficient to warrant Commission intervention.

3 WHERE ARE WE GOING?

Stanford economist Paul Romer noted in 2004 that 'A crisis is a terrible thing to waste'. That hardship and trials present opportunities and a chance to define a 'new normal' is indeed nothing novel. And while a crisis cannot be permanent, as the EU started to move away from crisis management, a new challenge emerged following Russia's invasion of Ukraine. Consistent with the response to the pandemic, the Commission used the flexibility of the State aid toolbox and adopted a Temporary Crisis Framework.[58] The legal basis is the same as during the pandemic, with Russia's aggression and its effects being recognised as a 'serious disturbance' under Article 107(3)(b) TFEU, and Member States being able to support companies to address damage directly caused by this 'exceptional occurrence' under Article 107(2)(b) TFEU.

para. 43; Case T-677/20, *Ryanair and Laudamotion v. Commission (Austria – Austrian Airlines; Covid-19)*, EU:T:2021:465, para. 61.

54. Case T-388/20, *Ryanair v. Commission (Finland – Finnair; Covid-19)*, EU:T:2021:196, para. 41.
55. Case T-388/20, *Ryanair v. Commission (Finland – Finnair; Covid-19)*, EU:T:2021:196, para. 41; Case T-657/20, *Ryanair v. Commission (Finland – Finnair; Covid-19)*, EU:T:2022:390, para. 30.
56. Case T-378/20, *Ryanair v. Commission (Denmark – Scandinavian Airlines (SAS); Covid-19)*, EU:T:2021:194, paras 23-24; Case T-677/20, *Ryanair and Laudamotion v. Commission (Austria – Austrian Airlines; Covid-19)*, EU:T:2021:465, paras 54-57.
57. Case T-238/20, *Ryanair v. Commission (Sweden; Covid-19)*, EU:T:2021:91, para. 53; Case T-628/20 *Ryanair v. Commission (Spain – Spanish Airlines; Covid-19)*, EU:T:2021:91; para. 49.
58. Commission Temporary Crisis Framework for State Aid measures to support the economy following the aggression against Ukraine by Russia, in OJ C 131I 24.3.2022, p. 1, as amended by the First Amendment to the Temporary Crisis Framework for State Aid measures to support the economy following the aggression against Ukraine by Russia, in OJ C 280, 21.7.2022, p. 1 ('Temporary Crisis Framework').

When in the midst of yet another crisis, it is challenging to look beyond the immediate difficulties and delineate where we may end up between fundamental principles and flexibility. Already the response to the recent crisis tells us however that the State aid rules are likely to continue being advanced as a key means to drive the green transition. Indeed, the Commission has sought to ensure that also the temporary rules support the EU's flagship Green Deal. Under the Temporary Framework, Member States were encouraged to keep the importance of the green transition in mind, and large undertakings benefiting from recapitalisation aid are requested to report on how the support benefits green objectives, including climate neutrality by 2050.[59] The Temporary Crisis Framework goes further, and provides routes to fast-track the roll-out of renewable energy and incentivise investments in decarbonisation and energy efficiency.[60] While these temporary rules can contribute to green objectives, an even more important contribution is likely that the crisis frameworks have allowed the Commission to maintain its permanent State aid rules. This since the Green Deal will require the Commission to rely on traditional State aid instruments, with the new CEEAG in particular being key to accelerate and enable the considerable amounts of sustainable investments required.

The Commission's approach as described above – to allow for flexibility whilst upholding fundamental principles – is thus likely to offer a glimpse also of the State aid of tomorrow. This flexibility means that State aid policy can be adapted to accommodate changes in prioritised objectives, beyond the fundamental rationale of avoiding distortions of competition. While the rules must refrain from becoming subservient to political objectives, targeted interventions will be necessary to oil the wheels of the economy and deliver better as well as more sustainable and greener standards of living.

59. *Ibid.*, paras 10 and 44.
60. Temporary Crisis Framework, *see* in particular section 2.6.

CHAPTER 15

Should We Adapt the Centralised Enforcement System in the New Era?

Jacques Derenne[*]

1 THE ORIGINS

Back in 1955, under the auspices of the Belgian Minister of Foreign Affairs, Mr Paul-Henri Spaak, the idea and future of the European integration were, again, relaunched at the Messina Conference (1 to 3 June 1955). Referred to as the Intergovernmental Committee, a working group, the 'Spaak Committee', was created and vested with the paramount task of designing the future of the then European Economic Community. Among the various delicate topics was that of reconciling the dichotomy between the State as an economic operator and the State as a regulator of the market.

The results of the Committee were reflected in the Spaak Report of 1956,[1] where the completion of the common market was at the core of the proposals put forward, aiming at integrating the national markets into a single whole. This objective inevitably required the elimination of the main competition distortions such as all artificial advantages granted by the Member States through taxation, social security benefits, price regulations, working conditions and other means. In this sense, it was warned that any State assistance, in whatever form, was to be closely examined and declared incompatible as a general rule of it were to distort fair competition. In parallel, harmonisation of legislation was seen as a path to mitigate competition distortions, but

---

* The author is grateful to Ana Álvarez Vidal for her assistance in the drafting of this chapter, which contains the substance of the oral presentation made at the conference on 26 March 2022.

1. 'Rapport des Chefs de Délégation aux Ministres des Affaires Etrangères', Comité intergouvernemental créé par la Conférence de Messine, Bruxelles, 21 avril 1956 – *Report of the Heads of Delegation to the Ministers of Foreign Affairs*, unofficial translation of the main portions of the '*Brussels Report on the General Common Market*'. *See* http://aei.pitt.edu/995/1/Spaak_report.pdf.

also to boost the free movement of labour. In this sense, the Spaak Report encouraged to mitigate disparities among national legislation in a number of fields.

Overall, for the completion of the then called common market to be attainted, it was necessary to prevent Member States from engaging in subsidies races, provide aid to exports or to promote protectionism of their own economies. As the report indicated, 'it would be contradictory to establish this common market in the name of greater productivity which will result for our economies while at the same time maintaining the previous protective measures'.[2]

In this context, the Spaak Report entrusted the Commission with the task of distinguishing between different forms of State aid, while at the same time imposing on Member States the obligation to notify such aid, as well as the possibility for the Commission to examine a given measure on its own initiative or at the request of another Member State. In this way, the European Commission was already seen as a supranational, independent and exclusive authority whose role was *consubstantial* to State aid control, in the sense of the ancient Greek meaning of *ousia*, inextricably linked to its essence or substance.

2 THE EUROPEAN UNION SYSTEM

Such supranational and independent authority with the duty to assess the aid granted by Member States implied an ex ante control, now regulated in Article 108(3) Treaty on the Functioning of the European Union. Indeed, it is a fact that State aid control is part of the substance of competition policy as a way to control competition between Member States and, indirectly, competition between undertakings, in line with the central objective of integrating the European Union (EU) internal market.

In this context, the discussion has been constant over the need to strike a balance between the objectives of public policy that Member States aim at promoting and the potential distortive effects on competition that their intervention might produce. This is where the EU system intervenes, ensuring that undue distortions are avoided,[3] refraining negative spillovers on other Member States and preserving an adequate functioning of the internal market. This results from confronting the potential of trading against the obstacles to trade, monitoring closely the creation of 'national champions' by trading partners via subsidies and suppressing market failures without affecting an efficient functioning of the market.

3 STATE AID ACTION PLAN (SAAP) OF 2005

After the impactful accession of new Member States of 2004, the EU State aid policy was reviewed by the Commission in order to adapt it to the new scenario as well as to achieve a clearer, more predictable and better targeted framework which would

2. Spaak Report, p. 3 of the English summary.
3. Any State aid is a distortion of competition, therefore the objective is to avoid 'undue' distortions and accept those distortions which are weighed in by more positive externalities than negative externalities (aid compatible with the internal market).

guarantee more efficient State aid procedures.[4] The new approach also counted on a shared responsibility between the Commission and the Member States (and their national courts) to achieve that improved enforcement and transparency and for which the notification procedure had to be applied adequately. The underlying principles of the reform as a whole followed the aims to have less and better targeted State aid, with a finer economic approach[5] and more efficient procedures to improve the application, predictability and transparency of State aid.

In this context, the Commission examined, as part of the public consultation conducted, the possibility of instituting independent authorities in the Member States as enforcers of the State aid policy, more specifically 'whether independent authorities in Member States could play a role as regards facilitating the task of the Commission in terms of state aid enforcement (detection and provisional recovery of illegal aid, execution of recovery decisions)'.[6] However, it resulted in one of the measures raising more controversy among the responding stakeholders and the one more strongly opposed with 28 negative replies, including 8 Member States, 8 regions and several business associations.[7] The negative feedback emphasised, among other elements, on the possible conflict of interests that such independent national authorities would have considering the political and public national pressure, as well as the impact on bureaucracy and a likely unequal application in each Member State:

1. The *independence* of such national authorities: there might be a conflict of interest (the State controls the State); political and public pressure against national surveillance authorities might be high.
2. This measure could *increase bureaucracy* and slow down procedures.
3. There is a risk of implementation standards varying from one MS to another because national authorities could monitor with differing levels of rigour, leading to *uneven application* of State aid controls.
4. There is a general concern about the legality and operation ability of a full *delegation* of responsibility to independent authorities in MS. The final responsibility should remain with the EC in order to avoid any legal uncertainty.
5. Creating such authorities would be at variance with the *principle of the institutional autonomy* of the MS.

---

4. 'State aid action plan, Less and better targeted state aid: a roadmap for state aid reform 2005 – 2009', consultation document, COM(2005) 107 final of 7 June 2005. *See also* Competition Policy Newsletter, 2-2005, pp. 3-16.
5. *See* Jacques Derenne & Massimo Merola (eds), 'Economic Analysis of State Aid Rules: Contributions and Limits', Proceedings of the Third Annual Conference of the Global Competition Law Centre (GCLC), College of Europe, 21-22 September 2006, Lexxion, Berlin, p. 220.
6. Results of the consultation on the State aid action plan (SAAP) – Detailed summary, 9 February 2006, p. 26.
7. 'This proposal had the *highest disapproval level* of all the proposals for modernising State aid practices and procedures. [...] *15 respondents* (6 business associations, 5 MS, 2 law firms, 1 region and 1 non-business association) *confirm their support* for the proposal while *28 respondents* (8 MS, 7 regions, 3 law firms, 2 institutions, 6 business associations, 1 company and 1 mixed entity) *question it*. In general, the private sector is in favour of independent national authorities, but it often calls for more details or clarification; the public sector, on the contrary, disagrees with the idea of creating independent national authorities' (*ibid.*, p. 26).

6. *Comparison* with the *experience of accession MS*: this experience was different; it was limited in time and scope.[8]

Therefore, the idea was disregarded and the reform followed the support expressed for a strong central role of the European Commission and a lack of power delegation to national instances.

4 REVOLUTION: FROM EX ANTE TO EX POST?

The next update of the State aid framework, apart from the exceptional intervention and communications to tackle the financial crisis, was launched in 2012 with the Commission Communication on State aid Modernisation programme (SAM).[9] With the Europe 2020 sustainable growth strategy as guiding light, one of the objectives of the SAM was 'to focus Commission ex ante scrutiny on cases with the biggest impact on internal market whilst strengthening the Member States cooperation in State aid enforcement'.[10] This aim put the focus on the use of an extended general block exemption regulation (GBER), already developed in the SAAP but which however only caught less than half of the measures and about 32% of the budget under its scope.

The newly adopted texts in the context of the modernisation included three interdependent objectives:

> First, the updated system aimed at supporting the objective of sustainable growth and helping to improve the quality of public spending, which implied working on the revision and rationalisation of certain existing texts (environmental guidelines, regional aid, risk capital, rescue and restructuring of undertakings in difficulty).
>
> Second, the target was to focus on cases with the most significant impact on the internal market, for which it was required to have a closer scrutiny of large amounts of aid that could distort competition, launch sector enquiries and also to revise regulations such as the GBER or *de minimis*. In this sense, the modernisation framework shifted the weight from an ex ante control to an ex post one for most of the cases, thereby implementing nearly all new measures (representing about 65% of the total expenditure) under the 2014 GBER and leaving only the more challenging measures for the deep scrutiny of the Commission.[11] In this way, the SAM brought a drastic reduction of

8. *Ibid.*, pp. 26-27.
9. EU State Aid Modernisation (SAM), COM(2012) 209 final of 8 May 2012, pp. 9.
10. *Ibid.*, point 8.
11. More than 97% of all State aid measures are now implemented by Member States without the need for prior approval by the Commission. This is mainly the effect of the extension of the GBER, although about 40%/45% of State aid in value are still notified and approved by the Commission (individual aid or aid schemes not falling under the GBER): *see* Commission's press release of 6 October 2021, IP/21/5027. The 2021 State aid scoreboard indicates that new block-exempted measures (GBER, ABER (Agricultural Block Exemption Regulation), and FIBER (Fishery Block Exemption Regulation)) represented +98.8% of total new measures in 2019 (this percentage decreased since March 2020 because of the massive increase in notified COVID-19 measures).

notifications that diminished from 578 in 2013 to around 150 in 2019. While this application of the GBER plays the role of a 'collective' ex ante control,[12] it also inevitably limits State actions and makes them significantly more rigid.

Third, the reviewed regime also aimed at simplifying procedures, especially the analysis of cases with only a limited impact on trade, as well as improving the quality of information provided by Member States and ensuring a strict compliance with procedures and substantive rules.

The next stage of modernisation then commenced in 2019 with the 'Fitness Check' of the 2012 SAM package, including an evaluation of GBER and *de minimis*, regional aid and the remaining instruments and further adding a revision of the railways guidelines and short-term export credit insurance. The conclusions, published at the end of 2020,[13] showed that overall the State aid rules are still fit for purpose, but certain clarifications, revisions, simplifications and adjustments are to be welcomed in order to keep up with the development of some markets and technologies.

5 TODAY

In light of the above, recent illustrations that confirm the initial wisdom of the Founding Fathers design in 1957 can be identified.

The different crisis that the European Union has (and is) surmounting play a key role in shaping the State aid policy. Already in the context of the financial crisis the then Commissioner in charge of competition policy, Ms Neelie Kroes, together with the Ministers of Finance, realised in 2008 how a centralised EU vision and coordinated actions at the national level were urgently needed, avoiding any intergovernmental approach (against the intentions of some Member States who wanted to 'deactivate' competition rules). That crisis, in a pattern that we have seen repeat in the following ones, required some procedures to be adjusted as reflected in the six financial crisis communications adopted by the Commission until 2013. However, even if the crisis during the framework constituted a derogation from some general State aid principles and requirements, a strong ex ante control was firmly maintained in order to avoid the *jungle* that would be created if State aid control was to be abandoned ('State aid rules are part of the solution, not part of the problem'),[14] as it was also considered with

12. Judgment of 5 March 2019, *Eesti Pagar*, C-349/17, EU:C:2019:172, para. 65: '... it follows from [the GBER], that the Commission, in essence, exercised *ex ante*, by adopting that regulation, all the powers conferred on it by Article 107(3) TFEU with respect to all such aid as satisfied the criteria laid down by that regulation, and only with respect to such aid'.
13. Commission Staff Working Document - Fitness check of the 2012 State aid modernisation package, railways guidelines and short-term export credit insurance, SWD(2020) 257 final of 30 October 2020, pp. 135 and annexes - press release of 30 October 2020. *See also* C. Barbu-O'Connor et al., 'Impact Assessment' (Chapter 6, pp. 88-102) in 'The Future of EU State Aid Law - Consolidation and Expansion', J.-J. Piernas-López, L. Hancher and L. Rubini (eds), EU Law Live Press, 2022, p. 283.
14. Neelie Kroes, Competition Policy Newsletter, 2008; Briefing to Economics and Finance Ministers on financial crises measures on 2 December 2008, MEMO/08/757.

respect to the COVID-19 outbreak through the Temporary Framework.[15] A similar approach is currently taking place through the Temporary Crisis Framework for State Aid measures to support the economy implemented to mitigate the effects from the aggression against Ukraine by Russia.

Closely related, but at the level of non-EU countries, the new 'Regulation of foreign subsidies distorting the internal market', which entered into force on 12 January 2023,[16] will grant the Commission the exclusive competence to assess aid (rather, 'subsidies') given by a non-EU country and affecting the internal market in order to fill the legislative gap that existed from the lack of implementation of the State aid rules in third countries. This regulation introduces three new tools, two (entering into force on 12 October 2023) based on a prior authorisation by the Commission subject to specific thresholds for mergers and public procurements and one (entering into force on 12 July 2023) in the form of a general market investigation tool by the Commission. The procedural aspects of the application of the Regulation are detailed in the Implementing Regulation.[17] The EU legislator agreed that the Commission will be the exclusive enforcer of the regulation, although Member States will be involved via the advisory procedure. This is the last testimony of the virtue of prudence (the 'phronesis' – φρόνησις, under the meaning of Aristotle's Nicomachean Ethics) shown by the Founding Fathers in 1957.

Within the rules governing non-EU countries we also find the paradoxical case of the United Kingdom (UK) after Brexit and its apparent tendency to use domestic legislation to overcome certain aspects of the Trade and Cooperation Agreement signed with the EU. In the same vein, the UK Subsidy Control Act 2022, which entered into force on 4 January 2023, establishes the Competition and Markets Authority (Subsidy Advice Unit of the CMA) as the 'independent' authority in charge of reviewing Subsidies of Interest and Subsidies of Particular Interest, voluntarily and mandatorily respectively. However, the CMA has only an advisory role, the final subsidy decision being taken by the administration concerned. The Competition Appeal Tribunal reviews subsidy decisions following judicial reviews which may be brought by any interested party, unless the subsidy is the result of a decision contained in the primary legislation of the devolved parliaments or Westminster. One may raise doubts about the alleged 'independent' character of the CMA in a subsidy context: as shown by the EU State aid control, a true and effective control can only be made by a supranational authority truly independent from the State concerned to the extent that the decision-making process should be made in the interest of the Union (for the EU) and 'against' the interest of the State concerned.

15. Temporary framework for State aid measures to support the economy in the current COVID-19 outbreak (https://competition-policy.ec.europa.eu/system/files/2021-11/TF_consolidated_version_amended_18_nov_2021_en_2.pdf), now phased out since 30 June 2020.
16. Regulation (EU) 2022/2560 of the European Parliament and of the Council of 14 December 2022 on foreign subsidies distorting the internal market.
17. Commission Implementing Regulation on detailed arrangements for the conduct of proceedings by the Commission pursuant to Regulation (EU) 2022/2560 of the European Parliament and of the Council on foreign subsidies distorting the internal market.

6 CONCLUSION

Against all the above background, the EU way forward is marked by a lack of decentralisation (which would be contrary to the *essence* of State aid control), but reinforced by an increase of resources and powers for the Commission (and, more specifically, to DG Competition).

However, the extreme extension of the ex post control (through the GBER even though it represents an ex ante control legally) is not in line with the *essence* of State aid control. It is perhaps realistic in view of the number of cases and the lack of resources of DG Competition. But, this extension implies a too much rigid system: the Member States' main objective is often to avoid by any means any Commission's control (even if the latter could be made efficiently and quickly) and they are too much tempted to follow the rigid framework of the GBER, losing any creativity which should rather be required for their national measures in view of the evolving and unprecedented economic issues.[18] This creates an efficiency gap to the detriment of the beneficiaries and the consumers ultimately.

In parallel, a better national enforcement is still needed, as well as harmonised procedures, following the example in the State aid field of other areas such as the damages directive in antitrust. However, we can doubt of the genuine intentions of the Member States to adopt efficient EU legislation to control and sanction their illegal behaviours as they do for cartels and abuses of a dominant position by undertakings. This unbalance is the fundamental original sin of EU competition law.

Overall, the steps forward require a firm deterrence on Member States and beneficiaries to apply remedies to unlawful aid, while improving the prevention and detection tools by the legislators.[19]

---

18. The COVID-19 and Ukraine crises confirm this tendency: the Member States responses are 'shaped' by the interpretative communications of the Commission. This is good for coordination. This is less appropriate, to a limited extent, for the 'tailor made' response by Member States to the economic difficulties.
19. Both in terms of *remedies* (*see* J. Derenne, C. Barbu-O'Connor & C. Chilaru, 'Remedies in State Aid' in 'Remedies in EU Competition Law – Substance, Process and Policy', Proceedings of the 2019 Annual Conference of the Global Competition Law Centre (GCLC) of the College of Europe, D. Gerard & A. Komninos (ed.), Kluwer Law International, June 2020, p. 350, pp. 95-118) and of *better involvement of the 'interested parties'* in the procedure of State aid control (*see* Concurrences-On Topic, 'Les tiers et le contrôle des aides d'État / The Role of Third Parties in State Aid Cases', Concurrences n° 4-2022).

www.ingramcontent.com/pod-product-compliance
Lightning Source LLC
Chambersburg PA
CBHW071242230926
51849CB00001B/195
* 9 7 8 9 4 0 3 5 0 0 9 6 6 *